much academic learning and a practitioner's insight both the strengths and weaknesses of the three main current approaches before offering his own canonical-hermeneutical theory of translation. Future editions of the Bible and their readers will no doubt owe a great debt to Straus' contribution to this important field."

—**Ashley Null**, chair, Wittenberg Center for Reformation Studies, Wittenberg, Germany

"*The Word as word* is a gift: from an experienced translator of the New Testament comes a rich consideration of the art of translating Holy Scripture. The labor of and reflection upon the translation of ancient texts is often separated by specialization. In *The Word as word*, Michael Straus offers a rare and needed combination of philological and contextual precision, historical and theological awareness, and humane and pastoral sensitivity. Translation, as *The Word as word* explores it, lives with and moves from ancient words that have and continue to announce the Word."

—**Jonathan A. Linebaugh**, Anglican chair of divinity, Beeson Divinity School

"Written with verve and élan, *The Word as word* challenges us to rethink the assumptions about language, culture, and revelation implicit in different approaches to biblical translation. Michael Straus sets forth a bold vision for Scripture translation that takes seriously the effective history of the text in tradition and the life of the church. The result is a provocative and important contribution to New Testament studies."

—**Susan Eastman**, associate research professor emerita of New Testament, Duke Divinity School

"Almost everyone is interested in the different translations of Scripture. Michael Straus' *The Word as word* provides a stimulating and penetrating investigation into the art of translation through a canonical-hermeneutical approach. This book is not only important for exegesis, but for any translator of the New Testament. The translation of Colossians demonstrates the importance of translation on interpretation through history and tradition. Readers will be delighted by the history of English translations going back to Wycliffe."

—**Arthur Just**, professor of exegetical theology, Concordia Theological Seminary, Fort Wayne

"I heartily endorse Michael Straus' book as a rare reflection in translation studies. As a translation theorist, Straus takes full account of the apostles' and church fathers' concept of the inspired word (including the Trinity). In a clearly structured sequence, he offers different perspectives on the range of other translation approaches, in a spirit of humility and immersive understanding. The result is a greater appreciation of how form, register, and even the use in later church tradition of theological language may be employed in translation, all without falling into the pit of 'translationese.'"

—STEFAN FELBER, author of *Zwischen Babel und Jerusalem: Aspekte von Sprache und Übersetzung*

"What is the relationship between the Word of God living, Jesus Christ the Incarnate Son of God, and the Word of God written, the message which authoritatively proclaims him to a lost world? In what combination do the Holy Scriptures have both divine and human attributes as the living Word of God to which they uniquely witness, including the supernatural power to inspire its readers? Should the living Word's use of the written word in shaping the ongoing life of the Church effect the Church's subsequent understanding of it? In short, as a book of the Church, both as its product and as its source, should the Bible be read with the eyes of faith, as that faith has developed through the centuries? Or should the Bible be read "like other books . . . without reference to the adaptations of the Fathers or Divines; and without regard to a priori notions about its nature and origin," as Benjamin Jowett urged in *Essays and Reviews* (1860)? Such questions have dominated biblical hermeneutics ever since Jowett's time. Rarely, however, have such penetrating queries be made of the related task of biblical translation. Should the translator simply seek to recapture the initial exchange between the text in its original language and its first readers, like any other ancient text? Or should the translator recognize the impact of a sacred text on the unfolding linguistic contexts in which the text has been read and which the text has also shaped over the centuries? Moreover, should a translator weigh the importance of how prior translations have shaped the experiences of readers and, therefore, also their expectations for new versions? In *The Word as word*, Michael Straus grasps the nettle of these thorny issues firmly in favor of the latter. Himself a gifted translator of the New Testament, Straus assesses with

The Word as word

The Word as word

A Canonical-Hermeneutical
Approach to Translation

Michael Straus

◆PICKWICK *Publications* · Eugene, Oregon

THE WORD AS WORD
A Canonical-Hermeneutical Approach to Translation

Copyright © 2024 Michael Straus. All rights reserved. Except for brief quotations in critical publications or reviews, no part of this book may be reproduced in any manner without prior written permission from the publisher. Write: Permissions, Wipf and Stock Publishers, 199 W. 8th Ave., Suite 3, Eugene, OR 97401.

Pickwick Publications
An Imprint of Wipf and Stock Publishers
199 W. 8th Ave., Suite 3
Eugene, OR 97401

www.wipfandstock.com

PAPERBACK ISBN: 978-1-6667-7702-4
HARDCOVER ISBN: 978-1-6667-7703-1
EBOOK ISBN: 978-1-6667-7704-8

Cataloguing-in-Publication data:

Names: Straus, Michael [author].

Title: The Word as word : a canonical-hermeneutical approach to translation / Michael Straus.

Description: Eugene, OR: Pickwick Publications, 2024 | Includes bibliographical references and index.

Identifiers: ISBN 978-1-6667-7702-4 (paperback) | ISBN 978-1-6667-7703-1 (hardcover) | ISBN 978-1-6667-7704-8 (ebook)

Subjects: LCSH: Bible—Translating. | Bible—Criticism, interpretation, etc. | Bible—Versions.

Classification: BS449 S77 2024 (paperback) | BS449 (ebook)

VERSION NUMBER 04/24/25

Permissions

The Symbol GreekU fonts used in this work are available from www.linguistsoftware.com/lgku.htm (+1.425.775.1130)

Scripture quotations taken from the Amplified Bible are copyright © 2015 by The Lockman Foundation. Used by permission.

Scripture quotations taken from the Holy Bible, New International Version®, NIV® are copyright © 1973, 1978, 1984, 2011 by Biblica, Inc™. Used by permission of Zondervan. All rights reserved worldwide.

Scripture quotations from the NET Bible® are copyright © 1996–2017 by Biblical Studies Press, LLC. http://netbible.com. All rights reserved.

Scripture quotations taken from the Revised Standard Version of the Bible are copyright © 1971 by the National Council of the Churches of Christ in the United States of America. Used by permission. All rights reserved worldwide.

Scripture quotations taken from the New Revised Standard Version Bible are copyright © 1989 by the National Council of the Churches of Christ in the United States of America. Used by permission. All rights reserved worldwide.

Scripture quotations taken from the New Revised Standard Version Updated Edition are copyright © 2021 by the National Council of Churches of Christ in the United States of America. Used by permission. All rights reserved worldwide.

Scripture quotations from The Holy Bible, English Standard Version® are copyright © 2001 by Crossway, a publishing ministry of Good News Publishers. Used by permission. All rights reserved.

Scripture quotations from Eugene Petersen, The Message, are copyright 2002 by Eugene Peterson. Used by permission of NavPress. All rights reserved. Represented by Tyndale House Publishers.

Scripture quotations taken from The Holy Bible, New Living Translation (NLT) are copyright © 1996 by Tyndale House Foundation. Used by permission. All rights reserved.

Scripture quotations taken from *The Cotton Patch Version of Paul's Epistles* are copyright © 2014 by Smyth & Helwys Publishing, Incorporated. Used by permission.

Scripture quotations taken from the Douay-Rheims translation are from the 1899 American edition. Usage is online and in the public domain.

Scripture quotations taken from J. B. Phillips, *The New Testament in Modern English*, are copyright © 1962 by HarperCollins. Used by permission.

Scripture quotations taken from N. T. Wright, *The Kingdom New Testament*, are copyright © 2011 by HarperCollins. Used by permission.

Scripture quotations from The Good News Translation in Today's English Version are copyright © 1992 by The American Bible Society. Used by permission.

Scripture quotations taken from F. F. Bruce, *The Letters of Paul: An Expanded Paraphrase*, are copyright © 1965 by W. B. Eerdmans. Used by permission.

Scripture quotations taken from The Living Bible are copyright © 1971 by Tyndale House Foundation. Used by permission of Tyndale House Publishers. All rights reserved.

Scripture quotations taken from David Bentley Hart, *The New Testament: A Translation*, are copyright © 2017 by Yale University Press. Used in accordance with the publisher's guidelines.

Scripture quotations taken from Michael Straus, *The New Testament: A 21st Century Translation*, are copyright © 2019 by Wipf & Stock. Used by permission. All rights reserved.

Scripture quotations from Nestle-Aland, *Novum Testamentum Graece*, 28th edition, 3rd corrected printing, edited by Barbara and Kurt Aland, Johannes Karavidopoulos, Carlo M. Martini, and Bruce M. Metzger in cooperation with the Institute for New Testament Textual Research, Münster/Westphalia, are copyright © 2012 Deutsche Bibelgesellschaft, Stuttgart. Used by permission.

Scripture quotations from *The Greek New Testament*, 5th edition, edited by Barbara Aland, Kurt Aland, Johannes Karavidopoulos, Carlo M. Martini, and Bruce M. Metzger in cooperation with the Institute for New Testament Textual Research, Münster/Westphalia, are copyright © 2014 Deutsche Bibelgesellschaft, Stuttgart. Used by permission.

Contents

List of Abbreviations | ix

Introductory Summary | 1

Structure of the Book | 12

The Word as word

    I. Theoretical and Interpretive Principles | 17

        a. Recurrent Terminology | 17

        b. Linguistic Theory as a Point of Departure | 19

        c. Relationship to Historical-Critical Approaches | 22

        d. Effective History, the Canon, and the Creeds | 31

    II. Elements of a Canonical-Hermeneutical Translation Approach/Test Case | 35

        a. Navigating among Prevailing Translation Approaches | 37

            i. Literal | 38

            ii. Dynamic or Functional Equivalence | 42

            iii. Paraphrase | 48

        b. Excursus on "Classical" Formulations | 50

        c. Excursus on Translation Committees | 53

        d. Literary Characteristics | 58

            i. Genre and Occasionality | 60

            ii. Relationship to Other Writings | 69

            iii. Varieties of Register | 79

Contents

   e. Detailed Analysis of Key Words and Phrases | 111
      i. Christ Presented in Elevated Language | 112
      ii. Affirmative Use of Christological Language as Doctrine | 136
      iii. Negativizing Rhetoric | 143
   f. The Translation Tradition | 157
      i. The WYC/TYN/KJV Tradition and Its Continuity | 159
      ii. Dynamic Equivalence, Paraphrase, and Hybrid Approaches | 172
      iii. Specialized Versions | 198
   g. Methodological Conclusions | 202
      i. Elements Relating to Linguistic and Literary Analysis | 202
      ii. Elements Relating to the Translation Tradition | 203

III. Application of the Methodology to the Text | 206
   a. Words and Phrases | 206
   b. Formal Matters | 208
      i. Chapter and Verse/Punctuation | 208
      ii. *Ekthesis* | 210
      iii. Capitalization and Italics | 211
      iv. *Nomina Sacra* | 213
   c. References and Allusions | 214

IV. Research Contributions and Epilogue | 217
   a. Research Contributions and Suggestions for Future Research | 217
   b. Epilogue: Prolegomena to Any Future Translation | 218

Appendix: To the Colossians | 225
Acknowledgments | 235
Bibliography | 237
Subject Index | 259
Ancient Document Index | 275

List of Abbreviations

AB	Anchor Bible
ACCS	Ancient Christian Commentary on Scripture
Aeg	*Aegyptus*
AmJT	*American Journal of Theology*
ACNS	Anglican Communion New Service
AMP	Amplified Bible
ASV	American Standard Version
AugStud	*Augustinian Studies*
BA	*Biblical Archaeologist*
BDAG	Danker, Frederick W., Walter Bauer, William F. Arndt, and F. Wilbur Gingrich. *Greek-English Lexicon of the New Testament and Other Early Christian Literature*. 3rd ed. Chicago: University of Chicago Press, 2000
Bib	*Biblica*
BibInt	*Biblical Interpretation*
BibInt	Biblical Interpretation Series
BNTC	Black's New Testament Commentaries
BSNA	Biblical Scholarship in North America
BT	*The Bible Translator*
CBET	Contributions to Biblical Exegesis and Theology
CBQ	*Catholic Biblical Quarterly*
CGL	*The Cambridge Greek Lexicon*. Edited by James Diggle. Cambridge: Cambridge University Press, 2021
ChrCent	*Christian Century*
CPV	*The Cotton Patch Version of Paul's Epistles*. By Clarence Jordan. Piscataway: New Century, 1968.

List of Abbreviations

CTM	*Concordia Theological Monthly*
DBH	Hart, David Bentley. *The New Testament: A Translation*
DRA	Douay-Rheims
ERV	English Revised Version
ESV	English Standard Version
EvQ	*Evangelical Quarterly*
ExAud	Ex Auditu
ExpTim	Expository Times
FFB	Bruce, F. F. *The Letters of Paul: An Expanded Paraphrase*
GBS	Guides to Biblical Scholarship
GNB	Good News Bible
GNT	Greek New Testament
HTR	*Harvard Theological Review*
ICC	International Critical Commentary
Int	*Interpretation*
JAAR	*Journal of the American Academy of Religion*
JBL	*Journal of Biblical Literature*
JBP	Phillips, J. B. *The New Testament in Modern English*
JEH	*Journal of Ecclesiastical History*
JETS	*Journal of the Evangelical Theological Society*
JFSR	*Journal of Feminist Studies in Religion*
JR	*Journal of Religion*
JSNT	*Journal for the Study of the New Testament*
JSNTSup	Journal for the Study of the New Testament Supplement Series
JSOTSup	Journal for the Study of the Old Testament Supplement Series
JTS	*Journal of Theological Studies*
JTSA	*Journal of Theology for Southern Africa*
KJV	King James Version
L&N	Louw, Johannes P., and Eugene A. Nida, eds. *Greek-English Lexicon of the New Testament: Based on Semantic Domains*. 2nd ed. New York: United Bible Societies, 1989
LNTS	The Library of New Testament Studies
LSJ	Liddell, Henry George, Robert Scott, Henry Stuart Jones. *A Greek-English Lexicon*. 2 vols. Oxford: Oxford University Press, 1940
MSG	The Message
MTSR	*Method and Theory in the Study of Religion*

List of Abbreviations

NA²⁸	*Novum Testamentum Graece*, Nestle-Aland, 28ᵗʰ ed.
NEB	New English Bible
Neot	*Neotestimentica*
NET	New English Translation
NICNT	New International Commentary on the New Testament
NIDNTT	*New International Dictionary of New Testament Theology.* Edited by Colin Brown. 4 vols. Grand Rapids: Zondervan, 1975–78
NIGTC	New International Greek Testament Commentary
NIV	New International Version
NLT	New Living Translation
NovT	*Novum Testamentum*
NRSV	New Revised Standard Version Bible
NRSVue	New Revised Standard Version Updated Edition
NTL	New Testament Library
NTOA	Novum Testamentum et Orbis Antiquus
NTS	*New Testament Studies*
NTTSD	New Testament Tools, Studies, and Documents
OED	*The Compact Edition of the Oxford English Dictionary.* 2 vols. Oxford: Oxford University Press, 1971
OED Supp	*A Supplement to the Oxford English Dictionary.* Vol. 3 of *The Compact Edition of the Oxford English Dictionary.* Edited by R. W. Burchfield. Oxford: Clarendon, 1987
PGL	*Patristic Greek Lexicon.* Edited by Geoffrey W. H. Lampe. Oxford: Oxford University Press, 1969
RevExp	*Review and Expositor*
RSV	Revised Standard Version
SBR	Studies of the Bible and Its Reception
SCS	Septuagint and Cognate Studies
SJT	*Scottish Journal of Theology*
SNT	Straus, Michael. *The New Testament: A 21ˢᵗ Century Translation*
SNTSMS	Society for New Testament Studies Monograph Series
ST	*Studia Theologica*
STI	Studies in Theological Interpretation
SUNT	Studien zur Umwelt des Neuen Testaments
SymS	Symposium Series
TBei	*Theologische Beiträge*

TDNT	*Theological Dictionary of the New Testament*. Edited by Gerhard Kittel and Gerhard Friedrich. 10 vols. Translated by Geoffrey W. Bromiley. Grand Rapids: Eerdmans, 1964–76
Them	*Themelios*
TLB	The Living Bible
TNTC	Tyndale New Testament Commentaries
TYN	The Tyndale Bible
UBS[5]	*The Greek New Testament*, United Bible Societies, 5th ed.
VE	*Vox Evangelica*
WGRWSup	Writings from the Greco-Roman World Supplement Series
WTJ	*Westminster Theological Journal*
WUNT	Wissenschaftliche Untersuchungen zum Neuen Testament
WYC	Wycliffe, John. *The Complete Wycliffe Bible: Old Testament, New Testament & Apocrypha*
ZEC	Zondervan Exegetical Commentary on the New Testament

Introductory Summary

THE GOAL OF THIS book is to provide theoretical and practical justification for a translation methodology applicable to the New Testament that remains rooted in the literal Greek; considers its paleographic and philological characteristics as well as its sociohistorical context; understands the text as part of a canonical whole; reflects its reception and effective history in church doctrine and liturgy; accounts for any "classical" formulations in its translation tradition; and at the same time speaks with contemporary literary style. Such a methodology goes beyond existing approaches. It respects the textual faithfulness of a purely literal approach, yet at the same time recognizes translatable "free space around" the text within which meaning may be revealed.[1] And while the methodology advanced here credits the importance of historical-critical research into the "world behind the text," it neither limits textual meaning to what is "imagin[ed]" to be present in the minds of ancient writers,[2] nor translates with the goal of "reproduc[ing]" the same in the minds of modern readers.[3] Instead, it provides a pathway to translating the Scriptures as a living text with words grounded in the literal language yet modern in phraseology, reflective of church history yet without compromising traditional understandings.

Scripture is here understood to be the divinely communicated Word of God made incarnationally present in the words of the Bible,[4] with on-

---

1. Gadamer, *Philosophical Hermeneutics*, 211.
2. Piñero and Peláez, *Study of New Testament*, 345; Hagner and Young, "Historical-Critical Method," 15.
3. Nida and Taber, *Theory and Practice*, 200.
4. Augustine, *De Trinitate* 2.9. As further explained herein, the particulars of the translation methodology advanced here focus on New Testament texts, but their hermeneutical assumptions operate within a "whole Bible" canonical framework.

going effects in the continuum of church history and tradition.[5] Jesus' personhood as the Word of God is thus essential to his revelation, as the truths about Jesus, including that he *is* the truth, are grasped through textual mediation.[6] Consistent with this perspective, I take as an analytical point of departure the perception that the act of understanding is itself linguistic as the mind "think[s] through" unspoken thought.[7] Augustine of Hippo used the term *verbum interius* to describe this as inner thought.[8] He then analogized the "processual" relationship between inner thought and its verbal expression to that of the Father and the Son.[9]

As such, when the Word as communicated to the mind of the writer is expressed in the words of the Bible, it "does not lessen itself by its emergence into exteriority," any more than Christ in the incarnation was diminished in his divinity.[10] In his own analysis of the *verbum interius*, Thomas Aquinas similarly concluded that "the formation of the word does not pass away when the word itself is formed, but when it is being actively understood, the word is in continual formation."[11] Augustine's and Aquinas' views are likewise consistent with the Reformers' understanding of Scripture as the *viva vox evangelii*, with ongoing presence and effect in the world by way of the church's kerygmatic mission.[12]

More recently, and building on Augustine's Trinitarian analogy for purposes of his own philosophical linguistics, it was Hans-Georg Gadamer's insight that

> the human relationship between thought and speech corresponds, despite its imperfections, to the divine relationship of the Trinity. The inner mental word is just as consubstantial with

---

5. Mueller-Vollmer, *Hermeneutics Reader*, 38–39.

6. Watson, *Text and Truth*, 27. John 14:6; cf. Luke 1:1–4. Knowledge of the utterance and effect of divine speech likewise depends on textual reporting. See, e.g., Gen 1:3, 6, 9, 11, 14, 20, 24; Ps 33:6; Isa 55:11; John 11:43, 18:6; Acts 9:3–6.

7. Gadamer, *Truth and Method*, 422.

8. Augustine, *De Trinitate* 15; Augustine, *De doctrina christiana* 1.13.

9. Augustine, *Sermones*, 119.7.

10. Risser, "Hermeneutics and Linguisticality," 9–10; Arthos, *Inner Word*, 224; J. Smith, *Fall of Interpretation*, 143; Gadamer, *Truth and Method*, 420.

11. Aquinas, *De natura verbi intellectus* §277 (quoted in Arthos, *Inner Word*, 372). He thereby "bring[s] the whole weight of the Christian mystery into the phenomenon of linguistic understanding." John Arthos, email to author, 2020.

12. Arthos, *Inner Word*, 133; Just, *Heaven on Earth*, 199–200; Thiselton, *Two Horizons*, 100.

thought as is God the Son with God the Father [and] has its being in its revealing.¹³

As Gadamer further explained, a reader seeks understanding of a text's meaning by engaging in dialogue with it—a dialogue whereby he "*participates in an event of tradition*, a process of transmission in which past and present are constantly mediated."¹⁴ In the particular case of a New Testament text, its meaning is revealed as it unfolds in church history through credal, liturgical, and sermonic expression.¹⁵ To be sure, there has been an enormous diversity of such writings over the past two millennia. And there will always be differences of view as to any given expression's consistency with Scripture. But exploring such diversity is the very point of a dialogic engagement with the text. Such a dialogue is likewise consistent with the Reformers' rejection of a formal magisterium that purported to regulate that exploration.¹⁶ Tradition is thus an essential element of the Word of God's trajectory through time. And properly understood, tradition neither replaces nor undermines the text, but rather is integral to the revelation of its normative inner word.

These linguistic insights are clearly of great importance in biblical exegesis, where the goal is to capture and convey scriptural truths as those not limited by time and circumstance. Yet there has been no systematic effort to consider the potential relevance of a cross-temporal approach to the art of translation, such that insufficient methodological attention has been given to how a contemporary translation might more fully reveal the living nature of biblical texts. My working premise in that regard is that the Word of God is understood to be actively present in the world through the biblical texts' ongoing reception, interpretation, and application. If so, then there may be an "excess of meaning" present in them beyond that which might have been perceived on first reading.¹⁷ And as such, the interrelating effects of time and tradition on

---

13. Gadamer, *Truth and Method*, 421. Further, "the Word . . . is equal to the Father, since it is perfect and expressive of the whole being of the Father." Aquinas, *Commentary on John*, 15. See also John 1:1; Col 1:15.

14. Gadamer, *Truth and Method*, 290–91 (emphasis in original).

15. Gadamer, *Truth and Method*, 419n40 (citing Aquinas, *De natura verbi intellectus* §277); Just, "Today in Our Hearing"; J. Smith, *Fall of Interpretation*, 143; Thiselton, *Two Horizons*, 300.

16. Klein et al., *Introduction to Biblical Interpretation*, 43, 47.

17. Gadamer, *Philosophical Hermeneutics*, 102, 210. See also Watson, *Text and Truth*, 50: "If the gospels are regarded as canonical, communally authoritative texts, then there can be no question of confining these texts to an immobilized past."

textual understanding—what Gadamer termed "effective history" (or *Wirkungsgeschichte*)[18]—should be reflected not only in exegesis, but also as the words are presented in translation. I therefore propose a translation methodology characterized by dialogic engagement with the biblical texts as they take effect in church history and tradition; and I test its viability by application to Paul's Letter to the Colossians.

The need for a translation methodology that takes account of a New Testament text's trajectory through church history and tradition is further supported by arguments that certain post-Enlightenment, historical-critical approaches to exegesis have skewed the focus too far towards biblical texts' contextual origins, seeking to "reconstruct" their meaning as then understood. At least as initially conceived, historical-critical analyses proceeded on a rationalist model of autonomous interpreters seeking to understand the message of a distant text. That model was itself premised on the epistemological assumption that meaning should be sought primarily in the *mens auctoris*; and that authorial intent might be discerned "free of judgment and prejudice."[19] However, such a purportedly objective approach posited that modern readers and biblical texts stand "isolated from each other by a gulf of historical time."[20] One result was a subordination of understandings that began in early faith communities and continued as the biblical texts were received, interpreted, and applied by a globally expanding church.[21]

We and the Scriptures are now better seen to be "in a state of relatedness to each other" in the continuum of history.[22] My project thus relates to Markus Bockmuehl's proposed reframing of New Testament studies to take fuller account of the Bible's reception history and theological readings, as well as its sociohistorical origins and philological characteristics. As he points out, excessive reliance on historical-critical methodologies risks devaluing the continued interplay of the biblical texts with church doctrine.[23] This is the same vital interplay present in church liturgy.[24]

18. Gadamer, *Gadamer Reader*, 59.
19. Stuhlmacher, *Historical Criticism*, 43.
20. Mueller-Vollmer, *Hermeneutics Reader*, 38; Stuhlmacher, *Historical Criticism*, 62.
21. Luz, *Matthew 1–7*, 97: "Historical-critical scholarship distances the text to be interpreted not only from the interpreter and his or her faith but intentionally also from the entirety of the biblical testimony."
22. Mueller-Vollmer, *Hermeneutics Reader*, 39; Eberhard, "Mediality," 413–14; Steinmetz, "Superiority of Pre-Critical Exegesis," 11.
23. Bockmuehl, *Seeing the Word*, 76–77.
24. Just, *Heaven on Earth*, 183: "The historic liturgy is completely biblical." See also 272–74.

Gadamer's philosophical linguistics are likewise important to the theory. Gadamer argues that meaning is accessed by dialogic engagement with a text, with consciousness of how "our language bears the stamp of the past and is the life of the past in the present."[25] Such a process requires readers to reflect on their own "situatedness within the flow of history,"[26] conscious of how historical effects give rise to their own preconceptions. The interpretive goal is not to eliminate the tension between the ancient text and the language of the present, but consciously to find words expressive of the relationship between the two.[27]

Awareness of biblical texts' living history is therefore as essential to the task of translation as it is to exegesis. For one thing, many of the earliest expressions of the faith based on the original Greek text as well as its Latin formulations were canonized in the course of the church's efforts to resolve the christological, Trinitarian, and iconoclastic controversies of the first millennium.[28] And within the framework of a lengthy English translation tradition, these core doctrines of the faith have long been expressed in particular Greco-Latinate and Anglo-Saxon wordings which thereby sustain theologically important usages. For example, doctrines of righteousness, justification, redemption, grace, forgiveness, and faith, or considerations of Christ's sonship, image, blood, flesh, death, and resurrection, are persistently articulated with words having an embedded textual reception over multiple centuries and in multiple English-speaking communities. Importantly, these "classical" formulations have been retained in such academically informed and broadly church-sponsored translations as the RSV, NRSV, and NRSVue.[29] As such, they have ac-

---

25. Gadamer, *Philosophical Hermeneutics*, xxviii; cf. Faulkner, *Requiem for a Nun*, 49: "The past is never dead. It's not even past."

26. Thiselton, *New Horizons*, 6; Thiselton, *Two Horizons*, 100–101, 131–32; Gadamer, *Truth and Method*, 273; Hagner and Young, "Historical-Critical Method," 13, 16; Klein et al., *Introduction to Biblical Interpretation*, 192–201; Stuhlmacher, *Historical Criticism*, 87.

27. Gadamer, *Truth and Method*, 273; Luz, *Matthew 1–7*, 98: "The distanced text is always already present with the interpreter"; Ricoeur, *On Translation*, 6: The "great primary words [of a language] are themselves summaries of long textuality where whole contexts are mirrored."

28. See generally Kinzig, *Faith in Formulae*; and J. Kelly, *Early Christian Creeds*.

29. See New Revised Standard Version Bible, "New Revised Standard NRS," para. 6: "Rooted in the past, but right for today, the NRSV continues the tradition of William Tyndale, the King James Version, the American Standard Version, and the Revised Standard Version." For scholarly purposes, the NRSV has been described as "the basic default text of the English Bible," in Stuhlmacher, *Biblical Theology*, xxii.

quired an "authoritative" status,[30] even as newly developed philological, text-critical, and sociohistorical analyses are incorporated into further translation refinements.[31]

Translation *itself* is thus a historical phenomenon, realized within a "flow of history" of which both text and translator are integral parts.[32] Consistent with such an awareness, the translation methodology advanced here also builds on an exegetical tradition that understands the Hebrew Scriptures as the framework for Jesus' own hermeneutic, by which he claimed that it was he to whom the Law and the Prophets testified,[33] and indeed that the Law was fulfilled in him.[34] This understanding is further laced throughout the New Testament writings in the form of quoted passages[35] and interpretive material.[36] The Law and the Prophets thus provided the grounds for the global interpretation of Israel's history given by Peter in his preaching at Pentecost,[37] Stephen's dying sermon,[38] and much of the Letter to the Hebrews.[39]

This unifying approach to the Scriptures was sustained as the canon expanded to include the New Testament writings.[40] Faced with perceived errors and heresies, whether in the form of a Marcionite rejection of the Old Testament's content or a gnostic subordination of the person of Christ, the early church's bishops and theologians found it necessary to determine which texts were constituent of the faith. Over time, the result was the larger canon of both Old and New Testaments. An essential canon-formative criterion was whether the content was in "material agreement" with the church's *regula fidei*, a formulation that was itself

---

30. Gadamer, *Truth and Method*, 285–90; Watson, *Text and Truth*, 49, 66n22.

31. While secondary to my broader analysis, I similarly rely on current research concerning a text's philological, text-critical, sociohistorical, and literary characteristics. See especially sects. II.2.d–e, and III, *infra*.

32. Thiselton, *New Horizons*, 6; Stuhlmacher, *Historical Criticism*, 89; cf. Wittgenstein, *Zettel*, §173: "Only in the stream of thought and life do words have meaning."

33. E.g., Luke 4:16–21; 24:13–27; John 5:39.

34. E.g., Matt 5:21–26.

35. E.g., Matt 1:22–23; 2:14–15; 3:1–3; Heb 1:5–13.

36. E.g., Acts 2:14–36 (relying on Joel 2:28–36); Heb 3:1–7 (contrasting Christ and Moses); Rev 19:10: "The testimony of Jesus is the spirit of prophecy."

37. Acts 2:14–26.

38. Acts 7.

39. E.g., Heb 7–9.

40. Detailed examination of canon formation is beyond the scope of this work, but an emerging sense of unity may be seen in such verses as 2 Pet 3:15–16.

Introductory Summary

traceable to apostolic teaching.[41] And a core element of that teaching was that Christ is the "constitutive bond" between Old and New Testaments.[42] The fathers thereby took the "wholeness" of Scripture as their premise and rejected an "atomistic exegesis of isolated texts."[43]

Within this framework, Christ is understood to be the "interpretative key for understanding the Old Testament,"[44] a hermeneutical principle that remained vital in the church's developing doctrines and liturgy. For example, Jerome defended his approach to the Scriptures by providing numerous examples of apostolic renderings of Old Testament passages that interpretively express their typological fulfillment in the New.[45] Based on his own understanding of biblical wholeness, Augustine held that all Scripture "proclaims Christ and enjoins love."[46] A unitary perspective is likewise reflected in Martin Luther's aphorism that "Holy Scripture is that which 'urges Christ.'"[47] And as traditionally formulated in the Anglican communion, "The Old Testament is not contrary to the New: for both in the Old and New Testament everlasting life is offered to Mankind by Christ."[48]

Canonical integrity has therefore long been a consistent element of the biblical texts' *Wirkungsgeschichte*—something also evident in Brevard Childs' interpretive model, which involves "hearing the whole of

---

41. Stuhlmacher, *Historical Criticism*, 26; Stuhlmacher, *Biblical Theology*, 756; Barton, "Many Gospels, One Jesus," 181. See Irenaeus, *Adversus haereses* 3.1.1; Tertullian, *De praescriptione haereticorum*, 13, 20–22. See also Bokedal, "Bible Canon," 8 (apostolicity as a "canonical signal pertaining to eye-witness authority and Jesus' teachings" [citing Luke 1:1–4; 10:16; Acts 1:1–3]); Bockmuehl, "New Testament Doctrine," 41; Klein et al., *Introduction to Biblical Interpretation*, 40 ("apostolicity" as the key to determining orthodoxy); cf. Brewer, "Welcome" (early imagery establishing apostolicity of the four Gospels).

42. Stuhlmacher, *Historical Criticism*, 27.

43. Thiselton, *New Horizons*, 154, 156 (citing Irenaeus, *Adversus haereses*, 1.8.1; 2.28.3).

44. Thiselton, *New Horizons*, 150; Voelz, *What Does This Mean*, 260–61.

45. Jerome, *Letter to Pammachius* 7–10. See Venuti, *Translation Studies Reader*, 494–95.

46. Augustine, *De catechizandis rudibus* 4.8. See also his *De doctrina christiana* 1.16.40, 1.40.44 (the ultimate meaning of Scripture is *caritas*); and *Ennarationes in Psalmos*, 144.8: "the Old and New Testaments [are] the narration of the past and the promise of the future." R. Williams, "Augustine," 19: for Augustine, "the Psalms are the words of Jesus, the Word who speaks in all scripture."

47. Hengel with Deines, *Septuagint as Christian Scripture*, 54 (translating Luther's dictum, *ob sie Christum treibet*); Calvin, "Bible and the Word," 161: "If we would know Christ, we must seek him in the Scriptures."

48. Church of England, "Articles of Religion," art. 7. See Burnet, *Exposition*, 91–105.

Christian Scripture in light of the full reality of God in Jesus Christ."[49] The presence and interwovenness of Old Testament language and imagery in the New Testament should therefore be clearly and even explicitly revealed in translation.[50] Revealing such unity in translation is further supported by the identification of *nomina sacra* in some of the earliest extant manuscripts, whereby the divine name was presented in a scribally distinctive manner that effectively incorporated its ancient Jewish treatment into the gospel of Jesus' lordship.[51]

In short, I propose a canonical-hermeneutical approach to translation that relies on modern paleographic, philological, and sociohistorical scholarship at the same time as it accounts for textual understandings reflected in the past as well as ongoing life of the church. Such an approach recognizes that the New Testament's "place in history clearly comprises not just an original setting but a history of lived responses to the historical and eternal realities to which it testifies."[52] And because the text has continued effects in the present, its living history should be revealed in translation as much as in preaching, teaching, and worship. In that regard as well, translation is related to exegesis in those instances where interpretive decisions must be made among linguistic alternatives as to which there may be credible grammatical arguments.[53] A contemporary version should therefore seek to capture, recapitulate, and incorporate the living sweep of the timeless Word in words that cross time. And it should do so with attention to literary style, to avoid being "lifeless[ly] cast in 'translationese.'"[54] Such a version would thereby serve faith communities by providing a further bridge across the societal and linguistic distance between past and present, "the once and now."[55]

---

49. Childs, *Biblical Theology*, 87. See also Childs, "Old Testament as Scripture," 714: "By its peculiar shaping of the tradition, the canon provides the hermeneutical key for the later generations of Christians to appropriate the ancient testimony for itself."

50. As explained in sect. II.d.ii.2. For present purposes, I focus on Septuagint phraseology.

51. Hurtado, *Earliest Christian Artifacts*, 133. Nomina sacra thus gave "textual expression to a devotional pattern" whereby Christ is identified as the same God of creation and Israel. Bokedal, *Formation and Significance*, 87; Bokedal, "Early Rule-of-Faith," 66–69.

52. Bockmuehl, *Seeing the Word*, 65.

53. Gadamer, *Gadamer Reader*, 170: "Every translation, even the so-called literal translation, is some kind of interpretation."

54. Steiner, *After Babel*, 364. See also Alter, *Art of Bible Translation*, 11, 17 (noting the literary deficiencies of "gravely flawed modern translations of the Bible").

55. Gadamer, *Philosophical Hermeneutics*, 22.

Introductory Summary 9

With that background, I test the theory's proposed methodology by application to Paul's Letter to the Colossians, illustrating how a given biblical text's effective history might usefully be elicited in translation. I focus the test in particular on the so-called "Colossian Hymn" (1:15–20), which was of material importance in the development of church doctrine, including through a number of faith formulae canonized by conciliar decrees.[56] The passage was especially relevant in the christological and Trinitarian struggles of the fourth and fifth centuries, as well as in the iconoclastic disputes of the eighth and ninth centuries.[57] And apart from its presence in the creeds, much of Colossians' language and imagery is also reflected in hymns and other liturgical elements.

Given its continued importance in doctrine and worship, the Colossian Hymn thereby serves well as an exemplary application of the model. In that connection I further examine how it has been presented over the course of its lengthy English translation tradition. That tradition builds in the first instance on Jerome's late fourth-century Latin version,[58] where much of its imagery and phrasing was carried into Middle English by way of John Wycliffe's incorporation of numerous Latinate forms in his fourteenth-century translation from the Vulgate. Importantly for an effective history analysis, William Tyndale's subsequent sixteenth-century translation from the Greek was highly consistent with the Jerome/Wycliffe renderings, while adding literary elegance. And the King James Version in the early seventeenth century retained some 70 percent of Tyndale's Old Testament phrasing and 80 percent of the New, while also providing scholarly expertise.[59] I therefore trace the letter's translation tradition to

---

56. There are other texts that might also have served this purpose, such as John's Prologue. But for reasons of space and practicality, I narrowed the test to Colossians.

57. J. Kelly, *Early Christian Doctrines*, 217. See also Morgan, "Critical Study," 216: "The conciliar definition of Jesus . . . is sufficiently true to [the New Testament's] intentions to test the claim of any . . . biblical interpretation to be Christian in a traditional sense."

58. Jerome's Old Testament Vulgate was based on the Hebrew texts. His New Testament was largely based on Greek texts but also involved revisions to Old Latin forms, which were in turn based on the Greek. See generally Plater and White, *Grammar of Vulgate*, 5–10.

59. These percentages are based on a comparative count of identical words found in several Old and New Testament books. See Tulsa 2011, "King James Version," under "Ronald Mansbridge: The Percentage of Words in the Geneva and King James Versions Taken from Tyndale's Translation," estimating a possible statistical error of 2 to 3 percent in making such comparisons, but concluding that they serve as a useful "rough figure." Others have found even higher percentages using more refined methodologies. See Nielsen and Skousen, "How Much" (King James retained 76 percent of Tyndale's Old Testament language and 84 percent of the New).

examine the extent to which it remains inertially present in contemporary translations.

In this context I also examine methodological reactions against the WYC/TYN/KJV translation tradition, most notably in the dynamic equivalence theories of Eugene Nida, which are dominant in a number of important contemporary translation projects. His methodology seeks to render the text in a manner fully "intelligible" to the modern reader, without necessary regard to particular characteristics of the original Greek or the text's presence in church history and tradition. Nida's dynamic equivalency theory in fact *denies* the relevance of "writings of the early Church Fathers" or of "creeds" in determining textual meaning.[60] Yet as Stefan Felber cogently argues, Nida's method "distanc[es] form and meaning"[61] and thereby diminishes the role of "biblical language and [the] theology of the word and the sacraments as the *media salutis*."[62]

I therefore emphasize the importance to modern translation of acknowledging and retaining the text's effective history in church history and tradition. And I argue that this can be accomplished without compromising modern intelligibility or stylistic elegance. To that end I bring the book full circle within itself by engaging dialogically with my own prior translation of Colossians.[63] In that instance, I recognized that in its "inspired literalism" the KJV set a linguistic gold standard.[64] At the same time, I found myself aligned in spirit with individual translators such as J. B. Phillips and David Bentley Hart, both of whom brought new life to the text as the Word found personal expression in their versions. I therefore aimed as well for colloquial energy without jettisoning traditional understandings.[65]

But in my research for this book, I realized there was room for reexamination of my own critical horizons in producing that translation. I thus turned to Colossians again, but this time with greater openness to several aspects of the text's formal characteristics as well as its effective

---

60. Nida and Taber, *Theory and Practice*, 8, 31.

61. Felber, "Chomsky's Influence," 255. See also Felber, "Moratorium," 218 (criticizing Nida's conception of language as "naïve").

62. Felber, "Chomsky's Influence," 260. To be sure, dynamic equivalency is by definition a trade-off in which attention to lexical detail is sacrificed for fluidity of expression. But where formal elements are essential to inner meaning, a bad dynamic version may fail for the reasons Felber points out.

63. Straus, *New Testament*, 432–39.

64. Alter, *Art of Bible Translation*, 5, 10.

65. Robert Alter, email to author, 2019.

history, allowing for any changes in translation that might result. I found that application of the translation methodology advanced here justified substantial revision, this time taking fuller account of intrascriptural language and imagery from the LXX; the social composition of the Colossian community; contemporaneous philosophies and religious practices; hymnic aspects of the text; *nomina sacra*; the letter's effective history in faith formulae; and the trajectory of its translation tradition (which in theory now included my own prior version). I then produced a revised translation in reciprocal engagement with that earlier one.[66] As such, the book's own structure might be said to reflect a "hermeneutical spiral."[67]

I conclude the book by identifying its research contributions as well as areas for future exploration. And I provide an epilogue in the form of "prolegomena to any future translation,"[68] offering principles distilled from its methodology. These guidelines are not meant to be proscriptive, but rather suggestive of factors a translator might take into account in applying such an approach. As I note there, one goal has been to explore ways in which the New Testament texts may be more expansively presented within a church framework. The methodology advanced here therefore leaves great room for periodic revisiting of the text in light of newly discovered historical materials as well as further linguistic developments, all while remaining true to essential elements of the translation tradition. And it is likewise fully open to be seen where the methodology might lead a given translator—save my submission that his overarching goal should be a continued filling of the "free space around" the text,[69] whose very meaning lies "in its revealing" of the Word's "inner mental word."[70]

---

66. See the appendix hereto.

67. See Osborne, *Hermeneutical Spiral*. Such self-reflection is likewise consistent with the mediality of διαλέγομαι. See Eberhard, "Mediality," 412–14 (citing Gadamer, *Truth and Method*, 103).

68. *Pace* Immanuel Kant.

69. Gadamer, *Philosophical Hermeneutics*, 211.

70. Gadamer, *Truth and Method*, 421.

Structure of the Book

IN SECT. I, I provide a theoretical basis for my translational approach. In sect. I.a, I preface the discussion with a glossary of certain terminology as used in the book. In sect. I.b, I discuss certain linguistic theories that provide a theoretical basis for an interpretive/hermeneutical approach that takes account of the "effective history" of Scripture as the *viva vox evangelii*. In sect. I.c, I address the relationship of this approach to historical-critical methodologies. And in sect. I.d, I address its relationship to canonical and credal developments in church history and tradition.

In sect. II, I turn to the construction of a novel methodology built on the foregoing interpretive principles. In sect. II.a, I survey a range of current translation approaches: in sect. II.a.i, the literal; in sect. II.a.ii, the dynamically equivalent; and in sect. II.a.iii, the paraphrastic. I also offer an excursus in sect. II.b on "classical" formulations; and another in sect. II.c on translation committees. I then focus on the elements of a translation methodology that would take account of a given text's paleographic and philological characteristics; its sociohistorical setting; its intrascriptural relationships; its trajectory in subsequent faith formulations; and its translation tradition.

As noted, I use Colossians to test the viability of such a methodology as applied to translations of the New Testament. In sect. II.d.i, I therefore discuss Colossians' epistolary genre. In sect. II.d.ii, I address its relationships with other writings. And in sect. II.d.iii, I examine the varieties of register, tone, and style employed by the writer. In sect. II.e, I undertake a more detailed examination of certain of its key words and phrases with reference to the letter's philological and sociohistorical aspects; intrascriptural references or allusions; and effective history in conciliar and other church materials. In that context, I identify alternative translation options and explain how the methodology of this book aids in selecting among them. This part of the analysis is subdivided into three subsections. In subsect. II.e.i, I address the letter's distinctive use of elevated terminology to describe Christ and its effective history in the christological and Trinitarian struggles of the fourth and fifth centuries and the iconoclastic disputes of the eighth and ninth centuries. In subsect. II.e.ii, I address other doctrinal language in the letter. And in subsect. II.e.iii, I discuss the use of negativizing rhetoric to counter alternative understandings of who Christ is.

In sect. II.f, I examine the text's translation tradition as another essential aspect of its *Wirkungsgeschichte*, focusing on the Colossian Hymn (1:15–20) as the letter's most distinctive portion from a linguistic, doctrinal, and stylistic perspective. I divide this part of the analysis into three subsections. In subsect. II.f.i, I examine the translation tradition that commenced with Jerome's Latin Vulgate, was extended into Middle English with Wycliffe, further developed by Tyndale, and continued thence to date. In subsect. II.f.ii, I examine translations made applying dynamic equivalence theories as well as those taking other approaches, including my own prior effort. In subsect. II.f.iii, I discuss certain specialized approaches, including the amplified and interlinear. And in sect. II.g, I draw conclusions concerning the relevance of the translation tradition to the canonical-hermeneutical methodology of this book.

As the next stage in the process, I address practical issues in applying the methodology. In sect. III.a, I discuss general principles involved in determining appropriate English wording. And in sects. III.b–c, I address alternative ways in which a given text might be presented in the receptor language consistent with the methodology of the book, such as the use of *nomina sacra*; intrascriptural quotations; marginal references; capitalization; italics; sense-divisions; and distinctive grammar or syntax.

In sect. IV.a, I summarize the book's contribution to current research and offer suggested areas for further research. In sect. IV.b, I offer as an epilogue non-proscriptive factors that might be considered by a future translator seeking to apply its methodology.

The appendix then sets forth a translation of Colossians applying the proposed methodology.

The Word as word

I. Theoretical and Interpretive Principles

THE GOAL OF THIS work is to present a translation methodology that may be utilized by modern translators of the New Testament. Such a methodology remains rooted in the literal Greek text; considers its paleographic and philological characteristics as well as its sociohistorical context; understands it as part of a canonical whole; reflects its reception and effective history in church doctrine and liturgy; accounts for any "classical" elements of its translation tradition; and at the same time speaks with contemporary stylistic energy. I preface the first part of the discussion with a glossary of terminology. From there I identify linguistic theories that function as a point of departure for developing a canonical-hermeneutical approach to translation. I then comment on the relationship of the book's' proposed methodology to historical-critical approaches, canon theory, and credal expressions of the faith.

a. Recurrent Terminology

As used here:

Apocrypha refers to those texts included within the Septuagint/LXX version of the Old Testament but not uniformly accepted as canonical.

Canon refers to Old and New Testament texts that have been collected, arranged, and adopted for normative purposes by a given tradition.

Dynamic/functional equivalence refers to a translation methodology that prioritizes the intelligibility of a text in its receptor language.

Effective history, or *Wirkungsgeschichte*, concerns the historicity of understanding. It refers to the interrelating action of history and tradition in forming one's cognitive perspective, such that an ancient text should be approached with a *wirkungsgeschichtliches Bewußtsein*—a mode of thought that is conscious of its own being affected by history.

Genre refers to the linguistic structure of a particular variety of text, such as a letter, novel, or poem.

Hermeneutics refers to the manner in which one understands and interprets a text. With respect to the Bible, it concerns a means of access to its "inner word" through dialogic engagement with the text with consciousness of one's situatedness in the continuum of church history and tradition.

Inner word/verbum interius/verbum cordis interchangeably refer to thought as divinely communicated to the mind. In the case of a biblical writer, such thought finds expression in the living words of Scripture, with meaning revealed as the words are actively understood.

Literal refers to a translation methodology that prioritizes the formal characteristics of a text in its source language, including its vocabulary and imagery.

Paraphrase refers to a translation methodology that, as with dynamic/functional equivalence, prioritizes intelligibility in the receptor language, but also allows for more expansive means to achieve that result, including through the greater use of restructured syntax, colloquialisms, or parachronisms.

Register refers to the linguistic and syntactical features used in creating a text that belongs to a particular genre.

Septuagint/LXX refers to the Greek version of the books of the Old Testament.

Style concerns the ways in which a writer describes people and things or conveys meaning, and includes his vocabulary, sentence structure, and/or figures of speech. Style may therefore also refer to a text's literary and aesthetic qualities.

Text refers to words expressed in writing for communicative purposes.

Tradition refers to the continuity of linguistic and cultural transmission in a process that mediates between past and present.

Translation/translation methodology refers to the critical methodology by which one engages with the literal text of the source language, its contextual setting, and its effective history in order to present the same in a given receptor language.

Translation tradition refers to the continuity of a text's translation history.

As uncapitalized, *word* concerns the linguistic nature of thought, as well as its verbal or written expression.

As capitalized, *Word* means the Word of God and may be used variously to refer to the Son of God; the Scriptures in the form of the

Old and New Testaments as a canonical corpus; or God's communications in general.

b. Linguistic Theory as a Point of Departure

Certain Patristic, Scholastic, Reform, and Contemporary linguistic views provide an interlocutory point of departure in developing a translation methodology that understands biblical language to be transformatively active in the teaching and worship of the church. Augustine, for example, understood the Scriptures to function within the generally "revealing" nature of language, but with the special purpose of providing access to divine self-disclosure.[1] In meditating on the nature of the Trinity, Augustine perceived an analogy in the relationship of the Father and the Son to that of thought and language. He adopted the term *verbum interius* to describe that which exists in the mind before its expression.[2] He then argued that just as the Father and the Son are one, so too are thought and word, even if the former is imperfectly realized in the case of human speech and writing.[3]

Such a relationship had also been perceived by the second-century apologist Justin Martyr, who wrote that Christ "was begotten of the Father by an act of will; just as we see happening among ourselves: for when we give out some word, we beget the word; yet not by abscission so as to lessen the word, [which remains] in us when we give it out."[4] Gregory of Nazianzus wrote to similar effect that the Son "is 'Word' because he is related to the Father as word is to mind."[5] Further, as the analogy was elaborated in the Scholastic period by Thomas Aquinas, "thinking when it happens in silence is truly speaking, just as He is called a Word with respect to His person."[6] Aquinas thus focused on Christ's personhood as Word in comparing the procession of our thoughts into words. He

---

1. Decock, "Pre-Modern Interpretation of Scripture," 64–65, 71. See also Voelz, *What Does This Mean*, 234: "The sacred Scriptures are the words of God in human words."

2. Augustine, *De Trinitate* 15.24–25; Augustine, *De doctrina christiana* 1.13.

3. Augustine, *Sermo* 119.7: "My word was with me and proceeded into voice. The Word of God was with the Father and proceeded into flesh" (as translated in Jordan, "Words and Word," 187).

4. Martyr, Πρὸς Τρύφωνα Ἰουδαῖον Διάλογος 61 (quoted in Schaff, *Nicene and Post-Nicene Christianity*, 365). See Arthos, *Inner Word*, 83 (citing Col 1:19).

5. Gregory of Nazianzus, *On God and Christ*, 109.

6. Aquinas, *De natura verbi intellectus* §277 (as translated in Arthos, *Inner Word*, 359).

suggested that just as Christ's salvific purpose was perfected by his sufferance of human form,[7] so too are our mental words perfected in the act of verbal or written formation.[8] Aquinas thereby "bring[s] the whole weight of the Christian mystery into the phenomenon of linguistic understanding."[9]

In one sense the analogy is imperfect because the procession of the Son from the Father is atemporal, whereas the generation of language from thought is sequential.[10] As a result, "our understanding does not grasp what it knows in one instant of thought [but must discursively] draw out from itself what it thinks."[11] Yet even though we think, speak, and hear words successively, we make *sense* of them as "the parts of a whole . . . by understanding the whole itself," i.e., by "projection of the whole of meaning."[12] In other words, it is only because of the temporality of human understanding that an atemporal reality like the Trinity must be "unrolled in order to be perceived and enumerated."[13] Accordingly, the *verbum interius* "is more than a mere metaphor,"[14] but is instead explanatory of the processual nature of human language.[15]

These Patristic and Scholastic linguistic insights resonate with the Reformers' understanding that the Scriptures unfold through history in a continuing dynamic, consistent with the "living Word" ethos of Isa 55:11; Rom 10:14–17; and Heb 4:12. It is thus the task of the preacher to allow himself to be addressed by God in the Person of the Word through the textual mediation of the divinely inspired written words of the Bible.[16] And in a processual manner similar to that understood by Augustine

7. Heb 5:8–9.

8. Aquinas, *De natura verbi intellectus* §277: "Our word [has] its complete existence [*perfectum esse*] in its becoming" (as translated in Arthos, *Inner Word*, 372).

9. John Arthos, email to author, 2020.

10. Augustine, *De catechizandis rudibus* 2.3; Arthos, *Inner Word*, 42–43.

11. Gadamer, *Truth and Method*, 422.

12. Arthos, *Inner Word*, 230–31 (quoting Aquinas, *Commentary on Aristotle*, §1229); Voelz, *What Does This Mean*, 103.

13. Augustine, *De Trinitate* 9.5 (as translated in Arthos, *Inner Word*, 114). As Gadamer phrased it, the unity of the "*one* word that we say to one another and that is said to us (theologically, 'the' Word of God) . . . always unfolds step by step in articulated discourse." Gadamer, *Truth and Method*, 457–58 (emphasis in original).

14. Gadamer, *Truth and Method*, 421.

15. Lonergan, *Verbum*, 33–34: "The intelligibility of the procession of an inner word is not passive nor potential; it is active and actual" and in this respect is "an image, and not a mere vestige, of the Blessed Trinity."

16. Calvin, "Bible and the Word," 161.

and Aquinas, the Reformers held that the *viva vox Jesu* is present in the world through the preaching of the kerygma,[17] taking effect through the congregation's active reception and understanding.[18]

Hans-Georg Gadamer appropriated this extended analytical history in developing his own hermeneutical perspective on the relationship between thought and language. Picking up principally on the Trinitarian analogy, Gadamer states that the "greater marvel of language is not that the word becomes flesh and emerges into an external existence, but rather that what so emerges and is externalized is always already a word" before being spoken or written.[19] As he further explains:

> The human relationship between thought and speech corresponds, despite its imperfections, to the divine relationship of the Trinity. The inner mental word is just as consubstantial with thought as is God the Son with God the Father [and] has its being in its revealing.[20]

Moreover, any such revealing of the atemporal "inner word" occurs as it takes effect in the world where, "being actively understood, [it] is in continual formation."[21]

A translation made from the "processual" point of view that the inner meaning of a text is learned "in its revealing" does not ignore the particulars of its historical origins. Rather, it reflects the living presence of the Word in present-day words. A biblical text's paleographic and lexical elements as well as its sociohistorical context thus remain important to contemporary understanding, but so too does its revelatory interpretation and application in church history and tradition. Importantly, while the inner word of the text remains stable, understanding it "never comes

---

17. Just, "Today in Our Hearing," 199–200: "Christ's 'kerygmatic presence' . . . means "that when the word of Christ is truly preached, then Christ is present'" (quoting Old, *Biblical Period*, 186). Thiselton, *Two Horizons*, 100: "The task of the preacher . . . is so to 'translate' the text that it speaks anew to his own time."

18. Gadamer, *Truth and Method*, 422; Arthos, *Inner Word*, 358 (citing Isa 55:10–11).

19. Gadamer, *Truth and Method*, 420. Cf. Wittgenstein, *Philosophical Investigations*, 107e (§329): "When I think in language, there aren't 'meanings' going through my mind in addition to the verbal expressions: the language is itself the vehicle of thought."

20. Gadamer, *Truth and Method*, 421. Further, "the Word . . . is equal to the Father, since it is perfect and expressive of the whole being of the Father." Aquinas, *Commentary on John*, 15 (§29). See also John 1:1 and Col 1:15.

21. Gadamer, *Truth and Method*, 419n40 (citing Aquinas, *De natura verbi intellectus* §277). See also J. Smith, *Fall of Interpretation*, 143.

entirely to an end."[22] Instead, what is "linguistically articulated has free space around it which it fills in constant response to the word addressing it."[23] In the following section, I discuss how the foregoing hermeneutical principles relate to historical-critical interpretive approaches.

c. Relationship to Historical-Critical Approaches

As noted, the biblical translation theory advanced here appropriates a range of hermeneutical insights concerning the relationship of thought and language, whereby meaning is actively revealed in the enlivening words of the Word of God. The theory functions in parallel with suggestions that excessive reliance on historical-critical methods may elide much of church history and tradition and thus fail adequately to capture such meaning.[24] To put this in broader context, so-called "pre-critical" exegesis relied in the first instance on the historicity of the Scriptures, but with allowance for metaphor, typology, and allegory where the literal meaning cannot have been intended,[25] or where figurative interpretation functioned in harmony with the literal.[26] Typological as well as allegorical readings of the Old Testament assumed the historicity of the persons involved.[27] But typological and allegorical readings also examined the Scriptures for their overall meaning, discerning relationships among people and events that might not have been in the minds of the original authors, yet are revealed in the person and proclamation of Christ as the subject matter of all Scripture, the same God of creation and Israel.

Typological readings thus allow the literal and the figural to be interpreted cohesively, the latter illuminating the former without denying its reality.[28] In allegorical readings the historical sense is also present, but

22. Gadamer, *Philosophical Hermeneutics*, 211.

23. Gadamer, *Philosophical Hermeneutics*. See also Pannenberg, *Systematic Theology*, 1:15: "Exposition of scripture continues with reference to its content and truth."

24. See, e.g., Bockmuehl, *Seeing the Word*, 76–77.

25. E.g., Origen, *De principiis* 4.16–18. "Historicity" in this context refers to the actuality of the events described and is thus distinct from ways in which "history" may be otherwise understood in modern scholarship.

26. See *De principiis* 4.13; Stuhlmacher, *Historical Criticism*, 27–30; R. Williams, "Augustine," 23, noting that as Augustine read the Psalms, "the 'spiritual' reading of at least these portions of scripture does not evade or relativize the 'historical' sense."

27. O'Keefe and Reno, *Sanctified Vision*, 100.

28. Frei, *Eclipse of Biblical Narrative*, 34, 39; J. Kelly, *Early Christian Doctrines*, 71; Mathison, *Shape of Sola Scriptura*, 85; Thiselton, *New Horizons in Hermeneutics*, 163–64.

plays a lesser role in comparison with the symbolic or spiritual meaning to be elicited.[29] Taken to excess, however, allegorical readings could become "ossified in the commentaries of scholastic tradition, the catenae [and] glossa ordinaria."[30] Indeed, this chain of interpretive writings "'became almost synonymous with [church] tradition.'"[31] The Reformers thus recognized that tradition had at times departed from earlier understandings. They addressed this distancing of interpretation from the literal text *not* by rejecting typological readings altogether, but by seeking to recover their proper function.[32] And allegorical readings were understood to be "legitimate only where the allegorical intention is given in Scripture itself."[33] In Luther's and Calvin's views, a literal reading of the Scriptures was therefore required in order to obtain a proper understanding of the gospel proclamation within the unified purpose of the Scriptures as a whole.[34]

In a broader philosophical/epistemological shift, the ensuing Enlightenment vouchsafed the independence of rational analysis from the

---

29. J. Kelly, *Early Christian Doctrines*, 70. I use *allegorical* here in "the very broad sense that the text is taken to mean something other than what on the surface it says," although the term did not have a precise scope in antiquity and could "be applied to a variety of quite different exegetical techniques" including parables, types, or "spiritual" readings. Alexander, "Jews and Judaism," 45.

30. Stuhlmacher, *Historical Criticism*, 31. See Piñero and Peláez, *Study of New Testament*, 11–13, discussing the quadruple interpretive approach of Bernard of Clairvaux and others. Whether the hermeneutic of some of the later fathers led to "questionable and artificial allegorizations" does not, however, "invalidate the basic principles." Thiselton, *New Horizons*, 155–56. Accordingly, there is a growing appreciation of Patristic insights, as evidenced by the published as well as projected volumes of the Ancient Christian Commentary on Scripture.

31. Klein et al., *Introduction to Biblical Interpretation*, 43 (quoting McNally, *Early Middle Ages*, 29).

32. Klein et al., *Introduction to Biblical Interpretation*, 47.

33. Gadamer, *Truth and Method*, 175; Thiselton, *Two Horizons*, 115. See, e.g., Gignilliat, "Paul," 145, analyzing Paul's allegorical interpretation of the story of Sarah and Hagar in Gal 4:21–31 as a "Christianly" reading "in light of the literal sense of the whole redemption narrative."

34. Stuhlmacher, *Historical Criticism*, 32–35; Gadamer, *Truth and Method*, 175. See also Just, *Heaven on Earth*, 225, noting that in 1 Cor 10:1–4, "St. Paul interprets the exodus and the manna and water provided in the desert *Christologically* and *sacramentally*" (emphasis in original). As Anthony Thiselton summarizes it: "On the one hand, [the Reformers] rejected the need for tradition in reaching a proper understanding of Scripture. On the other hand, however, they argued, first, that the understanding of individual passages depended on the witness of Scripture as a whole; and secondly, that Protestant credal formulae provided a guide concerning the understanding of this unity of the Bible." Thiselton, *Two Horizons*, 300.

authority of a received magisterium.[35] Historical-critical analysis soon flourished by opening up the biblical texts to purportedly objective scrutiny as to their sources, forms, and redaction history.[36] The texts' authors and recipients were likewise made the subject of sociological reconstructions of the cultural, political, and/or economic settings in which particular books were written.[37] Further, as additional manuscripts were discovered and their variant readings collated, text-critical research sought for a base text; while lexicographical and semantic efforts were undertaken to ascertain word meanings.[38] And the Bible was increasingly interpreted with reference to "the world behind the text," i.e., truths meaningful at a given time and in a given place.[39]

At least as initially conceived, historical-critical exegesis therefore focused with "grammatical and lexical exactness in estimating what the original sense of a text was to its original audience," on authorial intention, and on individual books rather than an interrelated canonical corpus.[40] Post-Enlightenment scholarship has in fact yielded valuable insights concerning Judaism's and Christianity's historical origins; the sources, forms, and edited characteristics of the scriptural manuscripts;[41] and Jesus himself.[42] By way of social-scientific approaches and a hermeneutic of suspicion, greater attention has also been paid to the cultural

---

35. Thiselton, *Hermeneutics*, 136–38; Klein et al., *Introduction to Biblical Interpretation*, 51–54; Pontifical Biblical Commission, *Interpretation of the Bible*, 1.A.

36. Although I do not rely on the terms here, such methods may also be described as *diachronic* and *synchronic*, the former examining the sources, forms and editing history of a given text; and the latter examining its lexicographical structure and literary characteristics as it now presents itself. See generally Klein et al., *Introduction to Biblical Interpretation*, 73–75, 192–201. And these may complement one another. Thiselton, *Two Horizons*, 125: "Diachronic description depends on synchronic description."

37. Piñero and Peláez, *Study of New Testament*, 425–40.

38. Piñero and Peláez, *Study of New Testament*, 441–71. These efforts had a genesis in Johann Reuchlin's 1506 publication of a Hebrew grammar, followed by Erasmus' 1516 publication of the first modern edition of the Greek New Testament.

39. Piñero and Peláez, *Study of New Testament*, 345: The focus of such research is "the particular situation in space and time of the documents contained in the NT." See also Hagner and Young, "Historical-Critical Method," 12.

40. Frei, *Eclipse of Biblical Narrative*, 7; Hagner and Young, "Historical-Critical Method," 14.

41. Thiselton, *Hermeneutics*, 138–47.

42. See generally Bockmuehl, *Cambridge Companion to Jesus*.

contexts of the writings and their possibly embedded gender, race, and/ or power-based presuppositions.[43]

But to the extent historical-critical scholarship called into question the historicity or exegetical significance of Old Testament people and events, figural meanings of the text could be lost *even though* they provide a "common pattern of occurrences and meaning together."[44] As more recently understood, the assumption that one might objectively "understand what an ancient text *means* [by] understanding what *it meant*" has yielded to the recognition that interpretation involves "a *conversation* with ancient texts," whereby the interpreter's own "prejudices and presuppositions" have an "ongoing impact of interpreter on text and text on interpreter."[45] And in that conversation greater attention is now being paid to understanding "the whole in reference to the parts and the parts in reference to the whole."[46] As such, an apostolically understood canonical unity remains relevant to exegesis, yet now in harmony with research into the semantics, lexicography, and *Sitz im Leben* of the texts.

What has been less recognized is that these scholarly developments have important implications for translation as well as exegesis. This is because certain contemporary approaches to translation *also* proceed from Enlightenment-derived, "time-bound" premises;[47] and may therefore suffer from epistemological defects similar to those implicated by an over-reliance on historical-critical analysis. Thus, a number of significant translation projects seek to "reproduce" in a modern receptor language the same experience had by a text's original readers or listeners. Or as

---

43. Bockmuehl, *Seeing the Word*, 50–55; Kerridge, "Reading of Ephesians," 8. See also Pontifical Biblical Commission, *Interpretation of the Bible*, 1.E.

44. Frei, *Eclipse of Biblical Narrative*, 34 (emphasis in original). One result was that the two Testaments were "pitted against each other in a manner unlike that experienced in the church since Marcion." Stuhlmacher, *Historical Criticism*, 38.

45. Hagner and Young, "Historical-Critical Method," 13, 16 (emphases in original). Gadamer, *Truth and Method*, 297: It was "the naïve assumption of historicism . . . that we must transpose ourselves into the spirit of the age, think with its ideas and its thoughts, not with our own." Luz, *Matthew 1–7*, 96: "A major problem of historical-critical exegesis today lies in isolating a text in its own time and its own situation of origin and thus preventing it from speaking to the present time."

46. Hagner and Young, "Historical-Critical Method," 16; Thiselton, *Two Horizons*, 22–23; Bokedal, *Formation and Significance*, 51. See also Luz, *Matthew 1–7*, 97: "The interpretations of the early church, of the Middle Ages and of the subsequent era up to the Enlightenment are of permanent importance because of their understanding of an individual biblical text from the wholeness of the faith."

47. See Klein et al., *Introduction to Biblical Interpretation*, 53.

Eugene Nida describes the essence of his "dynamic equivalence" methodology, the goal is "a translation in which the message of the original text has been so transported into the receptor language that the response of the [modern] receptor is essentially like that of the original receptors."[48] To do so, however, requires "placing the [translator] imaginatively within the world in which a text came into existence."[49]

The above insights into the "processual" nature of language therefore have particular impact in this context, where the "living Word" of God—the *viva vox Jesu*—is understood to unfold in human history through the church's kerygmatic mission.[50] As such, neither the incarnation itself nor the Word as present in biblical text and liturgy are simply matters of past history whose meaning must be accessed by a form of imaginative reconstruction, but rather events with ongoing transformative effects in the present.[51] As Gadamer expressed it:

> The proclamation of salvation, the content of the Christian message is itself a unified event in sacrament and preaching, and only brings to expression what happens in Christ's redeeming act. It is yet a single work out of which proclamation continually goes forth.[52]

Gadamer thereby countered the hermeneutical approach offered by Friedrich Schleiermacher to the effect that a modern interpreter bridges the gap between those of the distant past and today by a form of "reproductive repetition of the original intellectual act of the author's production of the meaning on the basis of congeniality of spirit."[53] In contrast, Gadamer viewed understanding *itself* as of a historical nature, with interpretations of the past "as much a creature of the interpreter's own time and place as the phenomenon under investigation was of its own period in history."[54] A

---

48. Nida and Taber, *Theory and Practice*, 200.
49. Hagner and Young, "Historical-Critical Method," 15 (emphases omitted).
50. Arthos, *Inner Word*, 133; Just, *Heaven on Earth*, 199–200.
51. Just, *Heaven on Earth*, 127: "The past is never lost, since the entirety of salvation history is recapitulated every Lord's Day, and indeed every single day, for the baptized already have been buried and raised with Christ" (Rom 6:3–4).
52. Gadamer, *Truth and Method*, 427.
53. Gadamer, *Gadamer Reader*, 51. Schleiermacher's approach apparently reflected his sense that only through immediate experience could he perceive the truths of "the faith of my fathers." As he explains, "Of all that I praise, all that I feel to be the true work of religion, you would find little even in the sacred books." Schleiermacher, *On Religion*, 9; but see Gadamer, *Truth and Method*, 187 (describing this as "a divinatory process").
54. Mueller-Vollmer, *Hermeneutics Reader*, 38; Gadamer, *Truth and Method*, 302–7.

modern reader and an ancient text are therefore "not two alien entities that are isolated from each other by a gulf of historical time," but rather "stand in a state of relatedness to each other" within the continuum of history.[55]

Gadamer similarly rejected the suggestion of Wilhelm Dilthey that one might find the meaning of a given text through a purportedly scientific interpretive methodology applicable to biblical texts as well as other written forms. According to Dilthey, such understanding might be attained by "imaginative projection," whereby the present-day interpreter "negates the temporal distance that separates him from his object and becomes contemporaneous with it" in order to access the *mens auctoris*.[56] Yet that methodology also falls into the same epistemological error of assuming that a present-day observer is essentially an autonomous subject able to engage with a text without regard to the "horizon" of his own presuppositions.[57]

Gadamer refers to these presuppositions as "prejudices," though not in a pejorative sense.[58] He simply means those that arise out of one's own situation in a continuum of culture and history:

> We all stand in the life-stream of tradition and do not have the sovereign distance that the natural sciences maintain in order to conduct experiments and to construct theories.[59]

Without rejecting the importance of the text's cultural and historical origins, Gadamer posits that one's engagement with an ancient text is necessarily dialogic in nature. Such a text is not so much an object to be interpreted as the occasion for "*participat[ion] in an event of tradition*, a process of transmission in which past and present are constantly mediated."[60] As the basis for this mediating function he relies on what he calls the *wirkungsgeschichtliches Bewußtsein*—a mode of thought that is conscious of its *own* "being affected by history."[61]

---

55. Mueller-Vollmer, *Hermeneutics Reader*, 38–39; Arthos, *Inner Word*, 104: "Understanding is not the grasping of a fixed object by a sovereign subject." See also Eberhard, "Mediality," 413–14.

56. Gadamer, *Philosophical Hermeneutics*, xiv–xv. See also Van Leeuwen, "On Bible Translation," 300; Vanhoozer, *Meaning in This Text*, 47, 106.

57. Cf. Scalia, *Matter of Interpretation* ("originalist" hermeneutic for interpreting the US Constitution).

58. Gadamer, *Beginning of Philosophy*, 46.

59. Gadamer, *Beginning of Philosophy*, 28.

60. Gadamer, *Truth and Method*, 290–91 (emphasis in original).

61. Gadamer, *Truth and Method*, 301; Gadamer, *Gadamer Reader*, 59 ("consciousness of history being always at work in consciousness"); Gadamer, *Beginning of*

Tradition is thus the result of the mediation of text and interpretation. Referring explicitly to the writings of St. Paul, Gadamer characterized tradition as the incremental process by which a certain "excess of meaning that is present in the [ancient text] itself ... surpasses ... the horizon of understanding" of the original author by virtue of the varying interpretations it receives over time.[62] Such meaning is thus revealed in "the event of proclamation."[63] He therefore argues that it would indeed be "a false honor" to the New Testament authors to suggest that the "salvation-meaning of a scriptural text" is limited to their "'actual' horizon[s]."[64] This does not exclude authorial intent as an interpretive starting point. But as the Reformation scholar David Steinmetz has pointed out, "The meaning of historical texts cannot be separated from the complex problem of their reception, and the [historical-critical] notion that a text means only what its author intends it to mean is historically naïve."[65]

It likewise follows that a translational approach that centers meaning on how a text was understood at the time of writing may well be inconsistent with the view of the Scriptures as the living Word of God expressed in words with ongoing life in the church's teaching and worship. The translational theory presented here therefore posits a dialogue between the words of the text and its extension in church history and tradition in order more fully to reflect the ongoing, active presence of the Word. To be clear, it is *not* the case that the *verbum interius* of the text changes over time, or that biblical meaning is malleable.[66] Rather, tradition neither replaces nor undermines the text, but instead reflects the unfolding of the Word of God throughout church history. As such, it is *integral* to the revelation of the text's "inner word."

While Gadamer therefore recognized that an excess of meaning may be elicited by dialogic engagement, he is nevertheless insistent on the ultimate safeguard of the text in "protect[ing] interpretation from anachronisms, from arbitrary interpolations and illegitimate applications."[67] As

---

Philosophy, 28: "Insofar as we are historical creatures, we are always on the inside of the history we are striving to comprehend."

62. Gadamer, *Philosophical Hermeneutics*, 102, 210; Watson, *Text and Truth*, 50.
63. Gadamer, *Truth and Method*, 427.
64. Gadamer, *Philosophical Hermeneutics*, 210.
65. Steinmetz, "Superiority of Pre-Critical Exegesis," 11.
66. Watson, "Toward a Literal Reading," 211; J. Smith, *Fall of Interpretation*, 143. See also 2 Pet 1:20.
67. Gadamer, *Philosophical Hermeneutics*, 209.

relevant here, Scripture *itself* thereby imposes limits both on interpretation and translation, since "the text represents the basis of all exegesis, which in turn presupposes the truths of faith."[68] Moreover, the church's own tradition of interpretation safeguards textual meaning, deriving as it does from apostolic teaching and preaching.[69] Indeed, early formulations such as the Apostles' Creed closely track the *regula fidei*.[70] And, as applied over time, "the saving message preached in every sermon is the crucifixion and resurrection of Christ."[71] As such, the living Word of God is continuously made present in carrying out the church's salvific mission.[72]

A notable defect of a hermeneutical approach that has its principal focus on discerning textual meaning within the temporal understandings of the author and his original audience is that it thereby fails to take into account the text's interpretation, translation, and reception in the continuum of church history and tradition. And yet these are necessarily present in what Gadamer describes as the "horizon" of modern listeners and readers.[73] It follows that Nida's *translation* methodology discussed above suffers from the same epistemological flaws as does an *exegetical* overreliance on historical-critical methods. In neither context can the Scriptures be fully understood by a contemporary "reconstruction"[74] of the thoughts or perceptions of those present at the time of first expression

---

68. Gadamer, *Gadamer Reader*, 169; Eberhard, "Mediality," 430: "Despite a text's freedom from its original context, its meaning is not drifting arbitrarily because of the limits the text itself and the tradition of interpretation impose on it" (citing Gadamer, *Hermeneutik I*, 301).

69. Tertullian, *De praescriptione haereticorum* 13, 20–22. See J. Kelly, *Early Christian Doctrine*, 33–35, 49: "The authority of the fathers consisted" in their having "faithfully and fully expounded the real intention of the Bible writers." Steinmetz, "Superiority of Pre-Critical Exegesis," 11: "The original text as spoken and heard limits a field of possible meanings." Compare also Church of England, "Articles of Religion," art. 6 with Fourth Session of the Council of Trent, first decree, for which see generally Burnet, *Exposition*, 71–90.

70. J. Kelly, *Early Christian Doctrines*, 40; Mathison, *Shape of Sola Scriptura*, 25–26, 46; Stuhlmacher, *Historical Criticism*, 26–27; Thiselton, *New Horizons*, 156, also noting that the fathers' emphasis on "the centrality of Christ as a hermeneutical principle or key" leads to the Reformation principle of *sui ipsius interpres*, i.e., that Scripture is its own interpreter.

71. Gadamer, *Truth and Method*, 427.

72. See Pannenberg, *Systematic Theology*, 1:238, noting Gerhard Ebeling's understanding that "the content of revelation has a soteriological character."

73. Gadamer, *Philosophical Hermeneutics*, 102, 210.

74. Or "reproduction," as per Gadamer, *Truth and Method*, 296.

without also taking account of meaning as expressed in doctrinal, liturgical, and other developments thereafter.

Moreover, while a number of New Testament writings are formally addressed to local communities and their concerns, not all are. Beyond that, even where there is a focus on local concerns, these are not invariably unique to those audiences but are in large part common to humankind. And again, a fundamental methodological failure of an interpretive approach that is overly focused on the circumstances at the time when, and for the audience where, the text was first written is that the Gospels, letters, and other materials soon circulated widely, foreseeably addressing a readership continuously expanding in time and place.[75] Indeed, we ourselves may fairly be understood as within the universe of originally intended readers.[76]

Such a continuity of scriptural understanding is in fact revealed in the texts' translation history. As more fully explored in sect. II.f, *infra*, numerous word choices made at the outset of the English translation tradition, at least, have been sustained for some 700 years. Most importantly, in passages that are sources for essential doctrines of the faith, Greco-Latinate, Anglo-Saxon, and other wordings have been carried through for centuries in expression of the theological inner word of the relevant texts. For example, doctrines of justification, redemption, sin, forgiveness, and faith, or references to Christ's sonship, image, blood, flesh, death, or resurrection, are persistently articulated with words received over multiple centuries and in multiple communities, even as their meaning is continuously explored.[77] And this is particularly noticeable with respect to the continued use of many "classical" formulations in such academically informed, church-sponsored translations as the RSV, NRSV, and NRSVue, where prior understandings may be preserved even as newly analyzed philological, text-critical, and sociohistorical materials are incorporated.[78]

---

75. Bauckham, "Gospels Written" (with respect to the Gospels); D. Smith, *Epistles for All* (with respect to the Epistles), esp. 5–18 (discussing and responding to critiques of the view that early Christian writings were intended for open rather than distinct faith communities); Bird, *Colossians*, 40: "The early Christians . . . had a sense of being a worldwide movement."

76. Stefan Felber, email to author, 2021.

77. See, e.g., Silva, "Faith versus Works."

78. Note also that the Ancient Christian Commentary on Scripture relies on the RSV in tracing the use of Scripture by the church fathers. See Gorday and Oden, *Colossians*, xxxiii.

As with exegesis, translation is thus itself a historical phenomenon, realized within a linguistic "flow of history" of which both text and translator are integral parts.[79] A contemporary translator should therefore translate with consciousness of how "our language bears the stamp of the past and is the life of the past in the present."[80] A translational approach that takes account of the text's canonical framework and its effective presence in faith formulae and a translation tradition may thereby provide a more expansive access to textual meaning than would historical-critical approaches operating alone. And such a methodology would serve faith communities by assisting to bridge the sociolinguistic distance between past and present.

d. Effective History, the Canon, and the Creeds

Consistent with the linguistic and hermeneutical principles discussed above, understanding a given biblical text does not primarily depend on an imaginative reconstruction of the *mens auctoris*, but rather a dialogic participation in its kerygmatic presence in the world. The goal of that dialogue is to reach an understanding of the text's *verbum cordis*, with such meaning perceived by virtue of its "unfolding" in church history and tradition.[81] In this section I will examine how an effective history hermeneutic thus requires understanding biblical texts within a canonical framework and with a view to their role in the development of credal and other affirmations of the faith.

It is a given that many of the terms used in the New Testament reflect phraseology and images from the Old Testament, as well as other books within the New Testament itself. These therefore have meanings that must be understood within the intrascriptural sweep of biblical history.[82] As such, the hermeneutical principles outlined above call for examination of the effective history of the Jewish Scriptures in the New Testament, as

---

79. Thiselton, *New Horizons*, 6; Stuhlmacher, *Historical Criticism*, 89.

80. Gadamer, *Philosophical Hermeneutics*, xxviii; Ricoeur, *On Translation*, 6.

81. Arthos, *Inner Word*, 12; Watson, *Text and Truth*, 199: "This history is a *Heilsgeschichte*, a history set in motion and determined by God's word."

82. In this regard, there are two aspects to "intrascripturality." In some instances, one may detect a linguistic influence, such as by parallel wording. In others, the relationship concerns different works within the canon that address similar doctrinal issues. Both are relevant to the methodology advanced here, with the former more evident in the use of particular words and phrases, the latter in marginal citation or exegetical comment.

well as a given New Testament text's own further history in the developing canon. If we perceive the text's inner word "in its revealing," then it is properly viewed with reference to "the dogmatic unity of the canon," i.e., considering the individual part as an element of a disclosive whole.[83] Gadamer thus understood the "concept of a canon in New Testament theology" as something "legitim[ized] . . . in the *wirkungsgeschichtliches Bewußtsein*."[84] The reason is that the essence of the divine communication in *both* Testaments is Jesus Christ as their common subject matter (*die Sache*)—with the Bible's "twofoldness" reflecting "a mutually constitutive relationship" in that revelation.[85]

Another way to approach meaning is to identify the question "behind the text," i.e., that which it purports to answer.[86] Again, using Colossians here as an exemplary text, Paul employs an elevated series of predicates concerning Christ. Among other things, Christ is named as "the Radiant Image of the Invisible God" (Col 1:15); "the Source and Beginning" of the Church (1:18); he in whom "the Totality of the Pleroma of Divine Perfection took up its dwelling" (1:19); and the one through whom God would "reconcile all things back to himself" (1:20). Indeed, the entire letter is suffused with plenary expressions. Thus, Paul prays that the Colossians be filled with all wisdom and knowledge of God (1:9). And he tells them that the fullness of Deity dwells bodily in Christ (2:9), who is the Firstborn over all creation (1:15) and the Head of the Church (1:18), such that they as members are fulfilled in him (2:10).

The question behind this text would therefore seem to be, "Who is Christ?" While this may have been a "Mystery hidden in past ages and generations" (1:26), it was revealed by Jesus himself both pre- and post-resurrection.[87] His identity as the same God of creation and Israel is thus

---

83. Gadamer, *Truth and Method*, 421; Gadamer, *Gadamer Reader*, 48; Stuhlmacher, *Biblical Theology*, 199, 367, 800–801.

84. Gadamer, *Gadamer Reader*, 59. See also Calvin, "Bible and the Word," 161 ("The writings of the apostles contain nothing that is not simply a natural explanation of the law and the prophets"); Calvin, *On the Christian Faith*, 59–60. Cf. Augustine, *De civitate Dei*, ch. 17 (tracing prophecies and fulfillment).

85. Watson, *Text and Truth*, 179–80; C. Campbell and Pennington, *Reading the New Testament*, 3.

86. Gadamer, *Truth and Method*, 370: "The meaning of a sentence is relative to the question to which it is a reply, but that implies that its meaning necessarily exceeds what is said in it."

87. E.g., John 5:39; Luke 24:13–32, 44 ("This is what I told you while I was still with you: Everything must be fulfilled that is written about me in the Law of Moses, the Prophets and the Psalms" [KJV]); Tertullian, *De praescriptione haereticorum* 20–21, 37

woven into the New Testament writings and reflected in the apostles' teaching.[88] This understanding prevailed in Patristic thinking, beginning at least with Justin Martyr.[89] And it was maintained in the form of the *regula fidei* emerging by the second century "as a compendium of the faith proclaimed and taught in the New Testament writings."[90] As Markus Bockmuehl notes, "the frame of the canon" is "already an implied reading of the two-Testament Scripture's constituent parts, *indeed an effect of the text.*"[91] Christological readings of the Old Testament are therefore a "natural extension" of the text, knitting it into a "unitary canon."[92]

(source of true doctrine is Christ himself); J. Kelly, *Early Christian Creeds*, 2; Stuhlmacher, *How to Do Biblical Theology*, 3.

88. E.g., Acts 2:14–36 (relying on Joel 2:28–36); Rom 3:2 (the Jews were entrusted with the "oracles of God"); 1 Cor 8:6 (one God, the Father, and one Lord Jesus Christ); 15:3–4 (delivering the gospel as received); Heb 3:1–7 (contrasting Christ and Moses); Rev 19:10 ("the testimony of Jesus is the spirit of prophecy"). See Stuhlmacher, *How to Do Biblical Theology*, 3–4, 11.

89. *Dialogus cum Tryphone*, 85.1-2 (Kinzig, Faith in Formulae, §104b3): εἰς δὲ μόνον τοῦτον τὸν ἡμέτερον Χριστόν . . . ὡς καὶ ὁ ψαλμὸς καὶ αἱ ἄλλαι γραφαὶ ἐδήλουν καὶ κύριον αὐτὸν τῶν δυνάμεων κατήγγελλον. Clement of Alexandria, *Stromata* 6.15: κανὼν δὲ ἐκκλησιαστικός ἡ συνῳδία καὶ συμφωνία νόμου τε καὶ προφητῶν τῇ κατὰ τὴν τοῦ κυρίου παρουσίαν παραδιδομένῃ διαθήκῃ. See also Origen, *De principiis* 4.13.

90. Stuhlmacher, *Historical Criticism*, 26; Bokedal, "Rule of Faith," 234–35; J. Kelly, *Early Christian Doctrines*, 40; J. Kelly, *Early Christian Creeds*, 2, 85–86.

91. Bockmuehl, *Seeing the Word*, 22–23 (emphasis added); Bockmuehl, "New Testament Doctrine," 40–41. I recognize that for some contemporary commentators, "Old Testament texts are to be interpreted 'in their own right.'" Watson, *Text and Truth*, 181; Thiselton, *Hermeneutics*, 77; Stuhlmacher, *How to Do Biblical Theology*, 1; cf. Stuhlmacher, *Biblical Theology*, 773, commenting on Brevard Childs' caution "that the independent witness of the Hebrew Bible must not be prematurely fused with the likewise independent witness of the New Testament." And some scholars challenge the notion that Christ is the hermeneutical key for understanding the Old Testament, on grounds that it robs the Old Testament of its distinctive role in the canon. See, e.g., Seitz, *Character of Christian Scripture*. But it may simply be that those influenced by "a historically-oriented hermeneutic . . . lack the analytical tools to grasp the phenomenon of a *Wirkungsgeschichte* that propels canonical texts far beyond their immediate circumstances of origin." Watson, *Text and Truth*, 320. See also M. Wilson, *Our Father Abraham*, 109–10 (discussing neo-Marcionism); Baker, *Two Testaments*, 51–52 (same).

92. Frei, *Eclipse of Biblical Narrative*, 2. Canon formation as such is beyond the scope of this work, but the testimony of Jesus as Messiah "connects the New Testament inextricably with the Old," such that this one "center" unifies the complex "canonical process." Stuhlmacher, *How to Do Biblical Theology*, 11, 62–63, 81. Bokedal, *Christ the Center*, 9: "Christ is held [by Luther] to be the *scopus* of Scripture, the central figure and point of view." Stuhlmacher, *Biblical Theology*, 10: there is a "continuity of confession between the Old and New Testaments." Cf. P. Zahl, *First Christian*, alleging a radical "discontinuity" within the canon.

The textual language must likewise be construed in the light of its effective history in developing church doctrine and liturgy. For example, taking Colossians as a test case for present purposes, the Niceno-Constantinopolitan Creed is laced with the letter's phraseology.[93] So too the Chalcedonian Statement and the Athanasian Creed.[94] Most particularly, as the church engaged with the implications of Col 1:19 and 2:9 concerning the fullness of Deity dwelling bodily in Christ, it credally affirmed him to be "perfect in godhead and perfect in manhood," with "the distinctive character of each [divine] nature being preserved."[95] And while the word "Trinity" does not appear anywhere in the Scriptures, "the first credal text to affirm the procession of the Holy Spirit from the Father and the Son" relies on language from Colossians as a source.[96]

In short, the hermeneutical principles discussed above lead directly to consideration of a given text's situatedness within the canon and its continuing effective presence in church history and tradition. I therefore address in the next section the elements of a translation methodology that builds on and applies such principles towards a dialogic revealing of the text's inner word.

---

93. Kinzig, *Faith in Formulae*, §184e.

94. Arthos, *Inner Word*, 74–87 (citing Col 1:19; 2:9–10).

95. Kinzig, *Faith in Formulae*, §215. See also Schaff, *Nicene and Post-Nicene Christianity*, 595–99, noting parallels between similar language in Athanasian Creed, §29–37 and Augustine's formulations in *De Trinitate*. In *Expositio fide* 1.8.14, John of Damascus described the relationship as one of περιχώρησις (in English, circumincession)—a nonphysical interpenetration of the Persons. See Straus, "Psalm 2:7," 222–29.

96. Kinzig, *Faith in Formulae*, 3:98. See Victricius of Rouen, *De laude sanctorum* §2 (Kinzig, *Faith in Formulae*, §462): *Sic confitemur, quia sic credimus individuam trinitatem, ante quam nihil potest attingi nec mente concipitur, per quam omnia visibilia et invisibilia sive throni sive dominationes sive principatus sive potestates. Omnia per ipsum et sine illo factum est nihil* [quoting Col 1:16]. See also Thiselton, *New Horizons*, 160 (citing Col 1:15 as part of a "Trinitarian ground-plan" in Pauline texts).

II. Elements of a Canonical-Hermeneutical Translation Approach/Test Case

IN THIS SECTION, I apply the linguistic and interpretive principles outlined above to the task of developing a canonical-hermeneutical approach to translation. Christianity itself may in large measure be seen as a faith-in-translation.[1] Just as the church's inception at Pentecost was a verbal realization of the Great Commission,[2] so too are translations of the Word into the words of all nations a further dissemination of the gospel "in various languages."[3] A translation methodology that embraces the effective history of the Old Testament in the New and that of the canonical writings in their ecclesial life thus serves to edify faith communities by providing intelligible words essential to the Church's "ongoing recapitulation of the event of salvation in the kerygma."[4]

A translation methodology premised on the Bible's canonical integrity likewise rejects the view that the Old and New Testaments exist or operate independently of one another. Themes of promise and fulfillment, of obedience and disobedience and/or of judgment and redemption find recurrent and developing expression across the books that were ultimately collected as canon, as do the myriad quotations, paraphrases or allusions to Old Testament books in the New Testament.[5] And the presence of *nomina sacra* in some of the earliest manuscripts is likely further evidence of an intentional textual continuity of reverence for the divine

---

1. Marcos, *Septuagint in Context*, 346: "From the beginning [Christianity] was a religion that favoured translation of the Bible into vernacular languages." Nichols, "Translating the Bible," 28.

2. Matt 28:18–20; Mark 16:15–17.

3. Acts 2:4: ἑτέραις γλώσσαις.

4. Arthos, *Inner Word*, 358; Bockmuehl, *Seeing the Word*, 64–68; Gadamer, *Relevance of the Beautiful*, 148–49. The academically informed methodology of this book thus operates broadly within a church framework; translations undertaken outside that context therefore might not avail themselves of all of its aspects.

5. This can, of course, be overdone. See Alter, Review of *Great Code*.

name from Old Testament to New Testament.[6] Indeed, further usage of *nomina sacra* in Patristic writings may also reflect "an 'embryonic creed of the first Church.'"[7] An effective history methodology should therefore take account of ongoing developments in church tradition, where the underlying text becomes woven into credal and liturgical materials, thus creating open space for appropriate language to be drawn from such materials when rendering the text into the receptor language.

Where there is—as in English—an extensive translation tradition, a canonical-hermeneutical methodology will reveal not only the intratextuality of Old and New Testament citations, allusions and themes within the original forms of the texts and in developing church tradition, but also the same as expressed in that translation tradition.[8] It may thus on occasion be appropriate for a new translation to incorporate passages from prior versions *in haec verba* in order to sustain that effective history in circumstances where it has become embedded in church liturgy and tradition by reception, e.g., where the English forms of certain passages are *themselves* essential elements of the text's *Wirkungsgeschichte*.[9] And the same is true with respect to particular credal formulations or other liturgical language.

Any contemporary translation also arises in the context of recent efforts to revisit biblical interpretation from reader-oriented, feminist, womanist, queer and/or liberationist perspectives. While I do not focus here on such sociohistorical aspects of the Scriptures' formation, an effective history methodology should in principle be applicable to translations undertaken from different theological standpoints.[10] My point is

---

6. Bokedal, *Christ the Center*, 348–49.

7. Bokedal, "Rule of Faith," 252 (quoting Roberts, *Manuscript, Society and Belief*, 46).

8. To be sure, the English translation tradition is more extensive than that of other languages, such that translation into those languages may raise epistemological issues that lie beyond the scope of this work. See, e.g., Nichols, "Translating the Bible," concerning biblical translation into Indonesian.

9. This is consistent with Brevard Childs' view that "the effect of the canonical collection is to provide a new intertextuality which relates these various witnesses within a literary corpus." Childs, *Old Testament Theology*, 851–52.

10. As Francis Watson observes: "To dissent from an authoritative translation is not to concede that the text itself is unstable and that its meanings are many. It is to recognize that, although all translations are approximations, some approximations capture the single sense of the text much more accurately than others, and that progress and improvement are therefore possible." Watson, *Text and Truth*, 112. See also Ullmann, *Semantics*, 49: "There is usually in each word a hard core of meaning which is relatively stable and can only be modified by the context within certain limits."

that a translation undertaken in dialogic engagement with the philological and sociohistorical elements of the text as well as its effective history in church doctrine and liturgy has the possibility of exploring its substantive meaning in *myriad* ways.

In the following sections I therefore provide suggestive elements of a canonical-hermeneutical translation methodology, interweaving particulars of Paul's Letter to the Colossians to test the methodology's operation and applicability. As a threshold matter, I examine three prevailing translation approaches: literal, dynamically equivalent, and paraphrastic/hybrid. I then offer an excursus on some of the practical ways in which translation methodologies are applied, examining differences between individual efforts and those by multiple translators functioning as part of committee-structured projects. Next, I identify relevant literary and linguistic categories that should be considered in applying a dialogic hermeneutic to a given biblical text, testing that argument by more specific analysis of Colossians' genre and register. I then engage in a more detailed examination of words and phrases in that letter, applying the foregoing methodological principles to a central portion of the text. In that context, I explain how the methodology may resolve interpretive conflicts and aid in revelation of the text's inner word. Finally, I seek to draw conclusions applicable not only to Colossians but potentially to other New Testament materials.[11]

a. Navigating among Prevailing Translation Approaches

Traditional approaches to translation theory have tended towards binary distinctions between the "original" and the "translation," prioritizing the former over the latter; or between "literal" and "dynamically equivalent/sense-for-sense" renderings, suggesting a need to choose one over the other. Other approaches expand beyond the dynamically equivalent into freer paraphrase, or take a more hybrid and eclectic tack.[12] There are of course problems in maintaining strict distinctions of this sort. And as discussed in this section, there are strengths and weaknesses to each.

---

11. Whether the methodology is fully applicable to other genres within the New Testament, or even within the epistolary genre, therefore remains open for further research, as noted in sect. IV.a, *infra*.

12. There are also theories that focus on particular translation concerns, such as those relating to gendered language, racial tropes, wealth/poverty distinctions, and/or Western ethnocentrism. See, e.g., Neufeld, *Social Sciences*. It is beyond the scope of this book to explore such theories, but its methodology does call for translators to approach a text conscious of the "horizon" of their social and cultural environment.

Notwithstanding the limitations of any given approach analyzed below, the canonical-hermeneutical approach argued for here recognizes some utility in each, often depending on the particular genre and register of a given biblical text.

i. Literal

Under a "literal" approach (sometimes referred to as "formal correspondence"), a translator follows the text's formal structure and layout and tries "to preserve as much as possible of its grammatical form, sentence and clause structure, and consistency of word usage" as possible.[13] Accordingly, the translator renders each word into an English equivalent and adjusts the word order and/or provides such linking verbs or similar terms as may be needed to conform to the syntactical rules of the receptor language.[14] For example, Greek does not fully depend on word order for meaning in the way that English does,[15] but rather a good deal more on inflected forms. The relative absence of inflection in English therefore calls for more expanded phrasing in order to express modes and relationships that are otherwise contained within the grammatical structure of the Greek source vocabulary.[16]

Moreover, there are some Greek words that have no English equivalent—the particles μέν and δέ for example, which can function as pathway markers to help a reader navigate through the text. But this barely scratches the surface of how complex Greek particles can be.[17] Moreover, even where a given word has an English analog as to meaning, it may well have more than a single meaning in Greek, or more than a single English analog. That would be true for even the most obvious words, where one might translate θάλασσα as ocean, sea, etc. The same goes for other common words, such as those for dirt, earth, ground, soil, sky, table, road, or

---

13. Wonderly, "Crib, Transposition," 8. A "literal" approach is also sometimes referred to as "word-for-word," although the latter term is more accurately applied to an interlinear translation. See sect. II.f.iii.2, *infra*.

14. Warren, "Modern Theoretical Approaches," 165.

15. Word order does, at the same time, have more impact in Koine than in Attic Greek. Even so, Jerome recognized that "much that is beautifully expressed by the Greeks does not, if transferred literally, resound in Latin; and conversely, what sounds pleasing to us, if converted by strict word order, would displease them." Jerome, *Letter to Pammachius* 11.

16. Belloc, "On Translation," 39.

17. See generally Denniston, *Greek Particles*.

Elements of a Canonical-Hermeneutical Translation Approach/Test Case 39

numerous other concrete things existing in the world. The art of translation therefore lies in understanding the dynamic nature of the process. As Gadamer explains, one

> transforms [a text into another language by] reproducing that which was meant from among the multiplicity of possible meanings, and this represents still another hermeneutical relation. Every translation, even the so-called literal translation, is some kind of interpretation.[18]

A translation might therefore technically be described as "literal" even where a different English word is used for the same Greek word. Yet one still needs reasons for translating/interpreting the same Greek word differently. Thus, where there are credible lexical options for a given word or phrase and translating one way or another may have theological and doctrinal implications, translation and exegesis come into close relationship with one another. A translator should therefore provide sufficient information to a reader or interpreter to alert him to those options and enable him to consider different readings. All of these can be identified or explained in marginal notations.

But it is also the case that "it is always possible *to say the same thing in another way.*"[19] This suggests the value of periodic translations into the receptor language, whether styled "literal" or not, because in every generation a decision ought to be made whether to retain or vary prior word choices. Hence "each age translates anew."[20] That is *not* to suggest that the truths of Scripture are unstable or that all readings have validity, but rather that a translator of sacred texts must be particularly sensitive both to the letter and the spirit, grounded in the former but taking care not to kill the latter.[21] For example, even though the King James Version is sometimes described as quintessentially "word-for-word" or "literal,"[22] its

---

18. Gadamer, *Gadamer Reader*, 170. See also Gadamer, *Truth and Method*, 386 ("the translator will seek the best solution—a solution that can never be more than a compromise"); Ricoeur, *On Translation*, 22 (translation aims for "equivalence without identity"); Belloc, "On Translation," 36: "There are, properly speaking, no such things as identical equivalents."

19. Ricoeur, *On Translation*, 25 (emphasis in original).

20. Steiner, *After Babel*, 262.

21. 2 Cor 3:6; cf. Kagan, "2015 Scalia Lecture," at 8:29: "We're all textualists now."

22. As is also the case with the ESV, which is self-described as a continuation of revisions to William Tyndale's version, placing itself in what it calls "the classic mainstream of English Bible translations over the past half-millennium" ("Version Information," in ESV [2001]) and adopting an "essentially literal" translation methodology with an emphasis on "'word-for-word' accuracy" ("Translation Philosophy," in ESV [2001]).

translators did not use the same English word to translate the same Greek word every time. Instead, they explain that they "have not tied [them]selves to a uniformity of phrasing, or to an identity of words" because "there be some words that be not the same sense everywhere."²³

Moreover, as more fully explained in the discussion of the English translation tradition in sect. II.f.i, *infra*, in making their word choices the KJV translators built on an existing translation history that in critical ways reflected prior decisions how particular Greek terms might be rendered. To pick one example, the word εἰκών in Col 1:15 is rendered "image" in the KJV, consistent with John Wycliffe's usage in the first English translation, which was in turn taken from Jerome's use of *imago* to translate εἰκών from the Greek. At the same time, the KJV *also* uses the word "image" in Heb 1:3, even though the Greek uses a different word for the concept, i.e., χαρακτήρ rather than εἰκών. Moreover, in this passage from Hebrews the KJV adds a modifying adjective "express" that does not appear in the Greek at all, but is arguably closer to the meaning of χαρακτήρ. So while sometimes the KJV translators used a different English word for the same Greek word, sometimes they used the same English word for a different Greek one.

Again, keeping to this same example, Jerome rendered χαρακτήρ in Heb 1:3 as *figura*. Wycliffe translated the Latin term as "figure." William Tyndale, working directly from the Greek, rendered it as "the very image." And the 1599 Geneva Bible used "the engraved form." While we lack records explaining why the KJV translators opted for the phrase "express image" rather than Wycliffe's term "figure," Tyndale's "the very image," or the Geneva Bible's "engraved form," the relevant point is that generalized descriptions of a translation method as "literal" do not themselves provide guidance as to any specific word choice. Yet because verses such as Col 1:15 and Heb 1:3 were critical in the church's formulation of credal language to resolve certain doctrinal disputes, a contemporary translator sensitive to the effective history of the text should consider its linguistic trajectory both in faith formulae and the translation tradition in finding present-day words that further the text's "revealing."²⁴

And when it comes to less concrete vocabulary—e.g., theological terms—there can be considerable room for lexical variance, such that the multiplicity of literal meanings is simply a starting place. Take the word

---

23. "Preface," in KJV (1611).
24. See Gadamer, *Truth and Method*, 421.

σάρξ, for example. It might refer to animal flesh,[25] to the human body as a whole,[26] to corrupted human nature,[27] to one's physical presence,[28] or even to ethnic/racial identity.[29] To use the same English word would reflect a lack of appreciation of the range of meanings in the Greek. As such, it may sometimes be appropriate to use different words to translate the same Greek word even when used in a similar context, in order to reflect that variability.

One notable example of the limits of taking a purely literal approach to translation is the phrase πιστίς Χριστοῦ, one that has itself been generative of volumes of scholarly commentary.[30] As the KJV translates Gal 2:16, "A man is not justified by the works of the law, but *by the faith of Jesus Christ.*" But as the NIV translates it, "We . . . know that a person is not justified by the works of the law, but *by faith in Jesus Christ.*" And as the NET translates it, "We know that no one is justified by the works of the law but *by the faithfulness of Jesus Christ.*" Or yet still as the MSG translates it, "We know very well that we are not set right with God by rule-keeping but only *through personal faith in Jesus Christ.*" Even further, as the AMP expounds, "Yet we know that a man is justified *or* reckoned righteous *and* in right standing with God not by works of the Law, but [only] *through faith and [absolute] reliance on and adherence to and trust in Jesus Christ (the Messiah, the Anointed One)."*[31]

These differences arise out of the distinction between the objective and subjective senses of the genitive construction. Does the verse in question refer to the faith one reposes in Christ Jesus, who would thus be the "object" of the faith; does it refer to the faith Jesus placed in the Father, in which case Jesus is the "subject" having faith; does it refer to the faithfulness with which Jesus lived his life, where Jesus is also the

---

25. 1 Cor 15:39.
26. 1 Pet 4:1; Col 1:24.
27. Rom 8:5–12.
28. Col 2:5.
29. Rom 11:14.
30. E.g., Bird and Sprinkle, *Faith of Jesus Christ*; Silva, "Faith versus Works"; Gathercole, *Where Is Boasting*; J. Barclay, *Obeying the Truth*.
31. See also Rom 3:22; Gal 2:20, 22; and Phil 3:9; as well as similar instances in Acts 3:16 (ἡ πίστις ἡ δι' αὐτοῦ); Rev 14:12 (οἱ τηροῦντες τὰς ἐντολὰς τοῦ θεοῦ καὶ τὴν πίστιν Ἰησοῦ); Jas 2:1 (ἔχετε τὴν πίστιν τοῦ κυρίου ἡμῶν Ἰησοῦ Χριστοῦ τῆς δόξης). Nor are the questions limited to verses concerning the "faith of Christ." They would likewise arise in verses referring to the "righteousness of God," e.g., Rom 1:17; or the "love of Christ," e.g., 2 Cor 5:14.

"subject" as to the manner he exercised faith; or does it refer to something more general, such as a faith system that is "of Christ"? Depending on which one chooses, we are either saved by virtue of our reposing faith in Christ, or by his having reposed his faith in the Father, or as members of a faith community whose center is Christ such that we are "of" him. Any or all of these have major theological implications and, indeed, much of Christian history from the Reformation onward has turned on such varied understandings.[32]

Even the Greek word πιστίς itself need not invariably be translated by the English word "faith." The word includes concepts of trust, commitment, loyalty and/or obedience—all of which may factor into the experience of an individual believer, of a particular church congregation, of the church as a whole, or of Jesus himself.[33] And where there is a range of permissible meanings but each with potentially distinctive theological significance, the choice made will often depend on the doctrinal position one brings to it—one's own "horizon," to use a Gadamerian phrase. The word ἱλαστήριον would be such an example, where it may be translated as propitiation (KJV, ASV, ESV), sacrifice of atonement (NRSV, NIV), expiation (RSV), sacrifice (NLT), seat of mercy (TYN), or reconciliation (GN). As Gadamer urges, in order to convey the text faithfully a translator must therefore pay careful attention to the presuppositions he brings to it. The point here is that a translator taking a canonical-hermeneutical approach to such theologically freighted words as "faith/trust" or "propitiation/atonement" should focus not only on the literal Greek and contextual setting, but also on textual meaning as revealed in church history and tradition by operation of the *viva vox evangelii*.

ii. Dynamic or Functional Equivalence

The popular approach to translation known as "dynamic" or "functional equivalence" owes its prevalence to Eugene Nida. Current examples are

---

32. Hays, *Faith of Jesus Christ*, 141–62. See also Reasoner, *Romans in Full Circle*, 39–40. To be sure, even where there are credible grammatical arguments for different readings, the doctrinal options are not always equally weighted. See Watson, *Text and Truth*, 112. For example, Eugene Nida asserts that "most scholars" agree that the phrase δικαιοσύνη θεοῦ in Rom 1:17 refers to the "process by which God puts men right with himself" rather than to "God's own personal righteousness." Nida and Taber, *Theory and Practice*, 2. But Nida clearly overstates his case. See Van Leeuwen, "On Bible Translation," 300–301.

33. See Hays, *Faith of Jesus Christ*, 119–32.

the NIV, TLB, and NLT.[34] Essentially, Nida challenged what he perceived to be an overemphasis on the part of Bible translators "to reproduc[ing] stylistic specialties [in the text], e.g., rhythms, rhymes, plays on words, chiasmus, parallelism, and unusual grammatical structures."[35] As a counterweight to such approaches, Nida argued that a translator should present the source text in a form consistent with the cultural patterns of the receptor language in order to achieve maximum intelligibility on the part of a given receptor audience. He thus proposed shifting the focus from "the form of the message to the response of the receptor":

> Correctness must be determined by the extent to which the average reader for which a translation is intended will be likely to understand it correctly. . . . We are not content merely to translate so that the average receptor is likely to understand the message; rather we aim to make certain that such a person is very unlikely to misunderstand it.[36]

The overarching goal is "a translation in which the message of the original text has been so transported into the receptor language that the response of the [modern] receptor *is essentially like that of the original receptors.*"[37]

In the first instance, Nida's argument assumes that it is possible to identify the "original receptors." Yet even within the relatively small confines of a church locality such as Colossae, there is no certainty as to the composition of the community to which the letter is nominally addressed. See sect. II.d.i, *infra*. More importantly, his argument suffers from a fundamental circularity, at least in the context of the biblical

---

34. It is not always easy to categorize a given translation as reflecting one or another theory. See generally Rhodes, *Complete Guide*. For purposes of this analysis, I have generally adopted any self-descriptions provided by the translators themselves.

35. Nida and Taber, *Theory and Practice*, 1.

36. Nida and Taber, *Theory and Practice*, 1.

37. Nida and Taber, *Theory and Practice*, 200 (emphasis added). Nida's basic premise is that all languages share certain basic structures called "kernels," out of which more complex surface structures are built; and that translation essentially involves breaking down the source language into its core elements and restructuring them in accordance with grammatical rules of the receptor language. Nida and Taber, *Theory and Practice*, 33. In that regard he reflects the influence of Noam Chomsky's "distancing of form and meaning," such that "meaning was located no longer in the surface structure but in the deep structure of a sentence of text," it being the task of translation to "transform" the source language into the receptor without "adding, deleting or changing the meaning." Felber, "Chomsky's Influence," 255. Nida thus offered a "three-stage model," graphically illustrating translation as the process of "transferring" such "kernels" from one language to another. Nida and Taber, *Theory and Practice*, 33.

writings. As David Smith explains with respect to Paul's letters, the "original" intended audience of such texts included not only those present at the time of writing, but also the expanded readership of a *corpus Paulinum* as it became more definable during the period AD 60–150, as well as the unknowable others to whom the writings would be circulated in the future.[38] To be consistent with the theory, a dynamically equivalent translation would therefore need to incorporate the hypothetical "responses" not only of listeners and readers living in scattered settings of the first and second centuries, but also those of subsequent readers and listeners.[39] And it would likewise need to incorporate the text's effective history in the form of understandings reflected in commentaries and creeds, as well as in translations throughout the continuum of history.[40] But this is precisely the opposite of what Nida argues.[41]

Nida's assumption that a translator will be able to have a firm grasp of how the text was to have been understood by its first hearers or readers therefore falls into the epistemological trap discussed above concerning certain historical-critical approaches, i.e., that the translator as subject purports to examine the text as object without recognizing the mutuality of discourse involved in understanding, or the conceptual horizons/prejudices he brings to the task. As Raymond van Leeuwen observes, Nida's translation approach is thereby flawed with its suggestion that "we and the other are essentially the same, so much so that we accommodate the other to our pre-understandings and situation."[42]

It is certainly true that protean translators in prior eras such as Tyndale and Luther aimed for fluidity and naturalness of expression, such that their phrasings were language formative as well as faith encouraging. Yet their translations were focused on the meaning of the original text rather than the capacities of the receptors, with the translation serving

38. D. Smith, *Epistles for All Christians*. See also Bauckham, "Gospels Written."

39. This is not to say that a translator should not consider how a text might have been understood at the time of writing, given the need to ground the text. As discussed in sect. II.d, *infra*, historical-critical analysis therefore remains important. The point is that presumed early understandings should not impose a limit on meaning.

40. Luz, *Matthew 1–7*, 97: "The interpretations of the early church, of the Middle Ages and of the subsequent era up to the Enlightenment are of permanent importance because of their understanding of an individual biblical text from the wholeness of the faith."

41. See Nida and Taber, *Theory and Practice*, 8 (rejecting the relevance of "writings of the early Church Fathers" or of "creeds" in determining textual meaning).

42. Van Leeuwen, "On Bible Translation," 296. See also Belloc, "On Translation," 39; Ricoeur, *On Translation*, 22.

not "as a mere aid to understanding but as an authoritative replacement."[43] In contrast, as Stefan Felber points out, Nida's approach has the risk of diminishing the "performative" function of biblical language as itself "the *media salutis, i.e.*, the means of salvation."[44] Moreover, Nida's approach may even fail to give sufficient weight to the literal text, at least where the underlying form is relevant to its substantive meaning. Sometimes the strangeness of how thoughts are conveyed in the source language may be the very point.[45] If the medium is unfamiliar, one might therefore lose the meaning by purposefully obscuring the difficulties.[46] With respect to passages of Scripture that express the ineffable, it may in fact do injustice to the text if its "mystery" is overly subordinated to "intelligibility."[47]

It is worth noting that when Nida applies his own methodology to the task of translation he is led into some plain errors. With respect to Colossians, for example, he makes the flat statement that "there are no OT quotations or allusions in the letter,"[48] a demonstrably incorrect statement, as shown in sects. II.d-e, *infra*. And beyond failing to perceive canonically essential elements of Colossians, Nida seems to read his own theology into the letter in a manner that avoids important language in the actual text. He would thus translate διὰ τοῦ αἵματος τοῦ σταυροῦ αὐτοῦ in 1:20 as "through his Son's death on the cross" rather than "through the blood of his cross,"[49] a plain departure from a key term in the literal text. In a similar vein, Nida would translate σωματικῶς in 2:9 as "in his

---

43. Nichols, "Translating the Bible," 29.

44. Felber, "Chomsky's Influence," 260. Felber also observes that one of the negative effects of Nida's method in a German context has been "the replacement of a sacred writing style by a fluid journalistic style," with a resulting "abandonment" of "the language-shaping power of Luther." Felber, "Moratorium," 216 (quoting Felber, "Bibelübersetzung"). And the effective role of Luther's translation in the German language is paralleled by the WYC/TYN/KJV's role in the development of the English language.

45. In other words, sometimes "the medium is the message." McLuhan, *Understanding Media*.

46. Rohrbaugh, "Foreignizing Translation," 14, argues in favor of a purposefully "foreignizing translation" as a "deliberately alien rendering that forces the reader to confront the cultural otherness of the text." The occasional use of languages other than English may be one way to achieve this. See, e.g., Straus, *Book of Revelation*.

47. Indeed, language itself may impose limits with respect to the "unsaid and inexpressible." Risser, "Hermeneutics and Linguisticality," 2 (quoting Gadamer, "Grenzen der Sprache," 358).

48. Bratcher and Nida, *Translators Handbook*, 2.

49. Bratcher and Nida, *Translators Handbook*, 27.

humanity" rather than "bodily/corporeally,"[50] a phraseology that bears no relationship to any translation of which I am aware.

It thus appears that Nida's *own* doctrinal horizon affected his choices of which words to use and—more seriously—which to omit. This again illustrates the epistemological defects of his methodology, because a translation presented in the name of dynamically equivalent "intelligibly" may well be laden with undisclosed presuppositions. As Gadamer stressed, in order to engage in honest dialogue with a given text, one must examine one's presuppositions, remaining open to any changes in understanding that might result. A principal risk of a dynamic equivalence approach in the biblical context is therefore that it encourages a translator to make imaginative projections (in Dilthey's sense) about the "react[ions]" of the "original receptors," without the benefit of the text's interpretive history in the church and without appropriate self-reflection. This can be a particular problem when dealing with theological terms, hence the doctrinal/credal focus of the translation methodology outlined here. For example, the following is a comparison of how the word καταλλαγή is translated in various verses by the NLT on the one hand with how it is translated in certain other versions.

	NLT	KJV	NIV	Hart
Rom 5:11	making us friends of God	atonement	reconciliation	reconciliation
Rom 11:15	God offered salvation	reconciling	reconciliation	reconciliation
2 Cor 5:18	reconciling people to him	reconciliation	reconciliation	reconciliation
2 Cor 5:19	the wonderful message	reconciliation	reconciliation	reconciliation

It is unclear how Nida's approach would guide a translator here. What, in other words, is the measure for determining how these verses were understood at the time of writing? To be sure, these are terms that have special meaning in Christian doctrine. They mean something more—a good deal more—than just "making friends" with someone, which the NLT offers as a "dynamic equivalent."[51] Yet as Anthony Thiselton observes in his recent commentary on Colossians, the Greek

---

50. Bratcher and Nida, *Translators Handbook*, 54.

51. The GNB, overseen by Nida, is to the same effect: "We were God's enemies, but he made us his friends through the death of his Son."

word καταλλαγή had an established secular meaning "denot[ing] the re-establishment of an interrupted or broken relationship," with former hostility now overcome. He therefore argues for the traditional English word "reconciliation" in Col 1:20, such that its use as a "theological term" would not require specialized knowledge or result in a lack of intelligibility.[52] The risk in too free a rendering along the lines of Nida's approach is that the force of the doctrine otherwise doesn't come through.

Nida's further argument is that "if we assume that the writers of the Bible expected to be understood, we should also assume that they intended one meaning and not several, unless an intentional ambiguity is linguistically 'marked.'"[53] But Nida's reductionist assumption fails to account for words' polysemic nature *both* as used in a given textual context *and* as understood across time and place. Stefan Felber pointedly criticizes this aspect of Nida's approach as overly "positivistic," with a resulting "denigration of ambiguity, metaphor and poetry."[54] By overweighting "intelligibility," a translator may thereby subordinate essential elements "of tone, of savour, of rhythm, of spacing, of silence between the words, of metrics and of rhyme."[55]

It is also unclear what Nida means by "intentional ambiguity." The apparent suggestion is that a translator should imaginatively reconstruct the *mens auctoris*. If so, then the approach risks limiting the text's reach to the immediate context in which it was written. As Lawrence Venuti saliently observes, "Nida's [equivalent effect] principle assumes that a textual effect is an invariant, an assumption that is put into question . . . by the variability of reception across diverse cultural constituencies and historical periods."[56] And as Gadamer points out, "temporal distance . . . is not a yawning abyss but is filled with the continuity of custom and tradition," such that "new sources of understanding are continually emerging that reveal unsuspected elements of meaning."[57]

Applying an effective history hermeneutic to the text, doctrinal truths are thus grounded in apostolic teaching even as they continuously unfold in church history and tradition.[58] In other words, there is no nec-

52. Thiselton, *Colossians*, 41–42.
53. Nida and Taber, *Theory and Practice*, 7.
54. Felber, "Chomsky's Influence," 259.
55. Ricoeur, *On Translation*, 38.
56. Venuti, *Translation Studies Reader*, 496.
57. Gadamer, *Truth and Method*, 295–98.
58. See Stuhlmacher, *Historical Criticism*, 89: "The biblical texts can be fully

essary inconsistency between an author's wish to be understood by his immediate audience and a recognition that explaining spiritual matters is not the same thing as writing an engine repair manual.[59]

iii. Paraphrase

To paraphrase is to provide a version of a word or sentence that does not displace but rather stands alongside the original, using other words for the purpose of restating or interpreting the original in order to help explain it.[60] There can be a great virtue in doing so, hence the popularity of such translations as Eugene Peterson's The Message. Even so, the farther one departs from the text, the greater the risk (in theory at least) of importing personal opinion or bias. It is true that historically there have been ecclesial correctives to errors or even heresies by virtue of the interpretive reception a translation will or will not be given by a given faith community.[61] But in the context of translation, what are the outer boundaries of paraphrase, or of adding information not contained in the literal text for the purpose of making the text's meaning clear? When is an idiomatic, colloquial, or slang rendering going too far?

The answers these questions may depend on how one understands the nature of a sacred text. As relevant here, without "definitive textual attestation" we could not grasp the truths about Jesus, including that he *is* the truth. Such textual mediation depends "foundationally" on the Scriptures and is also reflected in the words of "the Christian community, its preaching, its sacraments, its forms of life."[62] This parallels Gadamer's view that "consensus" may be reached about the subject matter of a text

---

interpreted only" through "genuine dialogue with the tradition of the text and . . . an awareness of the history of the text's interpretation and effects which determines it."

59. But see Nida and Taber, *Theory and Practice*, 1 (arguing that biblical translation should aim for the kind of "complete intelligibility" one finds in an aircraft operation manual). Cf. Van Leeuwen, "On Bible Translation," 300: "Nida's image evokes Scriptures as a 'handbook,' or technical manual—presumably one that contains life or death instructions on how to obtain eternal salvation."

60. Etymologically, the word comes from the Greek, where it means "to say using other words." "παραφράζω," LSJ 2:130. It was carried virtually intact into Latin as *paraphrasis* and thence into Middle French as *paraphrase*.

61. Morgan, "Critical Study," 213–14: "Credal elements" concerning Jesus' divinity "provide the contours of a doctrinal criterion of authentic Christianity" (citing Vincent of Lérin, *Commonitorium* 2.6).

62. Watson, *Text and Truth*, 27.

(*die Sache*) when we "participate in a continuum of tradition already shaped in part by the classic status accorded to the text."[63]

In his pithy essay "On Translating," Martin Luther addressed the question whether a translator could legitimately add any word(s) not present in the literal Greek text in order to best convey meaning in his own language. Defending his German translation of Rom 3:28, he readily conceded that he added the adverb *allein*[64] to the verse, even though there is no equivalent in either the original Greek or the Latin version thereof.[65] A plain English rendering of the underlying text would be, "We know that a person is justified by faith apart from works of the law." In Luther's version it reads something like, "We know that a person is justified *solely* by faith/by faith *alone*, apart from works of the law." Yet as Luther explained:

> I also know that in Romans 3, the word "*solum*" is not present in either the Greek or Latin text . . . [but] it conveys the sense of the text—if the translation is to be clear and accurate, it belongs there.[66]

To be sure, Luther's version is no loose paraphrase. But it does illustrate the use of explanatory language in a manner consistent with the inner meaning of the text as discerned by comparison with other portions of the Scripture, *sui ipsius interpres*.[67] In that regard, careful exegesis may be the key to the occasional paraphrastic translation of such "core" doctrinal passages. Benjamin Jowett addressed this point in his essay "On the Interpretation of Scripture," where he is highly skeptical of overreliance on etymology and grammar to resolve obscure words or passages, noting that "the difficulties of the New Testament are for the most part common to the Greek and the English." He argues that rather than "haggle" minutely over particles and tenses a translator/interpreter would more fruitfully focus on developing an understanding of "theological terms, such as faith (πίστις), grace (χάρις), righteousness (δικαιοσύνη),

---

63. Watson, *Text and Truth*, 45.

64. Or thus in his 1522 translation, *alleyn durch den Glauben*. Luther, "Open Letter on Translating."

65. I.e., λογιζόμεθα γὰρ δικαιοῦσθαι πίστει ἄνθρωπον χωρὶς ἔργων νόμου and *arbitramur enim justificari hominem per fidem sine operibus legis*.

66. Luther, "Open Letter on Translating," 9–10.

67. Clement of Alexandra also held to this interpretive approach. *Stromata* 7.16: "The truth is not found by changing the meanings, but . . . in establishing each one of the points demonstrated in the Scriptures again from similar Scriptures."

sanctification (ἁγιασμός), the law (νόμος), the spirit (πνεῦμα), the comforter (παράκλητος), &c."[68] Translation of the "great primary words" of the Scriptures may therefore sometimes *require* elaboration, such as "when we reformulate an argument which has not been understood."[69] To some extent, this may therefore be the essence of paraphrase properly handled.

b. Excursus on "Classical" Formulations

While each of the above general approaches to translation may be useful with respect to particular words, phrases, and images, the translation methodology advanced here does not rely on a unified or governing approach in that sense. Instead, applying the canonical-hermeneutical principles outlined above, it becomes clear that biblical translation requires more particularized attention to a range of factors, including paleographical and philological elements of the text, the presence of words and imagery of the Old Testament in the New, the trajectory of the text in conciliar statements and other faith formulae, and the text's own translation tradition. The goal here is not to displace other versions, but rather to provide further access to the text's inner word "in its revealing" through the continuum of church history and tradition.

In other words, as illustrated in sect. II.f, *infra*, where a translation such as the RSV is largely an updating of the English used in the KJV to eliminate so-called archaisms, to reflect text-critical developments, or to clarify obscure or convoluted passages, then it is really the inertial weight of the underlying translation that carries the meaning. Viewed this way, "tradition" is likewise consistent with Gadamer's "concept of the classical," whereby certain texts retain authoritative/normative significance *notwithstanding their historicity*.[70] A strong translation tradition is thus an essential element of the text's *Wirkungsgeschichte*, protecting it against "arbitrary interpolations and illegitimate applications."[71]

It follows that a translator should be familiar with, and consider when it is appropriate to retain, such "classical" formulations. Continuity of certain words or phrases may be *exactly* what is called for in order to

---

68. Jowett, *Interpretation of Scripture*, 47; cf. Robert Alter, email to author, 2019.
69. Ricoeur, *On Translation*, 25.
70. Gadamer, *Truth and Method*, 285–90.
71. Gadamer, *Philosophical Hermeneutics*, 209.

reflect consistent understandings of the text's truth content.[72] This might be the case, for example, with passages such as John 1:1, where the existing form of words has purposefully been followed in a nearly unbroken line for centuries. And where the cadences of a verse have become embedded over hundreds of years in literature as well as liturgy, subsequent translators might reasonably shy away from changing the language. Compare these translations from John 1:1, listed chronologically from old to new:

WYC	In the beginning was the Word
TYN	In the beginning was the Word
KJV	In the beginning was the Word
RSV	In the beginning was the Word
NRSV	In the beginning was the Word
NIV	In the beginning was the Word
ESV	In the beginning was the Word

The point is that over the course of nearly seven hundred years of English translation history *none* of these important versions changes the form originally provided by John Wycliffe—who was not even translating from the Greek, but from the Vulgate. Instead, when Tyndale and those who followed *did* translate John 1:1 from the Greek, they did so in exactly the same way Wycliffe had done from the Latin. Now, the Greek in John 1:1 is unquestionably straightforward—'Ἐν ἀρχῇ ἦν ὁ λόγος. So is the Latin—*In principio erat Verbum*. The translations that adhere to the classical WYC/TYN/KJV formulation are thus indisputably faithful to the literal Greek and exemplify a consistent strand of the translation tradition.

But that doesn't mean that the verse is self-explanatory, let alone that its meaning is easy to grasp. It's not. Who or what is the Word, for example? Much credit is due in that regard to David Bentley Hart for simply transliterating the Greek ὁ Λόγος as "Logos" rather than translating it as "Word." He thereby calls on the reader to embrace, reflect, and meditate on ὁ Λόγος in all of its depth and complexity of meaning. Even if that meaning is not fully apparent to all readers, Hart is also right that λόγος "in certain special instances is quite impossible for a translator to reduce

---

72. Gadamer, *Truth and Method*, 280: "Acknowledging authority is always connected with the idea that what the authority says is not irrational and arbitrary but can, in principle, be discovered to be true," and indeed "superior."

to a single word in English, or any other language."⁷³ His transliteration is therefore literal in the sense of faithfulness to the central Greek word; but also varies the phrasing of the verse as a whole, now reading, "In the origin there was the Logos." In general, Hart's use of "Logos" rather than "Word" does help signal the "mystery" inherent in the Scriptures to which Jerome referred and encourages a reader to engage in his own dialogue with the text in a search for the *verbum interius*. In that sense, he further explores the "excess of meaning" to which Gadamer refers.

How does one square such an exploration with the importance of *also* maintaining the effective history of the text in the form of authoritative translations? In other words, if the Word "is proclaimed ever anew" as it unfolds in church history,⁷⁴ then can it be proclaimed "anew" with the same words used for hundreds of years? The hermeneutic employed here seeks to allow room for *both*, at least in the English translation tradition, where freshly coined expressions provide fuller understanding without compromising, and often working in harmony with, standard formulations. The virtue of revisiting and/or expanding on the "classical" is in fact that any newness of expression can be presented either directly in the form of a distinctive translation, or by way of exegesis on the traditional form. In both cases, as Gerhard Ebeling observed, the goal is a dialectical process of understanding whereby the Bible speaks to the changing present:

> Identity and variability belong inseparably together and are linked to one another in the process of interpretation, whose very nature is to say the same thing in a different way and, precisely by virtue of saying it in a different way, to say the same thing.⁷⁵

The methodology of this book therefore does not suggest that every new translation involve alteration of or variance from prior versions in order to justify itself. Many classically authoritative and normative

---

73. Hart, *New Testament*, 549–51. He does allow that the Chinese Bible's use of *tao* (道) for Λόγος in John 1:1 might, within the complexity of its literary and religious meanings, be "about as near as any translation could come to capturing the scope and depth of the word's religious, philosophical, and metaphoric associations, while also carrying the additional meaning of 'speech' or 'discourse.'" Hart, *New Testament*, 550. But this does confirm the difficulty of rendering the word as Word, as it were.

74. Gadamer, *Truth and Method*, 419; cf. Thiselton, 101: "'Although preaching may say the same thing as the text, it in no case says the identical thing'" (quoting Fuchs, *Zum hermeneutischen Problem*, 95).

75. Ebeling, *Problem of Historicity*, 26 (quoted in Gadamer, *Philosophical Hermeneutics*, xxvi–xxvii); Gadamer, *Truth and Method*, 427; Steiner, *After Babel*, 178.

passages may well appear similar to others. At the same time, the "free space around" the text allows for novel expressions of its substantive meaning. And such latitude exists regardless of the particular genre or register of the text, i.e., whether narrative, epistolary, hymnic, etc. That said, the concerns of this book in capturing the text's effective history may be at their most acute where the text reflects a less tangible *verbum interius*; where the writer seeks to convey that which is ineffably beyond words; where the subject is the nature of God, "who alone has immortality, dwelling in light inaccessible, whom none among mortals has ever seen nor could see."[76] Almost by definition, it is in such cases that the text is at its most open, with understanding sought in "the infinity of dialogue."[77]

c. Excursus on Translation Committees

Having now surveyed a range of biblical translation theories and methodologies, it seems clear that no one theory or methodology will be suited to all possible textual forms. That said, it is undoubtedly true that many important and valuable insights can arise out of a multiplicity of scholars engaging with the texts, including through refinement of the form based on manuscript analysis, corrections to vocabulary and syntax, or incorporation of newly discovered social, historical, or archaeological facts. To that end, Nida and Taber provide extensive guidelines for the "Organization of Translation Programs" in an appendix to their monograph.[78]

The nature and structure of translation committees are the essence of these organizational principles. As more fully detailed therein, such committees are multiply layered, consisting of a governing editorial committee of three to five persons with "good Biblical backgrounds"; a review committee of eight to ten scholars with technical expertise in the relevant language; a consultative group of twenty-five to fifty persons representative of ecclesial constituencies; translation consultants of unspecified number; a stylist; plus support staff in the form of secretaries and administrators.[79] These guidelines are meant to be applicable to transla-

---

76. 1 Tim 6:16.
77. Gadamer, *Truth and Method*, xxxiv.
78. Nida and Taber, *Theory and Practice*, 174–88.

79. This is obviously not a cheap process. Indeed, the guidelines suggest that members of the review committee be offered a "per-page remuneration." Nida and Taber, *Theory and Practice*, 186.

tions into languages that have a literary tradition (which may or may not include prior biblical translations), as well as languages that have no such tradition.[80] They are thus presented as fully applicable to any new translation that might be undertaken in English, where the literary history is long and complex and numerous translations are readily available.

Nida's concept of a governing committee structure with multiple inputs has in fact been widely adopted, as is evident from the structure of committees responsible for the most popular of today's English versions, including those of the NLT, ESV, NIV, NRSV, and the NRSVue.[81] It is of course of primary importance for any major translation project to include the best scholars in a given area.[82] And the committee process itself calls for a significant number of drafting, review, editing, and other exchanges. As proposed by Nida and Taber, individual books are allocated to persons based on their relevant scholarly focus, with the same book often being assigned to more than a single scholar. There are no public records of translation committee deliberations, however, and therefore no reliable way of assessing the general extent to which controversial interpretive views are surfaced, reviewed, and accepted or rejected by consensus decision.

---

80. The guidelines reflect a mission-driven desire to translate the Bible into languages previously lacking the text, or even in some cases any written form of language. It is beyond the scope of this work fully to examine distinctions between Nida's sociolinguistic methodology as operative in such contexts and that developed here within an extensive translation tradition.

81. See New Living Translation, "Meet the Scholars" (four-member coordinating team, six senior translators, ninety-three scholars, one stylist); Bible Researcher, "ESV Translators" (fourteen-member oversight committee, fifty review scholars, "more than" fifty-member advisory council); Biblica (for NIV), "Committee on Bible Translation" (fifteen-member translation committee); Zondervan (for NRSV), "Translation Committee" (thirty-member translation committee); NRSVue, ix (seven general editors and fifty-six book editors, with some general editors also serving as book editors). Study Bibles incorporating and elaborating on a given translation are likewise comprehensive. See, e.g., Attridge, *Harper Collins Study Bible* (two general editors, four associate editors, one consulting editor, ninety-one contributors).

82. Even so, experience teaches that self-selecting entities (whether corporate boards of directors, translation committees, or private clubs) tend to turn to those most like themselves. In the present context, that tendency may even be fostered by the guidelines' specific provision that members of translation committees should be chosen based on informal recommendation. Nida and Taber, *Theory and Practice*, 179–80: members to be chosen by "talking with leading churchmen, professors, writers and others who are most likely to know those best able to do the job." This may explain why there is often considerable overlap in membership from translation committee to translation committee, i.e., many of the same people keep reappearing.

The guidelines also provide for stylistic input, although the scope of the stylist's task is not clearly spelled out and therefore most likely varies from publisher to publisher. As a general matter, the guidelines recognize that a person performing that role within a committee structure "is usually not a top-flight specialist in style but only someone who seems to be much more competent than perhaps the rest of the committee."[83] Faint praise indeed. As one illustration of that guideline in practice, it is instructive to examine internal memoranda concerning certain stylistic issues involved in preparation of the New Living Translation.[84] To the extent the NLT is indicative of how a multiply layered committee might work, a stylist was involved during the planning stages in providing input as to the translation's general methodology. Thereafter, his editorial input was engaged to review and comment on initial drafts as prepared by the several scholars with responsibility for particular books, and after the same had already passed through further review as to substance. But consistent with the guidelines, the senior-most review committee of the NLT had the final say on style as well as content.[85] More generally, if the NLT can be taken as exemplary, the stylist's task appears to have been focused on proposing language that would assure clarity of expression, listenability, and accuracy of grammar and syntax, without necessarily aiming for a "literary" result in the broad sense.

In this connection it is noteworthy that Nida and Taber warn that it would be "most unfortunate" for the "basic draft" to be prepared by one person for further stylistic and/or substantive review by the larger teams, speculating that such a person would be "the constant center of attack" by reviewers, become "defensive," and thereby render "impossible" the "teamwork" that is the essence of their proposed structure.[86] Even so, they recognize that

> there are, of course, those rare individuals who have exceptional literary and scholarly gifts and who have almost single-handedly produced fine translations of the Scriptures. For the most part, however, even these persons have had the advice and help of

---

83. Nida and Taber, *Theory and Practice*, 158. See also 157, suggesting that the stylist "should not have too much acquaintance with the traditional forms of the Scriptures."

84. These materials are courtesy of Tyndale House Publishers.

85. Daniel Taylor, email to the author, 2020.

86. Nida and Taber, *Theory and Practice*, 184.

advisers who have been able to supply the required guidance in critical matters.[87]

Their proposed committee structure and process thus contrasts generally with the work of individual translators. As outlined in sect. II.f, *infra*, John Wycliffe is the historical paradigm for such persons as far as English goes. William Tyndale further enriched the translation tradition. Thereafter, the committee of King James translators refined the Bible's literary and scholarly quality, but in doing so preserved the lion's share of the individual progenitors' language—over 70 percent in the Old Testament and 80 percent in the New Testament. And close examination of the actual output of modern committee translation projects demonstrates that at least with certain key passages, it is *still* the language of those early "rare individuals" that persists, notwithstanding subsequent translators' stated methodologies and notwithstanding the nature and structure of committees that apply them. As a result, the substantive weight of the texts as presented in the persistent "single-handedly produced" wording of its translation tradition is received anew in the church by way of successive adoption, at least for those versions like the RSV/NRSV/NRSVue that describe themselves as an express continuance of the WYC/TYN/KJV lineage.

What tends to be lost along the way, however, is what Robert Alter describes as "the stylistic authority of the 1611 version."[88] By now putting style in a subordinate position in their proposed committee guidelines, Nida and Taber may therefore have *inverted* the proper order that a generation-to-generation revisiting of the translation tradition might call for. As a result, many committee efforts seem bland and forgettable, being "lifeless[ly] cast in 'translationese,'"[89] the "sort of English that nobody ever spoke in any century at all."[90] Alter in fact posits as a "reason for the gravely flawed modern translations of the Bible" that while translators "are almost all rigorously trained at a few premier universities" in the "tools of philological analysis" and other linguistic skills, "it seems unlikely that they would have had any serious exposure to the prose of Margaret Atwood or Philip Roth, and, going back a few decades, to the prose

---

87. Nida and Taber, *Theory and Practice*, 174 (though not identifying any such persons).

88. Alter, *Art of Bible Translation*, 10.

89. Steiner, *After Babel*, 364.

90. Phillips, "Translating the Gospels."

of Nabokov, Faulkner, Hemingway, or Virginia Woolf, on the evidence of their own use of the English language."[91] Moreover, Nida's guidelines do not appear to include persons with expertise in credal and liturgical theology and practice, even though these are vital elements of church history and tradition that are (at least as proposed herein) relevant to textual understanding.

It is perhaps fair to ask whether the unmemorability of many modern translations is attributable, at least in part, to Nida's influence, such that translation projects geared to a dynamic equivalence methodology have inadvertently "distanc[ed] form and meaning"[92] and thereby diminished the role of "biblical language and [the] theology of the word and the sacraments as the *media salutis*."[93] And to the extent that broad-based translation efforts have produced versions that are "lifeless[ly] cast in 'translationese,'" this may be one consequence of the translators heeding Nida's patronizing injunction that they should "eliminat[e] . . . expressions" that are "so difficult and 'heavy' (whether in vocabulary or grammar) as to discourage the reader from attempting to comprehend the content of the message."[94]

One question is whether at least in the case of more spiritual and ineffable language, such as that in John 1:1 or the Colossian Hymn, the gathering and sifting of philological and sociohistorical input by the members of a broad-based translation committee is sufficient to evoke the "mystery" of the Word in the receptor language. In such instances, more poetic and allusive language, atypical grammar, or interpretive paraphrase might be called for *in addition* to scholarly improvements to the text. And here the input of persons with expertise in credal and liturgical theology and practice might well be important. It is perhaps

---

91. Alter, *Art of Bible Translation*, 11, 17. See also Dryden, "Preface to Sylvae": "A good Poet is no more like himself, in a dull Translation, than his Carcass would be to his living Body. There are many, who understand Greek and Latin, and yet are ignorant of their Mother Tongue." Belloc, "On Translation," 36: "If the translator . . . is not a good writer in his *own* language, then the translation *must* be bad throughout, however well [he knows] the original [language]" (emphasis in original). Cf. Robert Alter, email to author, 2019 (commenting on Straus, *New Testament*): "There is a cleanness and clarity in the [translation's] language . . . that I admire. I can see that it will make these texts accessible and understandable to modern readers in a fresh way . . . [and the] English, unlike that of the sundry modern translation committees, is quite good and idiomatically apt."

92. Felber, "Chomsky's Influence," 255.

93. Felber, "Chomsky's Influence," 260.

94. Nida and Taber, *Theory and Practice*, 1–2.

instructive to compare the above, "classical" formulation of John 1:1 with certain individual translators' renderings:

Phillips	In the beginning God expressed himself
TLB	Before anything else existed, there was Christ
MSG	The Word was first
Hart	In the origin there was the Logos
Straus	The Word existed before all Time

That is not to say that an individual translator's writing is of necessity enlivening—in fact, it may be quite deadening—or that the "inner word" of the text is thereby any more fully understood than by way of "classical" formulations. Nor is it to suggest that an individual translator would not benefit from "the advice and help of advisers," as Nida's guidelines put it. On the contrary, a sensibly constituted committee of consulting scholars from a range of disciplines could be of critical benefit to an individual translator, not only by providing specialized input but also by reviewing and commenting on interim drafts. The real question is whether the kind of consensus and compromise that are essential to successful group functioning are as well suited to the task of filling translatable "free space" as would a faithful individual with superior literary skills who takes on the role of "decider," whether that be in a committee context or otherwise.

d. Literary Characteristics

As noted, formal aspects of the Greek text remain important in contemporary translation. In that context, I have chosen the letter to the Colossians as a fit test of the interplay between historical-critical research and the canonical-hermeneutical considerations advanced here, not only because it addresses a wide range of substantive issues, but also because it is written in a corresponding diversity of stylistic tones, from the prosaic to the most elevated. Colossians is not unique in that regard, but it is considerably more varied than many other New Testament texts despite its relatively short length. The letter is also rich in identifiable intrascripturality and intertextuality by way of its relationships to the LXX, other books in the New Testament, contemporaneous extra-biblical materials, faith formulae, and other elements of ongoing church tradition. As explained in this section, a translation methodology that gives life to a biblical text's distinctive expressive forms as well as its intra/intertextual relationships may be critical in sustaining the Scriptures' revelatory nature as they speak across time's continuum. Without delving too deeply into the field of linguistic analysis, some background and definition will be useful for purposes of my use of Colossians as an example of how the effective history methodology advanced here may be usefully applied to a variety of literary aspects.

Essentially, the terms "genre," "register," and "style" are used to analyze and/or categorize different linguistic forms, including but not limited to those found in written texts. While "there is no general consensus concerning the use of *register* and related terms such as *genre* and *style*," these terms are generally used to describe "different perspectives on text varieties."[95] What this means, using the terminology of the discipline, is that genre analysis tends to focus on the linguistic structure of a particular variety of text, whether a letter, novel, or poem. Analysis or identification of the register of a given text focuses on "core linguistic features [within the text] like pronouns and verbs" with a view to identifying the "communicative purposes and situational context" thereof.[96] *Genre* thus refers to a general literary general category and *register* to its specific modes of expression.[97]

Style, on the other hand, essentially focuses on "aesthetic preferences associated with particular authors or historical periods."[98] An understanding of varieties of register appearing in the *Greek* text may therefore be of use in crafting a translation that stylistically reflects those varieties in *English*. In other words, identification of a given register—whether

---

95. Biber and Conrad, *Register, Genre and Style*, 2, 21 (emphasis in original). Not all theorists use the terms *genre* and *register* the same way. Bhatia, "Generic View," and Swales, *Research Genres*, use genre but not register, for example; while Ure, "Introduction," and Heath and Langman, "Shared Thinking," use register but not genre.

96. Biber and Conrad, *Register, Genre and Style*, 2.

97. See Willi, *Languages of Aristophanes*, 8: "'Register' is the linguistic code that is used in the creation of a text that belongs to a 'genre.'"

98. Biber and Conrad, *Register, Genre and Style*, 2. "Style" can also be a means of discriminating between "good" and "bad" writing. See, e.g., Strunk and White, *Elements of Style*. It is also how a competent reader of English should be able to identify a passage as written by Hemingway rather than Faulkner, by Joyce rather than Mailer, or to characterize a text broadly as Shakespearean, Victorian, or Beat in nature. Further, it is the basis for assuring conformity with such guidelines as may be (i) adopted by a particular publisher or institution (e.g., University of Chicago, *Chicago Manual of Style*); (ii) required within a given profession (e.g., Harvard Law Review Association, *Bluebook*), or (iii) proposed as generally applicable (e.g., Modern Language Association, *MLA Handbook*).

hymnic, liturgical, didactic, rhetorical, paracletic, and/or prosaic—may also suggest an appropriate English style. Attention to varieties of register may thereby serve to mitigate a "distancing of form from meaning."[99] The hymnic would thus be rendered hymnically; the prosaic prosaically; the paracletic paracletically.

i. Genre and Occasionality

With the relatively recent discovery of "thousands of ancient letters," scholars have identified a number of characteristics which, taken together, provide some basis for categorizing this form of communication as "epistolary" in genre. Gordon Fee and Douglas Stuart identify six characteristics as typical of letters in antiquity: (1) the writer's name; (2) the name and/or location of the recipient; (3) a greeting; (4) a prayer, health wish, and/or expression of thanksgiving; (5) the body or substance of the letter; and (6) a final greeting and farewell.[100] But the list is not invariable. Sometimes a prayer wish is missing; sometimes the writer has included both a prayer and a giving of thanks; and sometimes the writer pens a "doxology" in lieu of either.[101] And Hebrews, though described in the canon as a "letter," reads less like a letter than a treatise.

As relevant to my use of Colossians as a "test case" for the proposed translation methodology, Paul's letters were generally longer and more complex in form than those typically found in antiquity, often consisting of: (1) opening identification of the sender and addressee; (2) initial greeting; (3) thanksgiving or blessing; (4) body of the letter, with a proposition, arguments, and a theological or doxological conclusion; (5) paracletic/ethical remarks; (6) closing greetings and messages; (7) comments about the writing and signature itself; and possibly (8) a closing blessing.[102] Paul likewise often moves from prayers or petitions to any

---

99. Felber, "Chomsky's Influence," 255.

100. Fee and Stuart, *How to Read*, 58–59; but see Witherington, *New Testament Rhetoric*, 20: New Testament epistles are best understood as "rhetorical discourses to be proclaimed orally when the messenger arrives with the document in hand, rolls it out, and dramatically delivers it."

101. See Fee and Stuart, *How to Read the Bible*, 59 (noting such distinctions among 3 John 2 (prayer); Galatians, 1 Timothy and Titus (no prayer stated); and 2 Corinthians, Ephesians, and 1 Peter (doxology)).

102. Witherington, *New Testament Rhetoric*, 112–13. While questions of authorship are not strictly speaking at issue here, as they have no clear effect on translation, my own position is that Colossians was in fact authored by Paul. That conclusion is

theological issue relevant to the recipients and then back again.[103] And further, because it was thought "in antiquity that a letter replaced or represented its author . . . [then in Paul's] case the letters represented the presence of the apostle, the missionary" and carried with them his special authority.[104]

Again, for present purposes Colossians serves as a useful methodological example because it includes elements common to other Pauline letters, such as greetings, thanksgiving, and prayer.[105] It is also of a general type referred to as "occasional," i.e., set in a particular time and place and addressing concerns of a local community, but possibly of more general import. Contemporary theologians have thus grappled with the question whether a given letter should be interpreted principally based on the particular needs and circumstances of the recipient community, or whether the letter was from the outset intended for general circulation as a source of doctrine and guidance.[106]

The analysis is not strictly binary, of course. Some letters are plainly written for general use in the larger church, while others are directed to particular individuals or communities yet also include discussions of such substance and depth as to be received and applied as the Word of God for the benefit of all. Indeed, *most* New Testament letters have some portions that are quite specific (such as greetings to this, that, or the other person (e.g., Rom 16:1–23), as well as others that virtually transcend time (e.g., 1 Cor 13; Col 1:15–20). As explained above, for exegetical purposes, it is important to understand the local context and purpose of a given

---

particularly supported by the reference in 4:16 to the circulation of the letter, which suggests a kind of transparency that would not be expected coming from someone other than the actual author; the details concerning his imprisonment; and the overlapping references to persons also referred to in the undisputedly Pauline letter to Philemon. See D. Campbell, *Paul*, 103–5. However, in recognition that Colossians' authorship remains a divided question among scholars (see generally Foster, *Colossians*, 74–93), I will for convenience refer to "Paul" as the author and the letter as "Pauline," regardless of whether the letter: (i) was scribed by Paul; (ii) was a joint effort by Paul and Timothy (as arguably stated in 1:1); (iii) was written by a close associate of Paul's after his death; or (iv) came into form on some other scenario.

103. Compare Col 2:6–23 with Rom 1:16–17; 1 Cor 1:9; 1 Thess 1:4–5; and 2 Thess 1:5–10.

104. Hartman, "On Reading," 138–39, describing "Paul's letters as apostolic ministerial writings."

105. Compare, e.g., Col 1:2–4 with 1 Thess 1:2–3; 2 Thess 1:3–4; Rom 1:8–17; 1 Cor 1:4–9; Phil 1:3–11.

106. See generally D. Smith, *Epistles for All Christians*.

letter. Yet a given text's *verbum interius* should not be wholly constrained by the time, place, and circumstances of the original writer or recipient.

Fee and Stuart therefore go too far with the broad assertion that "*all*" New Testament letters/epistles must be interpreted as first-century works "arising out of and intended for a specific occasion."[107] The fact is that "texts of Scripture do not have a single meaning limited to the intent of the original author."[108] While it is therefore true that Paul's writings appear to be "always generated by a specific *occasion* or situation that required this rhetorical instrument, this modality of his presence," they are nevertheless "official correspondence from an Apostle chosen by God to churches called into being by God."[109] One should thus avoid over-contextualizing so as not to diminish the authority of what even at the time were understood to be part of the "Scriptures."[110]

These exegetical questions have relevant implications for translation. The fact that a given text is marked by the occasion of its origin simply means that its interpretation—and thus translation—must take that occasion into account. But in the case of a canonical text, that *also* means that the "work is borne along into a future of indefinite duration by a communally-authoritative tradition."[111] Hence the living Word approach of the methodology advanced here, which imports into the field of translation theory recent suggestions of the need to refocus biblical theology by taking fuller account of the texts' reception and effective history.[112]

In the following section I analyze Colossians' epistolary-related components as an example of how genre analysis functions as a hermeneutical element with effects on translation. I thereby focus on how a translator might separate any "universal principles from context-bound

---

107. Fee and Stuart, *How to Read the Bible*, 60 (emphasis in original).

108. Davis and Hays, *Art of Reading Scripture*, 2; Beetham, *Echoes of Scripture*, 140.

109. L. Johnson, *First and Second Letters*, 93 (emphasis in original): "None of his letters is purely personal correspondence."

110. 2 Pet 3:16. See also 2 Tim 3:16; 2 Pet 1:21.

111. Watson, *Text and Truth*, 49; see also 66n22, discussing Gadamer's concept of *Okkasionalität*. See also M. Mitchell, "Particularity and Universality," 123, expanding on Nils A. Dahl's arguments as to the "'implicit catholicity'" of Paul's letters.

112. See generally Bockmuehl, *Seeing the Word*. Note that Bockmuehl's critique also suggests that aspects of the "New Perspective" on Paul suffer from over-contextualization within the framework of Second Temple Judaism. Compare, e.g., E. Sanders, *Paul*; and Stendahl, "Apostle Paul"; with Gathercole, *Where Is Boasting*; Thompson, *New Perspective*; Stuhlmacher, *Revisiting Paul's Doctrine*; Westerholm, *Israel's Law*.

or culturally limited applications."[113] Again, using the particulars of Colossians for illustrative purposes, it becomes clear that from a translation point of view, those portions of the letter that tend more towards universality virtually cry out to be presented in such a way as to capture what has aptly been described as Paul's "cosmic" message of redemption and reconciliation, extending globally from the earthly to the heavenly, across and beyond all time.[114] Correspondingly, those portions of the letter that are focused on possibly evanescent concerns might legitimately be rendered more prosaically.

The following is a brief background on the "situation" in Colossae as context for the analysis.

1. As a Letter to a Specific Community at a Moment in Time

While Colossians contains material of universal application, it is also true that the letter is addressed to a specific community with specific concerns. As noted, as a general matter, it is important to examine the historical and cultural setting of the biblical texts *in* time as a starting point for their interpretive trajectory and effects *through* time.[115] How one balances the two may well vary depending on the book in question, but the point is that inner meaning is not constrained by the immediacy of the text's historical origins. A translator should therefore seek to absorb a reasonable amount of such particulars without assuming the analysis ends there. As illustrated by the analyses of particular words, phrases, and imagery in sect. II.e, *infra*, I therefore also rely on such materials to provide additional interpretive material.

Colossians is a good example of the limits to what can be known of a given text's sociohistorical setting. One cannot, for example, confidently say much about Colossae itself. While its ruins lie in the western part of modern Turkey, they remain largely unexcavated.[116] There is thus only in-

---

113. Klein et al., *Introduction to Biblical Interpretation*, 426–28.

114. See, e.g., Pizzuto, *Cosmic Leap of Faith*; Helyer, "Cosmic Christology"; Gibbs, "Cosmic Scope." See also Foster, *Colossians*, 49; Ridderbos, *Paul*, 78–86.

115. See, e.g., Bockmuehl, "Form of God," 5n10, analyzing the *Sitz im Leben* of Philippians as relevant to "the conceptual background to Paul's own thought" (emphasis omitted).

116. Little of the former city is visible apart from some scattered blocks of stone and a mound that may reflect accreted ruins (search, e.g., for "Colossae" on Google Maps). But recent epigraphical and numismatic studies shed some light on the city's life. Harrison and Welborn, *Colossae, Hierapolis, and Laodicea*. For an overview of the research, see Foster, *Colossians*, 15–20.

direct information as to its history, population, commercial importance, and physical layout. That is also the case, of course, with many of the faith communities to whom Paul's, Peter's, Jude's, James', or other letters were addressed.[117] Either way, for purposes of this example, we do know that Colossae was located at the foot of Mount Cadmus, some ten miles southeast of the twin cities of Hierapolis and Laodicea (of Revelation fame), both cities also being mentioned in the letter. All three cities are in the Lycus River Valley, around one hundred miles east of Ephesus.[118] Once part of the so-called Phrygian Cities, they were included in the Roman District known as "Asia" in New Testament times.[119]

The Lycus River Valley as a whole was highly fertile, with considerable pasturage for sheep. As such, the area was a center for the wool industry and the related trade for dyeing woolen garments and Colossae itself was known for a purple dye that bore its name, *colossinum*.[120] Colossae had clearly been an important commercial center in the centuries preceding Paul's writing. Herodotus, for example, indicates that Colossae was "a great city in Phrygia"; and notes that Xerxes stopped at the city around 481 BC during his great march to Sardis and then Thermopylae.[121] Xenophon relates Cyrus the Younger's march through the Lycus Valley in 401 BC, which included a stop at Colossae, describing it as "an inhabited city, prosperous and large."[122] Indeed, the city's name itself suggests that it was once quite large in size—or else it was simply the site of a "colossus," i.e., a gigantic statue.

Of the other two Phrygian Cities, Laodicea was a financial and political center for the Asian District. Hierapolis was something of a tourist center because of the alleged medicinal benefits of its spas. But while Colossae was once a city of equal importance to both of them, by Paul's time it had apparently declined in size and importance. That decline may date to Laodicea's establishment in the first century BC, as Colossae

---

117. And it is certainly true as far as any knowledge we have as to the particulars of those churches described in Revelation—if they are even being presented as specific communities rather than archetypes.

118. Strabo, *Geography* 12.8.16. See also S. Johnson, "Laodicea," 5–6. The three appear to have been close enough so that at least Hierapolis and Laodicea would have been visible to one another along the Lycus Valley and/or across its river. See Banks, "Colossae."

119. Lightfoot, *St. Paul's Epistles*, 19.

120. Strabo, *Geography* 12.8.16; Pliny, *Natural History* 21.27.9.

121. Herodotus, *Histories* 7.30–32.

122. Xenophon, *Anabasis* 1.2.6.

apparently lost out to it in commercial competition. On top of all that, Colossae suffered considerable destruction through earthquakes occurring in AD 17 during the reign of Tiberius.[123]

One might therefore wonder what it was about the local church in this now-diminished city that drew Paul's attention. There is admittedly not much information about the Colossian church as it may have existed at the time of the letter. It is uncertain, for example, what was the ethnic composition of the local church, including what might have been the relative numbers of Jews and gentiles. Even though we do not know with certainty the precise mix of ethnicities or religious traditions within Colossae, significant numbers of Jews lived in the Phrygian Cities as a whole. Estimates are that by 62 BC—and thus some hundred years prior to the notional dating of the letter—the Jewish population of the region had reached fifty thousand.[124]

How that population was divided among the various population centers is unknown, but a number of commentators cite evidence in Cicero's oration "For Flaccus" concerning the amounts of gold seized from the Jews by Flaccus when he was proprietor of Asia as the basis for estimating that some eleven thousand Jewish men resided in the Laodicean region by the first century, to which must be added women and children,[125] making it a reasonable inference that Colossae itself had an identifiable Jewish population by Paul's time. Even if the local church had significant numbers of gentile converts (see Col 1:21), it therefore might well also have included many Jewish members, who would bring their own traditions and backgrounds with them.[126] As discussed below, the question is relevant both for exegetical and translation purposes, because there remains considerable uncertainty in identifying the so-called "Colossian heresy" that lies at the heart of the letter.

---

123. And it was again devastated by an earthquake in AD 60 during Nero's reign. Tacitus, *Annals*, 14.27. That does not mean that the town was completely destroyed by earthquakes, any more than earthquakes necessarily wipe out a settlement today.

124. Tacitus, *Annals*, 14.27.

125. Lightfoot, *St. Paul's Epistles*, 20; Sumney, "Those Who 'Pass Judgment,'" 387. One can also infer the presence of a meaningful number of diaspora Jews living in the region from the fact that Phrygians were among those present in Jerusalem at Pentecost (Acts 2:10).

126. Foster, *Colossians*, 23–30 (summarizing the arguments); J. Dunn, "Colossian Philosophy," 155 (characterizing the city's Jewish population as "a significant ethnic minority"); but see Bratcher and Nida, *Translators Handbook*, 2 (erroneously asserting that the Colossian church consisted of gentiles only and therefore misreading passages concerning the observance of Jewish ordinances).

2. As a Letter Addressed to a Specific Concern

A significant amount of the scholarship and commentary on Colossians has focused on the so-called "Colossian philosophy" or "heresy," on the theory that Paul's concerns were prompted chiefly by whatever this doctrine or set of doctrines was, just as his concerns in Galatians might be said principally to have been prompted by so-called "Judaizers" in that congregation. In other words, while there are other issues addressed in Colossians, the alleged errors found there are especially distinctive. And as discussed above, neither a purely literal nor a dynamically equivalent approach will assure a rendering of theologically freighted passages in such a way as to provide access to the text's inner meaning, i.e., to help answer the main question posed by the letter: Who is Christ? As a starting point, it thus becomes relevant to examine and even take some position as to the nature of the doctrinal issues addressed in order properly to express them.

One suggestion is that Paul's essential purpose was to respond to reports of gnostic or proto-gnostic beliefs that were infecting the Colossian church's understanding of who Jesus is, i.e., potentially undermining Paul's Christology. This argument dates from Joseph Lightfoot's contention that the Colossians were being influenced by a form of Jewish mysticism practiced by the Essene sect, but now coupled with "theosophic speculation."[127] Essentially, Lightfoot argued that the particular expression of those views was an amalgam of Essene beliefs and pagan philosophy of a sort that later became identified as "gnostic"—in short, "a single complex heresy."[128]

Martin Dibelius, however, speculated on the basis of certain inscriptions from Apollo's oracle at Claros—a site near Colossae—that the challenged doctrines arose more directly out of pagan beliefs than by way of any syncretistic model. He thus argued that the key to understanding the alleged error lay in Paul's *hapax legomena* use in Col 2:18 of the verb ἐμβατεύειν (to enter), which Dibelius understood "as a technical term approximating" μύειν (to initiate) and referring to the initiation practices described by Apuleius in book 11 of Ovid's *Metamorphoses*.[129] As such,

---

127. Lightfoot, *St. Paul's Epistles*, 73–113.
128. Lightfoot, *St. Paul's Epistles*, 74; Lohse, *Commentary on the Epistles*, 116.
129. Dibelius, "Isis Initiation." See also Easton, "Pauline Theology," 361, 372–73; Gibbs, "Cosmic Scope," 22; Evans, "Colossian Mystics," 189.

the error would lie in a restrictive form of initiation into the Christian faith, in derogation of the freely available gospel.

And more contemporary scholars continue to remain divided whether the doctrines Paul attacks in the letter should be characterized as proto-gnostic, gnostic, mystical Judaism, a particularized local syncretism, or something "purely" Jewish.[130] It is beyond the scope of this work to come down definitively on one side or the other. It is clear, however, that a translator will need to consider a range of historical evidence as well as any intrascriptural and intertextual references and allusions in order not only to choose relevant vocabulary but also to provide notational information. In the detailed analyses of sect. II.e, *infra*, I therefore discuss how a canonical-hermeneutical methodological approach assists in making such choices.

3. As a Means of Exhortation and Encouragement

a. Paul's Imprisonment

As far as Paul's own condition, the Letter to the Colossians indicates that he was in prison at the time of writing (Col 4:3). If so, it was most likely his captivity in Rome, where he was under house arrest. One of those who visited him appears to have been Epaphras, the founder/first evangelist to the Colossian church (1:4–8).[131] In that context he might well have reported to Paul on some form of doctrine or "philosophy" (2:4, 8, 18) that was affecting the congregation. Paul was also ministered to in Rome by another member of the local gathering, the runaway slave Onesimus (4:9), who then accompanied Tychicus as the bearer of the letter back to Colossae.[132] Paul's concern for Onesimus is the context for the uniquely personal letter to Philemon, also written from prison in Rome. All together, these factors support the suggestion in sect. II.d.iii.5, *infra*, that translation of such passages should reflect their pastoral tone.

---

130. See, e.g., Bird, *Colossians*, 24 (a combination of Jewish "ascetic-mystical piety," "dualism of Hellenistic cosmology," and "local pagan folk religion"); Royalty, "Dwelling on Visions," 329n5 (surveying divergent views); DeMaris, *Colossian Controversy*, 17 (arguing for a "distinctive blend of popular Middle Platonic, Jewish, and Christian elements that cohere around the pursuit of wisdom").

131. See Col 4:12; Phlm 23.

132. Col 4:7–9.

b. The Colossians' Fellowship

How healthy a congregation was the Colossian church? We can see that there were particular concerns raised by Paul about the apparent influx of false teaching which, whatever its source in other texts or sects, posed a challenge to Paul's own Christology. That much seems clear from chs. 1 and 2. But Paul also addresses matters of conduct and behavior in ch. 3, enjoining the Colossians to shun various enumerated "works of the flesh." And he issues certain "household" instructions concerning the relative roles of men and women, parents and children, masters, and slaves. How much of this paracletic/pastoral side of the letter reflects Paul's general care for his communities; and how much reflects particularized issues of sexuality, worship practices, or wealth disparities?

We do not have any intrascriptural materials (references in other letters, for example) that might help answer these questions. That said, even though Paul had not ever visited the Colossian church in person and was relying on reports, he nevertheless took the occasion to provide the congregation with pastoral guidance concerning forms of temptation common to people everywhere but perhaps also specific to that community. In that regard it is noteworthy that the spiritual risks identified in the opening chapters of the letter concern a failure to recognize not only the unique lordship of Jesus Christ, but also the goodness inherent in the creation mediated by him. False spirituality manifested by extreme asceticism—mortification of the flesh, denial of ordinary appetites, abstaining from food or sex (Col 2:23)—could well be the result of such errors. Or such misperceptions could lead to the opposite, e.g., indulgence based on the mistaken understanding that nothing done to satisfy those appetites can affect the spirit because the "material" is inferior in kind.[133] Hence Paul transitions directly from his rejection of false asceticism to a corresponding rejection of licentiousness (3:5–7).

The point is that pastoral injunctions concerning positive and negative behaviors *both* flow from his Christology:

> The apocalyptic question as to whom the lordship over the world belong . . . is formulated by Paul in terms of the alternative between the lordship of Christ and the lordship of the ruling powers of this cosmos. But whereas Christ has overcome these powers and is now exalted as cosmocrator, the same is not the case for the church and the Christian. The struggle is now reflected in the

---

133. See Schüssler Fiorenza, "Apocalyptic and Gnosis," 569–70.

life of the Christian who is called to freedom but is still, as one living in this world, in danger of losing this share in the lordship of Christ and of falling victim again to the cosmic powers.[134]

Whether the behaviors described were a specific problem in Colossae or simply those Paul wished to identify as potentially following on wrongful beliefs remains unknown. But it was clearly important to him to state the link between the two. Even so, despite Paul's pointed criticism of such influences and influencers in ch. 2, he is not alarmed in the way he seems to be in Galatians, where the tone is critical, even harsh (e.g., Gal 1:6–9; 3:1–4). So again, the translation methodology advanced here calls for a "voice" sensitive to communicating levels and varieties of emotional register.

ii. Relationship to Other Writings

As noted, from a canonical point of view it is important in translation as well as exegesis to take intrascriptural account of a given text's relationship to other materials. As discussed in this section, a New Testament translator will need to consider contemporary materials such as Jewish and/or Graeco-Roman writings as well as later credal/doctrinal/liturgical developments in the church. In this regard as well, Colossians provides a useful methodological example of how a modern translation might account for relationships between a given text and such materials.

1. Other New Testament Books

There are a number of parallel phrasings as well as similarities of concern between those expressed in Colossians and those expressed in other New Testament books. To be sure, we lack precise evidence of what other materials were extant or available to Paul at the time. But as discussed herein, where there are sufficient similarities of thought and/or style between passages of Colossians and other writings, these should be noted as intrascriptural references or, at times, incorporated into the translation itself.

The most particular similarities are found between Colossians and Ephesians. Scholars have vigorously debated the question whether one predates the other, as well as the related question whether one is

---

134. Schüssler Fiorenza, "Apocalyptic and Gnosis," 575.

dependent on the other in a literary sense.¹³⁵ Much note has thus been taken of the fact that both letters contain forms of Roman "household codes." The elements of such codes are more elaborated in Ephesians than Colossians,¹³⁶ which leads some to conclude that Ephesians was written later.¹³⁷ Variations on household codes also appear in other letters believed to have been written after Colossians.¹³⁸ In addition, there is a good deal of overlapping language concerning proper conduct, including behaviors to emulate as well as those to avoid.¹³⁹ And there are similar phrasings concerning worship practices.¹⁴⁰

In addition, there are parallel phrases in Ephesians concerning a theological issue central to Colossians: Christ as manifestation of the "fullness" of God/the Godhead,¹⁴¹ as well as possible comparisons involving the two letters' "cosmic Christology."¹⁴² It has also been theorized that the Letter to the Ephesians was in fact a letter for general circulation to the churches in Asia. The suggestion is that Tychicus was dispatched by Paul to carry several copies of this general letter with him to be left with various congregations, one of which was Ephesus¹⁴³ but another of which was Laodicea. And further that Tychicus also delivered the separate letters to the Colossians and to Philemon on this same journey (Col 4:7). As such, it would stand to reason that Paul wanted to be sure the Colossians had the benefit both of the letter directed to them and this general letter (4:16).¹⁴⁴

As also noted, Colossae was one of three principal cities in the Lycus Valley, Laodicea being another. A close connection of the Colossian and

---

135. See, e.g., Foster, *Colossians*, 101–4. This debate may truly be "academic" if one assumes—as may well be reasonable—that Paul or his associates kept copies of his letters, such that elements might be freely adapted and used in more than one. See generally Trobisch, *Paul's Letter Collection*. And perhaps such copies are even the "parchments" Paul urgently wished Timothy to bring from Troas (2 Tim 4:13).

136. Compare Col 3:18–25, 4:1 with Eph 4:25–32; 5:21–32; 6:1–9.

137. Sumney, *Colossians*, 2.

138. See Titus 2:3–10; 1 Pet 2:18—3:7.

139. Compare Col 3:1–15 with Eph 5:1–18.

140. Compare Col 3:16 (ψαλμοῖς ὕμνοις ᾠδαῖς πνευματικαῖς ἐν [τῇ] χάριτι ᾄδοντες ἐν ταῖς καρδίαις ὑμῶν τῷ θεῷ) with Eph 5:19 (λαλοῦντες ἑαυτοῖς [ἐν] ψαλμοῖς καὶ ὕμνοις καὶ ᾠδαῖς πνευματικαῖς, ᾄδοντες καὶ ψάλλοντες τῇ καρδίᾳ ὑμῶν τῷ κυρίῳ). See also Lightfoot, *St. Paul's Epistles*, 246–48.

141. Compare Col 1:19 and 2:9 with Eph 3:19.

142. See Bockmuehl, Review of *Cosmic Christology*, 441–45.

143. The salutation in Eph 1:1 is "to the Ephesians" and also more generally "to the faithful in Christ Jesus."

144. Lightfoot, *St. Paul's Epistles*, 37.

Laodicean assemblies would likely have arisen in various ways. For one thing, Paul's co-worker Epaphras appears to have been a local Colossian (Col 4:12) and apparently was an early evangelizer not only of the local church there but of the churches in Hierapolis and Laodicea (4:13). Paul also greets someone named Nympha and notes that the "home church" meeting at her house is not in that city, but in neighboring Laodicea (4:15). Further, Paul connects the two congregations by enjoining the Colossians to read a letter left for them at Laodicea and correspondingly to pass along to the Laodiceans the letter now sent to them—in other words, each is to read a letter initially delivered to the other.[145] Paul thus made it clear that he intended these letters "to be read and reread in the communities to which they were addressed, and in others as well."[146] The authorization for others to "read" the Letter to the Colossians in fact gave it a public character.[147]

There is also a clear relationship between the Letter to the Colossians and that to Philemon, to some extent in connecting various personages but also in localizing both letters in the churches of the Lycus Valley. There are open questions among scholars as to the authorship of a number of letters historically attributed to Paul; but Philemon has generally been understood to be of such a uniquely personal nature as almost certainly to have come from Paul's hand—and, indeed, it is the only letter that purports to have been scribed entirely by him.[148] As relevant here,

145. No one has ever found a Letter to the Laodiceans as such. There is extant a twenty-verse document titled *Ad Laodicenses*, purporting to be the lost letter to the church in Laodicea. However, none of the manuscripts containing it are earlier than the sixth century, and none are in Greek. The Latin text is reproduced in Lightfoot, *St. Paul's Epistles*, 287–89. Although the letter is widely considered to be a forgery and the product of the Western Church rather than the Latin translation of a Greek text, Lightfoot opines that it *did* originate in a Greek text, spurious though that text may have been (291). He even translates the work from Latin to Greek as a conjecture (293–94). But he also concludes that regardless of its origin, it is a noncanonical pastiche of other writings, no more than the "ghost of a Pauline epistle" (300).

146. Hartman, "On Reading," 139; Foster, *Colossians*, 476. See also 2 Cor 1:1 and 2 Thess 2:2, 3:17.

147. Childs, *Church's Guide*, 161: "Paul's letters, however occasional in nature, were received as apostolic, authoritative directives and were soon circulated among his churches [Col 4:16]"). D. Smith, *Epistles for All Christians*, 37–38: "Colossians is the clearest example of a Pauline text that was meant to be read in more than one locale." Whether there was an actual collection or "edition" of Paul's letters, a *corpus Paulinum*, in separate circulation from an early date remains contested. Bokedal, *Formation and Significance*, 268.

148. Others have his signature together with a few closing words and/or blessings, e.g., Col 4:18.

there is extensive overlap between the persons named in Phlm 2, 23 and various of those in Col 4:7–17, particularly Onesimus, the runaway slave who is the actual subject of the letter to his former master, Philemon. And the salutations in Colossians virtually mirror those in Philemon.

In short, while it is not my purpose to provide a full exploration of factual, doctrinal, and linguistic relationships between this particular letter and other New Testament materials, not limited to Pauline letters, these examples confirm the importance of examining such relationships when applying the translation methodology advanced here.

2. The Septuagint

As discussed in sect. I.b, *supra*, a translation methodology that builds on the linguistic insights of Justin Martyr, Augustine, Aquinas, Gregory of Nazianzus, Luther, and more recently Gadamer is *also* consistent with a "whole Bible" theology that understands the entire canon as a unity of revelation. This would apply not only to the effective history of New Testament texts in the living continuum of doctrinal development and church tradition, but also the effective history of LXX in such texts.[149] The LXX thus had its own trajectory of influence in the writings of the New Testament, where it was understood to provide "the form of the OT promise that Christ fulfills in the NT."[150] As such the early church perceived the "unfold[ing]" narrative of salvation through history,[151] with categories of promise and fulfillment, typological imagery, and intrascriptural references being essential to the "dialectical relation" of the two.[152] In Augustine's words, "In the Old Testament there is a veiling of

---

149. Although it bespeaks of legend, the story in the Letter of Aristeas concerning the origins of the LXX illustrates an early understanding of biblical translation. As described therein, the seventy-two persons selected to translate the law—six from each of the twelve tribes—brought copies from Jerusalem to Alexandria and undertook their work separately from one another, yet their respective results varied not a word. Hence Augustine's conclusion that the translation was accomplished by means of divine inspiration, such that the translators were able to realize in Greek the message originally presented in Hebrew. Augustine, *De civitate Dei*, ch. 43. See also "Life of Moses II," 7, in Philo, *Works of Philo*, 40.

150. Glenny, "Septuagint," 277; Rösel, "Theology of the Septuagint," 242. See also Pontifical Biblical Commission, *Interpretation of the Bible*, 3.A.2.

151. Arthos, *Inner Word*, 12; Watson, *Text and Truth*, 199.

152. Childs, *Old Testament Theology*, 178; Stuhlmacher, *Biblical Theology*, 199, 367, 800–801. See also Kümmel, *Promise and Fulfillment* (on future fulfillment).

the New, and in the New Testament there is a revealing of the Old."[153] Nor is this a purely ancient interpretive understanding,[154] even if in tension with certain historical-critical approaches.[155]

There are, moreover, several examples of "spirit-guided apostolic freedom" in construing the LXX.[156] One commonly noted example is how Amos 9:11–12 is used in Acts 15:16–18, where the LXX version is used theologically to support James' argument in the Jerusalem Council that the gospel is for the gentiles as well as the Jews, even though "it is debatable whether this was the translator's intention."[157] The same is true of the citation in Matt 1:23 of the Greek translation of Isa 7:14 from the LXX to read "virgin" rather than "young woman," as the Masoretic Text reflects. And the same might be said of citations in 1 Cor 2:9; 9:10; Eph 5:14; Jas 4:5–6, and elsewhere to verses described as "Scripture" that do not clearly appear as such in the LXX, but may derive from older versions. Indeed, arguments made in verses such as Heb 1:6 concerning the superiority of the Son "could not have been made from the Hebrew text because the text that Hebrews cites is not even present in our M[asoretic] T[ext]."[158]

It thus behooves a translator to find ways to capture such usages in order more fully to reveal early understandings of the text. In some instances, similarities of wording between the LXX and New Testament materials make the connection inescapable.[159] Regardless, the New

---

153. Augustine, *De catechizandis rudibus* 4.8. Thiselton, *New Horizons*, 148–49: "Jesus died and was raised . . . as the fulfilment of God's purposes already partly disclosed in a pattern of redemptive suffering and vindication which constitutes a theme in the Jewish scriptures."

154. See, e.g., Hengstenberg, *Christology of Old Testament*; Ellis, *Paul's Use*; Wainwright, *Trinity in New Testament*; Hays, *Echoes of Scripture*; M. Wilson, *Our Father Abraham*; Schoeman, *Salvation Is from Jews*; Baker, *Two Testaments*. The relationship between such interpretive methods and midrashic or other rabbinical approaches, however, is beyond the scope of this work. For background, see Klein et al., *Introduction to Biblical Interpretation*, 23–31. See also Arthos, *Inner Word*, 34, noting the "value attached to the living character of the covenant voice."

155. E.g., Johann Semler's notion that the Old Testament is "a collection of crude Jewish prejudices diametrically opposed to Christianity" (quoted in Stuhlmacher, *Historical Criticism*, 39).

156. Hengel with Deines, *Septuagint as Christian Scripture*, 109; McLay, *Use of Septuagint*, 28–30, 148–58.

157. Dines, *Septuagint*, 144; McLay, *Use of Septuagint*, 18–19.

158. McLay, *Use of Septuagint*, 149.

159. Stuhlmacher, *Biblical Theology*, 748–50. A detailed exploration of the relationships between the Hebrew text and the LXX as used in the early church is beyond the scope of this work. At the same time, it seems clear that there was "a complex but

Testament writers' extensive usage of materials from the LXX reflects their purposeful "reading [of] biblical passages in their intra-scriptural context" and as "a literary unit."[160] Importantly, the "essential Jewishness of Christian faith"[161] and the resulting unity of the Scriptures is credally attributed to the one voice of the Holy Spirit, τὸ λαλῆσαν διὰ τῶν προφητῶν.[162] Note also that early Christian codices of the LXX render the Tetragrammaton as κύριος, with a number presenting it in *nomina sacra* form, i.e., with only the first and last letters together with a line over the top.[163] Given the likely sacral import of the *nomina sacra*, their usage in this context is a significant indicator of "the authority of the Septuagint as a witness to the biblical text."[164]

In short, a canonical hermeneutic is fully in harmony with an effective history approach, whereby the full corpus of canonical materials has a continuing impact on church tradition. The methodology advanced here therefore argues that in addition to other considerations, translation of the New Testament books should take into account formal and thematic aspects of Old Testament passages as rendered in the LXX, particularly to ways they were given fresh understanding in the New Testament. That formal connection has meaning, in other words, because it was "the

---

cohesive canonical process from which the Hebrew Bible, the Septuagint, and the two-part Christian canon of Old and New Testaments derive" (748).

160. Bokedal, "Early Rule-of-Faith," 58n14; Wagner, "Septuagint," 23; J. Kelly, *Early Christian Doctrines*, 68: "The continuity of the two Testaments [is] a commonplace with Christian writers." See, e.g., Clement of Alexandria, *Stromata* 6.15 (κανὼν δὲ ἐκκλησιαστικός ἡ συνῳδία καὶ συμφωνία νόμου τε καὶ προφητῶν τῇ κατὰ τὴν τοῦ κυρίου παρουσίαν παραδιδομένῃ διαθήκῃ); Melito of Sardis, *Peri Pascha*, 104 (Οὗτός ἐστιν ... ὁ διὰ νόμου καὶ προφητῶν κηρυσσόμενος) (Kinzig, *Faith in Formulae*, §107); Paul VI, *"Dei Verbum,"* §16 ("God, the inspirer and author of both Testaments, wisely arranged that the New Testament be hidden in the Old and the Old be made manifest in the New. For, though Christ established the new covenant in His blood, still the books of the Old Testament with all their parts, caught up into the proclamation of the Gospel, acquire and show forth their full meaning in the New Testament and in turn shed light on it and explain it").

161. Watson, *Text and Truth*, 17.

162. Niceno-Constantinopolitan Creed; compare also Niceno-Constantinopolitan Creed (Πιστεύω εἰς ἕνα Θεόν) with Deut 6:4–9 (the Shema).

163. Hengel with Deines, *Septuagint as Christian Scripture*, 41; Rösel, "Theology of the Septuagint," 245; Wagner, "Septuagint," 21. See also Vasileiadis, "Tetragrammaton into Greek," more broadly examining Greek renderings of the Tetragrammaton.

164. Glenny, "Septuagint," 265. Bokedal, "Early Rule-of-Faith," 66: By employing such orthography "as a form of supra-textual marker," the New Testament writers wove the corpus "into a coherent whole."

Greek Jewish Scriptures as witnessed to by the LXX . . . [that] were regarded as normative for life, belief and practice" in the early church.[165]

3. Credal and Liturgical Formulations

As noted, the dialogic approach advanced here depends in part on a translator's consciousness of his own "situatedness within the flow of history."[166] And while I test the validity of the approach by examining Colossians' effective history in church preaching, teaching, and worship over time,[167] it would likely require a separate study to trace all such effects.[168] But for purposes of my focus on the Colossian Hymn as exemplary of the letter's import in the development of the doctrine of Christ, there are a number of materials illustrative of that effect. These most notably include early affirmations of the faith in the *regula fidei* as well as more formulaic creeds generated in efforts to resolve christological, Trinitarian, or iconographic disputes. Of course, the New Testament itself is laced with passages expressive of the essential truths of the faith,[169] with numerous faith formulae building thereon.[170] And no formula is needed to confess that "Jesus is Lord," which Martin Hengel describes as "the basic confession."[171]

---

165. McLay, *Use of Septuagint*, 144; Stuhlmacher, *Biblical Theology*, 8.

166. Thiselton, *New Horizons*, 6.

167. Gadamer, *Gadamer Reader*, 59: "The concept of a canon in New Testament theology finds in the *wirkungsgeschichtliches Bewußtsein* a legitimation." "When we inquire into the truth of the word . . . the word is perduringly there: as the saving message, as blessing or curse, as prayer" (134).

168. Taking account of the effective history of New Testament texts is in fact the express purpose of the Blackwell Bible Commentary series. Rowland, "Pragmatic Approach." Several books have been published in that series, but Colossians is not (yet) one of them. See Maier, "Colossians and Philemon."

169. See, e.g., Rom 10:9: ἐὰν ὁμολογήσῃς ἐν τῷ στόματί σου κύριον Ἰησοῦν καὶ πιστεύσῃς ἐν τῇ καρδίᾳ σου ὅτι ὁ θεὸς αὐτὸν ἤγειρεν ἐκ νεκρῶν, σωθήσῃ. See also John 11:25–27; Mark 8:30; Acts 8:36–38; 10:43; 16:30–34; 1 Cor 15:3–4; Eph 4:4–6; Col 1:15–20; 1 Tim 3:16; 1 Pet 1:21; 1 John 2:22, 4:14–15. See J. Kelly, *Early Christian Creeds*, 8–10.

170. Clement of Alexandra, *Stromata* 7.6. See J. Kelly, *Early Christian Doctrines*, 42–43.

171. Hengel, *Son of God*, 13, 14, 59, 77 (also characterizing 1 Cor 8:6 as "a formula," and Rom 1:3–4 as "an early confession" and "common creed").

The earliest credos were often brief.[172] Yet all have their ultimate source in Christ, as Irenaeus made plain:

> I have pointed out the truth . . . which the prophets proclaimed . . . but which Christ brought to perfection, and the apostles have handed down, from whom the Church, receiving, and throughout all the world alone preserving them in their integrity, has transmitted them to her sons.[173]

From the canonical perspective of this book, it is therefore relevant that from the outset there was a clear affirmation of Jesus as the same God of creation and Israel proclaimed by the prophets and now revealed in the Son.[174] During the second and third centuries, various church fathers and localized communities elaborated on such statements by crafting their own summaries of the Christian faith.[175] They traced these summaries of belief ultimately to the apostles and thence to Jesus, restating them in the form of a "Rule of Faith"—κανών τῆς πίστεως/regula fidei.[176] These affirmations also took the form of catechetical responses to baptismal interrogatories, reflecting core elements of beliefs about the Father, the Son, and the Holy Spirit.[177] Further, the appearance of *nomina sacra* in some of the earliest extant manuscripts arguably reflects a purposeful reverencing of the divine name in continuity from Jewish liturgy, refined now in the form of binitarian and possibly even trinitarian affirmations.[178]

---

172. J. Kelly, *Early Christian Creeds*, 7, describes them as "creeds of a lesser sort, lacking the fixity and official character of the later formularies."

173. Irenaeus, *Adversus haereses* 5.praefatio.

174. See Bockmuehl, "New Testament Doctrine," 41: Jesus "is the one whom the New Testament affirms, precisely in his risen body, as saving Lord and Messiah of Israel (e.g. Rom 1:3–4; Acts 2:36)."

175. J. Kelly, *Early Christian Doctrines*, 95–101; J. Kelley, *Early Christian Creeds*, 167–204. The so-called "Old Roman Creed" is the most notable among these. J. Kelley, *Early Christian Creeds*, 100–166, discussing its nature and origins.

176. See, e.g., Irenaeus, *Adversus haereses*, 1.10.1; 3.4.1 (Kinzig, *Faith in Formulae*, §109b3, b7). As J. Kelly, *Early Christian Creeds*, 2 emphasizes, "The rule of faith must not be confused with the creed, but . . . the relationship between them was close." See also Kinzig, *Faith in Formulae*, 1:7.

177. J. Kelly, *Early Christian Creeds*, 13. See, e.g., Pseudo-Hippolytus of Rome, *Traditio apostolica* 21:11–18 (Kinzig, *Faith in Formulae*, §89a). The individual nature of such responses is why they were originally prefaced by "I believe," with "we believe" not being "attested before the fourth century, when it was introduced in relation to the first *declaratory* creeds." Kinzig, *Faith in Formulae*, 1:7 (emphasis in original).

178. Bokedal, *Christ the Center*, 16–17 (citing usages of Triune *nomina sacra* in Matt 28:19 [Codex Alexandrinus] and 1 Clem. 46:6 [possibly referring to 1 Cor 8:6 and Eph 4:4]).

These expressive affirmations took on a normative function apart from the missional or catechetical purpose of earlier confessional materials, in that they indicated an expressly canonical "demarcation of certain doctrinal content over against dissidents whose views were anathematized."[179] A further development of baptismal affirmations and/or the *regula fidei* into declaratory creeds having a more generalized role in the church took place in the context of the christological crises of the fourth century. These disputes centered on questions of the equal versus subordinate nature of Christ vis-à-vis the Father, with conflicting views and mutual accusations of heresy as to what it means to say (as does Colossians) that the Son is the "image of the invisible God." And other doctrinal disputes continued into the fifth century as to the nature of and relationships among the members of the Trinity.[180]

Resolution of such controversies was attempted in a series of general church councils or synods. These broad-based efforts principally involved the christological issues addressed at the Council of Nicaea (AD 325); refinements to Nicaea taken up at the Council of Constantinople (AD 381); Trinitarian formulations resolved at the Council of Chalcedon (AD 451); and disputes as to the relationship between visible imagery and Christ as the image of God considered at the Second Council of Nicaea (AD 757), with numerous other synodal convocations occurring throughout the same period and thereafter.[181] Where possible, the issues presented were addressed through the drafting and adoption of agreed credal formulations, "put forth not merely as epitomes of the beliefs of their promulgators, but as tests of the orthodoxy of Christians in general."[182]

In a general sense, a creed is "a formal pledge of allegiance to a set of doctrinal statements concerning God and his relationship to his creation in general and mankind in particular."[183] The developmental sketch

---

179. Kinzig, *Faith in Formulae*, 1:8–9; Kinzig and Vinzent, "Recent Research," 552–59.

180. J. Kelly, *Early Christian Doctrines*, 223–37, 310–43.

181. However, only seven such councils are considered "ecumenical" by both the Eastern Orthodox and the Roman Catholic Churches as setting forth orthodox doctrine.

182. J. Kelly, *Early Christian Creeds*, 205. These resolutions did not, however, last indefinitely. See, e.g., Anatalios, *Retrieving Nicaea*, 20–27 (tracing continuing doctrinal divergence after Nicaea); J. Kelly, *Early Christian Creeds*, 254–62 (same).

183. Kinzig and Vinzent, "Recent Research," 540. See also Kinzig, *Faith in Formulae*, 1:3–7 (usages of the terms σύμβολον τῆς πίστεως in the East and *symbolum fides* in the West for such affirmations).

above suggests that creeds may thus be seen as efforts to articulate in a systematic as well as authoritative way the essential meaning conveyed by biblical texts, those truths in which the believer places his faith and trust.[184] In effect, creeds might even be seen to reflect an understanding of the *verbum interius* of the entire Bible, both Old and New Testaments, to the extent they address who God is both in his eternal being and his temporal interaction with the world.

Once "canonized by the ecumenical council,"[185] such creeds became embedded in church liturgies on a widespread basis throughout a multiplicity of Christian traditions.[186] And in principle, the person making such affirmations gives present effect to the continued truths of the Scriptures, regardless of whether he employs elemental forms found in the Scriptures themselves, affirmations from early baptismal responses, the *regula fidei* as rearticulated by various church fathers, or credal formulations developed in the course of doctrinal struggles.[187] As such, these affirmations are *themselves* dialogic in nature, engaging the person who states his current belief interactively with the apostolic teachings and biblical texts that are the sources of the statements. On that analysis, credal

---

184. See Augustine, *Sermo* 213 (*Symbolum est ergo breviter complexa regula fidei, ut mentem instruat nec oneret memoriam; paucis verbis dicatur, unde multum acquiratur. Symbolum ergo dicitur, in quo se agnoscant Christiani*) (Kinzig, *Faith in Formulae*, §316e) (The *symbolum* is a briefly compiled rule of faith, intended to instruct the mind without overburdening the memory; to be said in a few words, from which much is to be gained. Thus, it is called a *symbolum* because it is something by which Christians can recognize each other); Pseudo-Augustine, *Sermo* 242 (*Symbolum, dilectissimi, breve est verbis, sed magnum est sacramentis*) (Kinzig, *Faith in Formulae*, §32) (The creed, dearly beloved, is brief in words but great in mysteries).

185. J. Kelly, *Early Christian Doctrines*, 217. See also Morgan, "Critical Study," 216: "The conciliar definition of Jesus . . . is sufficiently true to [the New Testament's] intentions to test the claim of any . . . biblical interpretation to be Christian in a traditional sense."

186. See, e.g., Kinzig, *Faith in Formulae*, pt. 4 (providing texts of liturgies into the ninth century).

187. To be sure, some traditions take the position that all that is necessary to doctrine is found in the words of the Scriptures alone, without recourse to the views of the church fathers, credal language, or other forms of explication. Perhaps a more nuanced view is that the purpose of exposition is to determine the sense of Scripture, not "add" to it. See Church of England, "Articles of Religion," art. 6: "Holy Scripture containeth all things necessary to salvation: so that whatsoever is not read therein, *nor may be proved thereby*, is not to be required of any man, that it should be believed as an article of the Faith, or be thought requisite or necessary to salvation" (emphasis added). Cyril of Jerusalem, *Catechetical Lectures*, 58 (lecture 5.12): "For the Articles of the Faith were not composed at the good pleasure of men: but the most important points chosen from all Scripture, make up the one teaching of the Faith."

statements and related writings are evidence of how scriptural understanding is achieved in "the infinity of dialogue."[188] To the extent such credal materials explicitly or allusively refer to particular words or passages, a translator should therefore examine them as possible sources for words and imagery, particularly with respect to theologically freighted passages. In sect. II.e, *infra*, I therefore discuss how that process might unfold.

4. Noncanonical Writings

While of less importance than resonances that might be detected with the Old Testament, there are certain passages in various New Testament books that appear to be atmospheric of language, or suggest background information, found in various noncanonical texts. Some of these may predate and others postdate letters like Colossians (to keep with the example examined here). Such materials might thus include Graeco-Roman as well as Judaic materials.[189] Others might be later gnostic texts.[190] And the temporal trajectory of a given biblical text in art, music, and literature itself may itself give rise to noncanonical material revelatory of its inner word.[191] For reasons of space I do not examine an exemplary range of such noncanonical materials in detail, but simply observe that it would be consistent with the hermeneutical principles of the translation theory advanced here for the same to be incorporated marginally or in wording, if and to the extent they provide historical-critical, contextual, and/or doctrinal insights.

iii. Varieties of Register

As noted, any biblical translation must be grounded in the Greek text itself as the stable reference for any further trajectory. That is not to say

---

188. Gadamer, *Truth and Method*, xxxiv. See Pannenberg, *Systematic Theology*, 1:15: "Exposition of scripture continues with reference to its content and truth."

189. See, e.g., Philo, "Concerning Noah's Work," "Life of Moses," "Eternity of World," "That Every Good Man"; Josephus, *Jewish Antiquities*, *Jewish War*; Apocalypse of Abraham; 2 Baruch; Martydom and Ascension of Isaiah; 1 Enoch; Prayer of Joseph; Testament of Solomon. See generally Charlesworth, *Old Testament Pseudepigrapha*.

190. See Pagels, *Gnostic Paul*, identifying several such texts.

191. Cf. Straus, *New Testament*, translationally incorporating biblically related passages from Shakespeare, Milton, and Handel.

there is no room for expressive variation. There clearly is, which is one reason a strictly literal effort may not capture the text's effective history. But the original text *does* operate as a guardrail to prevent dissolution of the inner word as the result of "an uncontrollable theory of inspiration or pneumatic exegesis."[192] Further, there may be formal elements of the text—its grammar, syntax, distinctive vocabulary, and possibly its orthography and visual format—that are expressive of its inner word and should thus be maintained in translation. So too might literary analysis aid in revealing intrascriptural aspects of a given text that should be reflected in translation, consistent with "the canonical character of the Bible" as a "single persuasive unit."[193]

In this section I therefore take as an example Colossians' literary and linguistic elements to test their relevance to a translator's dialogic engagement with the text. In this regard as well, the letter is illustrative of the kinds of diversities in tone or register that may be found in New Testament texts.[194] Such forms of expression have register-specific characteristics in their usage of speech-act verbs, vocabulary, syntax, and/or argument structure. The language of this particular letter might usefully be characterized as ranging across hymnic, liturgical, doctrinal, rhetorical, paracletic/pastoral, or prosaic registers. As explained herein, distinctive registers may also have canonical and hermeneutical implications to the extent expressive of the text's *verbum interius*. As such, a translator may need to reflect the same both formally and stylistically in a given receptor language.

1. Hymnic

Colossians is rich in examples of the kind of religious registers a translator should be alert to. In this section I consider how the processual hermeneutic described above may allow presentation of a text's hymnic aspects in such a way as to help reveal its inner word. I will focus on the so-called Colossian Hymn (1:15–20) as a particularly strong example of how form

---

192. Gadamer, *Philosophical Hermeneutics*, 210; cf. S. Zahl, *Holy Spirit*, 17, 20, discussing Luther's concerns about "enthusiasm" or *Schwärmerei* as "a chaotic and uncritical affirmation of the experiences of the human subject over and against God's objective Word," in contrast with a true "inner experience" of faith "ecclesially and biblically mediated through scriptural preaching and the sacraments."

193. Castelli et al., *Postmodern Bible*, 175.

194. See Biber and Conrad, *Register, Genre and Style*, 2.

and meaning may converge when language bespeaks the poetic, spiritual, or intangible.[195] As such, application of the methodology's governing linguistic theory suggests that paleographic and philological elements of the Greek text might appropriately be reflected in translation by way of incarnationally effective words and forms in the receptor language.

To be sure, there are ongoing scholarly debates as to the possibly hymnic nature and structure of particular passages in the New Testament. A number of passages do self-identify as a "song" or "hymn" or "psalm," such as the Magnificat (Luke 1:4–55), Benedictus (1:68–79), Gloria in Excelsis (2:14), and Nunc Dimittis (2:29–32), as well as those sung before the throne of God and throughout heaven (Rev 5:9–10; 15:3–4), some of which are expressly introduced as psalms/songs/hymns.[196] And the church at large has received these as "new liturgical texts . . . celebrating God," incorporating them into liturgy and music.[197] But others that are less explicitly identified have also been analyzed as hymnic in nature, including Col 1:15–20; Phil 2:6–11; and John 1:1–17; with additional consideration given to possibly liturgical structures in Eph 2:14–16; 1 Tim 3:16; 1 Pet 3:18–22; and Heb 1:1–4.

It is certainly clear that worship in the early church included "psalms and hymns and spiritual songs," as those gathered sang "to one another with grace in [their] hearts" (Col 3:16).[198] Larry Hurtado has made the further point that these forms of worship may have been shaped as much, if not more, by the Psalms than by classical forms of Greek ritual, given the frequent references to Psalms in early Christian texts. He also observes that the "Psalms don't follow Greek poetic/hymnic forms."[199] Re-

---

195. See Doty, "Paradigm Shift," 9; cf. Pamuk, *My Name Is Red*, 125–28, 267–68, 370, 397, distinguishing Islamic miniatures revelatory of Allah's perception from Renaissance imagery evocative of human sight.

196. E.g., Rev 5:9: "They sang a new song."

197. Pernot, "Rhetoric of Religion," 242–43 (citing the Canticle of the Lamb [Rev 15:3–4] and the Magnificat [Luke 1:47–55]).

198. See also 1 Cor 14:26; Eph 5:19–20. See generally Martin, *Carmen Christi*. Even non-Christians recognized that singing was fundamental to Christians' worship. See Pliny the Younger, *Letter to Trajan* 10.96.7: *Essent soliti stato die ante lucem convenire, carmenque Christo quasi deo dicere*.

199. Hurtado, "On 'Hymns.'" See also Foster, *Colossians*, 56 (noting musicality in Jewish worship); Pizzuto, *Cosmic Leap of Faith*, 99–100 (reviewing efforts to find parallels with Hellenistic materials "reflect[ing] Stoic and Platonic influences"); Baugh, "Poetic Form" (arguing that the "pattern" of Col 1:15–20 is "a simple chiasm much like poetry and prose from the OT and from other Semitic works"); Vawter, "Colossians Hymn," 72 (criticizing Ernst Käsemann's argument that Paul had "Christianized" a gnostic redeemer hymn).

gardless, it seems necessary to be alert to the importance of musicality in biblical texts, in part given the myriad instances of song and music in the Old Testament[200] as well as the inseparability of music from the worship practices of Greek religion.[201]

As a test case for application of the methodology, the Colossian Hymn is a good illustration of options that might be available to a translator both as to form and substance. This is in large part due to highly instructive disagreements whether the Colossian Hymn represents a separable paean sung in the church; whether it is derived from Semitic forms found in the Old Testament or Second Temple Psalmody; whether it bespeaks more of Hellenistic hymnology, including Stoic and Platonic materials; whether it is taken from confessional and/or liturgical materials; whether it is better characterized as a "prose hymn"; or whether it is more representative of such epideictic rhetorical forms as "prose encomia."[202] Matthew Gordley, for example, argues that the last lines of the two strophes of Col 1:15–20 end in spondees; and that since spondees have a "solemn and stately" feel characteristic of Greek hymnody, the passage should be seen as more of the nature of a hymn than not.[203] And Ralph Martin provides examples of alliteration of the initial and final syllables within a verse or between consecutive verses, e.g.

---

200. E.g., Exod 15:1–21; the Psalms; Song of Solomon. See also Ezra 3:11. It would require a separate treatise to explore the worship practices of ancient Israel, and there are many. See, e.g., Sendrey, *Music in Ancient Israel*; Brueggemann, *Worship in Ancient Israel*.

201. Furley and Bremer, *Greek Hymns*, 1:35; Pernot, "Rhetoric of Religion," 237; Willi, *Languages of Aristophanes*, 13, 16–17, 18–23, 23–27, and 35–37; Devlin, "Hymn in Greek Literature," 3. In Greek religion more broadly, a religious register can include invective and aischrology. See generally Worman, *Abusive Mouths*. But neither is relevant here.

202. The literature concerning the Colossian Hymn has been described as "almost infinite." R. Wilson, *Colossians and Philemon*, 123. See, e.g., Gordley, *Christological Hymns*; Foster, *Colossians*; Edsall and Strawbridge, "Songs We Used to Sing"; Hurtado, "Christ-Hymns"; Hurtado, "Another New Article"; Andrie, "Christ Hymn"; Peppard, "Poetry"; Pizzuto, *Cosmic Leap of Faith*; Collins, "Origins of Christology"; Wright, "Poetry and Theology"; Schweizer, "Colossians 1:15–20"; Balchin, "Colossians 1:15–20"; Baugh, "Poetic Form"; Lohse, *Commentary on the Epistles*; Vawter, "Colossians Hymn"; J. Sanders, *New Testament Christological Hymns*; Nakagawa, "On Christology"; Martin, "Early Christian Hymn"; J. Robinson, "Formal Analysis."

203. Gordley, *Christological Hymns*, 121. See also Gordley, "Johannine Prologue," analyzing John's Prologue as a form of Jewish didactic hymn.

ἐξουσίαι/ἔκτισται (1:16), νεκρῶν/πρωτεύων (1:18), and κατοικῆσαι/ ἀποκαταλλάξαι (1:19–20).²⁰⁴

The answers to these questions may therefore impact how the text is presented in translation. As noted, when dealing with less prosaic passages, a translator should recognize the "free space around" the text and be prepared for the literary challenge—and opportunity—that may present. Taking Col 1:15–20 as a prime example, the passage does lend itself to a distinctive form of language, regardless of how the register is described. The context is a perceived threat to the church's developing Christology by way of a so-called "Colossian heresy," one element of which apparently involved subordinating Christ to or within the Godhead. Paul thus responds with a description of the "cosmic" scope of God's reconciliation of all things to himself through Jesus Christ as Lord, in whom the fullness of the Godhead is said to dwell. Given the nature of the language he uses—elevated, spiritual, nearly abstract—the form seems essential to the content.

The question then is what this implies for translation. A number of scholars, for example, take the position that Col 1:15–20 should be presented in a manner broadly poetic, arguing that the passage can fruitfully be analyzed on linguistic terms normally associated with poetry and song.²⁰⁵ A good deal of their analysis therefore focuses on the grammatical, logical, and possibly chiastic structure of the passage and, in particular, whether it effectively stands alone as a separable text either first expressed by Paul or derived from existing sources. James Robinson thus undertook what was arguably the first systematic analysis of the passage. After surveying certain suggestions as to the possible liturgical relationships between Col 1:15–20 and Hellenistic Jewish "primal man" theology, he sought to "reconstruct" what he argued was its original pre-Pauline form, upon which Paul elaborated as part of his response to a perceived heresy threatening the Colossian church.²⁰⁶ He postulated a deliberate structure along the lines of Semitic *parallelismus membrorum* found in Proverbs.²⁰⁷ Based on parallels in terminology and vocabulary, he divided

---

204. Martin, "Early Christian Hymn," 196n10; but see Peppard, "Poetry," 324, arguing that such traits may simply reflect "language that is well-crafted."

205. See, e.g., Wright, "Poetry and Theology"; Baugh, "Poetic Form"; Balchin, "Colossians 1:15–20"; J. Robinson, "Formal Analysis"; but see Peppard, "Poetry," criticizing the use of versified indentations.

206. J. Robinson, "Formal Analysis."

207. This grammatical form can be seen as a general characteristic of certain Hebrew writings, e.g., Prov 10:1, but it may also be employed in examination of New Testament passages, e.g., Matt 5:3–11. But see Bockmuehl, "Form of God," 4n7, pointing

the passage between a "strophe A" and "strophe B," with italics and "A" or "B" numbered markings to indicate such relationships:

v. 15 *Who is* the image of the invisible God, *the first-born* of all creation;	A1
v. 16 *For in him were created all things in heaven and on earth,*	A2
Visible and invisible	A3
Whether thrones or dominions	A4
Or principalities or authorities;	A5
All things through him and *to him have been created,*	A6
v. 17 *And he himself is* before all things,	A7
And all things in him have come together,	A8
v. 18 And he himself is the head of the body the church;	A9
Who is the beginning, *the first-born* from the dead,	B1
That he might in all things himself might be pre-eminent;	B2
v. 19 *For in him* was pleased all the fullness to dwell,	B3
v. 20 And *through him* to reconcile *all things to him*	B4
Making peace by the blood of his cross,	B5
Through him whether those *on earth*	B6
Or *those in heaven.*	B7

Just looking at Robinson's proposed structure, it is clear that others might focus on different parallels or resonances. Thus, a number of scholars argue (in my view persuasively) that the passage might better be understood as *tripartite*, with part or all of vv. 17a–18 standing as a "hinge" strophe. Stephen Baugh, for example, centers his chiastic structure on v. 17b, arguing that vv. 15–16 and 18b–20 are parallel in presenting Christ as the preexistent agent both of God's first and new creations; that vv. 17a and 18a identify him as the head of the first creation and head of the church; while v. 17b functions separately as the "focus" of the entire passage, tying both creation and redemption together on the basis that "all things find their unity in him."[208]

John Balchin illustrated several parallels, setting related verses in tandem and providing the relevant verse numbers, as follows:[209]

ὅς ἐστιν εἰκὼν (15)

---

out the limitations of such an analysis.

208. Baugh, "Poetic Form," 236–37 (quoting Beasley-Murray, "Colossians 1:15–20," 170).

209. Balchin, "Colossians 1:15–20," 67, does concede that these claimed relationships are "different from any Hebrew *parallelismus membrorum* that we might name."

Elements of a Canonical-Hermeneutical Translation Approach/Test Case

ὅς ἐστιν ἀρχή (18)
πρωτότοκος πάσης κτίσεως (15)
πρωτότοκος ἐκ τῶν νεκρῶν (18)
ἐν αὐτῷ . . . τὰ πάντα (16)
   ἐν αὐτῷ . . . πᾶν (19)
ἐν τοῖς οὐρανοῖς . . . ἐπὶ τῆς γῆς (16)
   ἐπὶ τῆς γῆς εἴτε τὰ ἐν τοῖς οὐρανοῖς (20)
τὰ πάντα δι᾽ αὐτοῦ καὶ εἰς αὐτὸν (16)
   καὶ δι᾽ αὐτοῦ ἀποκαταλλάξαι τὰ πάντα εἰς αὐτόν (20)
καὶ αὐτός ἐστιν πρὸ πάντων (17)
ἵνα γένηται ἐν πᾶσιν αὐτὸς πρωτεύων (18) and/or
αὐτός ἐστιν ἡ κεφαλὴ (18)

Regardless of alternative forms of presentation, there are important substantive parallels among the verses as to the manner in which Christ as the subject is described. Thus, Scot McKnight focused on "the repetition of 'firstborn' (*protokos*) in each 'stanza' (1:15, 18b), the repetition of the reason (*hoti*) in each stanza (1:16, 19), the repetition of 'all things' in each stanza (1:16, 20), and the 'refrains' of vv. 17 and 18a" as essential to any such analysis.[210] Consistent with that approach, two parallel verses, 15 and 18, are introduced by "the one who," i.e., ὅς ἐστιν, a use of the relative pronoun that Ralph Martin has identified as "a tell-tale mark of *liturgica*."[211] And to be sure, both verses concern the Son, consistent with the view that texts of a hymnic nature function as sung praise of a divinity.[212]

But no matter what the origins of the passage are or how one describes any parallelisms, virtually all scholars agree that its vocabulary and style are markedly distinct. It might best be described as "a Pauline composition that, while perhaps hymnic in content, is not properly a hymn but rather a poem that confesses and celebrates the role of the exalted Christ in both creation and redemption."[213] Scholars like Helyer who take this position argue that the passage is "hymnic" in the sense that it is written in an elevated vocabulary that may *itself* lift the reader/

---

210. McKnight, *Letter to the Colossians*, 144.

211. Martin, "Early Christian Hymn," 197.

212. Sanders notes that "ardor and enthusiasm" are often characteristic of hymns and that "early Christian hymnody tends to deal with a divine *drama*, a cosmic redemption, thus with an 'exalted' subject." J. Sanders, *New Testament Christological Hymns*, 4–5 (emphasis in original).

213. Helyer, "Cosmic Christology," 235. See also Strawbridge, *Pauline Effect*, 141; cf. Bockmuehl, "Form of God" (addressing a similar complex of issues in Phil 2:6–11).

believer to a closer contemplation of the one being praised,[214] whether addressed as God, Lord, Lord Jesus Christ, or other variations. And in this passage, as Ralph Martin concisely observed, the "correspondences" found by comparing vv. 15/18b, 16a/19, and 16c/20 "are not accidental, but designed, to bring out the main emphases in the two orders of creation and redemption."[215] The rhythmic nature of the passage thus reflects the mind of "an author steeped in the poetic background of the Old Testament, where not only hymns but prophetic productions were encased in parallel forms."[216] And in fact it is illustrative of this particular text's *Wirkungsgeschichte* that numerous church hymns have been written either incorporating or alluding to such passages.[217]

Because the text is poetic, elevated, and at least in the broadest sense "hymnic," I argue that it should be reflected as such both formally and substantively in translation. As Jerry Sumney puts it, the passage "possesses a more exalted style than regular prose" and can be considered "as poetic and liturgical, without identifying any genre more specifically."[218] For example, delineating and organizing the Hymn's verses in strophic or other forms might have the virtue of highlighting structural parallels of form and substance. As can be seen in sect. II.f.ii, *infra*, a number of translations do so.

But one should also be attentive to the uninterrupted flow of Paul's writing in passages like this where he seems almost carried away with the message he is inspired to convey. The default mode in translating from Greek to English is to adopt standard sentence structure and punctuation. That may make perfect sense where a passage reads like ordinary prose or dialogue. But where there is something more involved, as where

---

214. This conclusion also flows from the "rhetorico-poetic persuasiveness" analysis in Selby, *Wisdom of Words*.

215. Martin, "Early Christian Hymn," 197. So too the emphasis on "reconciliation" by use of the word "all" a total of eight times in vv. 15–20. See also Stuhlmacher, *Biblical Theology*, 440: The "reconciliation of the universe effected by God in and through Christ is the end-time counterpart to the redemption of Israel from slavery to guilt in Egypt."

216. Balchin, "Colossians 1:15–20," 68, noting that Jesus himself at times taught by way of "balanced statement that went well beyond single line parallelism" (citing Luke 11:31–30 and 17:26–30). See also J. Sanders, *New Testament Christological Hymns*, 4, noting "the rather close formal similarity" between the Colossian Hymn and certain analyses of the Old Testament "song of thanks."

217. See, e.g., Hymn Society, "Hymns for Colossians." This is true across denominations. See Donovan, "Hymns for Colossians."

218. Sumney, *Colossians*, 60–61.

the writer goes beyond the prosaic in order to convey something about the Deity, about timelessness, about that which is beyond words, then a translator should consider moving beyond ordinary syntactical conventions as far as punctuation, subject/verb agreement and the like. For example, the translation of the Colossian Hymn in the appendix does not "versify" it, but suggests its poetic nature by insetting the margins, italicizing the font, largely dispensing with punctuation, employing a couple of Greek letters, and adding *nomina sacra*. Again, this is only by way of a test application of the *viva vox Jesu* hermeneutic, but it is one admittedly novel way to convey the atemporal, aspatial *verbum interius* of which the passage is a plerophoric expression.

2. Liturgical

In addition to the hymnic characteristics noted above, Colossians is also a useful example of other forms of liturgical language and structure, including prayer, epithets, and *nomina sacra*, found throughout the Scriptures. The question is whether these too may be forms essential to expressing the text's inner word in a given receptor language. I therefore examine portions of Colossians more closely to help answer that question.

a. Prayer

Gentile members of the Colossian community might well have been steeped in Greek religious traditions and would thus understand prayer as a form of "discourse addressed to the gods."[219] In that tradition, this generally includes "asking the gods for something," a petition usually being present.[220] And Jewish members of the congregation would likewise be familiar with Hebrew prayers, which are also premised on requests and often coupled with praise.[221] It is beyond the scope of this work to engage in a comparative analysis of religious traditions and practices, but for present purposes I will premise a basic commonality as to the relative relationship of supplicant and supplicand. Thus, at a general level, prayers might begin by invoking the deity. In Greek religious practice this is often (though not invariably), with "ὦ" preceding the name of the

---

219. Pernot, "Rhetoric of Religion," 236.
220. Pulleyn, *Prayer in Greek Religion*, 15.
221. E.g., Pss 4, 10, 13, 17, 22, 25, 28, 39, 42, 43, 44, 51, 70, 71, 82, 85, 143.

god addressed.²²² Such forms can also be seen throughout the Psalms.²²³ Although the opening of Colossians does not begin with an invocation as such, Paul might be said to be invoking God variably as Lord, Jesus, or Father. Regardless, he does begin directly with prayerful thanksgiving (1:3). He then moves seamlessly into extended petitions for the Colossians—requests he makes to the Lord for them not only in the opening of the letter, but as it proceeds through prayerful stages of praise, argumentation, and encouragement.

A sense of reciprocal obligation on the part of God is of course absent from orthodox Christian faith, essentially replaced by a recognition that any gifts or benefits are a matter of grace. In a sense, the letter as a whole might therefore be seen as a form of prayer, in that Paul prays "ceaselessly" (1:9) that the Colossians may obtain a right understanding of who Christ is and live their lives free of the negative impact of a wrong understanding. But to the extent one might identify more specific examples of what might be characterized as a "prayer register," these would involve Paul's petitions for the Colossians to partake of the "fullness" reflected in the hymnic material discussed above. Thus, Paul prays in Col 1:9 that the Colossians "may be filled" with "all" wisdom and "all" knowledge, combining the concepts of fullness and completeness.²²⁴ Similarly, Paul prays in Col 2:2 that the Colossians' hearts might be encouraged εἰς πᾶν πλοῦτος τῆς πληροφορίας τῆς συνέσεως. Indeed, if there is a leitmotif in the letter it must be the continuous series of variations on the theme of fullness, entirety, and completeness, conveying a sense of abundance in Christ's own nature as well as believers' completeness in him as "the Body, the Church" (1:18), where "Christ is all and in all" (3:11).²²⁵

The style is therefore well-described as "plerophoric," i.e., one of fullness itself, expressed in a tone of completeness, confidence, and assurance.²²⁶ The text's form *itself* thereby reveals its substance, with lin-

---

222. Willi, *Languages of Aristophanes*, 16; Devlin, "Hymn in Greek Literature," 17.

223. E.g., Pss 4, 5, 6, 7, etc.

224. Adding to the tone of this register, there are in fact a number of lexemes from the root πλήρ in Col 1:9, 19, 24–25; 2:2, 9–10; 3:5, 16; 4:12, 17; and from πᾶν in 1:6, 9–11, 15–20, 23, 28; 2:2–3, 9–10, 14, 19–20, 22; 3:8, 11, 14, 17, 20, 22; 4:6–7, 9.

225. So too Eph 1:23 concerning "the Church, which is his Body, the Fullness of him who fills all in all."

226. Granados Rojas, "Word of God Incomplete," 72n28 (citing Bujard, *Stilanalystische Untersuchungen*, 143). Cf. also the usages of the word in Heb 6:11; 10:22. Another term might be "pleonectic," although that implies excess; Paul's specific use of πλεονεξία in 3:5 thus reflects a negative sense of "fullness."

guistic fullness reflective of the overflowing presence of the Godhead bodily in Christ.[227] Consistent with the "processual" understanding described above of the relationship between thought and word, Colossians' formulations might thus be seen as the Word's "filling" of human language with words expressive of that which is beyond words. It follows that to the extent God's fullness *in every sense* lies at the heart of the letter's divine communication, a translator applying the hermeneutic of an effective history approach should strive for plerophorically evocative words in his own receptor language.

b. Epithets

The Old Testament is filled with varied names for the God of creation and Israel, emphasizing one or another trait as may be relevant to a given passage.[228] In classical Greek worship it was also common for hymns and prayers to be laced with epithetical references to the gods.[229] Whether writing with a background in the Jewish Scriptures or with some awareness of the tradition of Greek religious thought, it is worth noting that Paul includes ascriptive references to God in Colossians, such that the same might reinforce a perception of the "sacred" nature of the divine being he described. From a translation point of view, it may be useful to present the same in such a way as to reflect these traditions, e.g., were the Lord to be described by use of a predicate adjective as in "the Lord is omnipotent," one might with equal validity incorporate the descriptor into his name as "the Omnipotent Lord." That might be an option with 1:1, using "Father God" rather than "God the Father."

c. *Nomina Sacra*

Nomina sacra are scribally distinctive presentations of certain words relating to the divinity. Orthographically, they appear as contractions or

---

227. Again, contrast this with dynamic equivalence theory's rejection of the importance of an original text's "stylistic specialties." Nida and Taber, *Theory and Practice*, 1.

228. See, e.g., Gen 22:14; 49:24; Exod 15:26; 16:13; 17:15; Isa 9:6; Jer 33:16. See generally Hemphill, *Names of God*.

229. Devlin, "Hymn in Greek Literature," 17; Pernot, "Rhetoric of Religion," 237–38. Some typical examples might be "grey-eyed Athena," "dark Erebus," "golden-haired Apollo, Lord, Healer, Swan of Pythos and Delos," "winged Chaos," or "almighty Zeus, high enthroned."

suspensions of the letters of divine names (such as Jesus or Father) or theologically associated words (such as cross). Contractions are most commonly formed by the first and last letters of a given word, while suspensions are formed using a given word's initial two letters; some forms, however, abbreviate with three or even four letters.[230] Contractions and suspensions are marked in manuscripts as such with a horizontal bar over what are thus abbreviated forms. It is beyond the scope of this work to explore in detail the nature, origins, and purposes of *nomina sacra*.[231] But in the same way that I propose utilization of initial capital letters in translating certain words to mark "elevated" language (sect. III.b.iii, *infra*), as well as the use of epithetical descriptors evocative of certain divine attributes (sect. II.d.iii, *supra*), in this section I consider the value of incorporating a form of *nomina sacra* in a translation to reveal them as effective modes of reverent speech.

Broadly speaking, *nomina sacra* began to appear in Christian manuscripts as early as the second/third centuries as contracted or suspended forms of divine names or names "intimately associated with the divine name."[232] By then, "these (originally) Greek short forms were present in basically all Christian Bible manuscripts" as a means of "weaving the Old and New Testament texts into a coherent whole."[233] They appear most commonly where the text refers to Jesus, Christ, Lord, God or Spirit, but also with Cross, Father, Son, and others.[234] As relevant to the test case

---

230. See generally Hurtado, *Earliest Christian Artifacts*, 95–134; Trobisch, *First Edition*, 11–13. Note that contraction using the first and last letters allows for determination of the case of the noun. Here is a typical example (with highlights added):

231. Tomas Bokedal, for example, has closely examined the relationship between the early Christian *regula fidei* and *nomina sacra* and the importance of the latter to biblical interpretation. Bokedal, *Christ the Center*, 317–55. And open issues remain concerning the origins of *nomina sacra*, including possible relationships with Jewish scribal practices, as well as their function. See Hurtado, *Earliest Christian Artifacts*, 95–134; Trobisch, *First Edition*, 13–17.

232. Bokedal, *Christ the Center*, 321.

233. Bokedal, *Christ the Center*, 303. See also Kenyon, "Nomina Sacra," discussing the Chester Beatty Papyri; Hurtado, "Origin of *Nomina Sacra*," 660, suggesting "an origin no later than the first century."

234. For convenience, Jesus, Christ, Lord, and God are sometimes referred to as

discussion here, *nomina sacra* appear in manuscripts of Colossians at least as early as the third century, notably in 𝔓46 (one of the so-called Chester Beatty Papyri). Again using Colossians as an example, *nomina sacra* likewise appear as the letter is presented in the fourth-century Codex Sinaiticus and the fifth-century Codex Alexandrinus.[235]

It has been theorized that adoption of a special orthography for certain names and words was doctrinal/theological in nature, reflecting early credal expressions of Christian devotion and belief.[236] When used together in particular texts, they thereby form "the main building blocks of the *regula fidei* formularies, demarcating the three articles of faith."[237] And by presenting the name of Jesus distinctively, the early church may purposefully have incorporated the reverential Jewish treatment of the Tetragrammaton into the gospel of Jesus' lordship.[238] Moreover, the horizontal crossbar over a given form may *itself* have functioned both as an editorial unifier and as a signal of distinctive pronunciation.[239] At a minimum, it is fair to say that *nomina sacra* "combine textual and visual features . . . intended to mark them off visually (and reverentially) from the surrounding text."[240] As such, the early church gave "textual expression to a devotional pattern in which Jesus features beside God,"[241] thus also confirming the validity of a canonically unified hermeneutic.[242] Their visual demarcation in translation as proposed herein would therefore carry into the present their early and important function in the underlying texts.

---

a "primary" group, with Cross, Spirit, Father, and others taxonomized as "secondary," "tertiary," and "quaternary" groups, and more, depending on dating and/or frequency, with the primary group alone accounting for some 2102 occurrences in 74 early manuscripts. Bokedal, *Christ the Center*, 329–34. See also 303, 320, 325–26, noting differences of form among various codices.

235. See https://greekcntr.org/collation/index.htm.

236. Bokedal, "Notes on *Nomina Sacra*," 288, 291; Bokedal, *Christ the Center*, 303, noting C. H. Roberts' suggestion that the *nomina sacra* may reflect an "'embryonic creed' engrafted into the text."

237. Bokedal, *Christ the Center*, 303–4.

238. Hurtado, *Earliest Christian Artifacts*, 106, 133. *Nomina sacra* also allowed for clear distinctions between references to "gods" and "God." See Bokedal, *Christ the Center*, 305, 341, noting the frequency and possible monotheistic interpretive significance of such distinctions.

239. Bokedal, *Christ the Center*, 351.

240. Hurtado, *Earliest Christian Artifacts*, 121.

241. Bokedal, *Formation and Significance*, 87; Bokedal, "Early Rule-of-Faith," 66–69.

242. Bokedal, "Notes on *Nomina Sacra*," 291.

The scribal use of *nomina sacra* continued in nearly all Greek and Latin Christian manuscripts up to the invention of movable type, but largely ceased in printed texts thereafter. *Nomina sacra* in forms that seem more purposefully related to Greek manuscripts do however appear in early printed editions in other languages. Thus, in "Luther's Bible of 1534, the Lord is rendered in German by HERR/HErr, God by GOtt and Jesus by JEsus"; and in the "Swedish Bible edition of 1703 . . . the Tetragrammaton is similarly rendered by HERren and Jesus by JEsus."[243] The KJV's small-caps use of LORD for the Tetragrammaton is an arguable exception to the general absence of *nomina* in English versions, in that it is an orthographically distinct form. The NRSVue retains this form where YHWH appears in the Masoretic Text,[244] although it does not use it in the New Testament where κύριος appears. Yet while such usage lacks the early manuscript format for *nomina sacra*, it does serve to mark the reverential nature of YHWH.[245]

That said, we do not know with certainty whether *nomina sacra* performed a liturgical function, such as being read aloud distinctively, as may have been the case with the divine name in Jewish worship; or in prompting a response, as is now the case in certain Christian traditions where the presiding minister and/or the congregants genuflect or cross themselves when the Lord's name is invoked.[246] The question thus arises whether it would be of value to reflect *nomina sacra* in a contemporary English translation in order to capture this element of the text's *Wirkungsgeschichte*. On balance, I suggest that presentation of some form of *nomina sacra* would in fact maintain a clear connection with understandings reflected in the earliest extant manuscripts; retain the

---

243. Bokedal, *Formation and Significance*, 86n11.

244. The editors of the NRSVue overstate this as "the traditional way that English versions render the Divine Name" (NRSVue, xi), since LORD has not been universally received in that form in the larger translation tradition.

245. Note that John Henry Newman provides a known instance of an author marking divine names by the use of capital letters in his own writings. Bokedal, "Notes on Nomina Sacra," 294.

246. There is in fact some doubt that lectors made "some gesture of 'obeisance' where the *nomina sacra* appear." Hurtado, *Earliest Christian Artifacts*, 132. And we have no way of knowing how the relevant names sounded when read aloud from texts marked with *nomina*. In Hebrew readings, for example, YHWH is sounded out as "Adonai" so as *not* to verbalize the sacred name. Yet for many Christians it is an essential element of worship *to* sound out Jesus' name, not only because it is the "Name above all names" (Phil 2:9–11), but because of the unique authority attached to it (Matt 28:19; John 14:13–14; Luke 10:17; Acts 4:30; Rom 10:13).

canonical and reverential functions they seem to perform; sustain a link to Christian tradition more broadly, including illuminated manuscripts, iconography, and other artistic forms; and in general help to avoid the "distancing of form from meaning"[247] that characterizes the dynamic equivalence method. In sect. III.b.iv, *infra*, I therefore build on the KJV's small-caps form for Lord as one way to do so.

3. Didactic/Doctrinal/Intrascriptural

Paul's letters are not written as explicit doctrinal treatises, nor are they an organized systematic theology in the way of later writers such as Thomas Aquinas, John Calvin, or Karl Barth. At the same time, Luke Timothy Johnson probably goes too far in asserting that there is not even a "generic 'Pauline letter,' but only a collection of unique missives,"[248] since there are in fact a number of formal and substantive similarities as well as intrascriptural relationships among many of the letters. In Romans, for example, Paul "explain[ed] the gospel at length and in a nuanced way,"[249] even if the letter was not meant as a comprehensive presentation of all issues concerning God, man, and salvation. And with respect to Colossians, Lars Hartman observes that its "length alone," not to mention its contents, suggests that it might be considered "as some sort of treatise."[250]

But whether "systematic" or not, there is such a range of material in Paul's letters that theologians and preachers have devoted lifetimes to understanding, explaining, and applying the doctrinal elements of "Pauline theology."[251] This material might include passages concerning who God is; who Jesus is; the relationship of Christ and the church; the work of the cross; false teaching; improper behavior; and proper behavior. Relevant intrascripturality is often noted in existing translations by marginal notes or cross-references, though not necessarily by direct literary reference or the use of parallel language. And as noted, beyond the intrascripturality of the New Testament books, there are essential intrascriptural links to the LXX.[252]

247. Felber, "Chomsky's Influence," 255.
248. L. Johnson, *First and Second Letters*, 93.
249. Thielman, *Romans*, 38–39. See, e.g., Longenecker, *Epistle to Romans*, 2016.
250. Hartman, "On Reading," 138.
251. See, e.g., Ridderbos, *Paul*.
252. See Beale and Carson, *Commentary*, xxii–xxviii, 841–70; cf. Foster, *Colossians*, 66–75.

The methodology advanced here calls for such relationships to be elicited in translation. Colossians again may serve as a good example of how identifying and sustaining in translation certain formal or structural aspects of the text may help in revealing its internal doctrinal message. For example, Col 1:15 reads ὅς ἐστιν εἰκὼν τοῦ θεοῦ τοῦ ἀοράτου, πρωτότοκος πάσης κτίσεως. It might be translated literally as "who is the *image* of the invisible God, the *firstborn* of every creature," as in the KJV. The key phrase εἰκὼν τοῦ θεοῦ seems inescapably taken from Gen 1:27 (κατ' εἰκόνα Θεοῦ) and must have called the creation passages to mind. Likewise, πρωτότοκος appears as a purposeful reference to Exod 4:22 (υἱὸς πρωτότοκός μου Ἰσραήλ) and/or Ps 88:28 LXX (κἀγὼ πρωτότοκον θήσομαι αὐτόν). These canonical relationships should therefore be expressly retained in translation. This might be by marginal notes, or, more distinctively, by incorporation of language identical to that found in a translation of the related Old Testament passage.

Going forward in the text's trajectory, moreover, important passages were adopted into credal statements or other doctrinal formulations.[253] A translation made consistent with an effective history hermeneutic should likewise reflect the same either by incorporation of credal language *in haec verba*, or by providing marginal notes. In other words, translating with attention both to the LXX's effective history in the New Testament and the New Testament's effective history in church tradition highlights the dialogic nature of doctrinal development.

4. Rhetorical

Certain scholars take issue with the notion that the epistolary form of various New Testament texts, including letters such as Colossians, provides the most defining framework for formal analysis. Their theory is that the "occasional" nature of such correspondence imposes a limit on one's ability to generalize from it. Focusing on what they discern as the rhetorical nature of such texts, some take the position that various of the letters are better understood within the framework of "persuasive discourse," including that of classical Hellenistic and Roman political and literary culture. The relevance of that question here is that from a formal point of view, rhetorical elements may be important to the Greek text's

---

253. McKnight, *Letter to the Colossians*, 39–65. See discussion in sect. II.d.ii, *supra*.

"revealing" of its inner word. If so, they may appropriately be considered in how the text is presented in the receptor language.

For example, Ben Witherington III asserts that "the dominant paradigm when it came to words and the conveying of ideas, meaning and persuasion in the NT era was rhetoric, not epistolary conventions."[254] With respect to the epistles, he points out that given the low literacy rates (10 to 20 percent at most across the Greco-Roman world of the first century), "literary documents in early Christianity were intended to be read aloud in the assemblies."[255] Indeed, Paul himself clearly meant his letters to be read aloud.[256] Hence the value of "hearing" the letters as persuasive expressions of one who was a rhetor as well as a writer.[257] Still, one should not overstate the argument. Paul himself criticizes overly florid speech, after all, and disclaims having used sophistic eloquence.[258] Instead, he claims he relied on the demonstration of the power of the Holy Spirit.[259] An overdependence on speech related analysis may also obscure recognized distinctions between the spoken and written word.[260] Nor are the letters "orations" in a Lysian, Ciceronian, or other classical mode. Pauline letters may even be said to be *sui generis*, shaped to some extent by rhetorical forms and the occasionality of their circumstances, but also universal in scope and theological in content.[261] Hence for present purposes, I will identify and assess the utility of rhetorical forms to

---

254. Witherington, *New Testament Rhetoric*, 5. See also 123: "The rhetorical forms of Paul's letters are more revealing of what Paul's letters are actually about than the epistolary forms and elements."

255. Witherington, *New Testament Rhetoric*, 97; Loubser, "Orality and Literacy," 64.

256. 1 Thess 5:27; Sampley and Lampe, *Paul and Rhetoric*, ix.

257. This may give a clue as to what his opponents meant when they said that his "letters are weighty and powerful" (1 Cor 10:10).

258. 1 Cor 1:2-5. Note too that Augustine rejected verbal displays as potentially deceitful. See Augustine, *Confessions*, 9.2.

259. 1 Cor 2:4. Even so, there are indications that Paul had at least some of the skills of oral advocacy, as reflected in his commanding "sweep of the hand" in Acts 26:1 to silence listeners as he began an essentially forensic speech defending himself before Agrippa. See Newbold, "Nonverbal Communication," 225-27, on the use of rhetorical gestures.

260. Sampley and Lampe, *Paul and Rhetoric*, 12-13, 144. See also Demetrius, *On Style*, §§224-26, 229.

261. So too, the Gospels evince generic aspects of narrative yet are also uniquely shaped by Jesus' manner of teaching as well as by Old Testament imagery and themes.

translation, but without suggesting that rhetoric is the dominant element of Paul's style and presentation.[262]

By way of background, Aristotle proposed three "species" of rhetoric: judicial, deliberative, and epideictic.[263] The judicial argument seeks to persuade the audience as to the occurrence of acts taken in the past; the deliberative as to acts to be taken by them in the future; and the epideictic as to their holding or reaffirmation of positions in the present. As a general matter, both judicial and deliberative arguments would include an introductory *exordium* seeking the good will of the audience; a *narratio* that might provide background and transitional elements; a *propositio* setting forth the issues and any propositions to be demonstrated; a *confirmatio*, which would include a *probatio* of the proposition(s) being advanced as well as a *refutatio* of contrary positions; and a *peroratio* and/or *conclusio* summing up the argument and appealing to the audience with pathos.[264] Epideictic speech might reflect similar forms, but also has as a central focus qualities of character that the speaker or writer wishes the audience to emulate.[265]

Regardless of which "species" of rhetoric is involved, argument is at the heart of persuasive rhetoric. Arguments may be elaborated in myriad ways, of course, including through stylistic flourishes; figures of speech such as analogies, comparisons, fables, parables, or metaphors; historical examples; citations to authority; presentation of opposing arguments and rebuttals to them, including through "rhetorical questions"; and/or the use of enthymemes (inferred propositions). The concluding portion could also include warnings or advice.[266]

Taking Colossians as a test case to see if such analysis might be relevant to translation, one can see suggestions of judicial argumentation, with Paul reminding the community of the validity of events (such as

---

262. See also Wedderburn, *Reasons for Romans*, 6–11, discussing epistolary, treatise-like, literary, ambassadorial, and other approaches to Romans.

263. Aristotle, *Rhetoric* 1.3.1–13. See Sampley and Lampe, *Paul and Rhetoric*, 25–47 (identifying all three species in the New Testament); Mack, *Rhetoric*, 34–35 (same).

264. Witherington, *New Testament Rhetoric*, 129–30; Mack, *Rhetoric*, 41–42; Dormeyer, "Hellenistic Letter-Formula," 66–67. Note that the so-called "New Rhetoric" would not confine the analysis to categories established in antiquity. Sampley and Lampe, *Paul and Rhetoric*, 6; Castelli et al., *Postmodern Bible*.

265. Mack, *Rhetoric*, 41–43, 47–48; Humphrey, *And I Turned*, 33n6; Pernot, "Rhetoric of Religion," 240–45. Cf. Witherington, *New Testament Rhetoric*, 127–28, describing 1 Cor 13 as "an excellent and poetic example of showpiece epideictic rhetoric in praise of love."

266. Mack, *Rhetoric*, 39–41; Kennedy, *New Testament*, 23–24.

Jesus' death and resurrection) occurring in the past (e.g., Col 2:13–15). And an important section of the letter encourages the Colossians as to acts to be taken deliberatively in the future (e.g., 3:1–25; 4:1). The letter also strives epideictically to persuade the Colossians of the truths of the faith in the face of contrary arguments, exhorting them to hold fast and/or reaffirm the core as presented by Paul (e.g., 2:8, 16–23).

As a formal matter, Paul employed rhetorical elements such as synonyms and repetitions, with the letter's multiple variations and repetitions of words rooted in "fullness," "filling," and "fulfillment,"[267] as well as those rooted in "all" and "every."[268] And in Col 1:29, Paul cumulates several nominative and verbal expressions of struggle, work, energy, and power.[269] He also uses military vocabulary and imagery in 2:5, where he commends the Colossians for their steadfast faith;[270] and in 2:15, where he employs the verb ἀπεκδύομαι, which can mean "disarm in battle," to describe Christ's defeat of powers and authorities.[271]

Rhetorical speech can also allow an image to perform a range of functions. Thus, Paul uses clothing vocabulary in Col 3:8–10 to contrast the "putting off" of old behaviors (ἀπόθεσθε . . . τὰ πάντα) with "being clothed" in the new (ἐνδυσάμενοι τὸν νέον), imagery that might have alluded to Roman law prescribing different clothing for persons of different class and status.[272] Or it might be an intrascriptural reference to "putting on Christ" at baptism (Χριστὸν ἐνεδύσασθε).[273] And his use of ἀπεκδύομαι in 2:15 noted above has the alternative meaning of "strip off," and thus might be intrascripturally allusive to the stripping off of Christ's clothes in the crucifixion. Finally, one can see in the numerous

---

267. I.e., Col 1:9, 19, 24–25; 2:2, 9–10; 3:16; 4:12, 17.

268. I.e., Col 1:6, 9–11, 15–20, 23, 28; 2:2–3, 9–10, 14, 19–20, 22; 3:8, 11, 14, 17, 20, 22; 4:6–7, 9.

269. κοπιῶ ἀγωνιζόμενος κατὰ τὴν ἐνέργειαν αὐτοῦ τὴν ἐνεργουμένην ἐν ἐμοὶ ἐν δυνάμει. Bird, *Colossians*, 69, recognizes the "emphatic" nature of the verse, but seems to miss its rhetorical validity, describing the Greek as "awkward and tautologous."

270. Compare Col 2:5 (βλέπων ὑμῶν τὴν τάξιν καὶ τὸ στερέωμα) with Xenophon, *Anabasis* 1.2.18 (ἰδοῦσα . . . τὴν τάξιν τοῦ στρατεύματος), and with 1 Macc 9:14 (εἶδεν Ἰούδας . . . τὸ στερέωμα τῆς παρεμβολῆς).

271. ἀπεκδύομαι, BDAG.

272. Sumney, *Colossians*, 199, citing passages in Suetonius, Appian, Livy, and Dio Cassius.

273. Gal 3:27. While there is no evidence that special baptismal garments were given at this early time in the church's development, cf. Pseudo-Hippolytus of Rome, *Traditio apostolica* 21:1–20 (ca. AD 215), it is not inconceivable.

hapax legomena of the letter a series of memorable words carefully employed for didactic or other purposes.[274]

All such forms of speech seem purposefully styled in aid of Paul's persuasive goals. Paul use of classical rhetorical elements is perhaps not surprising given the likelihood that he had a "Hellenistic education, consisting of more than the second stage of grammar school, which included the beginning of rhetorical studies."[275] His letters might well have been read by and sounded familiar to persons educated within Greco-Roman culture.[276] And by virtue of his training as a Pharisee studying "at the feet of Gamaliel,"[277] they would also be approachable by those immersed in the Jewish Scriptures, who might be accustomed to such forms of argumentation as midrashic and allegorical readings.[278] Jerry Sumney's recent commentary on Colossians, in fact, frames the entire structure of the letter as a series of "arguments," also noting the presence of metaphorical, poetic, and paracletic elements.[279]

The point here is that a translator should be attentive to identifying forms of persuasive rhetoric and then, if the form appears revelatory of the text's inner word, adopting receptor language that reflects such tones. Gary Selby's analysis of "non-rational" responses to scriptural texts is informative in that regard. Drawing on Aristotle's theory of *mimesis* in the *Poetics* as well as Longinus' analysis of "elevated" speech in Περὶ Ὕψους, Selby argues that the "poetic texts" of the New Testament represent the writers' attempts "to create . . . numinous experiences for their

---

274. E.g., φιλοσοφία (2:9), χειρόγραφον (2:14), ἀπεκδύομαι (2:15), νεομηνία (2:16), ἐμβατεύων (2:18), καταβραβεύω (2:18), δογματίζω (2:20), ἀπόχρησις (2:22), ἐθελοθρησκία (2:23), ἀφειδία (2:23), and πλησμονή (2:23).

275. Dormeyer, "Hellenistic Letter-Formula," 70: "Paul often employed the popular rhetorical modes of imagery, antithesis, diatribe, admonition, applied ethics, apology, self-recommendation, reproach and textual proof in his letters."

276. Witherington, *New Testament Rhetoric*, 99–104 (discussing Paul's likely education, rhetorical and linguistic skills) and 102 (noting the forms of argumentation in 1 Cor 9:7–14 and Gal 4:21–31); Granados Rojas, "Word of God Incomplete," 69–74 (analyzing rhetorical devices of "accumulation and reversal" in Col 1:24–29); Holloway, "Enthymeme," 335–39 (analyzing Paul's rhetorical use of enthymemes to make his points); Van W. Cronjé, "Stratagem" (analyzing Paul's use of ἐρώτημα as a means of argumentation).

277. Acts 22:3.

278. Gignilliat, "Paul," 135–46, analyzing Paul's allegorical method in Galatians with reference to Hellenistic rhetorical treatises as well as Palestinian rabbinical readings.

279. Sumney, *Colossians*, vii–viii. See also Harding, "Disputed and Undisputed," 159: Colossians is "dialogical in its argumentative strategies."

Elements of a Canonical-Hermeneutical Translation Approach/Test Case

audience."[280] Poetic arguments, moreover, do not proceed so much from "syllogisms [as from] enthymemes,"[281] i.e., arguments from probability. In this context, Ryan Stark describes a category of "mystical enthymemes" where, because both the writer and reader lack the ability fully to grasp the "missing premise that allows for a particular vision of God," the Spirit of God must itself "bridge the ontological gap, the metaphysical lacunae, between mortal understanding and God's providence."[282]

In addition to passages that open up what Gadamer might refer to as "free spaces," a good deal of Paul's writing exemplifies what Selby describes a form of persuasive liturgy. In that regard, the Colossian Hymn shares important elements with the extended "blessing" of Eph 1:3–14, a passage to which it has been compared.[283] Thus, "by its very nature . . . [the hymn] provides a communicative form through which a congregation expresses its praise to God."[284] The elevated language creates an "imaginative picture" that "transports" the listeners/readers "out of themselves," such that they are not merely giving intellectual assent to theological truths but "apprehend[ing] realities about God in their direct experience."[285]

As such, the language has "the sense-producing potential of *mimesis* and *phantasia*"[286]—a placing of the vision "before the eyes" of the audience.[287] A translation that is faithful to the language of such passages may

---

280. Selby, *Wisdom of Words*, 16; Humphrey, *And I Turned*. See also Castelli et al., *Postmodern Bible*, 170: "The essence of rhetoric, like that of poetry, is not communication but the creation of new states of being."

281. Gadamer, *Gadamer Reader*, 415 (citing Aristotle).

282. Stark, "Christian Mystical Rhetoric," 264.

283. McKnight, *Letter to the Colossians*, 17; Pizzuto, *Cosmic Leap of Faith*, 26–30.

284. Selby, *Wisdom of Words*, 119. See also 154–55, noting the group-binding effect that may be obtained through shared participation in liturgical expression, an effect that might serve to unify the local community in opposition to the false teachers and/or their doctrine. Cf. Aristotle, *Rhetoric* 1355a–57a (enthymemes require audience/listener participation for their completion); Eberhard, "Mediality," 429 ("Understanding means understanding by participation").

285. Selby, *Wisdom of Words*, 34, 121 (citing Longinus, Περὶ Ὕψους 39.1–3).

286. O'Gorman, "Longinus's Sublime Rhetoric," 73. Maier, "Vision," 321: "*Phantasiai* [vivid mental pictures] . . . place in the mind images by means of which persuasion is effected." See also Humphrey, *And I Turned*, proposing "vision report" as a form of rhetorical expression.

287. See Newman, "Aristotle's Notion." See also Selby, *Wisdom of Words*, 36 (citing Longinus, Περὶ Ὕψους 15.9–11); Witherington, *New Testament Rhetoric*, 204 (citing Longinus, Περὶ Ὕψους 15.1, 11); Humphrey, *And I Turned*, 36 (noting Quintilian's description of a rhetorical "move known as *demonstratio* as the expression of the matter

even create through visualized imagery a "vivid actuality" in the listeners, going so far as to become a vehicle for "ecstatic" transport.[288] It may likewise produce in the reader or listener a sense that God is speaking to them in the text, i.e., that the text "*is more than a 'docetic' or disembodied system of signifiers.*"[289] The result would thus validate Augustine's claim that faithful readers of Scripture "undergo the same type of inspiration as mystical writers," such that "spirited reading begins with prayer and ends with revelation."[290] And it would likewise validate this work's appropriation for purposes of translation theory of Aquinas' insight that the divinely communicated inner word "is in continual formation when being actively understood."[291]

There is a useful comparison here to Revelation, where the ineffability of the language allows for multivalent expression in translation, in part because the *verbum interius* there expressed is not limited to speech. Indeed, the vision there conveyed arguably *transcends* speech because it partakes of the infinite. Revelation thus confronts us with the limitations of human speech recognized by Augustine,[292] in that it appears to convey in language things seen and heard that cannot be fully expressed in words.[293] If the vision experienced by John could not be fully expressed in the original Greek, then a translation of the words used to express the inexpressible may well need to depart considerably from such language as he *did* employ, in order to afford the reader some access to John's atemporal spiritual perception.[294]

In that regard, Revelation may reflect the rhetorical "creation of [an] alternative world" that George Steiner finds to be the essence of language, permitting "ambiguity, polysemy, opaqueness [and] the violation of grammatical and logical sequences."[295] If so, Revelation may provide yet another example of how translating a text through ekphrastic description

---

in hand with words so that it appears to be borne up 'before the eyes' [*res ante oculos*] of the audience"); Maier, "Vision," 320–21 (stressing the importance of visual imagery in ancient rhetoric, including by emphasis on "vivid description," or *ekphrasis*).

288. Longinus, Περὶ Ὕψους 25.1.
289. Thiselton, *New Horizons*, 75 (emphasis in original).
290. Stark, "Christian Mystical Rhetoric," 261 (citing *De doctrina christiana*).
291. Aquinas, *De natura verbi intellectus* §277.
292. Augustine, *De catechizandis rudibus* 2.3.
293. And were in one instance forbidden to be expressed. See Rev 10:4.
294. Hence the imperfection of the Trinitarian analogy, as noted above.
295. Steiner, *After Babel*, 246.

and with lesser regard to grammatical constraints may provide access to its inner meaning. Take this version of Rev 6:1–17:

> Still watching I saw the Lamb open one of the seven seals when one of the four living creatures speaking as thunder roars said "Come!" and I beheld a white horse one on it with a bow given power to go conquering that he might conquer as the Lamb opened the second seal and the second living creature said "Come!" and I saw another horse this time red and on it one with a mighty sword taking peace away from the Earth men murdering men as the Lamb opened the third seal the third living creature said "Come!" and I saw a black horse one upon it with a pair of scales in his hand while a sound from the midst of the four living creatures said "A day's pay for a pound of wheat, a day's pay for three pounds of barley, yet leave no shortage of oil and wine" as the Lamb opened the fourth seal and the sound of the fourth living creature said "Come!" and I saw a horse green in pallor one atop it having the name Death all Hell following him with power killing a quarter of Earth's people with slashing Thracian blade famine death ravaging wild beasts even so the Lamb opened the fifth seal and looking I saw below the altar the souls of all slaughtered for the sake of the Word of God and his testimony crying out together with great voice "How much longer Holy Master and True until you judge vindicating our blood on all who dwell on the Earth?" each one wearing a long and lustrous white robe being told patiently to wait a little while longer until their ranks be complete continuously filling up with their fellow servants' souls the souls of their brothers and sisters slain as were they but when the Lamb opened the sixth seal seismic shudders seized the Earth the sun as sackcloth darkening the whole moon turning to blood the stars of Heaven falling to Earth as wind-shaken late Summer figs the whole Heaven splitting apart rolling up as a scroll every mountain and island upended from its roots the kings of the Earth the rulers the captains the rich the strong all slaves and all free hiding themselves in mountain dens and stone grottos shouting to the mountains and rocks "Fall upon us and hide us from the face of the one who sits on the throne and from the wrath of the Lamb, for the Great Day of his wrath is come and who can withstand it?"[296]

---

296. Straus, *New Testament*, 539–41. See also Straus and Reiland, *Revelation*.

Here again, application of the translation methodology of this book starts with a grounding in the text.[297] Yet the above is not a "literal" translation. For example, on reviewing the Greek it seems clear that whatever the experience of sight and sound was for the writer, it was not the same as any ordinary viewing of people, things, and natural events. Even though the events are expressed one after another—because that is all that language can do—they *also* "occur" in the eternal present, i.e., in the absence of time.[298] How to convey this in translation? While the Greek is written in reasonably linear syntax, in theory there is room to test the limits of its grammatical "free space" in order to reveal the atemporal inner word, even if incompletely.

The foregoing example thus dispenses with certain standard grammatical forms, such as punctuation. And as for vocabulary, the imagery of Revelation can seem more poetry than prose. This passage occasionally therefore leans on rhetorico-poetical devices such as alliteration ("when the Lamb opened the sixth seal seismic shudders seized the Earth the sun as sackcloth darkening"), even though no such form appears in Greek; or adds modifying language ("slashing Thracian blade") that likewise has no textual analog but is resonant of the ancient ῥομφαία; or reads paratactically ("the kings of the Earth the rulers the captains the rich the strong all slaves and all free") to suggest a simultaneity of vision. Of course, this is far from the only way the passage could be translated. At the same time, considering it in such a fluid manner not only allows for a new perspective on the written form but may also affect how it is heard if read aloud. And as with poetry, some biblical texts may be best appreciated aurally.[299] Whether that was originally the case with Rev 6:1–17 or Col 1:15–20 is unknowable. But the point is to keep the living Word lively.

---

297. As Gadamer would insist, even though the "translator . . . creatively 'interprets' the original creation . . . , *the text itself still remains the fixed point of relation* over and against the questionability, arbitrariness, or at least multiplicity of the possibilities of interpretation directed toward it." Gadamer, *Gadamer Reader*, 57, 168 (emphasis added).

298. Rev 10:6. See also Just, *Heaven on Earth*, 126–27, taking a "Christological view of time," whereby "the Church now lives in the eternal Sabbath rest of Easter Sunday." Cf. Hawking, *Brief Answers*, 37 ("And just as with modern-day black holes . . . the laws of nature dictate . . . that time itself must come to a stop"); Steiner, *After Babel*, 161 (conceptualizing "the grammar of the future tense [being] stopped" as an implication from thermodynamic theory that "cessation of any energy-yield from the motion of particles" results in a state of "no 'time'").

299. See P. Dunn, "What If I Sang," 91: "The identification of a poetic paratone raises questions about the ways in which different registers or performance situations may be marked in intonation."

Thus, to the extent a given text may be read to convey the "vivid actuality"[300] of its *verbum cordis* by the use of visualized imagery, a faithful translation might likewise be a vehicle for "ecstatic" transport. And such a translation would, under "an incarnational Christology in which revelation operates through the interwovenness of word and deed," produce in the reader or listener a sense that God is speaking to them in the text.[301] This is consistent with a hermeneutical engagement with the text as a form of dialogue with "the one who speaks to us in the Church."[302] Where the inner word is expressed in particularly elevated language, it thus seems incumbent on a translator to seek such inspiration as might allow him to forge as spiritually transporting a passage as he can.

5. Paracletic/Pastoral

Paul's ministry was closely linked with the worshipping communities he established, visited, or corresponded with in the exercise of his apostolic authority. A considerable portion of his letters addresses the needs, dilemmas, and disputes of those communities in very practical ways. This may justify Luke Timothy Johnson's description of Paul, "anachronistically, as a practical theologian."[303] Indeed, Paul's pastoral side has been given increasing attention.[304] Important portions of Colossians, for example, are thus taken up with pastoral concerns and advice, allowing it to serve as an example of how one might identify a pastoral tone for purposes of reflecting the same in translation.

Paul thus opens the letter with a heartfelt prayer for the Colossians to know God's will for themselves individually and as a community (Col 1:9-12). His prayers for them are constant (1:9), a characteristic also seen in his letters to the Thessalonians, Romans, and Ephesians.[305] Paul outlines the several goals he hopes for them—"that they may" know God (1:9), know God's will (1:9), live a productive/fruitful life (1:10), grow

---

300. Longinus, Περὶ Ὕψους 25.1.

301. Thiselton, *New Horizons*, 75. See also 74 (quoting Wittgenstein, *Zettel*, §117): "You can't hear God speak to someone else; you can hear him only if you are being addressed."

302. Gadamer, *Relevance of the Beautiful*, 142. See Heb 4:12.

303. L. Johnson, *First and Second Letters*, 92.

304. See, e.g., Rosner et al., *Paul as Pastor*, 109–22.

305. 1 Thess 1:2-3; Rom 1:9-10; Eph 1:15-16. Regular prayer would have been a deeply ingrained part of Paul's Jewish experience. See Deut 6:4-9.

in their understanding of who God is (1:10), partake of the power God would grant them (1:11), and be embraced within the family of God in the kingdom of light (1:12). All of this is a segue to the letter's hymnic paean to Christ's nature and glory (1:13–20).

Having established a core Christology,[306] Paul continues the letter with what can fairly be called pastoral counsel and encouragement to the local congregation. The letter includes what are referred to as "household code" guidelines (3:5–25; 4:1).[307] From there, Paul closes with personal greetings (4:2–18) that also seem pastoral in nature, even including the specific exhortation to Archippus (4:17). Can one therefore identify a "paracletic/pastoral" register or tone in these sections of the letter?[308] And how, if at all, should the same be brought out in translation? In other words, does adoption of a paracletic tone have relevance to accessing the text's inner meaning? For present purposes, it might be described as something comforting but also not without sternness where needed—basically the way one might think of parents exercising certain responsibilities of care for their children.

Seen this way, Paul's statement in 1 Thess 2:7 makes pastoral sense: "We were as gentle among you as a mother nursing her babes."[309] He goes on in 1 Thess 2:11–12 to say that "as would a father his children, we exhorted, encouraged, even implored each one of you to walk worthy of God, he who calls you into his own kingdom to partake of his glory."

---

306. Foster, *Colossians*, 41–45. Paul does not address Christology as crystally in other writings, which helps explain the importance of the letter's effective history in later doctrinal development.

307. Such guidelines also appear in later writings, e.g., Did. 4:9–11 and 1 Clem. 1:3; 21:6–9. And the importance of the household unit as the building block of the state dates at least to Aristotle, *Politics* 1.1252a. See Foster, *Colossians*, 400.

308. Another term might be "paraenetic," adopting the genre analysis of certain form critics. See, e.g., Dibelius and Conzelmann, *Pastoral Epistles*, 5–8. See also Starr, "Paraenesis." Yet "Paul's exhortation of the church is . . . only inadequately characterized by the Greek technical term that has established itself in the specialist literature . . . namely, 'paraenesis,'" which rather suggests a command. Stuhlmacher, *Biblical Theology*, 410. Moreover, "paracletic" has the overtone of encouragement more than mandate, thus reflecting with the actual usage of παρακαλέω in the letter (2:2; 4:8). And the term likewise resonates with the work of the Holy Spirit as Paraclete. Stuhlmacher, *Biblical Theology*, 710–15.

309. There is disagreement whether the key word here should be ἤπιοι (gentle) or νήπιοι (babies). NA²⁸/UBS⁵ picks the latter; the former is found in the Byzantine Textform. This is a good example of the limits of textual criticism, in that it is hard to say which one might choose even using the more difficult reading/*lectio difficilior* as a canon of construction. Would it be more awkward, in other words, for Paul to portray himself as a nursing mother, or as a baby? See Aasgaard, "Paul as a Child," 147–48.

Indeed, Paul frequently compares his relationship to the churches as that of a father to his children.[310] The same holds true with respect to his concern and care for specific individuals.[311] And in that light his household code instructions to parents in Col 3:21 reflect a sense of pastoral care: "Fathers, do not provoke your children, lest they feel beaten down."[312]

Note that this is quite a distance from the stereotype of Paul as a harsh authoritarian.[313] It reflects instead the attitude of "one who is concerned with his children and attentive to their abilities and needs."[314] Arguably, Paul even displays a nuanced understanding of the place of children in the family, sometimes conforming to but also deviating from "general attitudes in antiquity toward children."[315] Again, one might therefore convey such passages with the kind of language used with one's own children: tender where tenderness is called for, corrective where correction is needed.

Colossians also includes a number of general admonitions to the local assembly. In 3:1–4, for example, the language is more in the form of an exhortation than a theological or doctrinal statement, even though it is grounded in a series of truths about Christ, e.g., that he is seated at the right hand of God and will appear again in glory. Paul's point in this section, however, is to encourage the Colossians by explaining that *because of who Christ is* (rhetorically expressed in 3:1 as εἰ οὖν), they should be "setting [their] minds on heavenly not earthly things" (3:2).[316] As far as the register or tone he uses, it might again be described as comforting.

And just as throughout the letter Paul balances the positive and the negative, here too he balances his warnings not to fall back into the negatives of the believers' former lives (Col 3:5–9) with encouraging words

310. Rosner et al., *Paul as Pastor*, 4. See, e.g., 1 Cor 4:14–15; Gal 4:19–20.

311. See Phlm 10; Phil 2:22.

312. See also Eph 6:4: "Parents—don't drive your kids crazy with unreasonable demands, but raise them up in the proper discipline and instruction of the Lord."

313. See, e.g., Kilgallen, "Complicated Apostle": in his letters he "appear[s] pompous, cantankerous, superior, harsh."

314. Aasgaard, "Paul as a Child," 156.

315. Aasgaard, "Paul as a Child," 131. See also 159, concluding that Paul's use of metaphors placing himself in maternal as well as dependent roles "shows an apostle very much on a level with contemporary attitudes on parenting, children, and childhood . . . ," exhibiting a "sensitivity and openness" for which he is not generally given credit, but which may reflect "his understanding of Christ as a model for Christian service."

316. Such encouragements are not unique to Colossians. See, e.g., Gal 3:28; 5:22–23; Eph 2:14–15; Phil 4:8; Rom 12:9–21.

about their new lives, informing them that in Christ the former barriers between them as Jews and gentiles, slave and free, have been broken down (3:10–11).[317] To the extent there is a distinctive register at work, it might also be described as admonitory.[318] Translating in such a way as to capture that tone might well produce clearer understanding and response than were the words to be conveyed blandly or pedantically. It thus seems appropriate to use words that are more rather than less evocative of the behavior criticized, as a means of emphasizing the seriousness with which Paul viewed them.[319]

But perhaps in this context more than any other, questions will arise how to translate verses where the literal Greek suggests a meaning that may be inconsistent with contemporary sensibilities. How does the hermeneutic and methodology advanced here guide a translator? For example, in Col 3:19-20 Paul addresses the relationship of husbands and wives. This is his advice: αἱ γυναῖκες, ὑποτάσσεσθε τοῖς ἀνδράσιν. Read literally, this might be seen to implicate questions of subordination, inequality, or overly patriarchal structures.[320] In the first instance, one should of course remain rooted in the text, being prepared to translate bluntly even if the words ring harshly to modern ears—i.e., it is essential not to "twist" the Scriptures to say something they do not.[321] But it

---

317. As with the encouragements, the injunctions against wrongful conduct are not unique to Colossians; and lists of interpersonal sins are reasonably consistent in the letters. See, e.g., Gal 5:19-21; 1 Thess 4:3-7; 1 Cor 5:9-11; 6:9-10; Rom 1:28-31; 1 Pet 2:1; 4:2-3.

318. Sumney, *Colossians*, 107-8. See Col 1:28: νουθετοῦντες πάντα ἄνθρωπον.

319. For example, one might translate the list in Col 3:5 as "licentiousness, pollution, ardor, cupidity" in comparison to the NRSV's "fornication, impurity, passion, evil desire." Neither is clearly right; neither is clearly wrong. And the NRSVue has now changed the NRSV's "fornication" to "sexual immorality" in order to "update archaic language to modern equivalencies." NRSVue, xii. More difficult questions can arise when translation looks more like exegesis. One example would be a rendering of ἄστοργος in Rom 1:28-31 as "baby killers," where the Greek most literally means "without affection for kindred." See Straus, *New Testament*, 321.

320. See, e.g., Mouton, "Household Ethos," 177-80, noting the potential for an implied rhetorical effect modifying existing hierarchical and subordinating social structures. These questions also arise where ἡ κεφαλή appears in verses that concern male/female relationships, e.g., 1 Cor 11:3. When it is translated to mean "head," there may be a suggestion of male authority that is in tension with Paul's more general understanding of male/female equality in Christ, e.g., Gal 3:28. And where a male authority reading is challenged, the alternative translation "source" is usually what is proposed. See Payne, *Man and Woman*, 117-37; cf. sect. II.e.i, *infra*, concerning the description of Christ in Col 1:18a as the "Head of the Body."

321. See 2 Pet 3:16.

is equally important to be sure what the words say within the whole of Scripture. I do not suggest that there is an easy answer all the time. Debates over the Bible's position on homosexuality prove that.

Taking these verses as another test example, it is true that the verb ὑποτάσσω can have a sense of imposed order. Translating it as "submit" is not plainly wrong. Yet the word may also be read to cover a voluntary ordering, consistent with the general thrust of the root verb τασσω.[322] In that light, applying a canonical-hermeneutical approach, a translator might rely on Eph 5:21-24 as an intertextual reference, because spousal relationships are there set in the context of a general injunction about mutual deference within the church. Thus, Paul writes ὑποτασσόμενοι ἀλλήλοις ἐν φόβῳ Χριστοῦ, where ἡ ἐκκλησία ὑποτάσσεται τῷ Χριστῷ. And in the related passages of Eph 6:1-4, children are treated as persons with the ability to will in obedience, while their parents are asked not to push them too far. In keeping with Paul's pastoral tone, one might therefore opt for language reflecting a mutuality of respect among family members.

In Col 3:11 and 3:22—4:1, moreover, Paul addresses a range of persons of different and even contrasting religious, ethnic, social, and/or economic classes. For example, the reference there to Greeks or Jews concerns a core biblical division among peoples of the earth, with the related reference to those circumcised or uncircumcised concerning the covenantal marker of that distinction. From an effective history point of view, theological clarity suggests adhering to these same "classical" terms in contemporary translations, lest their canonical significance be lost.

Paul then identifies two other paired groups—those who are "barbarian, Scythian" on the one hand, and those who are "slave or free" on the other. On first blush the former pair seem nearly synonymous,[323] in that βάρβαρος typically referred to a non-Greek, identified

---

322. Gerhard Delling, "ὑποτάσσω," *TDNT* 8:39-46. I note that the *TDNT*'s focus on individual words and their etymologies has been criticized on grounds that words used in different contexts cannot be converted into distinctively biblical concepts. See generally Barr, *Semantics*. However, it is "precisely by reading [a word] in its various contexts [and] distinguishing those that imply a more 'theological' sense from those that are more neutral" that the "theologically-significant sense of the word is obtained." Watson, *Text and Truth*, 21. See also Thiselton, *Two Horizons*, 129 ("word-studies . . . constitute starting-points from which we arrive at the meanings of words-in-context"); cf. Ullmann, *Semantics*, 50 (noting the potential relevance of "cultural context" to word meaning).

323. And, indeed, are asyndetonically written.

onomatopoetically by the foreign-sounding nature of his language;[324] while Σκύθης referred to members of a particularly violent subset thereof.[325] Yet the term "barbarians" could be *also* used of those in regions distantly south of Greece, while "Scythians" were those distantly north.[326] As such they are not entirely congruent. Unlike the embedded significance of paired references to Jews and gentiles, the culture-specific nature of these terms provides an option to translate paraphrastically or parachronically as a way to reflect the passage's broad inner meaning that walls of separation are broken down in Christ.[327] For example, one might highlight the reconciliation in Christ of global "north/south" economic divides by using such terms as "privileged" and "untouchable." Harry O. Maier in fact suggests that Paul is here using imagery of the *Pax Romana*, which brought a form of peace to the nations that fell under Roman's imperial control, and that the terms are thus metaphorically evocative of Christ's reconciling us to God.[328]

Many translations of the second paired terms "tone down" δοῦλος by using a word like "servant" rather than "slave." While not an impermissible translation, it arguably ignores the reality of slavery in the first century, which reduced the enslaved to the status of property.[329] A translator attuned to the effective history of the biblical language might therefore consider using economic and class/caste terms that *also* resonate with the fundamental notion of inequality as a state that persists in the world, contrasting the same with how members of the church should relate to one another.[330] Thus, while ἰσότης as used in Col 4:1 is generally translated "fairness" (RSV, NIV, NLT, MSG), its etymology from ἴσος might also suggest economic "equity," a balancing of material wealth

---

324. The Greek term "barbarian" also incorporated societal distinctions of slavery versus freedom, which may thus be alluded to in 3:11. See Euripides, *Iphigenia in Aulis*, 1400: βαρβάρων δ' Ἕλληνας ἄρχειν εἰκός, ἀλλ' οὐ βαρβάρους, μῆτερ, Ἑλλήνων· τὸ μὲν γὰρ δοῦλον, οἳ δ' ἐλεύθεροι.

325. 2 Macc 4:47; 3 Macc 7:5.

326. Sumney, *Colossians*, 208–9.

327. To be sure, a number of terms in the Bible are culturally and historically bound and the referents are often not always known. Translating with a modern analog is one way to address the issue; but another is to preserve the literal language and provide marginal notes with explanatory or exegetical information.

328. Maier, "Sly Civility," 328–30; cf. Oxenham, "In Christ" ("In Christ there is no East or West, in him no South or North").

329. Foster, *Colossians*, 419; Sumney, *Colossians*, 206.

330. Sumney, *Colossians*, 235.

not unfamiliar in Paul's own praxis.³³¹ Whether Paul was suggesting that those who owned slaves compensate them as they would free persons in their employ is of course pure speculation. But at the same time, contemporary writings indicate that "ἰσότης does not merely represent what is reasonable, but in fact means equality between groups of varying status in ancient society."³³² If the passage is understood as such, it would at least call for slaves to be treated as equal members of the congregation—fellow servants of Christ—even if not for outright manumission.

The methodology proposed here therefore allows for flexibility, but always with the goal of discerning the *verbum interius* of the text. Some of the words used in Colossians, for example, call for adherence to their "classical" referents; some less so. And as noted, this is an area where translation and exegesis can overlap, requiring the translator to alert the reader to possibly novel renderings. The translation in the appendix, for example, reflects these alternate modes by rendering Col 3:10–11 as "there is no Greek or Jew, circumcised or uncircumcised, privileged or untouchable, labor or capital, but CHRIST is all and in all"; and 4:1 as "bosses, treat your employees with fairness and equity, knowing that you both have a Boss in Heaven."³³³ One hermeneutical goal might therefore be to provoke a thoughtful, dialogic interaction between the linguistic past and present.

6. Prosaic/"Everyday"

Of course, much Scriptural language falls outside of any of the above categories of genre/register/style. Not everything in a sacred text, in other words, must find expression in specialized language. That makes it no less valid as an element of Scripture, as Paul avers in 2 Tim 3:16 with

---

331. E.g., 2 Cor 8:13–15. See also Acts 2:44–45, 4:32; cf. Marx and Engels, *German Ideology*, 566. Focusing on inequality in general is thus consistent with the literal Greek, even if it also expands on possible understandings at the time of writing. See Gadamer, *Truth and Method*, 296 (temporal distance enables "new sources of understanding").

332. Standhartinger, "Origin and Intention," 128.

333. To be sure, translating κύριος as "Boss" is unconventional. But the verse is fairly applicable to non-compulsory employment as well as slavery. And Boss is a common term for one's earthly κύριος. See Foster, *Colossians*, 419 (this is "not simply a play on words . . . but a radical relativization of the power that earthly lords or masters possess"). The word is also rendered in the appendix with the novel *nomen sacrum* BOSS as a way to signal the early manuscripts' usage of the same Greek word for our Lord and Master in heaven. An alternate *nomen* form would be the more conventional LORD.

the broad statement that "*all* Scripture is inspired by God, beneficial for teaching, for refutation, for on-course correction, for instruction in righteousness."[334] If so, this is as much the case with descriptions of Paul's travels from city to city as for his transportation to the third heaven.

Taking Colossians again as an example of the range of categories, a fair amount of the text is simply prosaic, such as the salutations, greetings, exhortations, and miscellaneous instructions that comprise ch. 4. These can overlap with more pastoral passages and in general reflect Paul's particularized care for various individuals, his "newsy" updates about his stay in prison and his comments about travel plans. And as noted, final exhortations, greetings, or personal requests are a notably common and even charming feature in many of Paul's letters.[335] Although written in relatively simple prose and not entirely paracletic, they might therefore be described as "apostolically pastoral" in tone—a register perhaps unique to Paul. From a translation point of view, one might try to capture that colloquial flavor.

That said, not all prose is created equal. Some is good and a lot is dreadful. Hence even passages as "prosaic" as serial greetings are susceptible of individualized style, with distinctiveness a matter of personal craft. For example, this is one way to render the greeting in Col 4:12 that Paul relays from Epaphras, a founding member of the Colossian assembly who was then in Rome:

> Epaphras a servant of CHRIST JESUS greets you—he's also your *landsman*—always toiling on your behalf in his prayers to the end that you stand perfected, fully settled in all the Will of GOD.

Now, the word "landsman" is Yiddish and was originally used by Jews in the American diaspora to refer to those who had come from the same part of the "Old Country." Over time, it has come to be used of any fellow Jew.[336] Translation of the verse using that slang is thus an illustratively free rendering of ὁ ἐξ ὑμῶν.[337] And yet it is arguably in the spirit of the

---

334. To the same effect are general references in 2 Samuel 23:2, Mark 12:36, Luke 1:70, John 14:26, Acts 1:16, and 2 Pet 1:20-21 to prophets and apostles writing and speaking through the inspiration of the Holy Spirit.

335. E.g., Rom 16; Gal 5:26—6:6; 1 Thess 5:12-28; 2 Tim 4:9-21.

336. Rosten, *New Joys*, 203-4.

337. Note also the use of capitalizations and *nomina sacra* in that rendering, which are added as a possible way to maintain the sacramental nature of even so "prosaic" material as a series of greetings.

text, where the term is used inclusively of both Jews and gentiles, the latter now being "grafted in."[338]

As another experiment, one might use a "handwriting" font in larger than ordinary size for the last verse of Colossians. Why? For one thing, Paul says he wrote the verse with his own hand—suggesting that he used a scribal amanuensis for the rest (probably Timothy as referenced in Col 1:1). Second, Paul elsewhere refers to the "large letters" he penned in closing,[339] suggesting that he had difficulties with his vision. Presenting the last verse in large type along with the faux signature *Paul* is simply one way to reflect this distinctively personal aspect of the letter's closing. And if one assumes that the manuscript original was likewise signed by Paul, reflecting the same in translation is consistent with a methodological maintenance in the present of formal aspects from the past.

e. Detailed Analysis of Key Words and Phrases

A next stage in applying a canonical-hermeneutical approach would be to focus the lens with more detail on particular words and phrases that might raise contextual, philological, or theological issues relevant to translation. As suggested here, the proposed methodology would call on a translator to make decisions how to reflect intratextual, intertextual, and/or later interpretive materials in the translation. And again, the hymnic portions of Colossians can serve as a test case on how one might further elicit the *verbum cordis* of the letter concerning "who Christ is." These passages are exemplary of the interplay between historical, archaeological, and sociological insights into the historical context of the letter on the one hand, and the text's further trajectory in the life and traditions of the church on the other. The following, more detailed examination of key language in Colossians seeks to illustrate how an approach grounded in the text yet not limited to the particulars of its historical setting might avail itself of sufficient translational freedom in aid of providing the reader or listener with fuller access to textual meaning.

---

338. See Rom 9–11.
339. Gal 4:14–15, 6:11.

i. Christ Presented in Elevated Language

Colossians' distinctive formulations partake of ineffable language in the expression of its christological truths. On the hermeneutical understandings outlined in sect. I.b, *supra*, the biblical words are themselves "events" expressive of Word of God as divinely communicated to the mind of the writer. And under this work's guiding linguistic principles, the term "inner word" refers to the meaning so communicated. Again, by analogy to the relationship of the Father and the Son, the inner word as expressed in human words is the effective embodiment of that divine communication.[340] The *verbum interius* is therefore "more than a mere metaphor,"[341] but is instead explanatory of the processual nature of human language.[342] And the fact that thought is only imperfectly realized in human language by virtue of its temporality[343] is *actually* what allows a translator room to explore the "free space around" the text as a participant in its effective history.[344]

Where the text in effect seeks to express the inexpressible, translation is therefore integral to the "revealing" of the Scripture's *verbum cordis* because, "being actively understood, [it] is in continual formation."[345] As such, the Word is enabled to function transformationally in the lives of those who lack the original languages,[346] being uniquely alive in the

---

340. Augustine, *De Trinitate* 15.24–25; Aquinas, *De natura verbi intellectus* §277. See also Lonergan, *Verbum*, 33–34.

341. Gadamer, *Truth and Method*, 421.

342. Voelz, *What Does This Mean*, 234.

343. Augustine, *De catechizandis rudibus* 2.3; Arthos, *Inner Word*, 42–43.

344. Gadamer, *Truth and Method*, 290–91; Watson, *Text and Truth*, 45.

345. Aquinas, *De natura verbi intellectus* §277; J. Smith, *Fall of Interpretation*, 143.

346. Gadamer, *Gadamer Reader*, 170. While detailed exploration of the nature and function of liturgy is outside the scope of this work, a "living Word" approach also has implications for how one understands both private and corporate worship. For example, in some traditions scriptural readings serve liturgically as a form of participation in that which is sacred, whether in the form of daily lectionaries or through meditative practices such as *lectio divina*. See, e.g., the daily lectionaries of numerous Christian denominations; *Rule of St. Benedict*, 48; Paul VI, *"Dei Verbum,"* §25; Pope Benedict XVI, *General Audience of May 2, 2007*; Casey, *Sacred Reading*. Moreover, reading the Gospel "is a form of remembering Jesus' words and provides access for later believers to the life and ministry of Jesus. The mimetic form is mnemonic inasmuch as it bridges the divide between past and present." Parsenios, "Anamnesis," 7. This is likewise analogous to the anamnestic function of the Eucharist, in that "mimetic behavior makes something present." Gadamer, *Relevance of the Beautiful*, 98; Dix, *Shape of the Liturgy*, 243; Luke 22:19; 1 Cor 11:24–25. See also Just, *Heaven on Earth*, 78 ("the body and blood of Jesus are truly present with the bread and wine") and 227 ("the Lord's Supper is an eschatological event in which eternity is present because the eternal God is present with His grace").

world even though textually mediated.³⁴⁷ I therefore discuss below how a canonical-hermeneutical methodology is of special use in that revealing where the language is of a particularly elevated nature. I focus principally on christologically central language in the letter, which is both plerophorically expressive of the fullness of the Godhead dwelling in Christ and substantively essential to the text's effective history in the development of church doctrine and liturgy.

1. Christ as ὁ λόγος

Paul opens the letter by referring to "the word of truth of the gospel" (1:5), employing ὁ λόγος, a word with significant and varied usage throughout the Scriptures.³⁴⁸ For example, Ps 32:6's description of the workings of ὁ λόγος τοῦ Κυρίου is effectively present in Paul's description of Christ as the one by whom all things were made.³⁴⁹ But the extended expression of 1:5 is found uniquely in Colossians—the more common phrasing being "the truth of the gospel" (as in Gal 2:5, 14). By adding "the word of," Paul may be writing in counterpoint to the false λόγοι addressed later in the letter, i.e., the false words and philosophies of his so-called opponents (2:8, 20), as well as gnostic or mystical usages of λόγος.³⁵⁰

At the same time, Paul does not use λόγος in Col 1:5 precisely as Ὁ Λόγος is used in John 1:1 or 1 John 1:1, where it may embrace the Word, Speech, or Thought and likewise be identified with the person of Jesus. Yet these are also important to note in a translation applying a canonical-hermeneutic approach, whether by marginal notation or modification of the wording when presented in English. For example, one way to maintain the intrascripturality of 1:5 might be to use "truth" adjectivally rather than nominatively. The phrase would thus be "the True Word of

---

347. See Origen, *De principiis* 4.6: "If anyone, moreover, consider the words of the prophets with all the zeal and reverence which they deserve . . . , he will feel his mind and senses touched by a divine breath, and will acknowledge that the words which he reads were no human utterances, but the language of God."

348. See, e.g., L&N 33.98 (statement), 33.99 (speech), 33.100 (Word), 33.260 (gospel), and 89.18 (reason).

349. Ps 32:6 LXX: τῷ λόγῳ τοῦ Κυρίου οἱ οὐρανοὶ ἐστερεώθησαν.

350. Moore, "Gnosticism," para. 2: "According to the Gnostics, this world, the material cosmos, is the result of a primordial error on the part of a supra-cosmic, supremely divine being, usually called *Sophia* [Wisdom] or simply the *Logos*." See also the discussions of "wisdom" and "knowledge," *infra*.

the gospel," capitalizing both True and Word so as to allude to Christ as the True Word.

Paul also uses the term in Col 3:16, where he hortatively urges the Colossians to "let the λόγος of Christ dwell fully/richly in you." Does he refer to Christ as the Word in the sense used in John's Gospel? To the Scriptures as a whole? To the gospel message generally? To the entire complex of meanings and references?[351] Again, it would not be unreasonable to maintain an intrascriptural link between 3:16 and Paul's related use of λόγος in 1:5, where he plainly refers to the gospel message as essentially the word of the Word. In choosing a word (as it were) for translation purposes, it might be faithful to the sense of the verse to use the most open-ended option, i.e., the uncapitalized "word," which is what most translations do. Hence the plainest reading, i.e., "the word of Christ," is both the closest to its meaning and at the same time faithful to any intrascripturality.

2. Christ as ἡ σοφία

Paul further employs the word ἡ σοφία with reference to Christ as true Wisdom, most likely providing an intrascriptural reference to "Wisdom" as used in Prov 8. The word σοφία is in fact extensively present in the entire Scriptures, as well as classical Greek literature and Hellenistic Jewish works.[352] And as relevant to one of the letter's concerns, Christ as ἡ σοφία stands in direct counterpart to mystical and/or proto-gnostic uses of the word.[353] As Anthony Thiselton points out, dictionary and lexicon definitions generally "constitute starting points from which we arrive at the meanings of words-in-context."[354] Paul's disclosure of the truth that Christ is "the wisdom of God" should thus also be understood in

---

351. McKnight, *Letter to Colossians*, 329 (itemizing numerous options); Silva, *Biblical Words*, "λόγος," 26(same).

352. See Ulrich Wilckens, "σοφία," *TDNT* 7:465–526; "σοφία," L&N, 32.32; 32.37; 32.41; "σοφία," *PGL* 1244–46.

353. See "Myth of Sophia," in Moore, "Gnosticism": "According to Gnostic mythology ... we, humanity, are existing in this realm because a member of the transcendent godhead, Sophia [Wisdom], desired to actualize her innate potential for creativity without the approval of her partner or divine consort."

354. Thiselton, *Two Horizons*, 129: "If terminology alone had to furnish the criterion between Gnostic and biblical materials we would be confronted with a most chaotic situation."

contrast to the hiddenness and initiate-only access of false "wisdom."³⁵⁵ Paul therefore prays in Col 1:9 that they the Colossians come to know God's will "in all wisdom." And in 2:3 he writes that all the "treasures of wisdom" are found in Christ.

As noted, certain English renderings have achieved their own authoritative/normative significance by way of their effective history in textual reception, akin to what Gadamer refers to as "classical" status.³⁵⁶ The best way to sustain the canonical importance of the word may therefore simply be to translate σοφία as "wisdom," as it has been virtually throughout the translation tradition outlined in sect. II.f, *infra*.

In many instances a translator may rely on English derivatives as possible choices in order to take formal account of the original Greek expression. Here, however, there is no such reasonable derivative. Alternatively, one might therefore consider Latinate forms, as did Wycliffe in his renderings from the Vulgate. Thus, "sapience," derived from *sapientia*, would provide a translation history link to Jerome's Vulgate usage in Col 1:9 and thereby reflect the text's effective/translation history in that formative moment. Though valid, the word is admittedly highly obscure in English. The same would be true of "sagacity," from the Latin *sagax*. And conceptually related terms such as "discernment," "understanding," or "perception" do not carry as much intrascriptural weight as does "wisdom." Yet another alternative English rendering might be "knowledge." However, that is also the more traditional translation for the word γνῶσις which, while related to σοφία, is distinctly used elsewhere in the letter, as discussed below. The best option thus remains the classical choice, "wisdom," which is itself a compound formed from Proto-German and Old English. The point is that sometimes the most frequently used word may be the most appropriate, regardless of whether the relevant usage varies among hymnic, doctrinal, or paracletic registers.

3. Christ as the Source of ἡ ἐπίγνωσις/ἡ γνῶσις

The same "classical" result holds with respect to Paul's uses of the related words ἡ γνῶσις and ἡ ἐπίγνωσις, where "knowledge" (the most frequent rendering in the English translation tradition) does convey textual

---

355. Compare also Col 1:26–27 (τὸ μυστήριον τὸ ἀποκεκρυμμένον ἀπὸ τῶν αἰώνων καὶ ἀπὸ τῶν γενεῶν) with 1 Cor 2:7 (σοφίαν ἐν μυστηρίῳ τὴν ἀποκεκρυμμένην, ἣν προώρισεν ὁ θεὸς πρὸ τῶν αἰώνων).

356. Gadamer, *Truth and Method*, 285–90.

meaning. So too would the word "understanding."³⁵⁷ From a translation point of view, however, one should note that Paul cumulates several closely related words when he prays in Col 2:2–3 that the Colossians might be "confirmed in all richness of the full assurance of knowledge and gain a thorough understanding of the mystery of God, even our Savior, in whom lie all apocryphal treasures of wisdom and knowledge." Paul similarly prays in 1:9 that the Colossians be filled with the "knowledge of God's will"; and in 1:10 that they increase in the "knowledge of God." And there is an unmistakable intrascripturality between the combination of words in 2:2–3 and that in several Old Testament passages, where σοφία, σύνεσις, ἐπίγνωσις, and θησαυρός are likewise woven together.³⁵⁸ The same holds true for the cumulating usages in Rom 11:33.³⁵⁹

From a register point of view, these verses are *literally* plerophoric in both form and substance.³⁶⁰ As such, their formal characteristics, verbal relationships and even rhythm communicate the "fullness" of the Godhead as well as the Christian life, both of which are at the *verbum cordis* of the letter and a leitmotif of its linguistic expression. A translation should therefore strive to capture the plerophoric style that is expressive of that inner word, even if that means using thesaurus-like vocabulary.³⁶¹

Similarly, a register-sensitive hermeneutic should consider the import of the intensifying prefix ἐπι. Both γνῶσις and ἐπίγνωσις have an extensive history in the Greek language, including usages in classical Greek philosophy and literature, gnostic texts, the LXX, and Christian

---

357. One might also consider the rare English word "gnosis," which might directly focus on the contrasting forms of "false knowledge" that concerned Paul. A good example of where that might be helpful would be 1 Tim 6:20.

358. Compare Col 2:2–3 (εἰς πᾶν πλοῦτος τῆς πληροφορίας τῆς συνέσεως, εἰς ἐπίγνωσιν τοῦ μυστηρίου τοῦ θεοῦ, Χριστοῦ, ἐν ᾧ εἰσιν πάντες οἱ θησαυροὶ τῆς σοφίας καὶ γνώσεως ἀπόκρυφοι) with Prov 2:1–6 LXX (ὑπακούσεται σοφία τὸ οὖς σου, καὶ παραβαλεῖς καρδίαν σου εἰς σύνεσιν, παραβαλεῖς δὲ αὐτὴν ἐπὶ νουθέτησιν τῷ υἱῷ σου. ἐὰν γὰρ τὴν σοφίαν ἐπικαλέσῃ καὶ τῇ συνέσει δῷς φωνήν σου, τὴν δὲ αἴσθησιν ζητήσῃς μεγάλῃ τῇ φωνῇ, καὶ ἐὰν ζητήσῃς αὐτὴν ὡς ἀργύριον καὶ ὡς θησαυροὺς ἐξερευνήσῃς αὐτήν, τότε συνήσεις φόβον Κυρίου καὶ ἐπίγνωσιν Θεοῦ εὑρήσεις. ὅτι Κύριος δίδωσι σοφίαν, καὶ ἀπὸ προσώπου αὐτοῦ γνῶσις καὶ σύνεσις) and with Isa 33:6 (ἐν νόμῳ παραδοθήσονται, ἐν θησαυροῖς ἡ σωτηρία ἡμῶν, ἐκεῖ σοφία καὶ ἐπιστήμη καὶ εὐσέβεια πρὸς τὸν Κύριον· οὗτοί εἰσι θησαυροὶ δικαιοσύνης); 45:3 (δώσω σοι θησαυροὺς σκοτεινούς, ἀποκρύφους, ἀοράτους ἀνοίξω σοι, ἵνα γνῷς). See also 1 Macc 1:23; 2 Bar. 44:14; 54:13.

359. Ὦ βάθος πλούτου καὶ σοφίας καὶ γνώσεως θεοῦ.

360. See Col 2:2: εἰς πᾶν πλοῦτος τῆς πληροφορίας.

361. But of course, that's what a θησαυρός is for.

Elements of a Canonical-Hermeneutical Translation Approach/Test Case 117

materials, all of which may be relevant in construing the text.³⁶² Luke's prologue may be helpful here, in his usage of ἐπίγνωσις to emphasize the "catechetical" purpose of his Gospel.³⁶³ Lightfoot, moreover, suggests that ἐπίγνωσις is "a favourite word in the later epistles," and that a distinction might be made along the lines that "the compound ἐπίγνωσις is an advance upon γνῶσις, denoting a larger and more thorough knowledge," pointing to an alleged contrast between "γινώσκειν, γνῶσις [and] ἐπιγινώσκειν, ἐπίγνωσις as the partial with the complete in two passages, Rom. i. 21, 38, 1 Cor. xiii. 12."³⁶⁴ He further observes that "ἐπίγνωσις is used especially of the knowledge of God and of Christ, as being the perfection of knowledge."³⁶⁵

That said, Lightfoot concedes that it may be "just as hard to find any strict distinction between γνῶσις and ἐπίγνωσις in the NT as it is in the LXX and Philo."³⁶⁶ Either way, a number of versions in the English translation tradition render *both* words as "knowledge" in the several places they occur.³⁶⁷ One explanation might be that there is no correspondingly prefixed English word concerning "knowledge." In such a circumstance, a translator might try to come up with an intensifying neologism, something like "hyper-knowledge." However, another appropriate way to reflect any such nuance would with an adjectival modifier, such as "perfect" or "perfected," as is suggested in the translation in the appendix.

4. Christ as εἰκών τοῦ Θεοῦ τοῦ ἀοράτου

Paul writes in Col 1:15 that Christ is the "image of the invisible God." As noted above, the verse necessarily calls up the Greek of the LXX

---

362. See generally Rudolf Bultmann, "γνῶσις" and "ἐπίγνωσις," *TDNT* 1:689–719.

363. See Just, "Today in Our Hearing," commenting on Luke 1:1–4.

364. Lightfoot, *St. Paul's Epistles*, 137–38.

365. Lightfoot, *St. Paul's Epistles*, 138 (citing Prov 2:5; Hos 4:1; 6:6; Eph 1:17; 4:13; 2 Pet 1:2, 8; 2:20). See also "ἐπίγνωσις," *PGL* 519.

366. Bultmann, "γνῶσις" and "ἐπίγνωσις," *TDNT* 1:689–719.

367. See, e.g., Col 1:9–10; 2:3; Rom 2:20; 11:33; 15:14; 1 Cor 8:1, 7, 10, 11; 12:8; 13:2, 8; Eph 3:19; Phil 3:8; 1 Tim 6:20. This is true of translations of verses like Hos 4:6, where both words are generally translated as "knowledge" (e.g., "My people are destroyed for lack of knowledge: because thou hast rejected knowledge, I will also reject thee" [KJV]), even though both occur in the same verse, which suggests that some distinction should be made in translation in order to be faithful to the text (ὡμοιώθη ὁ λαός μου ὡς οὐκ ἔχων γνῶσιν· ὅτι σὺ ἐπίγνωσιν ἀπώσω).

concerning mankind's creation "in the image and likeness" of God.³⁶⁸ Indeed, it is clear that "the christological title . . . has not been independently formulated" but that the "original creation provides conceptuality for describing the new creation."³⁶⁹ Hence this canonically integrative verse adverts to the creation of Adam in disclosing the nature and being of the Second Adam. As Scot McKnight puts it, "We can understand Adam only through Jesus . . . [because Jesus] is the true *eikōn*."³⁷⁰ Again within a canonical framework, 1:15 also relates to the statement in Heb 1:3 that Christ is "the very Impress of God's Being."³⁷¹ That Christ thereby reveals the "unseen" God also ties the verse to John 1:18—"No one has ever seen God. But the Only-Begotten Son, who dwells in the heart of the Father, he has made him known." The attribution thus concerns Jesus' timeless being—his deity or divine essence—as made manifest/visible in the incarnation. Importantly, "all the emphasis is on the equality of the εἰκών with the original," such that "the being of Jesus as image is only another way of talking about His being as the Son."³⁷²

The verse presents a series of translation questions and as explained herein, the proposed methodology can usefully point the way to appropriate solutions. As far as word choice, the realistic options in English are the Latinate "image," which is part of the translation tradition beginning

---

368. Gen 1:27 LXX: ποιήσωμεν ἄνθρωπον κατ᾽ εἰκόνα ἡμετέραν καὶ καθ᾽ ὁμοίωσιν.

369. Watson, *Text and Truth*, 282.

370. McKnight, *Letter to the Colossians*, 146–47; cf. Macaskill, "Union(s) with Christ," 100–101, noting a Second Temple period understanding of Adam "not as an icon, but as a protological high priest within the cultic Eden."

371. The relevant word in Heb 1:3 is not εἰκών but χαρακτὴρ, but in both contexts it is Christ's identification with God that is at issue. This is therefore an example of the usefulness of bringing out a substantively parallel intrascriptural reference in the actual language of a translation, even though the one may not have directly influenced the other. See Strawbridge, *Pauline Effect*, 145; Foster, *Colossians*, 197. It might also be appropriate to annotate this verse with the effectively synonymous usage in an early third-century creed ascribed to Gregory Thaumaturgus, *Confessio fidei* (εἷς κύριος, μόνος ἐκ μόνου, θεὸς ἐκ θεοῦ, χαρακτὴρ καὶ εἰκὼν τῆς θεότητος) (Kinzig, *Faith in Formulae*, §117) (one Lord, the singular from the singular, God from God, express form and image of the Godhead). Another reference might be Paul's gloss on the "unknown god" of Greek cosmology (Acts 17:22–31). See also Irenaeus, *Adversus haereses* 1.10.1 (κατὰ τὴν εὐδοκίαν τοῦ πατρὸς τοῦ ἀοράτου) (Kinzig, *Faith in Formulae*, §109b3); cf. Plato, *Timaeus* 92c, describing the "cosmos" itself as "a perceptible god made in the image of the Intelligible" (εἰκὼν τοῦ νοητοῦ θεὸς αἰσθητός).

372. Gerhard Kittel, "εἰκών," *TDNT* 2:381–97; Hengel, *Son of God*, 23; Gorday and Oden, *Colossians*, 12: "He calls Christ the invisible image, not because God becomes visible in him but rather because the greatness of God is shown forth in him" (quoting Theodore of Mopsuestia).

with Jerome and continuing via Wycliffe; or the Greek-derived and more formally literal "icon."³⁷³ To decide this by applying a canonical-hermeneutical approach, it would be essential to consider the effective history of the verse as seen in the christological and Trinitarian crises of the fourth and fifth centuries, as well as the iconoclastic controversies that followed in the eighth and ninth centuries. The central dispute before the council held at Nicaea in AD 325 concerned the Arian position that Christ was a divine yet created being and thus "like" but not "the same" as the Father, perhaps on analogy to mankind's having been made καθ' ὁμοίωσιν, in the "likeness" of God.³⁷⁴ Relying on two verses from Colossians, the Arians argued that if Christ was "Firstborn" (1:16), then he was a created being; and that if he was the "Image of God" (1:15), then he was "like" but not in all respects the "same" as the Father and thus subordinate, even if divine.³⁷⁵ Nicaea's resolution addressed the substantive dispute as to what it meant to be the εἰκών of God with the credal statement that Christ was ὁμοούσιον—"consubstantial/of one substance," with the Father, not simply "like" him.³⁷⁶ The term ὁμοούσιος thus contravened the Arian position as to the nature of Christ as image "by asserting the full deity of the Son . . . [that] whatever belonged to or characterized the Godhead belonged to and characterized him."³⁷⁷

Even so, factions remained after Nicaea, generating a series of further synodal decrees with additional faith formulae. Of particular note is the Dedication Creed (the second creed of the Council of Antioch) in AD 341, which takes express language from Col 1:15 and provides the

373. The word "form" seems inappropriate because of the usage of μορφή in Phil 2:6, which is not a synonym for εἰκών and presents its own interpretive issues. See Bockmuehl, "Form of God."

374. Gen 1:27 LXX; cf. Babylonian Talmud, Ketubot 8a ("Who made humanity in His image, in the images of the likeness of his form").

375. Arius, *Epistula ad Alexandrum Alexandrinum*, 4 (ὁ δὲ υἱὸς ἀχρόνως γεννηθεὶς ὑπὸ τοῦ πατρὸς καὶ πρὸ αἰώνων κτισθεὶς καὶ θεμελιωθεὶς οὐκ ἦν πρὸ τοῦ γεννηθῆναι) (Kinzig, *Faith in Formulae*, §131a) (but the Son being timelessly begotten by the Father, and being created and founded before the ages, did not exist before he was generated), and *Epistula ad Eusebium Nicomediensem*, 5 (Καὶ πρὶν γεννηθῇ ἤτοι κτισθῇ ἤτοι ὁρισθῇ ἢ θεμελιωθῇ, οὐκ ἦν, ἀγέννητος γὰρ οὐκ ἦν) (Kinzig, *Faith in Formulae*, §131b) (before he was begotten, or created, or ordained, or established, he was not, for he was not unbegotten).

376. Kinzig, *Faith in Formulae*, §135c: Πιστεύομεν . . . εἰς ἕνα κύριον Ἰησοῦν Χριστόν . . . γεννηθέντα οὐ ποιηθέντα, ὁμοούσιον τῷ πατρί. See also Hilary of Poitiers, *De synodis* 84: *natum, non factum, unius substantiae cum patre [quod Graeci dicunt omousion]* (Kinzig, *Faith in Formulae*, §135d[3]).

377. Kinzig, *Faith in Formulae*, 1:238. See also Strawbridge, *Pauline Effect*, 170–73 (analyzing the effective history of 1:15–20 in the development of the credal formula).

gloss that Christ is the "unparalleled/matchless image of the Godhead."[378] These post-Nicaea disputes then led to a further refinement at the Council of Constantinople in AD 381, resulting in the language of the Niceno-Constantinopolitan Creed.[379] The "binding character" of the form vouchsafed at Constantinople in AD 381 is relevant here, since "of all existing creeds it is the only one for which ecumenicity, or universal acceptance, can be plausibly claimed."[380]

What lay at the heart of these disputes was the mystery of the incarnation, i.e., how one might understand the invisible God to be visibly present in the world—or, as expressed in Col 1:15, what it meant for Christ to be the "image of the invisible God."[381] And yet the Niceno-Constantinopolitan Creed still did not put that question to rest, but was rather a particular moment in the text's continuing *Wirkungsgeschichte*.[382] What remained, for example, were questions as to the nature of the incarnate person of Jesus—to what extent, for example, did a divine as well as human nature subsist within him? Were the two separate? Had they been somehow combined? Efforts to resolve these questions led to a statement of faith adopted at the Council of Chalcedon in AD 451 that both natures were present in one person without having been divided or mixed.[383]

These various formulations aimed to provide a "demarcation of certain doctrinal content over against dissidents whose views were anathematized."[384] Nevertheless they did not purport fully to capture the "Mystery of Christ" reflected in the Colossian Hymn, which Brian Daley describes as "the bridge between a transcendent, unimaginable God and a world of limited, visible things."[385] The post-Chalcedonian Church

---

378. Kinzig, *Faith in Formulae*, §141b: τῆς θεότητος . . . ἀπαράλλακτον εἰκόνα. See also Hilary of Poitiers, *Liber (II) ad Constantium Imperatorem* 11 (*qui est imago dei invisibilis*) (Kinzig, *Faith in Formulae*, §151e2).

379. Kinzig, *Faith in Formulae*, §184e.

380. J. Kelly, *Early Christian Creeds*, 296, setting aside the variant use of the *filioque* clause (358–67).

381. Questions of God's "physicality" are found in Jewish mystical writings, some of which may have been part of Paul's conceptual framework. Bockmuehl, "Form of God," 15–19. Speculations concerning God's form likewise continue in the writings of Christian mystics (22–23, referring to the *Wirkungsgeschichte* of Phil 2:6).

382. Daley, *God Visible*, 23: The creed "is one stage in a much longer process of staking out the course for orthodox Christology."

383. Kinzig, *Faith in Formulae*, §215.

384. Kinzig, *Faith in Formulae*, 1:8–9.

385. Daley, *God Visible*, 23.

Elements of a Canonical-Hermeneutical Translation Approach/Test Case 121

therefore continued to diverge on how to understand and therefore express this mystery. Thus in the so-called "iconoclastic controversies," the church struggled again over the implications of Col 1:15: whether Christ might "be represented by a material image in such a way that the image itself reveals something of the divine reality in sensible, earthly form, and so becomes an object worthy of Christian devotion."[386] On the one side were those who inferred from Chalcedon that Christ's two natures permitted devotion to his image; and on the other were those who considered such representations to be idols, veneration of which is condemned throughout the Scriptures.

The Second Council of Nicaea held in AD 787 attempted to resolve the controversy by distinguishing between "idols" and "icons." According to the council, the latter had long and traditionally been venerated, not as

> real adoration, which befits only the divine nature, but resembl[ing] the honor we show to the form of the precious and life-giving cross, and the holy Gospels, and the other sacred objects we set up for devotion.[387]

The council therefore anathematized the iconoclasts as "those who call holy icons idols."[388] But how does one police that dividing line? The condemnation of the iconoclasts demonstrates that it is not so easy to do. Indeed, despite its ecumenical status, the Second Council of Nicaea's pronouncements never found universal acceptance, being countered soon thereafter during the "Second Iconoclastic Period" at the Synod of the Hagia Sophia in AD 815, which characterized any form of devotion to images as "pointless and misleading."[389] And there is still no uniformity of belief or practice on the subject with respect to the sacred art and architecture of Protestant, Catholic, and Orthodox traditions, or their respective liturgical accoutrements.[390] But from a positive point of view,

---

386. Daley, *God Visible*, 21.

387. Daley, *God Visible*, 250, translating the council's *Acta* 1.135–36, which relies on Basil of Caesarea, *De Spiritu Sancto*, §18.45: "The honor paid to the image passes on to the prototype."

388. Kinzig, *Faith in Formulae*, §245a.7: Τοῖς ἀποκαλοῦσι τὰς ἱερὰς εἰκόνας εἴδωλα ἀνάθεμα. The council also "canonically" rejected the AD 754 Synod of Hierea's ban on *all* religious images, describing it as a "pseudo-assembly." Kinzig, *Faith in Formulae*, §245a.2; Daley, *God Visible*, 247–48. See also L&N 6.96–97, comparing and contrasting both terms.

389. Daley, *God Visible*, 252n78.

390. See, e.g., Schmemann, *Eucharist*, 11–16.

such diversity is simply evidence of the vitality of Colossians' effective history, i.e., the continued exploration in church tradition whether or to what extent images might function in "*sacramental* terms, mak[ing] present what they signify, without actually losing their earthly character."[391]

The foregoing thus confirms the importance of considering the text's effective history in assessing translation options, for whether one chooses image, likeness, form, or icon, each will resonate with one or another aspect of that history. In this particular instance, the conciliar framework seems of such importance to understanding, and would not itself emerge from a more literal rendering, that a translator might consider incorporating portions of the relevant credal language *in haec verba* into the translation. For example, in order to capture the "light" imagery of Nicaea's Φῶς ἐκ Φωτός, one might add the adjective "Radiant" to "Image." Or one might add the key credal language that as True God, Christ is both "consubstantial with the Father" and "eternally begotten not made." While these words do not appear in the text, they reflect important elements of its effective history through the "canonized" words of the creeds.[392]

I recognize that adding words to the text implicates difficult questions as to how much liberty can be taken in translation. Without shying away from that difficulty, the point here is not so much to validate the use of elaborative terms as it is to illustrate the importance of considering the validity or not of their presence in church history and tradition as evidence of the *viva vox Jesu*. The dialogic operation of an effective history hermeneutic, in other words, can drive translation outcomes in revealing the inner meaning of this critical verse.

5. Christ as ἡ κεφαλή

According to Col 1:18a, Christ "is the Head of the Body, the Church." The word ἡ κεφαλή most commonly means "head," but may also mean "source," as in a river's source.[393] The question is therefore whether ἡ

---

391. Daley, *God Visible*, 265 (citing 1:15; emphasis in original).

392. Kinzig, *Faith in Formulae*, §184e: πρὸ αἰώνων . . . ἐκ τοῦ πατρὸς γεννηθέντα. See also Amphilochius of Iconium, *On the Orthodox Faith*, 2 (εἷς υἱὸς αὐτοῦ ἀληθινός, ὁ μονογενὴς θεὸς λόγος, σύμφυτος, συναΐδιος, ὁμοούσιος) (Kinzig, *Faith in Formulae*, §181) (his one true Son, the only-begotten God-Word, of one nature, coeternal, consubstantial); J. Kelly, *Early Christian Doctrines*, 217.

393. "κεφαλή," *CGL* 2:799; "κεφαλή," *LSJ* 1:945.

κεφαλή as used in 1:18a should be translated not only as "head" but *also* as "source" with reference to the Church/the Body.³⁹⁴ From a canonical/intrascriptural perspective, Paul's description in 1:18 of Christ's lordship as it relates to the church is worth noting in comparison with his descriptions elsewhere. Thus in 1 Cor 12:27 and Eph 4:15–16, Christ is also referred to as the head, although in that context Paul is writing about the various functions of the members of the church body. Here the focus appears to be on Christ's controlling power.³⁹⁵ As such, "he directs the growth of the body [the church] to Himself."³⁹⁶ "Head" therefore seems to be the most reasonable alternative, in that it conveys not only a sense of authority but also multiple senses evoked in related passages describing Christ as "the inspiring, ruling, guiding, combining, sustaining power, the mainspring of [the church's] activity, the centre of its unity, and the seat of its life."³⁹⁷ And this choice seems especially appropriate given the immediately following reference to Christ as ἀρχή, discussed below.

6. Christ as ἀρχή

As noted above, if one translates Christ as the "Head" in the sense of Christ's ruling position vis-à-vis the church in 1:18a, then how should one translate his further status in Col 1:18b as ἀρχή, which *also* can refer to one having authority? The word in fact is so used in 1:16 concerning those who are who are simply ἀρχαί, a term referring sometimes to people of high stature (Luke 12:11; Titus 3:1), sometimes to good angels (Col 2:10; Eph 3:10), and sometimes to fallen angels (Col 2:15; Eph 6:12). In other words, the verse as a whole seems redundant if read to say something like "Christ is the Head/Ruler of the Body, the Church; and the Head/Ruler."³⁹⁸ This is the same kind of problem that would be raised if one were to translate ἡ κεφαλή as Source/Beginning, in which case we would end up with a similarly redundant verse reading, "He is the Source of the Body, the Church; and the Source/Beginning."³⁹⁹ In considering

---

394. "κεφαλή," *PGL* 749.

395. See also Eph 1:22–23; 2:16; 4:4, 12.

396. Heinrich Schlier, "κεφαλή," *TDNT* 3:673–81. This reading is also consistent with the usage in Col 2:10, where Christ is ἡ κεφαλὴ πάσης ἀρχῆς καὶ ἐξουσίας.

397. Lightfoot, *St. Paul's Epistles*, 157.

398. Cf. *Symbolum synodi Sirmiensis*, 27: Κεφαλὴ γάρ, ὅ ἐστιν ἀρχὴ πάντων, ὁ υἱός (Kinzig, *Faith in Formulae*, §148).

399. Payne, *Man and Woman*, 289–90, suggests that ἡ κεφαλή should be translated

alternatives to something like "Ruler," a translator will want to examine ἀρχή's intrascriptural usages and resonances. The word can mean first in time or in rank,[400] although it seems most often to be translated as "the beginning" (KJV, ASV, ESV, NLT, NIV, RSV, WYC).[401] And in that connection there seems to be a clear intrascriptural relationship of parallel material (rather than direct influence) between these verses and John 1:1 and 1 John 1:1.[402] Even if Colossians predates the Johannine material, it therefore doesn't seem unreasonable to think that Christ was already understood to have an originating priority, however it might be expressed.[403]

As relevant here, Paul may also be responding at least indirectly to an "errorist/heresy" view that Christ was a created being and/or a form of "emanation," and therefore not himself of equal rank with the "invisible God." The word ἀρχή as used in Col 1:18b could certainly be translated as "First" in order to distinguish Christ from those who are subordinate to him, albeit still first in their own realm.[404] At the same time, his priority might be conveyed by translating it as "Source" or "Beginning." As an alternative to translating ἀρχή as "First," "Source," and/or "Beginning," one might also incorporate an intrascriptural reference from Rev 1:8; 21:6; and 22:13 to Christ as "Alpha and Omega." Such a reference would be consistent with the "eschatological awareness of the earliest community" as an element of its "protology," such that the "beginning *had to* be illuminated by

---

as "head" in Col 1:18 as well as in Eph 5:23 "in order to preserve the 'head' and 'body' interrelated imagery," while at the same time suggesting it be translated as "source" in 1 Cor 11:3. Recognizing the apparent inconsistency, he would add a "note" that "by 'head' [Paul] means 'source'" in Col 1:18, and another note at Eph 5:23 that there "'head' means 'savior.'"

400. Gerhard Delling, "ἀρχή," *TDNT* 1:478–89. See also "ἀρχή," *CGL* 1:225; "ἀρχή," *LSJ* 1:252. And as noted below with respect to Col 1:16, the usage of ἀρχή here is a canonically important reference to the LXX version of Gen 1:1.

401. And the same is true with translations of ἀρχή as used in Rev 3:14, where Christ is described as ἡ ἀρχή τῆς κτίσεως τοῦ Θεοῦ.

402. See Strawbridge, *Pauline Effect*, 161–66.

403. Pizzuto, *Cosmic Leap of Faith*, 238–39; Burney, "Christ as APXH," 173–77. Although Col 1:18b is the only verse using ἀρχή with reference to Christ, he is also described in 1 Cor 15:20 as ἀπαρχή τῶν κεκοιμημένων—the "first fruits of God's harvest from those who've fallen asleep."

404. There is no article ἡ preceding ἀρχή in what NA[28]/UBS[5] consider the best manuscripts. However, there is a decent textual argument for including it based on the earliest manuscripts for Colossians, 𝔓46 and B (Vaticanus). In this instance it may not matter because "ἀρχή . . . being absolute in itself, does not require the definite article. Indeed, the article is most commonly omitted where ἀρχή occurs as a predicate." Lightfoot, *St. Paul's Epistles*, 157.

the end."⁴⁰⁵ One might even use the actual Greek letters A and Ω, as shown in the appendix.⁴⁰⁶ As such, the form is pervasive in Christian iconography.⁴⁰⁷ In short, a creative effective history approach may allow translation better to convey the text's canonical themes of origination and finality.

7. Christ as the One Who τὰ πάντα δι' αὐτοῦ καὶ εἰς αὐτὸν ἔκτισται

In Col 1:16, Christ's preeminence is further emphasized by asserting his role as the one "through whom and in whom all things were created." This phrase was important in the early church as an intrascriptural reference to Christ's role in creation⁴⁰⁸ and therefore his identity with the one God of the Old Testament.⁴⁰⁹ As noted, conflicts arose when the Arians suggested that while Christ as the Image of God in Col 1:15 was divine, Col 1:16 should be read to say that as one "born," he was nevertheless not equal to the Father in the Godhead.⁴¹⁰ When the Council of Nicaea rejected that position, it adopted the language of 1:16, construing it together with John 1:18.⁴¹¹ In so doing, the council correspondingly rejected gnostic formulations that Christ's generation was a form of emanation.⁴¹² Hence the resulting credal language, γεννηθέντα οὐ ποιηθέντα ... δι' οὗ

405. Hengel, *Son of God*, 69 (emphasis in original).

406. The colloquial English expression "from A to Z" is also resonant with that formulation, even if not a strict indication of its effective history.

407. At times together with the Greek letters X and P, as here:

408. Gen 1:1 LXX: Ἐν ἀρχῇ ἐποίησεν ὁ Θεὸς τὸν οὐρανὸν καὶ τὴν γῆν. See John 1:3: πάντα δι' αὐτοῦ ἐγένετο.

409. See Irenaeus, *Epideixis*, 6 (Χριστὸς Ἰησοῦς ὁ κύριος ἡμῶν ... δι' οὗ τὰ πάντα ἐγένετο) (Kinzig, *Faith in Formulae*, §109a2), and *Adversus haereses* 1.22.1 (Kinzig, *Faith in Formulae*, §109b4), referencing Genesis together with Colossians.

410. J. Kelly, *Early Christian Creeds*, 232–33 ("the Pauline text [thus] being interpreted to mean that He was included among creation"); Anatolios, *Retrieving Nicaea*, 18.

411. Anatolios, *Retrieving Nicaea*, 137.

412. See Alexander of Alexandria, *Epistula ad Alexandrum Thessalonicenseum*, 46 (Kinzig, *Faith in Formulae*, §132), condemning such views on the part of Sabellius and Valentinus.

τὰ πάντα ἐγένετο.⁴¹³ As noted, in order to capture that effective history, one might incorporate the relevant credal expression *itself* into the text (as in the appendix) and/or provide it in marginal notation.

8. Christ as the One Who τὰ πάντα ἐν αὐτῷ συνέστηκεν

The verb συνίστημι does not appear elsewhere in the New Testament in its active form. As a compound verb based on ἵστημι it means "stand together." It is used as such in Luke 9:32 for the simple statement that when Peter, James, and John beheld Jesus in his glory, they saw "two men standing with him." It otherwise appears only in 2 Pet 3:5, where the Earth is said to have been "put together out of water and through water." But in Col 1:17 it has theological significance, describing Christ as the one who actively holds all things together.⁴¹⁴ The verse was in fact critically important to a number of church fathers as evidence of Christ's equality within the Godhead.⁴¹⁵

Hebrews 1:3 expresses essentially the same thought, i.e., that the Son "sustain[s] the universe by the Word of his Power." Although the verb used in Hebrews is from φέρω not ἵστημι, it carries the alternative meaning "sustain."⁴¹⁶ It is thus congruent with the sense of Col 1:17 that *but for* God's maintaining the cosmos in its present form, the "elements" might "dissolve in fervent heat."⁴¹⁷ An additional nuance might be gleaned from the Vulgate. Jerome translated the verse as *omnia in ipso constant*, where *constare* means not simply to stand together but also to stand firm.⁴¹⁸ In context, the concept appears to be that all things "are held firmly

---

413. Kinzig, *Faith in Formulae*, §135c. The council's additional modifier μονογενῆ of the word "begotten" was apparently "accepted by all parties in the Arian quarrel [but] no special dogmatic significance was read into it." J. Kelly, *Early Christians Creeds*, 235.

414. Wilhelm Kasch, "συνίστημι," *TDNT* 7:896–98, suggests that in 1:17 the word means nothing more than "to exist," thus rendering 1:17 as "all things have their existence in him." But that is too mild a use of the word considering other references to Christ's role in creation and his involvement in its maintenance. See, e.g., Heb 1:3.

415. See Basil of Caesarea, *De fide*, Prologus 8.4 (ἐν ᾧ τὰ πάντα συνέστηκεν) (Kinzig, *Faith in Formulae*, §174f); Gregory of Nazianzus, *On God and Christ*, oratio 30.20; John of Damascus, *Expositio fide*, 1.3.

416. "φέρω," LSJ 2:1923.

417. 2 Pet 3:10; Heb 1:12. See Foster, *Colossians*, 211.

418. In later usage, particularly in the sciences, the word "constant" means invariable, not subject to change. Using "constant" in 1:17, however, would be in tension with 2 Pet 3:10 and Heb 1:12.

together" by or in Christ, a view that is thus central to Paul's Christology.[419] The verse also has a clear intrascriptural parallel with the creation story, where all things are placed in order.[420]

What word therefore seems most apt? David Bentley Hart translates the passage as "all things hold together in him."[421] One could quite reasonably combine Jerome's and Hart's renderings to produce something like "in him all things hold firm together." But the Latinate "cohere" also expresses the concept.[422] The word is derived from the intransitive verb *cohaere*, meaning "to be closely attached/stick together."[423] Any of these would certainly be better than Nida's dynamically equivalent rendering that in Christ "all things have their proper place,"[424] which fails adequately to account for the intrascriptural link to Genesis, the Patristic writings, or the English translation tradition.

9. Christ as πρωτότοκος πάσης κτίσεως

As noted, there is general recognition that for Paul questions of the universal, or "cosmic" nature of Jesus' lordship go beyond questions of soteriology and concern the subjection of all things and all creatures to

419. Sumney, *Colossians*, 70 (citing sources).

420. Gen 1. Such usage is also consistent with noncanonical materials to the effect that God holds the cosmos together. Thiselton, *Colossians*, 38 (citing Sir 43:26 ["all things hold together by (God's) word"]; and Philo, *Quis rerum divinarum heres* 23:188 ["hold together"]). See also Lightfoot, *St. Paul's Epistles*, 156 (putting it cutely that because of Christ there is "a cosmos instead of a chaos"); cf. Zwicky, "Rotverschiebung," 125 (theorizing the presence of "dark matter," from whose existence one infers a gravitational effect holding the universe together); NASA, "Dark Matter" (same).

421. Hart, *New Testament*, 398. See also Bruce, *Letters of Paul* ("it is through Him that everything holds together").

422. Lightfoot, *St. Paul's Epistles*, 144, uses the word in a more expansive, exegetical formulation: "in Him, as the binding and sustaining power, universal nature coheres and consists." Thiselton, *Colossians*, 31, renders the phrase as "in him all things achieve a coherent focus," adopting an adjectival form of the word but arguably depriving the verse of its cohesive force. And Montgomery, *New Testament*, 538, translates the phrase as "in him all things subsist," although in English that can also have the overtone of existing at only a minimal level.

423. See *Latin Dictionary*, s.v. "cohaere," https://www.online-latin-dictionary.com/latin-english-dictionary.php?parola=cohaere. The word does not appear in English until the sixteenth century, where its meaning was essentially the same as in Latin. However, its current usage is not so much "stick" as "hold/be held firmly together." *OED* Supp and *Merriam-Webster*, s.v., "cohere."

424. Bratcher and Nida, *Translators Handbook*, 25; cf. Idioms, "Place for Everything": "a place for everything and everything in its place."

him.[425] The Colossian Hymn expressly so states, as do numerous other passages.[426] Moreover, the predication of Christ as "Firstborn above all creation" became an essential element of the credal formulations thereby effected.[427] Several scholars have therefore focused on the sources of this view, with some arguing that the "cosmic Christology" of Colossians relies directly on Jewish Wisdom literature and/or Second Temple Psalmody.[428] Attention has also been paid to descriptors such as Wisdom, Son of Man, and the Kingdom that "imply the idea of pre-existence."[429] The New Testament's glosses on Ps 110:1 are likewise canonically relevant to consider in translation, where Jesus' lordship is said to encompass all powers and creatures, whether on earth or in heaven.[430]

Paul's description in Col 1:15 of Christ as πρωτότοκος πάσης κτίσεως thus reinforces Christ's priority as "firstborn" vis-à-vis the *totality* of "all things," including things on earth or in heaven, things seen/unseen and all thrones/dominions/powers.[431] There is an interesting parallel

425. Gibbs, "Cosmic Scope," 20, 20n1, criticizing the contrary views of Rudolf Bultmann.

426. E.g., 1 Cor 15:20–28; Eph 1:19–23; Phil 2:9–11; 1 Tim 6:13–16; Heb 1:1–13; 1 Pet 3:21–22; Rev 5:5–14; 19:11–16.

427. Niceno-Constantinopolitan Creed; Origen, *In Matthaeum commentariorum series*, 33 (*primogenito universae creaturae*) (Kinzig, *Faith in Formulae*, §116c); Ignatius of Antioch, *Epistle to the Smyrnaeans*, 1.2 (πρωτοτόκου πάσης κτίσεως) (Kinzig, *Faith in Formulae*, §98e); Justin Martyr, *Dialogus cum Tryphone* 85.2 (πρωτοτόκου πάσης κτίσεως) (Kinzig, *Faith in Formulae*, §104b3); Origen, *De principiis* 1.4 (*ante omnem creaturam natus ex patre est*) (Kinzig, *Faith in Formulae*, §100). See also *Constitutiones Apostolorum* 6.11.1–2: ἕνα μόνον θεὸν καταγγέλλομεν . . . , θεὸν καὶ πατέρα τοῦ μονογενοῦς καὶ πρωτοτόκου πάσης δημιουργίας (Kinzig, *Faith in Formulae*, §182a).

428. See Wright, "Poetry and Theology," 452: The hymn "presents a pattern easily recognizable in the context of mainline Judaism." But see Pizzuto, *Cosmic Leap of Faith*, 220n40: "While Jewish motifs . . . have paved the way for some of the Christological predications in the Col[ossian] hymn, they do not go far enough to account for the entire hymn."

429. Foster, *Colossians*, 200; Strawbridge, *Pauline Effect*, 151–52; Hengel, *Son of God*, 66–76; Gibbs, "Cosmic Scope," 15.

430. See, e.g., Rom 8:34; 1 Cor 15:25; Eph 1:20; Col 3:1.

431. Macaskill, "Union(s) with Christ," 95–97; Foster, *Colossians*, 203–8. See also Strawbridge, *Pauline Effect*, 155–57, discussing a possible relationship to "throne imagery" in the noncanonical Martydom and Ascension of Isaiah. Wasserman, "Gentile Gods," 736–37, takes the position that the terms rules/powers/authorities are best understood to refer to "divine intermediaries" who function as "bit players in a larger religious and political drama about favored and disfavored peoples, legitimate religious beliefs, and more- versus less-powerful deities" rather than "as unqualified forces of evil," as they are often construed. It is an ambitious argument, relying principally on noncanonical texts such as the Book of the Watchers, Jubilee, and 1 Enoch, but is flawed

to Rev 3:14, where Christ is ἡ ἀρχὴ τῆς κτίσεως τοῦ Θεοῦ, thus linking his preeminence in rule to his priority of origin as "firstborn."[432] In other words, πρωτότοκος concerns not only temporal but also ontological priority. Paul's point is that there is nothing left out, nothing that remains unsubordinated to Christ. As such, the proper translation of κτίσεως should be "creation," not just "creatures," even though the latter might be a legitimate rendering in another context.

In short, the "inner word" of the passage concerns Christ's preeminence. It is therefore also important to consider how to construe the genitive in Col 1:15. If read as a partitive genitive,[433] then Christ might be seen as a created being, i.e., one "of" many."[434] But construed as a comparative genitive,[435] Christ is ontologically superior with respect to all creation.[436] This understanding is fully consistent with the Messiah's sovereignty over all creation; and is likely an intrascriptural allusion to the Psalms that as Firstborn, he is placed "over" all.[437] Applying the foregoing analysis, a translator should at least provide a marginal reference to the relevant LXX language.

---

by her failure to cite Col 1:16; 2:10; or 2:15 or to grapple with military imagery in the letter. She likewise ignores Jude 6, which is in direct tension with her assertion that such powers are unrelated to "heavenly rebels" (738). And further, although she argues that the terms ἄρχων, ἐξουσία, and δύναμις in 1 Cor 15 "never appear together in the letters," the phrase πρὸς τὰς ἀρχάς, πρὸς τὰς ἐξουσίας, πρὸς τοὺς κοσμοκράτορας τοῦ σκότους τούτου in Eph 6:12 is sufficiently close in phrasing and sense as to undermine that claim, especially coming after the exhortation in Eph 6:11 to be armed with the weapons of God πρὸς τὸ δύνασθαι ὑμᾶς στῆναι πρὸς τὰς μεθοδείας τοῦ διαβόλου.

432. There is also notable intrascripturality throughout the LXX, where the word is used with respect to the priority of the firstborn, whether it be Israel as God's chosen (Exod 4:22), in obverse form as the focus of the angel of death (Exod 11:5; 12:29), or as those chosen for priestly service to the Lord (Num 8:16). See also Strawbridge, *Pauline Effect*, 153–54, discussing the reference in the noncanonical Prayer of Joseph to the angel Israel as the "first-born of all creation."

433. Smyth, *Greek Grammar*, 315–17 (§§1306–19).

434. Hence in gnostic thinking, one in a series of "emanations." Pagels, *Gnostic Paul*, 137.

435. Smyth, *Greek Grammar*, 279–80, 330 (§§1069–70, 1401–4); but see Payne, *Man and Woman*, 285n50, failing to recognize the genitive of comparison and therefore incorrectly criticizing the NIV's translation "over all creation" on the ground that "no Greek manuscript adds a preposition suggesting a relationship of authority."

436. C. Campbell, "Response to Macaskill," 110; Sumney, *Colossians*, 65.

437. Ps 88:28 LXX: κἀγὼ πρωτότοκον θήσομαι αὐτόν, ὑψηλὸν παρὰ τοῖς βασιλεῦσιν τῆς γῆς. See also Lightfoot, *St. Paul's Epistles*, 146: "The way had been paved for this Messianic reference of πρωτότοκος by its prior application to the Israelites, as the prerogative race" (citing Exod 4:22).

10. Christ as πρωτότοκος ἐκ τῶν νεκρῶν

Christ is not only "Firstborn above all creation" as per Col 1:15, but also "firstborn from among the dead" as per 1:18. In construing and translating this second usage of πρωτότοκος, it is important to note the context within 1:18, where Christ's status as firstborn from among the dead is in apposition to his role as "Head of the Body, the Church." That said, the sense in both instances is of a priority that is not only temporal but also originating/causational.[438] The verse as a whole emphasizes Christ's priority vis-à-vis the cosmos by virtue of his eternal Godhead; and parallels it to his priority vis-à-vis the Church by virtue of his incarnation, death, and resurrection.

The reference is temporal because Jesus' resurrection (unlike that of Lazarus, for example) did not involve a return to live but still to die. Instead, it was the defeat of death by Christ's unrepeatable death, resurrection, and ascension. And it is also originating/causational because there would be no resurrection but for Jesus' perfect offering as "forerunner" (Heb 6:20). Christ is thus "firstborn" in that regard because those who follow him in the "resurrection of life" (John 5:29) do so by virtue of, and temporally after, Jesus.[439] Colossians' hymnic assertion of this truth thereby finds a continuing, effective history in the church's confessional tradition. Under the hermeneutic of the proposed methodology, it should be noted as such in translation.[440]

11. Christ as ἐν πᾶσιν αὐτὸς πρωτεύων

As set forth in Col 1:18, Christ was made "preeminent" "in all things" as the beginning and firstborn from the dead. This itself is a central phrase emphasizing his "cosmic lordship."[441] In the context of Colossians, Paul

---

438. Foster, *Colossians*, 214–15.

439. As noted, there are limits to what language can convey when dealing with questions of time and the absence of time. The immediate perception of those who died in faith "before" Jesus' resurrection, "before" the parousia, or "before" the day of judgment may be one of timeless presence in heaven. That said, the Scriptures aver that *without* Jesus there is no resurrection to life, making him "firstborn" in that sense.

440. See, e.g., *Concilium Serdicense: Professio fidei ab episcopis occidentalibus promulgata*, §6: Ὁμολογοῦμεν . . . ὅτι καὶ πρωτότοκος ἐκ τῶν νεκρῶν (Kinzig, *Faith in Formulae*, §144a1).

441. Glasson, "Colossians," 156, suggests that Paul may be adopting or at least alluding to language in the apocryphal book Sirach concerning Wisdom:

uses language of "preeminence" both as a worshipful attribution *and* as groundwork to counter a possibly incipient heresy/error that would give "undue respect" to or otherwise exalt angels to the point of being worshiped in their own right as equal or even superior to Christ.[442] Were any but Christ to hold preeminence and/or be entitled to worship, it would follow that believers could only be "complete" by engaging in precisely the kind of ancillary liturgies—e.g., "worship of angels"—that Paul condemns.[443] Here the Latinate "preeminence" is consistent with Tyndale's "classical" usage, which was thus adhered to in the King James and versions thereafter.[444]

12. Christ as Indwelt by πᾶν τό πλήρωμα

It follows from all that is said of Christ that "completeness" can only be found in him. As the KJV renders Col 1:19, "It pleased the Father that in him should all the fullness of God dwell." While not compelled by the grammar, 1:19 seems best understood to imply God rather than the "Fullness" as its unstated subject. Most translations render the phrase accordingly, e.g., "it pleased the Father" (KJV) or "God was pleased" (NIV).[445] And such a reading is consistent with the similar phraseology in Ps 67:17 LXX—ὃ εὐδόκησεν ὁ Θεὸς κατοικεῖν ἐν αὐτῷ—which may well have been Paul's intrascriptural reference.

I came out of the mouth of the most High, the firstborn before all creatures:

I made that in the heavens there should rise light that never faileth, and as a cloud I covered all the earth:

I dwelt in the highest places, and my throne is in a pillar of a cloud.

I alone have compassed the circuit of heaven, and have penetrated into the bottom of the deep, and have walked in the waves of the sea,

And have stood in all the earth: and in every people,

And in every nation I have had the chief rule. (Sir 24:5–10 DRA)

442. Wessels, "Eschatology," 192.

443. Wessels, "Eschatology," 193 (citing Moule, *Epistles of Paul*, 94).

444. Jerome translates the verse *sit in omnibus ipse primatum tenens*. While being "preeminent" is not as directly derived from the Latin as holding "primacy" might be, it nevertheless resonates with the Vulgate's several denotations of priority.

445. The ESV translates the verse with "fulness" as the subject: "For in him all the fulness of God was pleased to dwell." But grammatically, this is a less favored reading. See Lightfoot, *St. Paul's Epistles*, 158–59; Foster, *Colossians*, 216.

Paul restates the idea in Col 2:9 to the effect that "in him dwells all the fullness of God bodily" (KJV). I address the meaning of "bodily" below. But for present purposes, the question is what Paul means in Col 1:19 and 2:9 by πλήρωμα, and further how to understand the adjectival modifier πᾶν. The word πλήρωμα has a range of meanings in Greek.[446] As used in the New Testament, the general sense is one of completeness and abundance or, as Lightfoot synthesizes it, "the full complement, the entire measure, the plenitude, the fullness."[447]

From an intrascriptural point of view, it is relevant to compare the usages in Col 1:19 and 2:9 with those in Ephesians. In Eph 1:23, Christ's fullness is linked to the Church, where the Church is described as "his Body, the Fullness of him who fills all in all." And Paul prays in Eph 3:19 that the members of the Church may be "filled with all the Fullness of God." While Colossians is focused on Christ's supremacy in the cosmos, Ephesians' theme is the Church's dependency on Christ for *its* "fullness." As used in Eph 1:23, τὸ πλήρωμα might thus be understood in the more generic sense of "completeness," while in Col 1:19 and 2:9, it is used with theological reference to the nature of God/the Godhead. The binitarian implication is therefore plain: "If all the fullness of the Godhead, bodily, is in Christ, then must the Father and the Son be confessed to be of one Godhead."[448]

Even so, we are facing a mystery. How are we do understand what "the fullness of God" means, let alone "*all* the fullness of God"? As noted, Colossians itself is written in a fully plerophoric style.[449] As such it signals a form of spiritual abundance that may be nowhere more evident than in this passage. And neither πᾶν nor πλήρωμα is explanatory by reference to anything visible, i.e., by reference to illustrative imagery. The verse thereby presses against the expressive limits of human language, such that cumulative words may assist in revealing the *verbum cordis* of the text, e.g., a description of the immensurable/immeasurable/incomprehensible nature of God/the Godhead. And in fact, the verse has an

---

446. See, e.g., Lightfoot, *St. Paul's Epistles*, 257–73; "πλήρωμα," BDAG 829–30; Gerhard Delling, "πλήρωμα," *TDNT* 6:298–305; Reinier Schippers, "Fullness," *NIDNTT* 1:733–41.

447. Lightfoot, *St. Paul's Epistles*, 260–61.

448. Gorday and Oden, *Colossians*, 31 (quoting Ambrose, *Of the Christian Faith*).

449. Hence the multiple words incorporating the roots πλήρ (1:9, 19, 24–25; 2:2, 9–10; 3:16; 4:12, 17) and πᾶν (1:6, 9–11, 15–20, 23, 28; 2:2–3, 9–10, 14, 19–20, 22; 3:8, 11, 14, 17, 20, 22; 4:6–7, 9).

Elements of a Canonical-Hermeneutical Translation Approach/Test Case   133

effective liturgical history in the Athanasian Creed that seeks to do just that.[450]

The language of Col 1:17 and 2:9 is thus more ontological than spatial. That itself may explain why on first blush it is difficult to grasp how such "fullness" could, in effect, be fit within the "body" of one person (see sect. II.e.ii *infra* on the use of σωματικῶς in 2:9). And this necessarily implicates the mystery of the incarnation.[451] It is central to the methodology advanced here that such theological concepts cannot themselves be fully conveyed in either literal or dynamically equivalent terms, but rather alluded to or evoked, perhaps by hymnic, poetic, or rhetorical language. Indeed, a dynamically equivalent translation of these verses may drain them of meaning.[452] No single word in translation can fully elicit the inner meaning of such texts, any more than the literal words of the Greek entirely capture the spiritual or immaterial sense of the thought they seek to express.[453] Applying the hermeneutic of this theory, the translation in the appendix therefore retains a grounding in the literal text while also providing modifiers that yield to the absence of linguistic bounds on the boundless. Hence a possible phrasing might be "the Totality of the Pleroma of Divine Perfection" (1:19)[454] and "the Immensurable Plenitude of Deity" (2:9).[455]

Finally, there are relevant Old Testament references to be considered in translating the verb κατοικέω, which has a sense of "dwelling." In the LXX, it consistently means "to inhabit." For example, God's glory filled the Tabernacle on those occasions that he met with the high priest in the holy of holies at the mercy seat, where God is said to "dwell between

---

450. See, e.g., Athanasian Creed, §9: *immensus pater, immensus filius, immensus spiritus sanctus* (Kinzig, *Faith in Formulae*, §434a).

451. John 1:16: ὅτι ἐκ τοῦ πληρώματος αὐτοῦ ἡμεῖς πάντες ἐλάβομεν καὶ χάριν ἀντὶ χάριτος.

452. See, e.g., L&N 59.32: "For Christ is completely like God" and "For just what God is, that is exactly what Christ is."

453. Cf. Rom 8:26: "The Spirit comes to our aid: because we do not really know what we should pray for or even how to pray for it, the Spirit itself pleads before God on our behalf, interceding with sighs and yearnings beyond our expression."

454. F. F. Bruce does something like this with "the totality of divine fullness," a rendering consistent with the description of his work as "an expansion." Bruce, *Letters of Paul*, 9. See also Steiner, *After Babel*, 29: "Translations are inflationary."

455. The word "plenitude" thus captures the *Wirkungsgeschichte* of the Vulgate's *omnis plenitudo divinitatis* as well as the *immensus pater, immensus filius, immensus spiritus sanctus* of the Athanasian Creed.

the cherubim enthroned on high."[456] There are likewise resonances with the notion that God was pleased to dwell among his people,[457] as also on Mount Zion, which is metonymically the temple.[458] Carrying the imagery forward, the verse would be intrascripturally related to Jesus' reference to "the temple that was his body."[459] Similarly, it is said that Christ makes his "dwelling among us."[460] As such, Colossians' assertion that God indwelt Christ bodily—what Scot McKnight calls his "covenanted presence"[461]—is a statement about the mystery of the incarnation. And the passage was thus of effective importance in the development of relevant faith formulae. References to Col 1:15–20 as a whole, moreover, appear *hundreds of times* in Patristic writings as they seek "to explicate more clearly the person and nature of Christ."[462] Incorporation of wording from that effective history by direct usage or by marginal notation would thus be hermeneutically consistent with the Gadamerian understanding that translation fills, without exhausting, the "free space" around the text.

13. ἀνταναπληρῶ τὰ ὑστερήματα τῶν θλίψεων τοῦ Χριστοῦ

In Col 1:24 Paul adds his own statement of "rejoicing" concerning a form of "fulfillment" that involves suffering. The verb ἀνταναπληρῶ is a rare compound, *hapax legomena* both in the New Testament and the LXX. To give effect to the double prefix it has been suggested that the sense is supplementation arising out of a mutuality or sharing between two persons.[463] On first blush it might appear, at least in English, that Paul

---

456. Exod 25:8, 22; Isa 37:16; Ps 99:1.
457. Exod 29:45.
458. Ps 68:16; Isa 8:18.
459. John 2:21.
460. John 1:14.
461. McKnight, *Letter to the Colossians*, 161.

462. Edsall and Strawbridge, "Songs We Used to Sing," 301; Strawbridge, *Pauline Effect*, 244–66, providing an extensive list of such references. Nor is the verse's *Wirkungsgeschichte* limited to the church, but also takes effect in Milton's *Paradise Lost*, 3.225: "The Son of God, in whom the fulness dwels of love divine."

463. Gerhard Delling, "ἀνταναπληρόω," *TDNT* 6:307. See Lightfoot, *St. Paul's Epistles*, 165: "Where one personal agent is mentioned in connexion with the supply and another in connexion with the deficiency, the one forming the subject and the other being involved in the object of the verb, the ἀντί can only describe the correspondence of these personal agents. So interpreted, it is eminently expressive here. The point of the Apostle's boast is that Christ the sinless Master should have *left* something for Paul the unworthy servant to suffer" (emphasis in original). Cf. "ἀνταναπληρόω," *CGL*, 1:137,

Elements of a Canonical-Hermeneutical Translation Approach/Test Case 135

is suggesting that Christ's suffering on the cross remained incomplete. However, the Scriptures never use θλῖψις to refer to Christ's own sufferings. The word is used instead to refer to "afflictions which result from union with him."[464] What Paul refers to must therefore be the continued experiences of the church as the Body of Christ, whether the same involve physical suffering through persecution, or any of the myriad hardships individual Christians may experience.[465] These are the sufferings in his physical body that Paul himself elsewhere catalogs at length.[466]

The relevant Greek word Paul uses is σάρξ, sometimes translated as "body" (as it is for example in the NLT). That wouldn't be an impossible translation in some contexts. But to avoid confusion within the same passage it should be rendered differently than σῶμα, which also means "body" and is clearly used in Col 1:24 *not* to refer to a physical body, but rather to the "Body of Christ." Σάρξ might thus be rendered as "flesh." Adding *nomina sacra* as further suggested below, the verse would read, "I rejoice now in the things I suffer for the sake of the Body of CHRIST, his Church, supplementing in my own flesh what still lacks of the Savior's afflictions." Colossians 1:24 thereby provides a complex and even mysterious sense of another form of "fulfillment" experienced by the believer, where eliciting the meaning requires attention to similar language in related passages.

14. Christological Nature of τό μυστήριον

Paul does not cloak the "mystery" of the gospel, but understanding how the word is used in Col 1:26 calls for examination of the broader context. Here, Paul contrasts the free access of the Christian faith to access by way of initiation rites of the sort involved in then-contemporaneous "mystery religions."[467] Thus, although "hidden" for ages (ἀποκεκρυμμένον),[468] the "mystery" of which Paul is a minister has now been fully revealed (Col

---

relating the poorest contributors to the wealthiest individual in a taxation group.

464. Delling, "ἀνταναπληρόω," *TDNT* 6:307.

465. See Heb 4:15. Cf. R. Williams, "Augustine," 20, citing Augustine, *Enarrationes in Psalmos*, 51.4 as a gloss on 1:24, illustrating a "Head-and-Body," *totus Christus* theology.

466. E.g., 1 Cor 4:11–13; 2 Cor 6:4–10; 11:24–30.

467. See McKnight, *Letter to the Colossians*, 196; Sumney, *Colossians*, 104.

468. The verbal form is the perfect passive participle, "were made apocryphal."

1:26–27).⁴⁶⁹ Any previously restricted access thus disappears.⁴⁷⁰ Yet even though the truth that the way of life is opened to the gentiles may have been hidden, it is now a "mystery" with a *positive* meaning as a spiritual truth that is "transcendental, incomprehensible, mystical [or] mysterious, in the modern sense of the term."⁴⁷¹

The relevant intrascriptural references include 1 Cor 15:51 ("Listen while I tell you a mystery") and Eph 5:32 ("Listen—this is a great mystery. I speak of Christ and the Church"). As far as the translation options, μυστήριον is defined in Louw and Nida as that "which has not been known before but which has been revealed to an in-group or restricted constituency."⁴⁷² Some translations influenced by dynamic equivalence thus choose "secret." But that is plainly incorrect in the context of the freely available "mystery" of the gospel. Given the positive sense of the word, there is both formal and intrascriptural justification for adhering to "mystery" as the standard English derivative form, while possibly providing marginal references to other usages of the word in the LXX.⁴⁷³

ii. Affirmative Use of Christological Language as Doctrine

Having hymned Christ's person, Paul integrates that spiritual description with additional doctrinal points he wishes to make, both in his affirmative assertions concerning the nature of Christ and his negativizing rejection of the teachings of his so-called "opponents." Again, exploration of the text's effective history can inform its translation.

1. ἐστὲ ἐν αὐτῷ πεπληρωμένοι

One essential and affirmative statement in this context concerns the believer's relationship to Christ. Having indicated in Col 1:19 that the fullness of the Godhead was pleased to dwell in Christ, Paul repeats the assertion in 2:9 and then incorporates believers into that fullness.

---

469. Brevard Childs sees this "mystery as no longer identical with Paul's gospel, but [a]s the worldwide extension of Paul's earlier 'secret' (1 Cor 2:7–13)," in that Paul is "now himself part of the content of this proclamation." Childs, *Church's Guide*, 93.

470. The dramatic analog is the rending of the temple veil that had separated the people from the holiest of holies. Matt 27:51; cf. 2 Cor 3:13–16.

471. Lightfoot, *St. Paul's Epistles*, 168.

472. L&N 28.77.

473. E.g., Dan 2:18–19, 27, 30, 47.

Elements of a Canonical-Hermeneutical Translation Approach/Test Case   137

Thus, immediately following Paul's assertion that the entirety of the Godhead—πᾶν τό πλήρωμα—dwelled in Christ "bodily" (2:9), he shifts to believers, the members of the church, his body.[474] He states in 2:10 that ἐστὲ ἐν αὐτῷ πεπληρωμένοι. The form πεπληρωμένοι is the nominative masculine plural perfect passive participle.[475] The construction ἐστὲ . . . πεπληρωμένοι is a periphrastic participial one and thereby emphasizes the completed action of the "filling."

The English translation tradition is relevant here in assessing the effective history of the verse and the range of possible renderings. Thus, Col 2:10 is translated variously as "ye are complete in him" (KJV), "you have been filled in him" (ESV), "you have come to fullness in him" (RSV), "in Christ you have been brought to fullness" (NIV), and "in him ye are made full" (ASV). "Completeness" is an alternative meaning for πλήρωμα, as chosen in the KJV; but in context Paul seems to be more focused on the act of filling or the state of being filled, even if "completeness" is the result. Another way to translate the verse might be "you are fulfilled in the Fountainhead, he who is . . ."

Such wording captures the sense of having been filled as well as the completeness that results from it, both of which are otherwise reflected in the translation tradition. The second part of the phrase is that Christ is ἡ κεφαλὴ πάσης ἀρχῆς καὶ ἐξουσίας. As noted above, ἡ κεφαλὴ is most commonly translated as "head/Head"[476] and that is a legitimate choice. But the meaning of ἡ κεφαλὴ here may go beyond just being the chief over all other principalities or powers. It may also mean "source." Hence using the word "Fountainhead" may be one way to convey the sense that all power and rule is not only subordinate *to* him (as in Col 1:15–16) but comes *from* him.

As also noted above, Paul's statements concerning the indwelling of the Godhead in Christ are effectively statements about the incarnation. But just as they resonate intrascripturally with passages concerning God's indwelling presence on Mount Zion and in the temple (e.g., Ps 68:16; Isa 8:18), so too do they provide a canonically unified fulfillment of those verses by way of Christ's presence in his people, the church. As such,

---

474. There seems to be an intrascriptural reference in Col 2:9–10 to Christ's indwelling of the Church, as his body in that sense. See Eph 1:22–23: τῇ ἐκκλησίᾳ, ἥτις ἐστὶν τὸ σῶμα αὐτοῦ.

475. The form would be the same in the middle, but that voice wouldn't make sense here.

476. E.g., in WYC, KJV, RSV, NIV, and NLT.

Christ now indwells the church as he had typologically indwelt Israel.[477] The church, in other words, "is also full of the divine presence," such that believers corporately "have become a locus of the presence of God, a temple."[478] As far as finding apt words for the constellation of words that develop the notions of fullness and filling, there may thus be no better options than simply to use appropriate variations on the root words "full" or "fill." One alternative would be some form of "complete," but there is a separate word in Greek that is better suited to that concept.[479] "Filling" words also contrast well with "emptiness"—or, to use what later became a gnostic term, "deficiency."[480] And to the extent Paul was aware of this "deficiency" as a proto-gnostic or perhaps Jewish mystical term, he thus made clear that no "intermediate" beings could reconcile mankind to God, but Christ alone.

2. ἐκλεκτοὶ τοῦ θεοῦ

In Col 3:12, Paul addresses the Colossians as ἐκλεκτοὶ τοῦ θεοῦ ἅγιοι καὶ ἠγαπημένοι, a passage generally translated as the "elect of God, holy and beloved" (KJV, ESV, NLT), but sometimes as "chosen people" (NIV). The adjective ἐκλεκτός is derived from the verb ἐκλέγομαι and is used not only with respect to Christians[481] but also the children of Israel.[482] Hence the effective history of passages from the LXX is highly relevant in applying the methodology advanced here, as a way of alerting the reader to potential interpretive issues. It would therefore be reasonable to use the word "elect" for ἐκλεκτοί. As such, the reader might appropriately be led to focus on such fraught theological questions as the meaning of election, foreknowledge, and/or predestination. These questions also implicate Israel's status, including the identity of those who "belong to Israel" (Rom 9:6). But the same lines of thought would also be triggered

---

477. 2 Cor 6:16.

478. Beetham, *Echoes of Scripture*, 154. See also Rev 21:22: "But I saw no temple in the city because the Lord God, Ὁ Παντοκράτωρ, he is its temple, he and the Lamb."

479. Cf. John 19:30: Τετέλεσται.

480. Lightfoot, *St. Paul's Epistles*, 269.

481. 1 Pet 1:1; 2 John 1, 13.

482. Compare Col 3:12 with Deut 14:2 LXX (σὲ ἐξελέξατο Κύριος ὁ Θεός) with Deut 7:6–8 LXX (λαὸς ἅγιος εἶ Κυρίῳ τῷ Θεῷ σου . . . καὶ ἐξελέξατο Κύριος ὑμᾶς . . . παρὰ τὸ ἀγαπᾶν Κύριον ὑμᾶς) with Isa 42:1 LXX (Ἰσραὴλ ὁ ἐκλεκτός μου) and with Acts 13:17 (ὁ Θεὸς . . . ἐξελέξατο τοὺς πατέρας ἡμῶν). See also Gottlob Schrenk, "ἐκλεκτός," *TDNT* 4:181–92.

by the phrase "chosen people"—if anything more acutely, given that term's multiple historical and political implications for many peoples and cultures.[483] One option is therefore to render the word as Chosen People, capitalized for the reasons discussed in sect. III.b.iii, *infra*.

3. ἡ θεότης

As noted, there is no express subject of Col 1:19. From a purely grammatical point of view, the subject might legitimately be taken as implied, i.e., "it was pleasing to God that." Alternatively, it might be stated as "all the Fullness was pleased," thus personifying the image. And Col 1:19 and 2:9 are logically be read *in pari materia*, such that "all the Fullness" in both instances essentially means "all the Fullness of the Godhead/Deity." The verses may in fact reflect a proto-Trinitarian insight or revelation in that Colossians depicts Christ as ontologically equal to God the Father (1:15–20; 2:9).[484] And as to his superiority, Christ is over every "potentate and power" (2:9–10), the Father having "put everything under his feet" (1 Cor 15:27).[485]

Even so, ἡ θεότης as used in Colossians is not self-explanatory, nor is it entirely clear how best to translate it. "Godhead" and "Deity" now sound somewhat antique and are not clearly embedded in the English translation tradition as "classical" formulations. Ben Blackwell renders it as "divine essence."[486] Henry Sylvester Nash lists various ways it has been expressed in other languages as well as English: "divine nature," "*deitas*," "*divina majestas*," "divine being," "*was Gottes ist*," "the Divine Personality."[487] The most popular translations are inconsistent in this regard, reflecting possible uncertainty whether there is a difference between the usage of θειότης in Rom 1:20 and θεότης in Col 2:9.[488] Thus, θειότης

---

483. Such concepts also have an effective history in politics. See, e.g., Melville, *White-Jacket*, ch. 36, final para.: "We Americans are the peculiar, chosen people—the Israel of our time; we bear the ark of the liberties of the world." See generally Gitlin and Leibovitz, *Chosen Peoples*.

484. See also Phil 2:6–8.

485. It is beyond the scope of this work, however, to examine possibly subordinationist views concerning the Son's submission to the Father within the Trinity, notwithstanding his coeternal nature.

486. Blackwell, "You Are Filled," 106–8.

487. Nash, "Θειότης," 1.

488. See Nash, "Θειότης," 24–25, concluding that by Patristic times "the two words occupy and hold the same theological territory," even if in earlier Greek usage there

in Rom 1:20 is translated variously as Godhead (KJV), deity (RSV), divine nature (ESV, NIV), great eternal power (TLB); while θεότης in Col 2:9 is translated variously as Godhead (KJV), deity (RSV, ESV), all of God (TLB), and Deity (NIV).[489] It is therefore difficult to derive a rule from these examples. Sometimes the word is translated the same way in both passages and sometimes differently; sometimes it is capitalized to convey a sense of abstraction or special dignity but sometimes not. In all such cases, however, "Deity" does not mean "divine," but rather "'God' or 'Godhead' or 'the being God.'"[490]

To the extent the word thus refers to the essence of "who God is," then perceiving a kernel of Trinitarian doctrine as the *verbum interius* of the verse may help guide one to a translation that is consistent with its credal history. The Niceno-Constantinopolitan Creed, for example, affirms that Christ is ὁμοούσιον/of one substance with the Father. That essential element of orthodox belief is further refined in the Chalcedonian Statement, affirming that Christ was fully divine and fully human—that is, *both* consubstantial with the Father according to the Godhead (ὁμοούσιον τῷ πατρὶ κατὰ τὴν θεότητα) *and* consubstantial with us according to the Manhood (ὁμοούσιον τὸ αὐτὸν ἡμῖν κατὰ τὴν ἀνθρωπότητα).[491]

As Robert Morgan points out (citing the Colossian Hymn), the "vital words of the council's definition can be accepted as an appropriate expression and necessary defense of what all the New Testament writers were saying or presupposed."[492] It thus seems essential to convey the same in translation. But given the ineffability of the Trinity, *whatever* terms are chosen will necessarily elude any limiting definition. One can therefore only suggest, not ultimately capture, who God "is." As such, "Deity" or

---

were certain philosophical distinctions made as between divine attributes and divine nature; L&N 12.13, making no clear distinction between the two.

489. The Vulgate translates the words as *divinitas* in both Rom 1:20 and Col 2:9. Lightfoot attributes this "to the poverty of the [Latin] language" and notes that the word *deitas* was "coined at a later date to represent θεότης." Lightfoot, *St. Paul's Epistles*, 181–82. Thus, the Latin word *deitas* apparently only came into use after Jerome published the Vulgate, which had otherwise used the phrase *plenitudo divinitatis* in Col 2:9. See Nash, "Θειότης," 30.

490. McKnight, *Colossians*, 229n59.

491. Kinzig, *Faith in Formulae*, §215. The Latin translation renders the phrase as *consubstantialem patri secundum deitatem et consubstantialem nobis eundem secundum humanitatem*, thus using a form of *deitas* rather than *divinitas*.

492. Morgan, "Critical Study," 214–17, referring to the Latin formulation *vere Deus vere homo*.

"Godhead" or even "Divine Essence" could be permissible options as alternative translations of ἡ θεότης.

4. σωματικῶς

Again, language is pushed to its limits with the revelation in Col 2:9 that the entirety/fullness of the Godhead/Deity/Divine Essence "dwells bodily" in Christ. The verb κατοικεῖ is in the present tense. Christopher Rowland suggests that as used here it reflects certain Jewish sources that contemplate the "presence of the fullness of divinity in bodily form," and that there is in such thinking a "corporeal aspect of God" which Paul now sees "manifest[ed] ... in the risen and glorified Christ."[493] Others read the verse as a reference to Christ's bodily life while on earth.[494] As Lightfoot puts it, the adverb "is added to show that the Word, in whom the pleroma thus had its abode from all eternity, crowned His work by the Incarnation," drawing a comparison between Christ in John 1:1 as the Eternal Word and the statement in John 1:14 that ὁ λόγος σὰρξ ἐγένετο.[495] And the verse is strongly present by way of its effective history in the creeds and writings of the church fathers.[496] But as Jerry Sumney observes, there is no reason to take the verse to "specify one particular moment of Christ's existence; it refers to both the incarnation *and* the present, risen existence of Christ."[497]

If one therefore assumes that the word concerns some kind of bodily form in the both/and sense that God was enfleshed in the man Jesus, who died and yet took on a risen body that apparently allows him to ingest food, walk on a road, pass through walls, and in general not be bound by time or space, then in a way we have no words for this. As such, it may remain best—even if still mysterious—to translate the word using an adverbial form for "body." Here too the English translation

---

493. Rowland, "Apocalyptic Visions," 82n35 (citing Apoc. Ab. §10f).

494. Blackwell, "You Are Filled," 110–11; Bird, *Colossians*, 77.

495. Lightfoot, *St. Paul's Epistles*, 182.

496. Niceno-Constantinopolitan Creed; Chalcedonian Statement; Athanasian Creed, §9.29–37; Ambrose, *De fide*, 1.16 (*plenus e pleno*) (Fullness of Fullness); *Letter of Six Bishops to Paul of Samosat*, §8 (πᾶν τὸ πλήρωμα τῆς θεότητος σωματικῶς) (Kinzig, *Faith in Formulae*, §126); Irenaeus, *Adversus haereses* 1.26.1; 3.11.1. See also Hardy, *Christology*, 351: "The Word did tabernacle among us, and it is said that in Christ dwelt all the fullness of the Godhead bodily" (quoting Cyril of Alexandria, *Epistula tertia ad Nestorium*).

497. Sumney, *Colossians*, 133 (emphasis added).

tradition is relevant. Wycliffe translated it in Col 2:9 as "bodilich" (meaning body-like).⁴⁹⁸ One might also say "corporeally," providing a Latinate resonance with the Vulgate's *quia in ipso inhabitat omnis plenitudo divinitatis corporaliter*.⁴⁹⁹ Moreover, the Latinate form would be familiar to those who attend churches that still use the Tridentine Mass. They might therefore see in it a reference to the Mass' words of institution: *Hoc est corpus meum*. It is not the only option, of course, because the same sacramental intertextuality holds with "bodily," the reference being to English words of institution used in other traditions: "This is my body."⁵⁰⁰ It would therefore be hermeneutically appropriate to use words or cognates that variously bring to mind questions concerning such mysteries as the incarnation; the memorial meal; the real presence of Christ in the elements; the transformation/transubstantiation of those elements (or not); the resurrection; or Christ's being seated at the right hand of God.

5. οἱ θησαυροὶ τῆς σοφίας καὶ γνώσεως ἀπόκρυφοι

In Col 2:3, Paul identifies Christ as the locus of "all apocryphal treasures of wisdom and knowledge," a rebuttal to the idea that one might gain privileged access to such treasures through self-mortifying asceticism, ritual observances, and the like. Paul's appropriation of the word γνόσις thereby undermines erroneous usages of the word, including in the form of gnostic or proto-gnostic doctrines that might have been present in the Phrygian region.⁵⁰¹ In 1 Tim 6:20 as well, Paul expressly condemns the oppositions of "the vain babble and contrarian ways of so-called *gnosis*" (τῆς ψευδωνύμου γνώσεως). Paul should thus be understood to draw an explicit contrast between the true knowledge of God and distorted pretenses or, as in Col 2:8, "empty and deceitful philosophy."

---

498. The word is derived from the Old English *bodig* or *bodeg* and referred originally to the trunk or main portion of an animal frame (as opposed to the head or limbs). See *Bosworth-Toller Anglo-Saxon Dictionary*, s.v. "bodig," https://bosworthtoller.com/search?q=bodig. Lightfoot, *St. Paul's Epistles*, 182, would use "bodily-wise," but that is not really a word. Even so, his point is that Paul's language is careful: he is not saying "ἐν σώματι, for the Godhead cannot be confined to any limits of space." For Lightfoot, "bodily-wise" thus means "with a bodily manifestation."

499. See also Hilary of Poitiers, *Liber (II) ad Constantium Imperatorem* 11: *in quo habitat omnis plenitudo divinitatis corporaliter* (Kinzig, *Faith in Formulae*, §151e2).

500. E.g., Church of England, *Book of Common Prayer*, 156.

501. See Bultmann, "γνόσις," *TDNT* 1:689–714.

Paul also makes a relevant distinction here between γνῶσις and σοφία. Lightfoot, himself both a classicist and a theologian, suggests the following as a useful guideline:

> γνῶσις is simply intuitive, σοφία is ratiocinative also; γνῶσις applies chiefly to the apprehension of truths, σοφία superadds the power of reasoning about them and tracing their relations.[502]

Against that background, Paul vouchsafes Christ as the only source for true knowledge and wisdom, adverting to mysteries that had previously been "hidden"—apocryphal—but are now revealed in him. And 1 Cor 2:7 is to the same effect.[503] This provides some justification for using the word "apocryphal" in translating the verse to reflect the literal Greek while also alluding to usages in other sources.

iii. Negativizing Rhetoric

As explained in sect. II.d.iii, *supra*, ch. 1 of Colossians is dedicated to opening invocations and prayers, followed seamlessly in vv. 15–20 by one of the New Testament's most singularly hymnic passages, laced with terms having no direct counterpart in the visible world but instead evoking "things invisible." Having limned a strongly affirmative description of Christ's preexistent nature[504] together with his "preeminence in all things" (1:18), Paul shifts in ch. 2 of the letter to a more polemical tone. Here he restates as doctrine the spiritual experience conveyed via the hymn; and then applies that doctrine to combat those seen to be teaching and/or practicing a contrary understanding of who Christ is. It is useful therefore next to focus on the question whether this subsequent portion of the letter evinces an identifiable rhetorical register consistent with its

---

502. Lightfoot, *St. Paul's Epistles*, 174. He adds, contrasting these theological concepts with how they might be considered in Greek philosophy, that "in Aristotle *Eth. Nic.* i. 1 γνῶσις is opposed to πρᾶξις, [whereas in] St. Paul it is connected with the apprehension of eternal mysteries, 1 Cor. xiii. 2, εἰδῶ τὰ μυστήρια πάντα καὶ πᾶσαν τὴν γνῶσιν."

503. Λαλοῦμεν Θεοῦ σοφίαν ἐν μυστηρίῳ, τὴν ἀποκεκρυμμένην. There may also be an intrascriptural link to Isa 33:6 LXX: Ἐν νόμῳ παραδοθήσονται, ἐν θησαυροῖς ἡ σωτηρία ἡμῶν, ἐκεῖ σοφία καὶ ἐπιστήμη καὶ εὐσέβεια πρὸς τὸν κύριον· οὗτοί εἰσιν θησαυροὶ δικαιοσύνης. Cf. the noncanonical 2 Bar. 44:14 ("treasures of wisdom . . . and stores of insight") and 54:13 ("treasures of wisdom") (Charlesworth, *Old Testament Pseudepigrapha*, 2.634).

504. I.e., as the one "timelessly present with God and himself very God" (John 1:1).

substance as critique, and whether that has implications for translation. I do so again by focusing on key words and phrases.

1. ἡ πιθανολογία

After briefly restating that "all apocryphal treasures of wisdom and knowledge" are found in Christ (Col 2:3), Paul warns the Colossians ἵνα μηδεὶς ὑμᾶς παραλογίζηται ἐν πιθανολογίᾳ (2:4). The latter word is provocative. In classical Greek the word might simply mean arguments based on probability.[505] It is a compound word made up of πείθω, "to persuade" and λόγος, "word," thus meaning "to persuade by means of words." Πείθω itself carries no necessary opprobrium and is used to refer to Paul's own efforts to persuade people of the truth of the gospel.[506] Yet here the word is not used in a neutral sense but carries with it a sense of enticement or even deception.

Thus, while Paul does not expressly refer to the Sophists, there might well be an allusive sense in which the false σοφία of his opponents and/or of the syncretic mysticism he addresses call to mind the legacy of such orators as Protagoras, Gorgias, Isocrates, and others. To be sure, we have to speculate whether or to what extent Paul or his readers and listeners were familiar with classical texts,[507] but in this context Plato's attempt to distinguish "philosophy" from "sophistry" could have formed a background, however submerged in the language, to misleadingly persuasive speech. Thus, in the Sophist, the interlocutor Xenos/Stranger describes sophistry as a form of art that "bewitches" the young by exhibiting in words a distant "image" of true reality.[508] In that context, the Colossian persuaders might likewise be thought of as failing to present the true "image" of God, but only a "shadow" (2:17). All told, a translator should consider whether at the heart of Col 2:4 is the apostle's concern that certain people skilled in persuasive speech and adept at the use of rhetoric might have been leading the congregation into false doctrine. Although the compound word in question does not include a reference to σοφία, a

505. E.g., Plato, *Theaetetus* 162e.
506. E.g., Acts 18:4; 19:8; 26:28; 28:23.
507. Some have detected classical references in the letters, as in Titus 1:12 concerning the Cretans' propensity for lying, an assertion also found in an opening line of Callimachus' Hymn to Zeus (Callimachus himself quoting from a lost poem by Epimenides). Similarly, the comparison of the Cretans to "slow bellies" has a parallel in Hesiod's *Theogony* 26.
508. Plato, *Sophist* 243c.

translator might intertextually capture the pejorative sense of the phrase by using a term such as "sophistic persuasion."

2. ἡ φιλοσοφία

Paul's use of the word "philosophy" in Col 2:8 is another of the several *hapax legomena* in this letter.[509] Paul does not appear to use the term in a technical sense to refer to a particular philosophical school or practitioner. And the word does not even appear in any canonical and deuterocanonical materials. It is present in 4 Maccabees,[510] however, as a claim that Judaism legitimately promotes the "traditional ideals" of Greek philosophy.[511] And as far as more or less contemporary uses of the word (i.e., not long before or after Paul), Philo suggests that the Sabbath is suited for philosophical pursuits.[512] Josephus also describes three prevailing schools of Jewish thought—the Pharisees, Sadducees, and Essenes—as encompassing the φιλοσοφίαι of the Jews, outlining their tenets as such.[513] Nor were these the only writers using the language of contemporary philosophy to assert the rational power and coherence of Judaism.[514]

It seems clear, however, that the term is used pejoratively in the letter, even if not directed to a particular "school" of philosophy. Paul therefore warns the Colossians in Col 2:8 against those who would "captivate" them by "philosophy and vain deceit."[515] And Paul likewise distinguishes true Wisdom and Knowledge from the false ἐπίγνωσις or σοφία of the mystics/errorists, whose "knowledge" is οὐ κατὰ Χριστόν (2:8). One might therefore translate the phrase by using words that might refer to

---

509. Many in fact occur in this same chapter, arguably reflecting a rhetorical register: χειρόγραφον (2:14), ἀπεκδύομαι (2:15), νεομηνία (2:16), ἐμβατεύων (2:18), καταβραβεύω (2:18), δογματίζω (2:20), ἀπόχρησις (2:22), ἐθελοθρησκία (2:23), ἀφειδία (2:23), and πλησμονή (2:23).

510. Which is, however, canonical in the Orthodox Church.

511. DeMaris, *Colossian Controversy*, 48.

512. "Life of Moses II," 39, in Philo, *Works of Philo*, 215–16.

513. Josephus, *Jewish Antiquities* 18.1.2–5.

514. See, e.g., Charlesworth, *Old Testament Pseudepigrapha*, 1.477–606 (wisdom and philosophical literature); 775–919 (fragments of lost Judeo-Hellenistic works).

515. The word καταβραβευέτω is *hapax legomena* in the New Testament and may reasonably be translated as "disqualify." But it also has the overtone of deceit in the context of bribery of judges. See "καταβραβευέτω," LSJ 1:185.

3. ἀρχαί and ἐξουσίαι

As discussed above, in Col 1:16–18 Paul establishes Christ as prior to/first over all "thrones or dominions, principalities or powers," and thus "preeminent." As a counterpoint to Christ's lordship, Paul now focuses on the negative consequences of those who may be giving credence to subordinate powers, most likely in this instance spiritual beings rather than natural rulers. Thus, he writes in 2:15 that Christ "divest[ed] all sovereigns and dominions, exhibiting them boldly in his triumph over them." The doctrinal point concerns Christ's defeat of the devil, who held captive those "who all their lives had been in bondage through fear of death" (Heb 2:14–15). And it has an important intrascriptural analog in Dan 7, where the vision concerns the subjection of "all dominions" to God's kingdom and the rule of his saints.[517]

Paul arguably makes this point rhetorically through his use of the word θριαμβεύω in metaphorical reference to the Roman "triumph," a processional victory celebration whereby captives are paraded in open display. Indeed, by appropriating a compelling image of Roman imperialism, Paul linguistically contrasts Christ's kingdom with the lesser kingdom of Rome, "implicitly challeng[ing] an imperial ideology centered in military domination."[518] The Latin *triumphus* is derived from θρίαμβος, a Bacchian festal procession. There may thus also be a linguistic echo of pagan mysteries, consistent with Paul's assertion that Christ has defeated all false gods. This argues for adherence to a more literal rendering in order to preserve textual meaning.

Further elaborating on the description of the humiliation of those whom Christ led captive, Paul also uses the word ἀπεκδυσάμενος, which suggests stripping the captives naked.[519] This is the same verb used in Col 2:10–11 to affirm the Colossians' "completeness" in Christ ἐν τῇ ἀπεκδύσει τοῦ σώματος τῆς σαρκός. As such, there is a clear linguistic

---

516. Cf. Pascal, *Provincial Letters*.

517. Dan 7:27 LXX/Theodotian: πᾶσαι αἱ ἀρχαὶ αὐτῷ δουλεύσουσιν καὶ ὑπακούσονται. But see Wasserman, "Gentile Gods," 737, 741, taking a more benign view of such powers as "lower-level functionaries" in "the providential plan of history."

518. Maier, "Sly Civility," 325–26.

519. DeMaris, *Colossian Controversy*, 138: "exposing them to public ridicule."

contrast between the positive and the negative consequences of such a "stripping off." Paul's wording also resonates with the vivid image of Christ's own humiliation, where he was "divested," literally stripped of his clothes—καὶ ἐκδύσαντες αὐτὸν (Matt 27:29)—and further endured "the shame of the cross" (Heb 12:2). As such, Paul plays rhetorically on the imagery as he contrasts the humiliation of the defeated powers and principalities with Christ's humiliation, whose shame was not a defeat but victory.[520]

By emphasizing Christ's humiliation of the defeated powers, Paul fully negativizes proto-gnostic or mystical views that were circulating concerning such powers.[521] Without attempting exhaustively to review the range of contemporary mystical and/or proto-gnostic doctrines, it is sufficient to note that noncanonical literature is rife with schema concerning the names, forms, sequences, and hierarchies of the multiple "emanations" said to proceed from the infinite down to base matter.[522] While, as noted, textual meaning may not be fully captured if limited to its original context, historical-critical insights into that setting are not irrelevant, particularly in the absence of other sources. Translating the passage using rhetorical imagery resonant of contemporary literature and of the Roman polity would thus be hermeneutically appropriate.

4. τὰ στοιχεῖα τοῦ κόσμου

If there is one phrase in the letter that has led to the widest disagreement as far as meaning and translation, it is probably Col 2:8's τὰ στοιχεῖα τοῦ κόσμου.[523] Intrascripturally, the phrase also appears in Gal 4:3 and 4:9. Whether its usage in Galatians sheds light on its usage in Colossians, or whether it is used distinctly in each letter, is also a question. I will therefore discuss the varied options and suggest reasons a translator applying an effective history hermeneutic might choose one or the other.

---

520. See also 1 Cor 2:8 (referring not the natural rulers of this world but the fallen spirits animating them); cf. Dan 10:13; Zech 3:1–2.

521. DeMaris, *Colossian Controversy*, 137: "In this clarification of the hymn the letter writer casts the ἀρχαί and ἐξουσίαι in a decidedly negative role."

522. See, e.g., Lightfoot, *St. Paul's Epistles*, 152–54, cataloging the literature on thrones, powers, angels, archangels, cherubim, seraphim, potentates, levels of heavens, rulers, and dominions.

523. See Hincks, "Meaning of the Phrase," 183: "Perhaps no other New Testament expression has divided commentators so evenly."

The word τὰ στοιχεῖα has been given a wide range of meanings and presents various intrascriptural as well as intertextual considerations. There is philological evidence that the word refers in some contexts to individual "units," such as letters of the alphabet, syllables, musical notes, lines, points, or other basic constituents of the physical world. It may likewise refer to components of the heavens, such as stars or planets.[524] There is also evidence that it was used, at least before the second century, to refer to the so-called four elements of the world—earth, air, water, and fire.[525] Philo of Alexandria, writing in the first century BC, also theorized an equilibrium of the "elements of the world."[526] He further "speaks of the seasons, of equinox in spring and autumn" as consistent with the proportionality of "the four elements."[527] And the late first-century AD philosopher Plutarch, while writing after Paul's death, described the Pythagorean philosopher Empedocles as having linked the "four elements [of] fire, earth, water, and air" to the changes of the seasons.[528] Based on such philological and literary evidence, the στοιχεῖα probably had something to do with the natural world.

Even so, some scholars detect a reference to "personal supernatural forces" and see the expression as "reflecting a common Hellenistic and Jewish view that angels were set over the four elements, the planets, and the stars."[529] It is unclear, however, the extent to which an association of spirits with celestial bodies had emerged by the time of the Letter to the Colossians, at least in terms of making them objects of worship.[530] But

---

524. Gerhard Delling, "στοιχεῖον," *TDNT* 7:670–87. See also Schweizer, "Slaves," 455; DeMaris, *Colossian Controversy*, 52.

525. This may be the way the word is used in Wis 7:17; 19:18; 4 Macc 12:13. See also Schweizer, "Slaves," 459 (also citing Ovid's *Metamorphoses*). It is less clear that this is how the word is used in 2 Pet 3:10, 12, where the reference to "the elements melting with fervent heat" at the day of the Lord need not be based on a particular theory of the constituent components of the visible world. Rather, it seems to refer there to the entire created universe, more or less "everything," an interpretation supported by "the Stoic idea of a cosmic conflagration in which the other elements will dissolve into the primal element of fire." Delling, "στοιχεῖον," *TDNT* 7:686.

526. "On the Eternity of the World," 21, in Philo, *Works of Philo*, 109–11. See also Schweizer, "Slaves," 459.

527. Schweizer, "Slaves," 460.

528. Schweizer, "Slaves," 462; cf. 1 En. 75:3: "signs, periods, years and days."

529. Arnold, "Returning to the Domain," 56, 56n5 (citing numerous sources).

530. DeMaris, *Colossian Controversy*, 52; Easton, "Pauline Theology," 360–61; but see Deut 4:19, warning the people not to be "drawn off" to worship and serve "the sun and the moon and the stars, even all the host of heaven."

such an understanding does account for those versions in the English translation tradition that render the phrase as "elemental spirits," "spiritual principles," or "elemental principles," rather than simply "elements" or "principles."[531] These readings find the key to meaning in the adjectival form "elemental" as a modifier of "spirits/principles/powers." Others take the opposite position, translating the word as a plural noun, whether "elements" or "rudiments."[532]

It therefore seems that neither philological and literary research nor the English translation tradition provides a clear answer. It may be that a broader literary and cultural context is of assistance. Various scholars in fact perceive a reference to "angels and demons," by analogy to the "powers and principalities" of Col 2:15 and/or Eph 6:12.[533] Hart, for example, renders the phrase as "the Elementals of the cosmos."[534] Now, the word "elementals" is highly obscure and Hart's capitalization of the word suggests that he may be referring (of all things) to medieval alchemical works describing four mythical beings known as gnomes, undines, sylphs, and salamanders, each corresponding to the more traditional four "elements" of earth, water, air, and fire, respectively.[535] I warrant that virtually no one reading Hart's translation would recognize that reference, apart perhaps from modern practitioners of the occult (Wiccans and the like),[536] or readers of the eponymous Marvel comic book series, featuring Hydron as lord of the waters, Magnum as master of the earth, Hellfire as wielder of flame, and Zephyr as mistress of the winds.[537] Notwithstanding Hart's unusual use of the term in this context, he justifies it "as a plausible reading

---

531. See, e.g., "elemental spiritual forces of this world" (NIV); "basic principles of this world" (NIV alternative option); "basic principles of the world" (NKJV); "elemental spirits of the world" (ESV); "elemental principles of the world" (ESV alternative option); "ruling spirits of the universe" (GN); "elemental spirits of the universe" (NEB); "elementary ideas belonging to this world" (NEB alternative option); "spiritual powers of this world" (NLT); "spiritual principles of this world" (NLT alternative option); "elemental spirits of the universe" (RSV). See also L&N 12.43: "the supernatural powers . . . having control over the events of this world" (citing Col 2:20).

532. See, e.g., "elements of the world" (WYC); "elements of the natural world" (NEB); "rudiments of the world" (KJV); "rudiments of the world" (ASV); "rudiments of the world" (alternative option RSV).

533. Arnold, "Returning to the Domain."

534. Hart, *New Testament*, 399.

535. See "Elemental"; see also Rastell, "New Interlude."

536. See Chauran, "Understanding Elementals."

537. See Marvel Database, "Elementals."

within the larger context of the Pauline theology of this age and the Age to come, and of Christ's conquest of the 'principalities and powers.'"[538]

In contrast, other interpreters see the phrase as a reference to ritual laws or other guidelines that might have been followed by people before coming to faith.[539] Despite all these possibilities, Frank Thielman reaches the bland conclusion that "the attested meaning of στοιχεῖα as the stuff of which the world is composed suggests that the most probable meaning of its occurrence in Galatians [and presumably also Colossians] is simply 'the world.'"[540] A number of the translations cited here do use "the world" or "this world" or "the natural world" in translating τοῦ κόσμου, consistent with Thielman's analysis. Yet oddly enough, no translation of which I am aware employs the easily transliterated form "cosmos."

Given the above uncertainties, a better understanding of τοῦ κόσμου seems necessary in construing just what "elements" are at issue. Clinton Arnold, for example, argues that there was "a common Hellenistic and Jewish view that angels were set over the four elements, the planets, and the stars."[541] And he suggests that the phrase "principalities and powers" used elsewhere in Paul's writing, including within Colossians, is a reference to those spirits, albeit as fallen (demonic) angels rather than obedient.[542] Yet the scholarly evidence seems clear that usage of the term to refer to angels or demons postdates Colossians.[543] Moreover, if that were the reference, we would expect such "elements" to be identified and/or listed with the "principalities and powers" of Col 1:16 and 2:15. But they are not. Moreover, the sources Arnold relies on are curious ones, such as a "Jewish magical document" called the Testament of Solomon.[544] For one thing, while that text does refer to spirits summoned by Solomon

---

538. Hart, *New Testament*, 399. I do not suggest that Dr. Hart's is a "wrong" translation, but it is peculiar. And then there is the bizarre argument of the late Anglican scholar Burton Easton to the effect that the curse referred to in Gal 3:13 was "a curse from the Stoicheia," whom he identified as the angels who mediated the Israelites' reception of the law and thereby "attached a curse to crucifixion, and when Christ was crucified . . . hurled it at his head." Easton, "Pauline Theology," 364–65.

539. Kruger, "Law and Promise," 321, analogizing to the "laws" followed by gentiles before inclusion through the gospel (citing Rom 2:14–15, 26–27).

540. Thielman, *From Plight to Solution*, 82.

541. Arnold, "Returning to the Domain," 56 (citing authorities). See also Bockmuehl, Review of *Cosmic Christology*, 442.

542. Arnold, "Returning to the Domain," 57.

543. See Delling, "στοιχεῖον," *TDNT* 7:684n100.

544. Arnold, "Returning to the Domain," 58.

who identify themselves with the "elements, world rulers of the darkness," the late dating of the work makes it a dubious source for any usage in Colossians.⁵⁴⁵

Where does this leave us, then, from a methodological perspective? Here the textual context itself may help. Immediately following this phrase Paul adds that those who pursue whatever the "elements of the world" are do so οὐ κατὰ Χριστόν—"not in accordance with Christ." There seems only one fair reading of this phrase, and that is that observance of the "elements of this world" is contrary to the exercise of faith. It is a reliance on things seen, rather than unseen. As such, there is a compelling canonical/intrascriptural relationship to Paul's urging the Colossians not to "let anyone take you to task for what you eat or what you drink or how you deal with feast days or new moons or Sabbaths, all of which are a shadow of things to come" (Col 2:16–17), but rather to rest in their "fulfillment" in him by faith (2:10).⁵⁴⁶

Read this way, Paul's focus seems to be on the "graven decrees that stood in hostility against us," whose violation and trespass led to death, yet which by forgiveness he "cancelled" when he "nail[ed]" them to the cross" (Col 2:14). And it follows that the "elements" in question were likely the Mosaic purity laws, perhaps in their expanded halakic form, as now being urged on or at least practiced by the Colossians (much as appeared to be the situation with the Galatians).⁵⁴⁷ Wesley Carr nevertheless puts forward a novel alternative interpretation to the effect that the reference is to certain "penitential *stelai*" that were common in the Asian District during that period and recorded individual confessions of wrongdoing graven in stone.⁵⁴⁸ This has the attraction of a more literal reading of the word "handwriting," χειρόγραφον, in 2:14. But if one were to focus on commands graven in stone, the transgression of which would be "against us," then the tablets of Moses would be a more likely allusion. And to the extent such transgressions were understood to be recorded in

---

545. DeMaris, *Colossian Controversy*, 80, indicating a likely late third-century date and otherwise noting proposed possible ranges from AD 100 to 400.

546. Hincks, "Meaning of the Phrase," 189; Vergeer, "Σκιά and Σῶμα," 384–85.

547. McKnight, *Letter to the Colossians*, 228 (suggesting these are "a clever reference to *diaspora-framed Jewish halakic practices understood now as having spiritual force contrary to the will of God*" [emphasis in original]); Gorday and Oden, *Colossians*, 29 ("'Elements of the world' are the observation of cultic days" [quoting Theodoret of Cyr, *Interpretation of the Letter to the Colossians*]); J. Dunn, "Colossian Philosophy," 163–64 (same).

548. Carr, "Two Notes on Colossians," 493–96.

"books" in heaven, Paul's imagery of the same being "blotted out" (KJV) is all the more vivid.[549]

Given the likely presence within the Colossian congregation of both Jews and gentiles, it seems reasonable to suggest that the "errors" or the "philosophy" that concerned Paul were less due to pagan or outside influences than to rituals and practices to which at least some of the Colossians were accustomed, and which were now influencing the whole community.[550] Thus in Col 2:20–22 Paul expressly describes them as purity and food ordinances that had been cancelled:

> So why, if you died with Christ to childish things do you still subject yourselves to man-made dogmas as though living worldly lives—"don't handle, don't taste, don't touch"—all concerning foods that perish in the eating? These are but human commandments and teachings.

All these are, in a very literal sense, "worldly," "earthly," or "mundane" rituals.

A final question that might be considered in applying a canonical hermeneutic is whether any intrascriptural usage in Galatians changes the analysis. As noted, it is an open question whether one letter has a literary dependence on the other.[551] But in both letters, Paul takes issue with any suggestion that a believer's completeness before God depends on observance of laws, rituals or other practices, regardless of whether the same arise out of the law of Moses,[552] halakic rules, ascetic principles,[553] or some combination of sources.[554] As such, Paul's rebuke of the Galatians in Gal 4:9–10 concerning their "reverting" to such "elements" by observing "solemn days, new moons, festal seasons and sabbatical years" is of a piece with his injunction to the Colossians not to let themselves be beguiled out of their reward by those would subject them to

---

549. See Rev 20:12 (ἐκρίθησαν οἱ νεκροὶ ἐκ τῶν γεγραμμένων ἐν τοῖς βιβλίοις κατὰ τὰ ἔργα αὐτῶν); Dan 7:10 LXX/Theodotion (βίβλοι ἠνεῴχθησαν). See Apoc. Zeph. 3:6–9.

550. Patristic understanding may also be helpful as part of the text's effective history. Thus, both John Chrysostom (349–407) and Ambrosiaster (believed to have written between 366 and 384) interpreted τὰ στοιχεῖα τοῦ κόσμου this way in their respective commentaries on Galatians. See McKnight, *Letter to the Colossians*, 25; Thornton, "Jewish New Moon Festivals," 99.

551. See the discussion in sect. II.d.ii, *supra*. See also Schweizer, "Slaves," 455.

552. As argued forcefully in J. Dunn, "Colossian Philosophy."

553. As argued with similar vigor in Sumney, "Those Who 'Pass Judgment.'"

554. As concluded in DeMaris, *Colossian Controversy*.

body-denying practices or (as in v. 20) to "mundane rituals."⁵⁵⁵ All of these are forms of worship that comprised "elements" of the law's guidance towards Christ (Gal 3:24), but may also have been part and parcel of Pythagorean soul-purifying rituals.⁵⁵⁶ Either way, τὰ στοιχεῖα τοῦ κόσμου should be translated from a methodological point of view not merely as the "stuff" of which the world is made, as Thielman suggests, but to evoke rituals or practices dependent on seasons, natural phenomena, or celestial movements.

5. The False πλήρωμα

As analyzed above, Paul's use of the word τό πλήρωμα is central to his hymnic presentation of Christ. The "fullness" of which he speaks in Col 1:19 and again in Col 2:9 is unique to Christ. It is "all the fullness" of the Godhead, the essence of Christ's preeminence over all things. But it is worth noting that these passages *also* function rhetorically to distinguish the true fullness of God from a "false fullness," i.e., a usage of the term in the gnostic sense of "the All."⁵⁵⁷ Without attempting fully to survey the various sources, it at least appears from materials unearthed at Nag Hammadi that a number of gnostic sources describe multiple "pleromas," effectively "emanations of the Father" and therefore lesser beings or states of being.⁵⁵⁸ The "gnostic pleroma," if we can refer to it this way, is subject to diminution as it is continuously "distributed, diluted, transformed and darkened by foreign admixture" with matter in its "descent through successive evolutions."⁵⁵⁹ The result is not a completeness at all but an

---

555. The Vulgate renders τὰ στοιχεῖα τοῦ κόσμου as *elementa mundi*, which would thus provide translation tradition support for using the word "mundane" in Col 2:20. It is also etymologically appropriate: the word first appears in English in the mid-fifteenth century as a derivation from the Middle English *mondeyne*, Anglo-French *mundain*, Late Latin *mundanus*, and ultimately the Latin *mundus*. *Merriam-Webster*, s.v. "mundane."

556. Schweizer, "Slaves," 465. And Thornton, "Jewish New Moon Festivals," 100, makes the interesting point that gentile Christians who might now be drawn to include in their worship practices "in observance of the Jewish Calendar . . . would (in an age where the boundaries between astronomy, astrology, and the worship of heavenly bodies were unclear and easily crossed) be reverting to something akin to their previous paganism."

557. Lightfoot, *St. Paul's Epistles*, 257–73.

558. Evans, "Meaning of πλήρωμα," 261.

559. Lightfoot, *St. Paul's Epistles*, 102.

ὑστέρημα, that is, a "deficiency."⁵⁶⁰ Contrast this with Paul's insistence on the absolute fullness of the Godhead abiding in Christ, who is not a changeable manifestation of God but the full embodiment of Deity.

Again, Paul urges in Col 2:8 that the "fullness" that the "errorists" seek is not "in keeping with Christ."⁵⁶¹ Given that the "false use" of πλήρωμα might be known to the Colossians from existing Jewish sources and/or possible proto-gnostic teachers or sects in the Asian District, Paul's appropriation of the term for his own purpose in describing a fullness that was entirely contrary to those beliefs has a negativizing rhetorical function in revealing the emptiness of the latter. It would thus be relevant to note certain relevant sources in order to provide a reader with contextual information.

6. ἐν ταπεινοφροσύνῃ καὶ θρησκείᾳ τῶν ἀγγέλων

Colossians 2:16–23 are key verses concerning the essence of what Paul's opponents were teaching—in other words, the "Colossian philosophy." As we saw in assessing Paul's warnings concerning τὰ στοιχεῖα τοῦ κόσμου, here he urges the Colossians not to be seduced by such practices as the "worship of angels" (2:18), avoidance of certain kinds of food or drink (2:21), self-abasing ascetic practices (2:23), and/or calendrical observance of particularized festivals (2:17). The reference to ταπεινοφροσύνην, humility, in this context suggests a distortion of the Christian virtue of humility that is elsewhere encouraged with the same word (3:12).

There is in fact no indication that the ascetic/bodily-mortifying practices at issue here were congruent with the dietary and other practices in the law of Moses. To be sure, there are myriad instructions in the law concerning dietary restrictions as well as feast days.⁵⁶² But these are not critiqued in the New Testament as such, being elements of the Mosaic covenant and thus "holy, righteous, and good."⁵⁶³ In contrast, the dietary and other restrictions practiced by mystery and other sects then present in the Lycus Valley of the first century are what appear to have been the source of Paul's concerns. For example, "initiation into the Isis cult involved a ten-day preparation period in which there were food and drink

---

560. Lightfoot, *St. Paul's Epistles*, 269.
561. Sumney, "Those Who 'Pass Judgment,'" 382.
562. E.g., Lev 11:1–47; Hos 2:12; 1 Chron 23:31; 2 Chron 2:3; 31:3.
563. Rom 7:12.

regulations."⁵⁶⁴ Hence the general sense in the letter that Paul may have been addressing a broader risk of syncretism among the Colossians.⁵⁶⁵

Whether such practices were purportedly advocated within a Mosaic framework or not,⁵⁶⁶ Paul takes aim at the specific temptation faced by the Colossians, i.e., that they were being urged into a form of ascetic abasement or self-mortification with the possible goal of glimpsing some form of alleged heavenly or angelic vision. And the particular phrase ἐν ταπεινοφροσύνῃ καὶ θρησκείᾳ τῶν ἀγγέλων, ἃ ἑόρακεν ἐμβατεύων in Col 2:18 has simply bedeviled commentators, with a resulting impact on translation. They continue to be split whether to express θρησκείᾳ τῶν ἀγγέλων as worship directed *towards* angels (objective genitive), or as worship engaged in *by* angels (subjective genitive); and whether the relative clause ἃ ἑόρακεν ἐμβατεύων refers to a vision or sight of angels in heaven engaged in such worship, or to something seen during initiation rites, or to something else perceived by close scrutiny.

The literal Greek of the text doesn't answer the question, because the grammar admittedly allows for multiple readings.⁵⁶⁷ One question is whether the persons engaged in various forms of ἐθελοθρησκία, or "self-imposed asceticism," (i) are *themselves* engaged in worshipping angels, or (ii) are seeking to be caught up to heavenly places where they might have a vision of *angels* engaged in the worship of God.⁵⁶⁸ Reading the entire set of verses *in pari materia*, however, what seems to be of concern is that some people—whether Jewish members of the local church who are maintaining certain practices as part of their understanding of

---

564. Sumney, *Colossians*, 150 (citing Apuleius, *Metamorphosis* 9.23, 28, 30).

565. See, e.g., Lightfoot, *St. Paul's Epistles*, 73–113 (mixture of Gnosticism and Judaism); Bruce, *Epistles to the Colossians*, 199–200 (same); W. Barclay, *Letters to the Philippians*, 94–99 (same).

566. See, e.g., Lohse, *Commentary on the Epistles*, 129 (pre-gnostic); Sumney, "Those Who 'Pass Judgment'" (forms of Judaism); J. Dunn, "Colossian Philosophy," 179 (same); Sokupa, "Calendric Elements," 186 (same); McKnight, *Letter to the Colossians*, 271–72 ("halakic mystics").

567. See DeMaris, *Colossian Controversy*, 64–65 (proposing several); Francis, "Humility and Angel Worship," 163: "The interpretation of nearly every word or phrase [in the passage] has been disputed"); but recognizing that a "noun joined to θρησκείᾳ in a genitive construction is most commonly the object of the verbal idea" (180).

568. Compare, e.g., Francis, "Humility and Angel Worship," 168–70, 176–77, with Lyonnet, "Paul's Adversaries," 150–52; Evans, "Colossian Mystics," 196–97; Schweizer, "Slaves," 465n39; Sumney, *Colossians*, 154–55; Rowland, "Apocalyptic Visions," 74–77. See also Beetham, *Echoes of Scripture*, 203–5 (compiling authorities); DeMaris, *Colossian Controversy*, 58–63 (same).

required worship; or Judaizers of the sort referred to in Galatians; or Jewish mystics related to the Essene sect; or gentiles importing proto-gnostic angelologies; or some syncretic blend of the foregoing—are judging/disqualifying other members of the congregation for failing to engage in ascetic practices and/or failing to abase themselves in some form of visionary or experiential "worship of angels."

That such practices did exist at the time seems clear from historical-critical research; and James Dunn notes that "there is some evidence for the worship of angels in Asia Minor."[569] With respect to the relative clause in Col 2:18 referring to that which such persons have seen while "treading the void of mystical sights," the essence of the practice does seem to relate to something "visionary."[570] But whatever is "entered into" and however that may occur is distinct from the kind of "lawful" vision that Paul himself had (Acts 16:9), that Peter had (Acts 10), or that is otherwise within the range of charismatic gifts displayed in the church (1 Cor 12).

For translation purposes, of course, one must choose. In this instance the choice seems to require taking a theological position, given the range of permissible grammatical and sociohistorical readings. If viewed from a canonical perspective, there is good reason to understand the phrase as an objective genitive because as such it alludes to pagan practices condemned throughout the Scriptures in the form of the idolatrous worship of created objects and beings, whether animate or inanimate, earthly, or spiritual.[571] The pejorative references to "humility" are thus of a self-abasing sort. Further, the relative clause of Col 2:18, which might be translated to reference "that which they have seen upon entering/entering into that which they have seen," should be read in harmony with such forms of angel worship (which might even include the unwitting worship of *fallen* angels). In other words, if the principal phrase is read as an objective genitive, then the

---

569. J. Dunn, "Colossian Philosophy," 172. See also Gorday, *Colossians*, 39: "Those who defend the law lead persons to worship angels, since they say that the law was given through them" (quoting Theodoret of Cyr, *Interpretation of the Letter to the Colossians*). Note that Plutarch, writing a short generation after Paul, cites Paul's use in Colossians of "*threskeuein*, as though from *thressa*, a Thracian woman," in commenting on Alexander the Great's Samothracian mother Olympias' participation in "the wild worship of Bacchus." He finds the word "to have been derived [from such practices], as a special term for superfluous and over-curious forms of adoration." Plutarchus, *Plutarch's Lives*, 4:160–61.

570. Bird, *Colossians*, 86–87.

571. See, e.g., Deut 4:19; 17:3; Jer 8:2; 19:13; Zeph 1:5. See also Rom 1:21–25.

relative clause should modify the angel worshipper in a way that relates to his having entered a false spiritual realm.[572]

Here the temptation would be to worship created beings who, exalted spirits though they may be, are nevertheless inferior to the Creator. And Paul's condemnation of such a practice (rather than the alternate reading that construes the passage as condemning those who seek to imitate the worship practices of angels observed by them in some sort of trance-like or visionary state) is thus fully in accord with the condemnation throughout the LXX of the idolatrous worship of "the host of heaven."[573] It would therefore be reasonable to render the passage in a way that brings out the canonical consistency of the verse, making it clear that the practice being condemned would be one engaged in, rather than seen by, the believer. One such version might therefore be "Do not let anyone cheat you of your prize by insisting you abase yourselves in pompous worship of angels—such a person is suffused with vanity in his carnal mind, treading the void of mystical sights."

f. The Translation Tradition

In translating a New Testament text, it is essential to examine not only its philological, sociohistorical, and credal/liturgical aspects, but also prior translations made within the continuum of history of which the translator himself is a participant.[574] As N. T. Wright explains, "The meaning of a text is in practice deeply intertwined with its own tradition of hearing and heeding, interpretation and performance."[575] Previous versions are therefore essential to a translator's *wirkungsgeschichtliches Bewußtsein*—his consciousness of his own "being affected by history,"[576] because if and

---

572. Lyonnet, "Paul's Adversaries," 156n12, suggests that the sense of the phrase is "to cross a threshold, especially of a sacred place" and "to tread on (sacred) soil." He also relates an alternative proposed translation of the relevant phrase as "riding in the clouds." Cf. Aristophanes, *Nubes* 224-25: ἀεροβατῶ καὶ περιφρονῶ τὸν ἥλιον.

573. Such warnings were also present in noncanonical works of first-century Judaism. See, e.g., Apoc. Zeph. 6:15; Apoc. Ab. 17:2; Mart. Ascen. Isa. 7:21; and LAE (a.k.a. Apoc. Mos.) 13-15. See also A. Williams, "Cult of the Angels," 429-32, surveying a range of Talmudic and other Jewish texts condemning such worship as "a purely heathen practice."

574. See Gadamer, *Truth and Method*, 290-91.

575. Wright, "Reading Paul," 65.

576. Gadamer, *Truth and Method*, 301; Gadamer, *Gadamer Reader*, 59 ("consciousness of history being always at work in consciousness"); Gadamer, *Beginning of*

to the extent they have been widely received, they may embody critically important expressions of the text's "inner word."

In other words, just as doctrinal and liturgical materials are elements of the text's verbally incarnate history, so too are its prior expressions in a given receptor language. As such, together they are formative of a contemporary translator's horizon. And, as explained herein, these expressions may themselves both shape and be shaped by dogma. This might be the case, for example, with respect to the varied ways one might translate phrases such as πιστίς Χριστοῦ, or theologically freighted words like ἱλαστήριον. Once the text is rendered into a given language, its translated form may import as well as influence theological understandings. And where there is a strong continuity of words and phrases, they provide a linguistic reference point for any future translation.[577]

As a further step in testing the viability of a canonical-hermeneutical methodology, I will therefore focus for exemplary purposes on traditional as well as nontraditional ways the Colossian Hymn has been translated into English. I use this passage as a "test case within a test case" because its Christology goes to the *verbum cordis* of the letter—i.e., who is Christ? In that connection, the Hymn presents translators with a number of options, including how one might employ the kind of analysis undertaken above with respect to the philological and sociohistorical aspects of particular words and phrases; intrascriptural references or allusions; doctrinal/conciliar formulations; rhetorically poetic/transporting/elevated language; and various formal aspects such as capitalization, italics, strophic formatting, and *nomina sacra*.

Colossians, as with other biblical texts, has of course been translated into myriad languages. As relevant here, the English translation tradition begins with John Wycliffe's fourteenth-century translation into Middle English of Jerome's late fourth-century Latin Vulgate. Jerome's version thus remains highly relevant as the source for Wycliffe's Latinate renderings. The next major development was William Tyndale's sixteenth-century translation from the Greek, where much of Wycliffe's forms continue to shine through. Thereafter, the seventeenth-century King

---

Philosophy, 28 ("insofar as we are historical creatures, we are always on the inside of the history we are striving to comprehend").

577. Stuhlmacher, *Historical Criticism*, 89: "The biblical texts can be fully interpreted only" through "genuine dialogue with the tradition of the text and . . . an awareness of the history of the text's interpretation and effects which determines it." Note that this is the opposite of what the application of a purely historical-critical translation theory would suggest.

James translators added scholarly input and further refinement, yet now with some 70 percent of Tyndale's wording retained in the Old Testament and over 80 percent in the New. I therefore start by tracing the Wycliffe/Tyndale/King James translation tradition to date in order to assess its effective history over the past seven hundred years, first grounding it in elements of the Vulgate.

i. The WYC/TYN/KJV Tradition and Its Continuity

1. Jerome

In the late fourth century and at the instance of Pope Damasus I, Jerome of Stridon undertook a Latin translation of the entire Bible, working from the Hebrew for the Old Testament and the Greek for the New.[578] To the extent he evinced a translation theory, it can be gleaned from his *Letter to Pammachius* concerning criticisms leveled at him for his allegedly free approach. In the course of defending his work, Jerome noted the general value of rendering texts on a "sense for sense" basis, avoiding overemphasis on "words and syllables" lest one lose "the meaning of doctrine."[579] At the same time, he stressed that "even the order of the words is a mystery" in the Holy Scriptures,[580] suggesting that the literal text remains important in order to safeguard against unconstrained paraphrasing.

To be sure, what Jerome meant concerning the "mystery" of word order in the Scriptures is not entirely free from doubt or disagreement.[581] At a minimum, however, he indicates that Scripture, unlike secular prose, has the special character of inspired expression; and that because what is expressed is understood to be a divine communication, the form in which that expression was first presented (whether in Hebrew or Greek) should be carefully respected.[582] Jerome's literal yet also sense-for-sense approach allows for doctrinal truths to be "revealed in th[e] syntax" yet "paraphrastically" expressed.[583] Indeed, if the formal language of the text were itself sacrosanct, it is hard to see how *any* translation could effectively

---

578. Jerome's translation also involved refinements to the Old Latin version.
579. Jerome, *Letter to Pammachius* 7.
580. Jerome, *Letter to Pammachius* 5.
581. Venuti, *Translation Studies Reader*, 490–92.
582. See Marlowe, "Literal Character."
583. Venuti, *Translation Studies Reader*, 498 (quoting Gadamer, *Truth and Method*, 384).

allow the reader to access the inner spiritual message.[584] I therefore understand Jerome to call for a translator to be sensitive to possible "mysteries" embodied in the words themselves, while being equally focused on the doctrinal substance to be expressed.

Against that background, this is Jerome's rendering of the passage in question:[585]

15 qui est imago Dei invisibilis primogenitus omnis creaturae
16 quia in ipso condita sunt universa in caelis et in terra visibilia et invisibilia sive throni sive dominationes sive principatus sive potestates omnia per ipsum et in ipso creata sunt
17 et ipse est ante omnes et omnia in ipso constant
18 et ipse est caput corporis ecclesiae qui est principium primogenitus ex mortuis ut sit in omnibus ipse primatum tenens
19 quia in ipso conplacuit omnem plenitudinem habitare
20 et per eum reconciliare omnia in ipsum pacificans per sanguinem crucis eius sive quae in terris sive quae in caelis sunt

As discussed herein, a number of Jerome's formulations acquired a "classical" status when rendered into derivative forms in English, thus becoming the effective source for myriad doctrinal expressions, scholarly research, liturgical formulations, literary references, and even elements of musical composition.[586] And his wordings have thus performed a critical "language-shaping" function in our own culture.[587] Taken as a whole, Jerome's language and the embedded meanings it has acquired over time thereby comprise core elements of any English translator's "horizon," including as the same continue in the translation tradition described below.

---

584. Cf. Nichols, "Translating the Bible," 27, noting Islam's apparent position that, strictly speaking, the Koran is "untranslatable."

585. Jerome did not include verse numbers in his translation, and verse numbers did not appear in any biblical text until the middle of the sixteenth century. Noble, *Wycliffe's New Testament*, xii. Numbering is therefore added for ease of comparison with other versions.

586. See Plater and White, *Grammar of Vulgate*, 9n1, 54–64, identifying the extensive range of theological "words which we owe to Christian Latin," such as those derived from *creatio, deitas, divinitas, humilitas, redemptor, regeneratio, sacramenteum, passio, salvatio, justificatio, testamentum, lex, verbum, voluntas, discipulus,* and *compassio*.

587. See Felber, "Moratorium," 216 (quoting Felber, "Bibelübersetzung," 199).

2. Wycliffe

The fourteenth-century Oxford scholar John Wycliffe was the first to translate the Bible into the English of his day, assisted by his secretary John Purvey.[588] He worked from the Latin Vulgate, as his only available text. His initial version—referred to as the "Early Version"—was handprinted around 1382 (this being some fifty years prior to Johannes Gutenberg's invention of movable type). He undertook the translation out of a concern that by restricting presentation of the Scriptures to Latin, a language foreign to nearly the entirety of English society beyond the clergy and the privileged, the church was frustrating the power of the Word. He opined that "the Scriptures are the property of the people and one which no party should be allowed to wrest from them."[589]

Whether it was Wycliffe's translation into the vernacular, or his holding of certain controversial doctrines that were problematic for the authorities at Oxford, he was sacked soon after its printing, dying two years later in 1384.[590] Thereafter, Purvey undertook revisions of the work, first in 1388 and then more comprehensively in 1395 (the "Later Version"). The translation found wide distribution, as evidenced by the fact that despite numerous copies being confiscated and burned, at least 150 manuscripts were available in the mid-nineteenth century, providing the basis for a definitive edition.[591]

As explained above, a key argument in favor of a canonical-hermeneutical translation methodology is that the biblical text-in-translation itself has a continuing impact on subsequent renderings and interpretations by way of its *Wirkungsgeschichte*. I start by highlighting in yellow those words that are plainly derived from Latin (including those in turn derived from Greek), as a way to begin tracing the effective history of Jerome's Vulgate on Wycliffe and Wycliffe's on further translations.

---

588. The Venerable Bede (AD 672–735) started to translate John's Gospel from the Vulgate into Old English and apparently got "as far as the words, 'But what are they among so many,' etc. [John vi.9]" before dying. Giles, *Venerable Bede's*, xx. Yet nothing remains beyond that fragment.

589. Noble, *Wycliffe's New Testament*, v. See also H. Kelly, "Bible Translation," discussing late medieval controversies in England over translations into the vernacular.

590. The pre-Reformation Roman Church maintained its condemnation of him even after his death. See "Session 8—4 May, 1415," in Council Fathers, "Council of Constance": "This holy synod . . . decrees that the said John Wyclif was a notorious and obstinate heretic who died in heresy, and it anathematises him and condemns his memory."

591. Forshall and Madden, *Holy Bible*, xxxii–xxxiii.

Wycliffe's translation of Col 1:15–20 reads as follows:

15 Which is the ymage of God vnuysible, the first bigetun of ech creature.
16 For in hym alle thingis ben maad, in heuenes and in erthe, visible and vnuysible, ether trones, ether dominaciouns, ether princehodes, ethir poweris, alle thingis ben maad of nouyt bi hym, and in hym,
17 and he is bifor alle, and alle thingis ben in hym.
18 And he is heed of the bodi of the chirche;[592] which is the bigynnyng and the firste bigetun of deede men, that he holde the firste dignyte in alle thingis.
19 For in hym it pleside al plente[593] to inhabite,
20 and bi hym alle thingis to be recounselid in to hym, and made pees bi the blood of his cros, tho thingis that ben in erthis, ether that ben in heuenes.

It will become clear that Wycliffe's phrasings and vocabulary continue to have a dominant influence on English translations, notwithstanding that he translated the text from a Latin translation of the Greek, while others translated from the Greek itself. And the continuity of the English translation tradition lineage from Wycliffe is certainly not limited to this one example from Colossians. Just compare his version of the Lord's Prayer in Matt 6:9–13 with the familiar language of the KJV (setting aside obsolete letters such as ꝫ for g and obsolete spellings):

> Oure fadir that art in heuenes,
> halewid be thi name;
> thi kingdoom come to;
> be thi will don in erthe
> as it is in heuene;
> ꝫyue to vs this dai
> oure ech dayes breed;
> and forꝫyue to vs oure dettis,
> as we forꝫyuen to oure dettouris;
> and lede vs not in to temptacioun,
> but delyuere vs fro yuel. Amen.

---

592. It is possible that "chirche/church" is derived from Late Greek κυριακόν, meaning the Lord's house, but if so then it is not via Jerome's Latin, which uses the Greek-derived *ecclesia*. The Middle English "chirche" is more likely derived from Old English via Old German.

593. Changed to "fulnesse" in the 1388 version. See *OED*, s.v. "pleroma."

There is no known document by Wycliffe or his colleague Purvey describing their translation approach. What is plain, however, is that their translation reads quite literally when compared to the Latin, each word having an English equivalent, with necessary adjustments to account for syntactical differences between the two. To be sure, Wycliffe wrote in the Middle English of the late fourteenth century and thus at a particular moment in the development of the language. His version is therefore also rife with words sourced from Old English, German, Dutch, or Old Norse, as seen in the etymologies of such key words (using his spellings) as thingis (German *Ding*), bifor (German *bevor*), firste (Old Norse *fyrstr*), bigynnyng (Dutch *beginnen*), ben (Old English *beon*), bigetun (Old English *begietan*), heed (Old English *hēafod*), heuen (Old English *heofon*), erthe (German *Erde*), and blood (German *Blut*). But as relevant here, Middle English contained, and Wycliffe employed, many Latinate terms also found in the Vulgate, such as ymage (*imago*), dignyte (*dignus*), dominaciouns (*dominari*), inhabite (*inhabitare*), visible (*videre*), power (*posse*), plente (*plenus*), recounselid (*reconciliare*), pees (*pacem*), and cros (*crux*).[594]

What is key however is that Wycliffe's language—including both his Latinate phrasings based on the Vulgate and his own choices in Middle English—remains the substrate of all that followed in English. For example, there are scores of phrases originating with Wycliffe that were incorporated in the KJV and continue substantially unchanged in its progeny, including: "My God, my God, why hast thou forsaken me"; "for God loved so the world that he gave his one begotten Son that each man that believeth in him perish not, but have everlasting life"; "Jesus wept"; "for the wages of sin is death"; "if I speak with tongues of men and of angels, and I have not charity, I am made as brass sounding, or a cymbal tinkling."[595] The resulting English translation tradition is thus an essential element in the text's effective history, impacting both the literal wordings and their interpretation and application in church history and tradition.

---

594. Wycliffe's occasional use of certain other important words of ultimate Greek origin, such as trones (θρόνος), entered Middle English via Old French, German, or otherwise, becoming part of his language on that basis.

595. Noble, *Wycliffe's New Testament*, 1088.

3. Tyndale

As noted, William Tyndale was not the first to translate the Bible, or portions of it, into a form of English. And there is no clear evidence whether he had access to let alone consulted Wycliffe's translation when he undertook his own version in the early sixteenth century. It may be that Wycliffe's language had by that time worked its way into English, consistent with "the language-shaping power" of biblical translations.[596] Regardless, it is the case that some hundred Wycliffe-isms—including such theologically essential terms as baptism, unction, allegory, mystery, liberty, and veil—appear in Tyndale's version. Tyndale was the first, however, to have worked directly from Hebrew and Greek texts and thus the first to have fully rendered them from the biblical languages into English.

It is also the case that Tyndale's literary talents "blazed a stylistic path" for later translators, including the scholars who produced the KJV.[597] That is so even when they weren't expressly copying him, but rather working from intervening versions (such as the Coverdale or Geneva Bibles) that had already adopted Tyndale's language. Indeed, as with Wycliffe, some of Tyndale's phrasings are memorably embedded in English culture, including: "in the twinkling of an eye"; "a moment in time"; "let there be light"; "the powers that be"; "my brother's keeper"; "the salt of the earth"; "a law unto themselves"; "filthy lucre"; "gave up the ghost"; "the signs of the times"; "the spirit is willing"; and "fight the good fight." And Tyndale also coined words of continuing theological import, such as Jehovah, Passover, atonement, mercy seat, and scapegoat.

Tyndale's translation of Col 1:15–20 reads as follows. To continue tracing relevant words in the translation tradition as it developed, I again show Wycliffe's Latinate words derived from Jerome in yellow, now adding in red those originally found in Wycliffe's Middle English:

> 15   which is the ymage of the invisible god fyrst begotten of all creatures.
>
> 16   For by him were all thynges created[598] thynges that are in heven and thynges that are in erth: thynges visible and

---

596. See Felber, "Moratorium," 216 (quoting Felber, "Bibelübersetzung," 199).

597. Alter, *Art of Bible Translation*, 2.

598. Tyndale here adopted a Latinate word found in the Vulgate but not found in Wycliffe, i.e., using "created" (for *condita sunt*) and "creatyd" (for *creata est*) in 1:16. I will therefore note such words in blue as from Tyndale when they appear in subsequent versions such as the King James, rather than in yellow as from Wycliffe. The ultimate continuity from the Vulgate is nevertheless relevant as an indication of the text's effective history.

Elements of a Canonical-Hermeneutical Translation Approach/Test Case 165

> thynges invisible: whether they be maieste[599] or lordshippe ether rule or power. All thinges are creatyd by hym and in him
>
> 17 and he is before all thinges and in him all thynges have their beynge.
> 18 And he is the heed of the body that is to wit of the congregacion: he is the begynnynge and fyrst begotten of the deed that in all thynges he might have the preeminence.
> 19 For it pleased the father that in him shuld all fulnes dwell
> 20 and by him to reconcile all thynge vnto him silfe and to set at peace by him thorow the bloud of his crosse both thynges in heven and thynges in erth.

Again, there is no way to determine with certainty whether Tyndale's use of certain core words and phrases also found in Wycliffe such as "image," "first begotten," "beginning," or "reconcile" are evidence of direct appropriation, usage via circulated texts, or simply choices by both men for similar linguistic reasons. In some instances, Tyndale and Wycliffe vary, such as Tyndale's choice of "created" and "creatyd" rather than "maad" in 1:16, or "preeminence" rather than Wycliffe's "firste dignyte" in 1:18, or "fulness" rather than "plente" in 1:19.[600] But whether the one directly influenced the other, or whether Tyndale's choices were entirely independent, once an English *ur*-version developed, it exercised a dominant, inertial influence on future efforts,[601] becoming the embedded source for wordings and interpretations of the text. For present purposes, however, there is a sufficiently striking alignment of words and phrases from Jerome/Wycliffe/Tyndale as to confirm the existence of a developing translation tradition.

4. King James Version

While it is true that the King James is presented as the product of a "committee" of fifty-four scholars, it is importantly the case that a large majority of the wording and phraseology they used was taken virtually

---

599. "Maieste" is derived from the Latin *majestas*, but I have not highlighted it as Latinate in this context since it does not appear in the Vulgate and therefore lacks the same relevance in analyzing the translation tradition.

600. While "plente" appeared in Wycliffe's Early Version, the word was changed by Purvey to "fulness" in the Later Version.

601. See generally Bloom, *Anxiety of Influence*.

intact from Tyndale's translation of nearly a century earlier. The King James scholars thus incorporated some 80 percent of Tyndale's wording from the New Testament and some 70 percent from the Old.[602] As David Trobisch observes, "Strictly speaking, the KJV is not a translation; it is a revision of older translations."[603] Yet there is also a certain uniqueness to the King James arising out of its stylistic harmony, appropriating prior vocabulary but at the same time adopting Hebraic or Greek concepts or word orderings to create a form of English that was not the common idiom of the period—or of any period for that matter—but rather an English made purposefully majestic and reverent.[604]

Even beyond its place in the church, many of the KJV's turns of phrase so permeate English language and literature as to be, like many words and phrases from Shakespeare, indelible if not unsurpassable. That is not to say that the compilers of the KJV were poets or playwrights or novelists themselves. They were instead primarily scholars of Hebrew and Greek who were as fluent in Latin as in English. But as such they were highly attentive to grammar, vocabulary, and rhetoric, unafraid to incorporate Wycliffe's and Tyndale's felicitous phrasings.[605] They also read their drafts aloud to one another as a critical part of the editing process. Listenability may therefore account for much of their version's memorability.[606]

As a result of its widespread reception in worship, the KJV achieved its own independent status in Christian communication, as least within Reformed communities.[607] And its long-standing use as the "authorized

602. Tyndale's work had already been substantially incorporated into versions known as Matthew's Bible, the Bishop's Bible, and the Geneva Bible. See Tulsa 2011, "King James Version," under "Ronald Mansbridge: The Percentage of Words in the Geneva and King James Versions Taken from Tyndale's Translation"; Nielsen and Skousen, "How Much."

603. Trobisch, "KJV," 227 (also noting the continued influence of Wycliffe).

604. Alter, *Art of Bible Translation*, 5, describing the KJV's methodology as one of "inspired literalism." At the same time, one should not think that the KJV is itself sacred either on grounds of linguistic purity or theological perfection. Indeed, the translators themselves never suggested that what they wrote should be frozen in time, their own efforts being only "to make a good [translation] better." "The Translators to the Reader," in KJV (1611). See also NRSVue, ix: "claim[ing this] well-known line" for itself.

605. See generally Norton, "KJV at 400."

606. Burridge, "Priorities," 202.

607. The Douay-Rheims version holds a similar place in the Catholic translation tradition, being the English version of Jerome's Vulgate rather than a direct translation from the original languages. Yet unlike the lineage of English translations that began with Wycliffe's translation from the Vulgate, the Douay-Rheims has not given rise to a similar translation tradition; nor has it had a similar impact on English culture

version" had the effect of enduing the KJV with a canonically normative function as much attributable to its "classical" formulations as to its role in the Anglican tradition. The KJV is thus distinctive in the scope of its "domestication,"[608] a receptive status evident in the celebrations marking its four hundredth anniversary.[609] Indeed, the effective history of the KJV demonstrates the "language-shaping power" of the translation tradition of which it is a part,[610] as well as the continued use of its wording in explicating the text.

The Colossian Hymn appears in the KJV as follows, with Wycliffe's Latinate wording in yellow, Wycliffe's Middle English in red, Tyndale's English in blue, and the KJV's innovations in green:

15 Who is the image of the invisible God, the firstborn of every creature:
16 For by him were all things created, that are in heaven, and that are in earth, visible and invisible, whether they be thrones, or dominions, or principalities, or powers: all things were created by him, and for him:
17 And he is before all things, and by him all things consist.
18 And he is the head of the body, the church: who is the beginning, the firstborn from the dead; that in all things he might have the preeminence.
19 For it pleased the Father that in him should all fulness dwell;
20 And, having made peace through the blood of his cross, by him to reconcile all things unto himself; by him, I say, whether they be things in earth, or things in heaven.

As is quite clear, the essential vocabulary from the Wycliffe/Tyndale translation tradition is virtually codified in the King James with respect to a number of the word choices essential to understanding and interpreting the passage. Moreover, the KJV translators *reincorporated* a number of Wycliffe's phrasings that had been absent in Tyndale, e.g., "church"

---

generally.

608. Steiner, *After Babel*, 366–67.

609. See, e.g., Burke et al., *King James Version*, collecting thirty scholarly essays on the KJV's "genius as Bible translation and its literary influence." See also R. Williams, "Celebrating"; Royal Shakespeare Company, "Written on the Heart." The King James' dominance continues even among those who praise more recent efforts. See Gopnik, "How to Read."

610. Felber, "Moratorium," 216 (quoting Felber, "Bibelübersetzung," 199).

rather than Tyndale's "congregation," "dominions" for Tyndale's "majesties," and "principalities" for Tyndale's "lordships." These reversions may have reflected the KJV's more hierarchical Anglican context. Either way, the KJV's incorporation or reincorporation of such words endowed them with a continuing influence in church history and tradition. But most notably, with respect to this exemplary passage as a whole, the KJV varies little from Wycliffe or Tyndale, substituting only "firstborn" in Col 1:15 and 1:18 for "first begotten" (in Wycliffe and Tyndale) and "consist" in 1:17 for "ben" (in Wycliffe) and "have their beynge" (in Tyndale). The point is that the KJV's refinements of the WYC/TYN translation tradition continue as necessary elements of a contemporary translator's "horizon."

5. Revised Standard Version, New Revised Standard Version, and New Revised Standard Version Updated Edition

The King James reigned essentially unchallenged for more than two hundred years as the dominant version in English-speaking Christendom. A detailed study of the history of corrections, revisions, and adaptations of the 1611 text is beyond the scope of this work. What is clear however is that the KJV had certain errors from the outset; and that the principal texts it relied on were not among the earliest now available. And the KJV editors themselves often noted in the margin their own uncertainties concerning wording in the texts they worked from.[611] Comprehensive efforts to undertake a thorough revision of the KJV began in earnest during the latter part of the nineteenth century with the 1881 publication of the English Revised Version, followed by its 1901 counterpart, the American Standard Version.[612] Yet these revisions were deemed "a magnificent failure," despite reflecting advances in linguistic and archaeological studies, essentially because the "style was rather cumbersome."[613] Following the

---

611. The scope of their notes was, however, limited so as to avoid the extensive interpretive notes of the Puritans' Geneva Bible, many of which were seen to be antimonarchical and were perforce "silenced" in the KJV, whose own dedicatory material could easily be seen to vouchsafe the divine right of kings and thus to confer authority as "His Majesty's version of Scripture." Naudé, "Role of Metatexts," 164–66, 170. The same may be said of its tilt towards episcopal authority (176–77).

612. See generally Bissell, *Historic Origin*, 345–97, extensively detailing the arguments for and against revision.

613. Scanlin, "Revising the KJV," 148. See, e.g., Keister, "Too Many," 68 (quoting Charles Spurgeon on the Revised Version of 1881: "Strong in Greek, but weak in English").

abortive ERV and ASV, efforts to come up with another revision accelerated during the twentieth century.[614] The most widely accepted of these was the Revised Standard Version, both academically informed and broadly sponsored by the National Council of Churches.

Yet as is clear on its face, the RSV's translation of Col 1:15–20 is essentially a formal update of the KJV, without substantive change:

15 He is the image of the invisible God, the first-born of all creation;
16 for in him all things were created, in heaven and on earth, visible and invisible, whether thrones or dominions or principalities or authorities—all things were created through him and for him.
17 He is before all things, and in him all things hold together.
18 He is the head of the body, the church; he is the beginning, the first-born from the dead, that in everything he might be pre-eminent.
19 For in him all the fulness of God was pleased to dwell,
20 and through him to reconcile to himself all things, whether on earth or in heaven, making peace by the blood of his cross.

The close tracking of the KJV is perhaps not surprising. The RSV was never intended to be a fresh translation from the Greek and Hebrew, but rather "an authorized revision of the American Standard Version, published in 1901, which was [itself] a revision of the King James Version, published in 1611."[615] Even so, during the forty years following publication of the RSV, developments in text criticism, philology, and other fields of biblical studies called for a further update. This time, responsibility for a New Revised Standard Version was expanded to include not only Protestant denominations but also the Roman Catholic and Greek Orthodox traditions, as well as input from a Jewish scholar. The editors

614. Scanlin, "Revising the KJV."

615. "Preface," in RSV (1952). Even so, the resulting version was the subject of considerable criticism, if not condemnation, for the poverty of its language. President Harry Truman's colorful views are worth noting: "We were talking about the Bible, and I always read the King James Version, not one of those damn new translations they've got out lately. I don't know why it is when you've got a good thing, you've got to monkey around changing it. The King James Version of the Bible is the best there is or ever has been or will be, and you get a bunch of college professors spending *years* working on it, and all they do is take the poetry out of it." Miller, *Plain Speaking*, 231–32 (emphasis in original).

who produced the NRSV thus provided considerable philological, sociohistorical, and text-critical expertise, while also working within a broad scope of church sponsorship.

Yet as Bruce Metzger stated on behalf of the NRSV's governing Committee, this further revision was also not intended as a fresh translation, but simply "an authorized revision of the Revised Standard Version."[616] The NRSV's stated methodological principle was thus to be "as literal as possible, as free as necessary" in order "to make the meaning clear in graceful, understandable English."[617] Here then is the NRSV's translation of the Colossian Hymn:

> 15 He is the image of the invisible God, the firstborn of all creation;
> 16 for in him all things in heaven and on earth were created, things visible and invisible, whether thrones or dominions or rulers or powers—all things have been created through him and for him.
> 17 He himself is before all things, and in him all things hold together.
> 18 He is the head of the body, the church; he is the beginning, the firstborn from the dead, so that he might come to have first place in everything.
> 19 For in him all the fullness of God was pleased to dwell,
> 20 and through him God was pleased to reconcile to himself all things, whether on earth or in heaven, by making peace through the blood of his cross.

Other than a small change,[618] the NRSV's wordings in this passage, at least, are virtually indistinguishable from the RSV. And the recent NRSVue text is identical to the NRSV's. The NRSV and the NRSVue thereby retain the theologically essential, "classical" formulations of the

---

616. "Preface," in NRSV (1989). See also New Revised Standard Version Bible, "New Revised Standard NRS," para. 6: "Rooted in the past, but right for today, the NRSV continues the tradition of William Tyndale, the King James Version, the American Standard Version, and the Revised Standard Version." This remains true with the 2021 publication of the NRSVue, even as it incorporates historical-critical research developed over the past thirty years. See National Council, "Version Information" ("the NRSVue, like the NRSV, follows 'in the tradition of the King James Bible'" and "is not a new translation," but rather a philological and text-critical "update").

617. "Preface," in NRSV (1990).

618. Verse 18 now reads "so that he might come to have first place in everything" rather than the somewhat more formal "that in everything he might be pre-eminent."

Elements of a Canonical-Hermeneutical Translation Approach/Test Case   171

WYC/TYN/KJV translation tradition. The NRSV's widespread usage as an English text reliably reflective of extensive historical-critical and other scholarly input—a usage likely to be continued by the NRSVue—is *itself* compelling evidence of the inertial force of the linguistically expressed interpretive understandings developed throughout the course of the text's effective history in the church.

6. English Standard Version

The English Standard Version also places itself in "the classic mainstream of English Bible translations over the past half-millennium,"[619] adopting an "essentially literal" translation methodology with an emphasis on "'word-for-word' accuracy."[620] Implicitly critical of the dynamic equivalence approach taken in other recent translations (discussed below), the ESV editors opine that "[a] 'thought-for-thought' translation is of necessity more inclined to reflect the interpretive opinions of the translator and the influences of contemporary culture."[621] As such, the ESV continued what was by then a well-established translation tradition, validated by acceptance in a range of ecclesial settings and the source of much that is treasured in written as well as spoken English. The ESV's claims are in fact quite modest, expressly limiting itself to corrections of past transcriptional errors; updating of obsolete vocabulary; but using the 1971 version of the RSV as its starting point rather than the NRSV in order to distance itself from certain of the NRSV's controversial changes.[622] This is the ESV's version of Col 1:15–20:

> 15 He is the image of the invisible God, the firstborn of all creation.
>
> 16 For by him all things were created, in heaven and on earth, visible and invisible, whether thrones or dominions or rulers or authorities—all things were created through him and for him.

---

619. "Version Information," in ESV (2001).

620. "Translation Philosophy," in ESV (2001).

621. "Translation Philosophy," ESV (2001). Note, however, that just because the ESV translators considered persons adopting a dynamic equivalence approach to be influenced by their own "interpretive opinions," so too would *any* translator who remains critically unaware of his "situatedness within the flow of history." Thiselton, *New Horizons*, 6. See Gadamer, *Truth and Method*, 301.

622. Such as the use of gender-inclusive language and the change from "virgin" to "young woman" in Isa 7:14.

> 17 And he is before all things, and in him all things hold together.
> 18 And he is the head of the body, the church. He is the beginning, the firstborn from the dead, that in everything he might be preeminent.
> 19 For in him all the fullness of God was pleased to dwell,
> 20 and through him to reconcile to himself all things, whether on earth or in heaven, making peace by the blood of his cross.

As reflected in this hymnic passage from Colossians, at least, nothing indicates any substantive gloss on any prior translation. This is not a criticism, but rather a further indication that theologically important formulations originating in the WYC/TYN/KJV translation tradition have a powerful and persistent effective history in shaping contemporary biblical translations, possibly even giving rise to a reluctance to vary the linguistic style. Thus, while one member of the ESV's Oversight Committee is an emeritus professor of English (as well as a Bible teacher), there is no indication of his role as far as style goes. That is not to say the ESV is poorly written. It's not. But it does stand out for the impersonality of its writing.

ii. Dynamic Equivalence, Paraphrase, and Hybrid Approaches

As described above, an extensive translation tradition established itself relatively early in the linguistic progression from Middle English to more modern forms. Indeed, the earliest translations in that tradition were themselves language-formative.[623] And as one moves through the twentieth century, Bible translations continued to proliferate not only in volume but also in theory. As more fully explained in sect. II.a.ii, *supra*, most notable among these developments is the dynamic equivalency's focus on "intelligibility" in the ears of the listener as a more central value than adherence to formal considerations or the cadences of traditional language. It would be overstating the case to suggest a rigid taxonomy of approaches. But for present purposes, the following illustrate some of the principal examples of certain contemporary approaches. Each is examined for any innovations evidencing a distinctive approach. But each is

---

623. See Felber, "Moratorium," 216 (quoting Felber, "Bibelübersetzung," 199).

Elements of a Canonical-Hermeneutical Translation Approach/Test Case

also examined for possible adherence to the WYC/TYN/KJV translation tradition, notwithstanding their stated methodologies.

1. Phillips

J. B. Phillips was a classically trained Anglican clergyman who was prompted to undertake a new translation of the New Testament based on his experiences with a youth group to which he ministered during World War II, where he concluded that most of his charge found the prevailing King James Version "not intelligible."[624] His general approach might be described as casual or almost conversational, yet without being a complete paraphrase. As he explained:

1. As far as possible the language used must be such as is commonly spoken, written and understood at the present time.

2. When necessary the translator should feel free to expand or explain, while preserving the original meaning as nearly as can be ascertained.

3. The Letters should read like letters, not theological treatises. Where the Greek is informal and colloquial, the English should be the same.

4. The translation (or in some cases, the paraphrase) should "flow" and be easy to read. Artificial "verses" should be discarded, though cross-headings can be introduced to divide the letters into what seem to be their natural sections.

5. Though every care must be taken to make the version accurate, the projected value of this version should lie in its "easy-to-read" quality. For close meticulous study, existing modern versions should be consulted.[625]

He further described his methodology as the "principle of producing equivalent effect," i.e., "producing the same effect on the modern reader as was produced in the first case in the minds of those for whom the Gospels were first written."[626] As such, Phillips appears to have anticipated

---

624. "Preface to the Schools Edition," in Phillips, "New Testament."

625. Phillips, *Letters to Young Churches*.

626. Phillips, "Translating the Gospels," 153. Phillips explained that in undertaking the task he sought a "translator's inspiration": "I have found imaginative sympathy, not so much with words as with people, to be essential. If it is not presumptuous to say so, I attempted, as far as I could, to think myself into the heart and mind of Paul, for

the "dynamic equivalence" approach that would be taken by Nida in the 1960s.[627] This is how he presented the passage under consideration:

> Now Christ is the visible expression of the invisible God. He existed before creation began, for it was through him that every thing was made, whether spiritual or material, seen or unseen. Through him, and for him, also, were created power and dominion, ownership and authority. In fact, every single thing was created through, and for him. He is both the first principle and the upholding principle of the whole scheme of creation. And now he is the head of the body which is composed of all Christian people. Life from nothing began through him, and life from the dead began through him, and he is, therefore, justly called the Lord of all. It was in him that the full nature of God chose to live, and through him God planned to reconcile in his own person, as it were, everything on earth and everything in Heaven by virtue of the sacrifice of the cross.

As can be seen, Phillips took some liberty with the text in seeking to convey its meaning. For example, rather than say, "the church," Phillips describes "the body . . . composed of all Christian people." Nor do his explanatory phrasings always help. Thus, he describes Christ as "the upholding principle of the whole scheme of creation." It is difficult to discern the meaning of this, at least as compared with a more literal reading to the effect that all things hold together/cohere in Christ. Regardless, these examples illustrate Phillips' tendency to be expansive as to possibly more technical or theologically charged words on the apparent assumption that the words—such as "church"—might not carry the meaning by themselves. One might question that assumption as to commonly used terms, particularly in light of their effective history in English language

---

example, or of Mark or of John the Divine. Then I tried to imagine myself as each of the New Testament authors writing his particular message for the people of today." "Preface to the Schools Edition," in Phillips, "New Testament." Cf. in this context the discussion in sect., I.b, *supra*, concerning post-Enlightenment, subjectivist efforts to grasp the *mens auctoris*.

627. Phillips' approach was itself anticipated by Helen Barrett Montgomery's translation in the 1930s. In a concise study of her work, Elizabeth Willett writes that Montgomery was motivated to undertake a fresh translation of the New Testament by her experiences teaching underprivileged youths, where she concluded that the "stately and old expressions which had such a charm for the literary-minded, were a bar and a hindrance to the less educated." Willett, "Feminist Choices," 402. She therefore introduced colloquialisms and formatted the text in ordinary paragraphs rather than columnar verses. Her linguistic analysis was perhaps unknown to Phillips or Nida, but for whatever reason and despite her originality and skill, her work remains largely uncredited.

Elements of a Canonical-Hermeneutical Translation Approach/Test Case   175

and culture over the centuries. But Phillips' purposes are also didactic, consistent with his own self-description as a "parson," and to that extent his translation often appears to be explanatory.

To be sure, Phillips' translation of the Colossian Hymn reasonably conveys Paul's descriptions of who Jesus is, even if it lacks the transporting/elevated register of the passage. But his translation of Matt 1:1–17—the genealogy of Jesus—lacks more than that. This is how he renders the *entirety* of the passage:

> The genealogy of Jesus Christ may be traced from Abraham, through forty-two generations, to Joseph the husband of Mary, Jesus' mother—fourteen generations from Abraham to David, fourteen more from David to the Deportation to Babylon, and fourteen more from Babylon to Christ himself.

His explanation for omitting virtually all the actual personages was that "I felt that though it was important for the modern reader to realize that the genealogy of Jesus went back right through Jewish history, the actual list of names as such was not important to them."[628] Phillips might well be criticized for "dumbing down" the Scriptures by eliminating the genealogy's theological significance as the realization of the promise in Gen 22:18 to Abraham that in his "seed" all nations would be blessed.[629] More importantly, Phillips thereby diminished the importance of the history of Israel not only in its typological significance,[630] but also with respect to the elements of salvation history in general.[631] Phillips' is thus a clear example of a translation that virtually omits the effective history of the Old Testament in the New.[632] That critique aside, I do not suggest that Phillips' translation lacks merit. On the contrary, it evidences strong literary and linguistic skills. Even though one might differ as to some renderings, the translation reflects Phillips' personality and faith in an engaging way, provoking reflection and shedding new light on familiar passages.

628. Phillips, "Translating the Gospels," 159.

629. This was the view taken by Dr. Emile Rieu in a conversation with Phillips. Rieu was a classicist who had translated the four Gospels as well as Homer. He told Phillips that he seemed to "write down" to the "man in the congregation." Phillips, for his part, said he took such persons to be the original audience for the works. Rieu responded that "the original audience of the Gospels found them just as difficult as we do." Phillips, "Translating the Gospels," 154.

630. See, e.g., 1 Cor 10:1–11.

631. See, e.g., Rom 9–11.

632. Cf. Straus, *New Testament*, 3–4, interlineating Matthew's genealogy with intra-scriptural descriptions of key figures in the descent from Abraham.

2. Bruce

Frederick F. Bruce was a preeminent twentieth-century scholar, serving as Rylands Professor of Biblical Criticism and Exegesis at the University of Manchester. He was a prolific author, particularly known for championing the historical reliability of the Scriptures.[633] In 1965, he published *The Letters of Paul: An Expanded Paraphrase*, "not . . . to set side by side the various synonyms by which a Greek word may be rendered, or to bring out the finer nuances of Greek moods and tenses . . . . [but] rather to make the course of Paul's argument as clear as possible." Bruce was not seeking to substitute or supplant existing translations—indeed, he holds up the English Revised Version of 1881 as one that "reproduces most accurately" the Greek grammar "without doing excessive violence to English literary usage."[634]

What Bruce felt was lacking, however, was a proper flow of Paul's thinking in order to make clear his train of thought. Bruce also sought to "fill in a gap" in contemporary readers' understanding by virtue of background information that Bruce assumed would have been familiar to Paul's first listeners and readers. His solution was to provide "an expansion," calling his work "a paraphrase, not a translation." Bruce concedes that it is "difficult to say where translation ends and paraphrase begins," but suggests that the latter "includes much more of [the paraphrast's] own interpretation and exposition than a translator would deem proper." Nevertheless, Bruce expressed confidence that had not "represent[ed] Paul as saying anything which he did not intend to say."[635] There is something circular about this position: even as Bruce states that he is providing his own interpretation, he also feels he knows Paul's "intent."[636] This is the same difficulty noted with respect to Nida's approach, which assumes the translator is able to discern the original writer's intent as well as the original listeners'/readers' understanding. Here is Bruce's version of Col 1:15–20:

> This Redeemer of ours is the very image of the God whom none can see; He is the Firstborn, prior to all creation and supreme over it, because it was through Him that the universe was created. Yes, all things in heaven and on earth, visible things and

---

633. E.g., Bruce, *New Testament Documents*.
634. Bruce, *Letters of Paul*, 9.
635. Bruce, *Letters of Paul*, 9.
636. Bruce, *Letters of Paul*, 12.

> things invisible, whether thrones or dominions or principalities or powers—they have all been created through Him and for Him. He Himself exists before them all, and it is through Him that everything holds together. He Himself, moreover, is the Head of His body, the church; He is the Beginning; He is also the Firstborn from the dead, so that His preeminence is universal, extending over the old creation and the new creation alike. It is God's good pleasure, in short, that the totality of divine fullness should take up its abode in Him. It is God's good pleasure, too, to reconcile the universe to Himself through Him, through the shedding of His life-blood on the cross. This reconciliation embraces earthly things and heavenly things alike.

To be honest, this passage is not all *that* extended and paraphrased. It could be that other passages in Bruce's translation/paraphrase reflect more of those characteristics. But focusing on the Colossian Hymn for exemplary purposes, Bruce doesn't depart much from other versions. Again, this may well demonstrate the inertial force of "classical" formulations, at least with respect to theologically significant terms, notwithstanding the translator's stated approach.

3. Good News Translation/Bratcher and Nida

In 1966, the American Bible Society published a new translation titled Good News for Modern Man, purposefully adopting Nida's dynamic equivalence methodology. Nida himself was the Executive Secretary of the ABS at the time and retained Robert Bratcher, a staff member, as the principal translator. At various points the version was renamed, first as Today's English Version and later as the Good News Translation (GNB). The work was mass marketed and became immensely popular, selling over one hundred million copies within a decade and winning endorsement from a number of denominations as well as the evangelist Billy Graham. It is self-described as "easy-to-read," fully accessible both to children and to adults for whom English might not be their native tongue.[637]

In 1977, the United Bible Societies published a *Translator's Handbook on Paul's Letters to the Colossians and Philemon*, co-authored by Bratcher and Nida, in which they elaborate on the GNB's word and phrase choices. While, as noted, the GNB was not the first translation to use a

---

637. See the home page of the Good News Bible (https://www.goodnewsbible.com); "About the Good News Translation" (https://www.biblestudytools.com/gnt/).

dynamically equivalent methodology, Bratcher and Nida's handbook is a fertile source for understanding its operation. Their translation of the hymn reads and is formatted as follows:

> 15 Christ is the visible likeness of the invisible God. He is the first-born Son, superior to all created things. 16 For through him God created everything in heaven and on earth, the seen and the unseen things, including spiritual powers, lords, rulers, and authorities. God created the whole universe through him and for him. 17 Christ existed before all things, and in union with him all things have their proper place. 18 He is the head of his body, the church; he is the source of the body's life. He is the first-born Son, who was raised from death, in order that he alone might have the first place in all things. 19 For it was by God's own decision that the Son has in himself the full nature of God. 20 Through the Son, then, God decided to bring the whole universe back to himself. God made peace through his Son's blood on the cross and so brought back to himself all things, both on earth and in heaven.

As we saw with Bruce's version, however, many of the GNB's phrasings actually track those in the WYC/TYN/KJV translation tradition. The literal text in traditional form may therefore have more of a hold than a blanket recourse to dynamic equivalence would suggest. But because the GNB had Nida's personal involvement, it is also worth examining how well the methodology actually meets his stated goal of presenting the biblical "message" in such a way that "the average reader . . . is very unlikely to misunderstand it,"[638] at least when applied to more elevated passages such as this. For one thing, it is unclear whether modernizing the language in fact leads to a better understanding of the inner word, i.e., "who Christ is," than may already arise out of more "classical" wordings. It may, in fact, make it *less* accessible.

For example, the GNB substitutes "likeness" for "image" in 1:15. Bratcher and Nida explain this usage as necessary to prevent a "likely . . . interpret[ation]" of the verse to suggest that Jesus himself was "either an idol or an icon."[639] But such an erroneous reading doesn't seem "likely" at all, given the uniform condemnation of idolatry throughout the Bible. Moreover, by using the term "likeness," which emphasizes the character of the First Adam as made καθ' ὁμοίωσιν, the GNB may well leave open

---

638. Nida and Taber, *Theory and Practice*, 1.
639. Bratcher and Nida, *Translators Handbook*, 22.

an Arian interpretation that Jesus as the Second Adam was *not* equal to God.[640] In other words, by skipping over the effective history of the verse as revealed in credal and doctrinal formulations, the GNB fails to give clear effect to the Nicaean expression that Christ is ὁμοούσιον with the Father.

Second, the GNB substitutes the colloquial expression that in Christ "all things have their proper place" as its translation of the relevant portion of Col 1:17. The translators justify the phrasing as a reference to "dovetailing" in "the construction of furniture," such that to say that everything in the universe has its fit place is intelligibly expressive of συνίστημι's core sense of "holding together."[641] However, it is one thing to say that the universe of things is generally well constructed, and another that it is Christ's active power that sustains its coherence. Hence by oversimplifying an admittedly difficult concept, the GNB may fail to convey the expressive inner word.

Further, to the extent the GNB chooses to elide "heavy" wording,[642] it may omit essential language that *would* give rise to understanding. Again, by dispensing with a word like "image," with clear intrascripturality in both the LXX and the New Testament as well as intertextual realization in credal and other doctrinal/liturgical materials, the GNB isolates the text from its canonical setting and decouples it from church history and tradition. None of this is to gainsay the value of presenting the text in the current vernacular by way of appropriate paraphrase or colloquially descriptive language.[643] It is rather to suggest that the inner meaning of numinous passages cannot be easily reduced to plain speech. Instead, consideration should be given to such verses' transporting nature and purpose, both formally from a rhetorical point of view and substantively from a doctrinal perspective. The continuity in reception of the WYC/TYN/KJV translation tradition is evidence that its language is indeed expressive of textual meaning; and nothing here is meant to suggest that it be discarded. At the same time, to the extent a more elusive text allows for "free space" to expand on its ecstatic effect, a contemporary translator seeking to explore that space should not default to surface "intelligibility," but rather seek such poetic-literary language as might itself be transporting.

---

640. Compare 1 Cor 15:45–47 with Arius, *Epistula ad Eusebium Nicomediensem*, 5.
641. Bratcher and Nida, *Translators Handbook*, 25.
642. Nida and Taber, *Theory and Practice*, 2.
643. Robert Alter, email to author, 2019.

4. New International Version

In addition to the GNB, a number of other translations have been undertaken applying dynamic equivalence theory. The NIV, for example, has as its stated goal is "to bring modern Bible readers as close as possible to the experience of the very first Bible readers: providing the best possible blend of transparency to the original documents and comprehension of the original meaning in every verse."[644] Its governing Committee on Bible Translation consists of a range of Old and New Testament scholars, but none with any apparent focus on literature or other creative arts.[645] The translation is lucid, if unoriginal:

> 15 The Son is the image of the invisible God, the firstborn over all creation.
> 16 For in him all things were created: things in heaven and on earth, visible and invisible, whether thrones or powers or rulers or authorities; all things have been created through him and for him.
> 17 He is before all things, and in him all things hold together.
> 18 And he is the head of the body, the church; he is the beginning and the firstborn from among the dead, so that in everything he might have the supremacy.
> 19 For God was pleased to have all his fullness dwell in him,
> 20 and through him to reconcile to himself all things, whether things on earth or things in heaven, by making peace through his blood, shed on the cross.

While the NIV is generally presented as "a completely original translation,"[646] it turns out that in this instance, at least, the NIV *preserves* virtually all the "classical" formulations of the English translation tradition. To be sure, the NIV as a whole is written much more fluidly than translations as clumsy as the RSV; and it takes a number of interpretive positions that reflect scholarly as well as sociopolitical considerations.[647] But again, the more important point is that the inertial weight of the

---

644. "Version Information," in NIV.
645. See Biblica, "Committee on Bible Translation."
646. "Version Information," in NIV.

647. These include using gender-neutral words such as "child" rather than "son," or "they" instead of "he"; and omitting words or phrases based on text-critical analysis, such as "through his blood" in Col 1:14, the word "begotten" in John 3:16, or the "longer ending" of Mark 16:9–20.

literal text coupled with the *Wirkungsgeschichte* of its translation tradition is such that in such elevated and doctrinally sensitive passages as the Colossian Hymn, the "dynamic equivalent" is nearly the same as what already exists.

5. Peterson (The Message)

The late Eugene Peterson was a Presbyterian minister whose goal was also to translate the New Testament into a form of English that would be both modern and readily understandable. Peterson had training in Greek as well as Hebrew and took the texts in their original languages as his starting point. From there he wrote his version, The Message, in a decidedly personal paraphrase, freely using slang expressions. His aim was for modern listeners and readers to hear the Word of God in the way he imagined it would have sounded to its original readers and listeners. He also hoped to pry people loose from their over-familiarity with the Bible as a result of having heard it for so long in standard translations approved for use in denominational worship services. To a large extent, he viewed translation as part and parcel of his task as a preacher, whereby he was "always looking for an English way to make the biblical text relevant to the conditions of the people."[648] This is how Peterson presented the passage in question:

> 15–18 We look at this Son and see the God who cannot be seen. We look at this Son and see God's original purpose in everything created. For everything, absolutely everything, above and below, visible and invisible, rank after rank after rank of angels—*everything* got started in him and finds its purpose in him. He was there before any of it came into existence and holds it all together right up to this moment. And when it comes to the church, he organizes and holds it together, like a head does a body.
>
> 18–20 He was supreme in the beginning and—leading the resurrection parade—he is supreme in the end. From beginning to end he's there, towering far above everything, everyone. So spacious is he, so roomy, that everything of God finds its proper place in him without crowding. Not only that, but all the broken and dislocated pieces of the universe—people and things, animals and atoms—get properly fixed and fit together in vibrant harmonies, all because of his death, his blood that poured down from the cross.

648. "Introduction," in MSG.

The Message is a hugely popular translation and its acceptance should be seen as part of the text's reception history in and of itself. In other words, its success almost necessarily arises out of the appreciation it finds among a wide range of Christians in many settings. As such, it presents the Word in a way that reaches a multitude of people who otherwise might not be reached, consistent with the kerygmatic mission of the church and the manner in which translation serves that purpose. But purely as a hermeneutical matter, Peterson's assertion that a given passage can now be heard in much the same way it would have been by its original listeners is open to question, as is its expression (in this passage at least) of the text's *verbum interius*.

In Peterson's translation of Col 1:19, for example, there is little in "So spacious is he, so roomy, that everything of God finds its proper place in him without crowding" that suggests the elevated nature of the Fullness of the Godhead dwelling in Christ. To some extent, the physicality of Peterson's image creates the strange picture of possible congestion among members of the Godhead, as though the Deity were a troika, not a Trinity—even though Peterson is certainly trying to say the opposite. Moreover, the phrase "everything of God" is essentially meaningless. And in other passages, Peterson seems to go out of his way to avoid what might be theologically loaded or "churchy" vocabulary, as in John 13:21, where in lieu of translating ἐταράχθη τῷ πνεύματι as something like "he was troubled in spirit" (KJV), he says that Jesus was "visibly upset." That doesn't touch the pathos of the situation and reduces Jesus' spiritual engagement to a purely emotional one.

Again, this is not at all to criticize the faith-driven purpose and effect of MSG. My point here is that by going to paraphrastic extremes, Peterson risks losing track of the inner word, at least in those instances where meaning depends a good deal on the literal form of the text. As such, his translation illustrates the limitations of a Nida-like methodology: if taken too far, the resulting text may be so far distant from essential aspects of the original that it falls short of its own stated goal of providing modern readers with access to the text's *verbum interius*.

That said, there is much value in using contemporary slang as well as unexpected, humorous, and seemingly irreverent formulations. For example, compare Peterson's translation of 2 Cor 4:17, "These hard times are small potatoes compared to the coming good times," with the KJV's, "For our light affliction, which is but for a moment, worketh for us a far more exceeding and eternal weight of glory." Peterson's may serve to convey the text's meaning—at least if contextualized as to doctrines of judgment and salvation, death and resurrection, so as not to trivialize the meaning of "good times."

6. Jordan (The Cotton Patch Gospel)

Clarence Jordan was the founder of an interracial farming community in the heart of Georgia. He was a popular teacher, also holding a PhD in New Testament Greek. His purpose in producing the rural-accented translation he called "cotton patch" was to "change the setting from first-century Palestine to twentieth-century America" so that the New Testament writers could "cross the time-space barrier and talk to us not only in modern English but about modern problems, feelings, frustrations, hopes and assurances; to work beside us in our cotton patch or on our assembly line, so that the word becomes modern *flesh*."[649]

This is a plainspoken way to view the task of the translator in bringing the "then to now" and the "now to then." The question is whether it goes too far in terms of distance from the actual text. In theory, that would be the case only if the inner word of the text is somehow lost, i.e., if the effort to engage the modern reader in a dialogue with the text has somehow left it stranded in the past. To be sure, Jordan himself was moved to undertake the translation out of his belief in the truths of Scripture, a criterion Luther proposed as essential to the task.[650] This is Jordan's translation of the Colossian Hymn:[651]

> He's a perfect photo of the Unseen God, and has got it over everything that ever was made, because he's the reason everything was put together, whether it's in heaven or on earth, whether seen or unseen, whether sitting on thrones or governors' chairs, on judges' benches or in sheriffs' offices. Through him and for him the whole business has been put together. He's the starting point of everything and he's got it all in the palm of his hand. Too, he is the boss of the body, his church. He is the source, the originator of the resurrection. The result is that he's tops any way you look at it. In him God put all his eggs in one basket and

---

649. *CPV* 7 (emphasis in original).

650. Luther, *Word and Sacrament I*, 94 (quoted in Tomlin, "Luther's Approach," 130).

651. In keeping with the ethos of the translation, however, he has the letter addressed to the church in Columbus, Georgia, not Colossae.

showed, through him, that he was friendly towards everybody. Indeed, by the blood shed at his lynching he brought about peace with all, both on the earth and in heaven.

Jordan's translation is purposefully at the extreme end of the freely colloquial. But to be honest, no one really speaks this way, not those who labor in the cotton fields, on the assembly lines, or anywhere else. And if one looks closely, Jordan sometimes weaves in traditional phrasing, such that when he then adds a colloquialism, the conflicting result is jarring. In other words, there is an internal stylistic inconsistency that suggests how much of a struggle it must have been to depart from traditional formulations. It is hard to guess what Nida's views on this translation might have been, but Jordan seems to adopt Nida's theory that translations should focus on a given cultural setting in order to maximize "intelligibility."[652] Even so, it is hard to see how Jordan's description of the eternally begotten Son as a "perfect photo" sheds light on Christ's imagery of the invisible God. For one thing, a photo is not consubstantial with its subject in form or in substance. And to say, for example, that "the whole business has been put together" through Christ is presumably true, but it may be no more effective in conveying the sense of εἰς αὐτὸν ἔκτισται (1:16) than other translations written less colloquially.[653]

Jordan's further translation of τὰ πάντα ἐν αὐτῷ συνέστηκεν (1:17) to the effect that "he's got it all in the palm of his hand" may likewise be no more compelling, and possibly less so, than it would be to say that "in him all things cohere." Perhaps more controversially, Jordan uses the term "lynching" to refer to the crucifixion (1:20); and substitutes "white" and "Negro" for "Jew" and "gentile" elsewhere, asserting that "there is no adequate equivalent of the latter."[654] And in an effort to describe the "mystery" now revealed as "Christ in you gentiles" (1:26), Jordan refers to "all races." The obvious problem with this substitution is that it is intended to make a political point, but does so at the expense of canonical unity and/or relevant aspects of the historical faith.[655]

---

652. Nida, "Sociolinguistics."

653. To be clear, I am not opposed to the colloquial. Far from it. See Rowan Williams' cover description of Straus, *New Testament*, as an "irresistibly colloquial and energetic version of Christian Scripture."

654. CPV 9.

655. There may also be a troubling (if unintended) analog here to the gnostic assertion that one should not take references to Jews and gentiles literally, on the alleged ground that Paul only meant them "allegorically"; and that the terms instead refer

Jordan readily concedes that in many places "it will appear that I have taken entirely too much liberty with the text.... But let me point out that this is a translation, not of Paul's *words*, but of his *ideas*."[656] Thoughts may well be the ultimate subject of a translation,[657] but under the "processual" hermeneutic of Augustine, Justin Martyr, Gregory of Nazianzus, Aquinas, and Gadamer, the expressive word should embody the inner one. Hence the need to avoid a "distancing of form from meaning."[658] Here, where the complexities of the history of Israel are in effect subsumed into the civil rights struggle in the United States, one might fairly question whether the text itself is as fit a vehicle for that message as might be exegetical lessons drawn from the text.

7. Wright (*The Kingdom New Testament*)

N. T. Wright is a prolific scholar of the New Testament and a former bishop in the Church of England, known widely for his theological analyses as well as his ability to speak and to write in an accessible manner. Consistent with those gifts he produced his own translation of the New Testament, published in the United Kingdom as *The New Testament for Everyone* and in the United States as *The Kingdom New Testament*. His stated goal is accessibility, in particular for those who have not and will not ever read a commentary (although he himself has authored a number of commentaries, including one on Colossians). At the same time, he considers his work to be "a translation, not a paraphrase," in which he "tried to stick close to the original" while still writing in "a less formal and academic, and a more deliberately energetic, style."[659] His translation of Col 1:15–20 reads and is formatted as follows:

> 15 *He is the image of God, the invisible one,*
>   *The firstborn of all creation.*
> 16 *For in him all things were created,*
>   *In the heavens and here on the earth.*
> *Things we can see and things we cannot—*
>   *Thrones and lordships and rulers and powers—*

---

symbolically to "*psychic* and *pneumatic* Christians respectively." See Pagels, *Gnostic Paul*, 6 (emphasis in original).

656. *CPV* 9.
657. See "Ars Poetica," in Horace, *Works of Horace*, line 133.
658. Felber, "Chomsky's Influence," 255.
659. Wright, *Kingdom New Testament*, xii–xiii.

> All things were created both through him and for him.
> 17 And he is ahead, prior to all else,
>> And in him all things hold together;
> 18 And he himself is supreme, the head
>> Over the body, the church.
> He is the start of it all,
>> Firstborn from realms of the dead;
>> So in all things he might be the chief.
> 19 For in him all the Fullness was glad to dwell
> 20 And through him to reconcile all to himself,
> Making peace through the blood of his cross,
>> Through him—yes, things on the earth,
>> And also the things in the heavens.

There are some notable aspects to Wright's translation. First, the passage is both versified and italicized in his version, as is his rendering of the hymnic passage in Phil 2:6–11 and the Magnificat. He thus presents these passages orthographically as forms of song or poetry, purposefully distinguishing them from the rest of the text. Moreover, he insets the margins of Col 1:17 and 18a further than those of other verses, thus taking a position aligned with some of the scholars discussed in sect. II.d.iii, *supra*, as to the hymn's strophic and/or chiastic structure.

Although Wright does not explain these formatting decisions in his short preface to the translation, he has written elsewhere about his reasoning. Building on the word ποίημα in Eph 2:10, he asserts that we are not just God's handiwork (αὐτοῦ γάρ ἐσμεν ποίημα), but literally his "poem."[660] He argues that "the writing of the earliest Christian theology, or some of it at least, [is] in the form of poetry."[661] Passages of this sort are thus presented in distinctive English forms, even though they do not appear as such in any Greek manuscript. In that regard, he is in harmony with the methodological view taken here that passages with a distinctively elevated and/or poetic register seek, like much poetry, to express matters beyond the everyday realities of life; and may legitimately be presented as such in translation, regardless of the form of the original.

---

660. Wright, "Poem Doubled," 3.
661. Wright, "Poem Doubled," 4.

8. Taylor (The Living Bible and the New Living Translation)

Kenneth Taylor was a Christian books publisher who, frustrated by what he saw as the opacity of some of the wording in traditional Bible translations, undertook his own "personal paraphrase" in the early 1960s. He explains his motivation as follows:

> The children were one of the chief inspirations for producing the Living Bible. Our family devotions were tough going because of the difficulty we had understanding the King James Version, which we were then using, or the Revised Standard Version, which we used later. All too often I would ask questions to be sure the children understood, and they would shrug their shoulders—they didn't know what the passage was talking about. So I would explain it. I would paraphrase it for them and give them the thought. It suddenly occurred to me one afternoon that I should write out the reading for that evening thought by thought, rather than doing it on the spot during our devotional time. So I did, and read the chapter to the family that evening with exciting results—they knew the answers to all the questions I asked![662]

Published as The Living Bible, it was not, in his view, a translation as such. It was, however, immensely popular, becoming the best-selling book in the United States in the early 1970s. While it is true that Taylor disclaimed his effort as a "translation," paraphrase can, where appropriate, be as valid a translation methodology as any other.[663] This is the TLB's translation (or paraphrase if one prefers) of the hymn:

> 15 Christ is the exact likeness of the unseen God. He existed before God made anything at all, and, in fact,
>
> 16 Christ himself is the Creator who made everything in heaven and earth, the things we can see and the things we can't; the spirit world with its kings and kingdoms, its rulers and authorities; all were made by Christ for his own use and glory.
>
> 17 He was before all else began and it is his power that holds everything together.
>
> 18 He is the Head of the body made up of his people—that is, his Church—which he began; and he is the Leader of all those who arise from the dead, so that he is first in everything;

---

662. "Origin," in "Living Bible."
663. See sect. II.a.iii, *supra*.

19 for God wanted all of himself to be in his Son.

20 It was through what his Son did that God cleared a path for everything to come to him—all things in heaven and on earth—for Christ's death on the cross has made peace with God for all by his blood.

On its face, Taylor's paraphrase is a translation, despite his disclaimer. Yet to the extent he paraphrased (or, in his words, "explained") the text, it is not immediately apparent that he makes this hymnic passage any more understandable than it is in any other version. What I mean is that the essence of the passage—its Christology—arguably remains just as elusive here as it does elsewhere. Indeed, it may be that by *over-colloquializing* the passage, some of the essential "mystery" is gone.[664] To say that "God wanted all of himself to be in his Son," for example, tells little about the fullness of the Godhead dwelling in Christ. This is a risk adverted to above, when important intrascriptural and other aspects of a text's effective history are omitted in translation.

In the 1990s Taylor undertook a wholesale revision of The Living Bible. He did so by availing himself of a Bible Translation Committee of ninety scholars of Greek and Hebrew.[665] The resulting version was published in 1996 by Tyndale House (of which Taylor was a founder and which his son and grandson continue to lead) as the New Living Translation.[666] The NLT like the TLB represents an undertaking by persons who understood the text to be, as the descriptions indicate, the "living" Word of God. As to their methodology,

> they kept the concerns of both formal-equivalence and dynamic-equivalence in mind. On the one hand, they translated as simply and literally as possible when that approach yielded an accurate, clear, and natural English text. On the other, the translators

---

664. Note that Taylor also paraphrases 1:26–27 as follows: "He has kept this secret for centuries and generations past, but now at last it has pleased him to tell it to those who love him and live for him, and the riches and glory of his plan are for you Gentiles, too. And this is the secret: *Christ in your hearts is your only hope of glory.*" But as explained in sect. II.e.i.14, *supra*, translating τὸ μυστήριον as "secret" arguably deprives the verse of its spiritual sense.

665. See "Introduction," in NLT.

666. The NLT's chief stylist has noted that "the whole process was complicated, including . . . a dual track of revising the LB and at the same time creating a brand new translation from scratch. The latter was eventually abandoned, but the revised LB came out in 1996 as the NLT. We immediately applied the more rigorous approach of the canceled new translation to the 1996 NLT and came up with the NLT second edition, which came out in 2004." Daniel Taylor, email to the author, 2020.

rendered the message more dynamically when the literal rendering was hard to understand, was misleading, or yielded archaic or foreign wording. Their goal was to be both faithful to the ancient texts and eminently readable. A part of the reasoning behind adapting the language for accessibility is the premise that more people will hear the Bible read aloud in a church service than are likely to read it or study it on their own.[667]

The last observation is a bit discouraging. To be sure, "faith comes by hearing and hearing by the Word of God,"[668] but it begs the question whether the NLT was at times "dumbed down" based on what might in fact be considered a condescending perspective on the part of the Bible Translation Committee to the "folks in the pew."[669] Worse, the committee's assumption runs the risk of becoming self-fulfilling, i.e., if the work is styled on the assumption that it will not be read in private, then it probably won't. This is how the NLT renders the Colossian Hymn:

> 15 Christ is the visible image of the invisible God.
> He existed before anything was created and is supreme over all creation,
> 16 for through him God created everything
> in the heavenly realms and on earth.
> He made the things we can see
> and the things we can't see—
> such as thrones, kingdoms, rulers, and authorities in the unseen world.
> Everything was created through him and for him.
> 17 He existed before anything else,
> and he holds all creation together.
> 18 Christ is also the head of the church,
> which is his body.
> He is the beginning,
> supreme over all who rise from the dead.
> So he is first in everything.
> 19 For God in all his fullness
> was pleased to live in Christ,

---

667. "Introduction," in NLT.
668. Rom 10:17.
669. This echoes Rieu's critique of aspects of Phillips' version, as noted above.

> 20 and through him God reconciled
> everything to himself.
> He made peace with everything in heaven and on earth
> by means of Christ's blood on the cross.

The question remains in what ways, if any, has this effort supplemented and/or rendered more "intelligible" what was previously available, or to what extent does it instead sustain the historical translation tradition? As the Bible Translation Committee explains its thinking:

> It is evident in Scripture that the biblical documents were written to be read aloud, often in public worship (see Nehemiah 8; Luke 4:16–20; 1 Timothy 4:13; Revelation 1:3). . . . Therefore, a new translation must communicate with clarity and power when it is read publicly.[670]

Without at all denigrating that stated goal, it is open to question whether it has been achieved. It is admittedly difficult to perceive any novel renderings, or to detect any greater intelligibility here than in other versions that might be "read aloud" at a church service. To some extent, felicity of expression is a subjective matter. But the above passage from the NLT is not particularly elevated in tone despite the Greek's hymnic register and the transporting nature of the christological vision it reflects.[671] Admittedly, focusing on the Colossian Hymn does not do full justice to the NLT as a whole (any more than it does to any of the other translations so examined). And yet it is illustrative how often passages that *should* call for more enlivening literary presentation are nevertheless rendered just as they were in prior translations.

Take Heb 1:1 as another example, where the Greek is written in an alliterative, polysyllabic, even stentorian style: Πολυμερῶς καὶ πολυτρόπως πάλαι ὁ θεὸς λαλήσας τοῖς πατράσιν ἐν τοῖς προφήταις. Despite the NLT's stated desire to emphasize the aural nature of the Bible, it leaves it at this: "Long ago God spoke many times and in many ways to our ancestors through the prophets." Here's a possible alternative: "From ancient days at multiple times in multiplex manner God spoke to our fathers through the mouths of his prophets." That is of course far from

---

670. "Introduction," in NLT.

671. The NLT's main translator of the epistles was Dr. Norman R. Ericson of Wheaton College. I have the benefit of seeing the chief stylist's editorial comments on Dr. Ericson's initial draft of Colossians. Taylor, "Chief Stylist's Edits." Comparison of that draft with the final version, however, shows that few of the stylist's suggestions were adopted.

the only solution and may well be less "accessible" than the NLT. But sometimes the verbal traits of the literal text matter.

9. Hart (*The New Testament: A Translation*)

Dr. David Bentley Hart is widely known for his pointed formulations of Eastern Orthodox theology in contrast to what he deems Western Orthodoxy. Among other things, he contends that the Reformers' understanding of God's foreknowledge was deeply flawed, leading to the allegedly erroneous doctrine that some shall be saved and others damned for eternity. In Hart's reading—as he titles one of his books—it is in fact God's plan "that all shall be saved."[672] Hart's 2017 translation of the New Testament is consistent with those views. His stated purpose in undertaking a new translation was to provide an alternative to the plethora of those shaped by what he deems preformed "doctrinal expectations" rather than fidelity to the Greek. He takes aim in particular at the consequences of what he describes as Jerome's "inept rendering of a single verse, Romans 5:12 ... , for the development of the Western Christian understanding of original sin."[673] He is referring to Jerome's translation of ἐφ' ᾧ πάντες ἥμαρτον as *in quo omnes peccaverunt*, to which he traces Augustine's doctrine of original sin, i.e., guilt inherited from Adam rather than incurred by one's own actions.[674] Hart translates the relative pronominal as "whereupon all sinned," which he interprets to mean that each newborn person has a capacity to sin and thereby incur his own, not Adam's guilt.[675]

672. Hart, *That All Shall Be Saved*.
673. Hart, *New Testament*, xv.
674. In the Douay-Rheims translation, the phrase reads "in whom all have sinned." The Puritan couplet that introduced schoolchildren to the letter *a* is similar.

New-England Primer. See also Church of England, "Articles of Religion," art. 9.

675. Hart reads ἐφ' ᾧ to refer to the immediately preceding word, θάνατος, and to mean "whereupon" rather than "because." As such, the verse means that "the consequence of death spreading to all human beings is that all became sinners." Hart, *New Testament*, 296. Grammatically, however, ἐφ' ᾧ as a neuter relative pronoun introduced by the preposition ἐπί refers to an earlier concept or phrase, rather than a single word.

Hart asserts that much of Christendom understands sin as it does *not* because the text compels such a reading, but because Jerome's mistranslation led to a doctrinal error that persists notwithstanding the text. To put it in Gadamerian terms, Hart alleges this be a prejudice/horizon of which most Protestant and Catholic Christians are unaware, one attributable to Augustine's reading of the Vulgate.[676] At the same time, Hart is candid in acknowledging his own Eastern Orthodox perspective as the horizon against which *he* reads the text, arguing that such a reading is justified both on grounds of coherence with the literal Greek, including as informed by Greek-speaking commentators such as Origen.[677] As such, Hart may be seen to be engaged in hermeneutical dialogue with the Western Church's tradition, "filling out" the text even as he seeks to dismantle others' interpretations of it.

Hart takes further aim at the "perilously hazy" results of translations produced by committees of scholars, which he describes as yielding "solutions [to textual and doctrinal difficulties] that prove the least offensive to everyone involved, thus "becom[ing] ineluctably mired in the anodyne blandness and imprecision of 'diplomatic' accord."[678] He does so not to champion his own writing style, however, stating plainly that his version "is not a literary translation of the New Testament, much less a rendering for liturgical use."[679] Here is how he presents 1:15–20:

> 15 Who is the image of the invisible God, firstborn of all creation, 16 Because in him were created all things in the heavens and on earth, the visible as well as the invisible (whether Thrones of Lordships or Archons or Powers); all things were created through him and for him; 17 And he is before all things, and all things hold together in him, 18 And he is the head of the body, of the assembly—who is the origin, firstborn from the dead, so that he might himself hold first place in all things—19 For in him all the Fullness was pleased to take up a dwelling, 20 And through him to reconcile all things to him, making peace

---

"ὅς," 1.k, especially 1.k.δ for ἐφ' ᾧ, BDAG 727. Read thus, it means that all sin "by virtue of" the separation from God occasioned by Adam's sin, with death thereby obtaining the power to rule (Rom 5:14).

676. Wycliffe's translation of the relevant passage as "in which man all men sinned" would likewise be defective in Hart's view.

677. Hart, "Reply."

678. Hart, *New Testament*, xiv–xv. Hart is, however, less dismissive of prior translations of Colossians than he is, for example, of those of Romans.

679. Hart, *New Testament*, xvii.

by the blood of this cross [through him], whether the things on the earth or the things in the heavens.

Hart does have distinctive readings of certain terms of critical theological import;[680] but at the same time his translation methodology is consistent with a more literal approach given his careful respect for the formal text.[681] He therefore attributes his admittedly halting English to alleged defects in the Greek.[682] But he also mines the English language for words that may be legitimate renderings of the Greek but are remarkably obscure, such as tilth, chaplet, and cuirasse. That said, whether one adopts his interpretive readings or not, his glosses on and explanations of word choices are now part of the text's *Wirkungsgeschichte* and should be taken into account by anyone coming to the task after him.

10. Straus (*The New Testament: A 21st Century Translation*)

I would be remiss if I failed to include my own translation in this analysis. I undertook the project without having let alone applying a developed translation methodology, such as a purposeful tilt towards the literal, the dynamically equivalent, or the paraphrastic. That said, my base commitment was to the Greek text as a safeguard against invented meaning. I considered intrascriptural and intertextual usages, the historical settings of the various books, commentaries, and other translation efforts. And I often found it necessary to take doctrinal positions into account, in particular when presenting detailed arguments such as those in Romans or Corinthians. But if I had an idealized goal, it would have been that expressed by Robert Alter:

> I would propose that for an English translation to make literary sense it somehow has to register the stylistic authority of the 1611 version, or, one might say, it needs to create a modern

---

680. The most important of which are addressed in his extended footnotes and excursus.

681. Hart does however render "fullness" as the subject of v. 19. This is almost certainly incorrect. The intrascriptural reference to Ps 67:17 LXX as well as the preferred grammar indicate that the implied subject is the Deity. See Lightfoot, *St. Paul's Epistles*, 158–59, analyzing the grammatical options as well as the doctrinal consequences of choosing one or the other.

682. Hart says he chooses to "write bad English" when he judges that a given biblical text is written in "bad Greek." Hart, *New Testament*, xviii. See also the critique in Wright, "Strange Words," and the rejoinder in Hart, "Reply."

transmutation of how the King James translators imagined the Bible should be rendered in English.[683]

Without purporting to have reached that goal, I nevertheless strove for some degree of literary interest and artistry. This required attention to genre and register, with stylistic distinctions depending on whether the material involved narrative, epistolary, or visionary elements. To that end I engaged in number of variations, including departures from standard grammar and syntax; use of colloquialisms; incorporation of other languages; provision of commentary or historical information in the text rather than in marginal notes; and the use of parachronisms.[684] As relevant to my focus on the Colossian Hymn as a methodological test case, my 2019 published version reads as follows:

> He is the Radiant Image of the Invisible God, the Offspring of Heaven, the Firstborn of all creation—because in him all things in Heaven and on Earth collectively were created, whether seen or unseen, thrones or dominions, rulers or powers. All things were created by him and for him. He himself is before all things and all things cohere in him. He is the Head of the Body, the Church, its source and beginning, firstborn from among the dead in order that he himself have preeminence in all things— because it was pleasing to God that the totality of the pleroma of divine perfection should take up its dwelling in him and that having made peace through the blood of the Savior's cross he would through him reconcile all things back to himself, whether things on Earth or things in Heaven.

But I would now translate the same passage quite differently. It appears within my new translation of the whole Letter to the Colossians in the appendix. But for convenience, it is also set forth below with highlighting using the same yellow, red, blue, and green conventions used above. The highlighting thus reveals certain "classical" words that remain as core elements in the continuum of the WYC/TYN/KJV translation tradition, notwithstanding wording outside that tradition.

---

683. Alter, *Art of Bible Translation*, 10.

684. There is a particularly large such range in Revelation. See Straus and Reiland, *Revelation* (illustrations, musical notations, hyperlinks, and non-English languages).

Elements of a Canonical-Hermeneutical Translation Approach/Test Case 195

He is the Radiant[685] *Image*[686] *of the Invisible God*[687] *consubstantial with the Father*[688] *eternally begotten not made*[689] *Firstborn*[690] *above all Creation*[691] *by whom*[692] *all things in Heaven and on Earth were created*[693] *be they seen or unseen*[694] *thrones or dominions rulers or powers*[695] *all were created by him*[696] *and for him who is himself before all things*[697] *and in whom all things*

685. Adapted from Niceno-Constantinopolitan Creed: Φῶς ἐκ Φωτός.

686. 2 Cor 4:4; Heb 1:3; Gen 1:27 (κατ' εἰκόνα Θεοῦ ἐποίησεν αὐτόν); Wis 7:26; Gregory of Nazianzus, *On God and Christ*, oratio 30.20; Second Decree of the Council of Antioch (τοῦ πατρὸς ἀπαράλλακτον εἰκόνα).

687. John 1:18; Irenaeus, *Adversus haereses* 1.10.1; Hilary of Poitiers, *Liber (II) ad Constantium Imperatorem* 11 (*qui est imago dei invisibilis*); Basil of Caesarea, *Epistula* 38.8; cf. Plato, *Timaeus* 92c.

688. Added from Niceno-Constantinopolitan Creed; Hilary of Poitiers, *De synodis* 84 (*unius substantiae cum patre* [*quod Graeci dicunt omousion*]); Athanasius, *Against the Arians* 1.1.9 (μονάδα δὲ θεότητος ἀδιαίρετον καὶ ἄσχιστον).

689. Added from Niceno-Constantinopolitan Creed; Chalcedonian Statement; Ps 2:7 (υἱός μου εἶ σύ, ἐγὼ σήμερον γεγέννηκά σε), 110:4 (σὺ εἶ ἱερεὺς εἰς τὸν αἰῶνα).

690. John 3:16; Rom 8:29; Heb 1:6; Exod 4:22; Num 3:12–13; Prov 8:22; Niceno-Constantinopolitan Creed; Origen, *In Matthaeum commentariorum series* 33 (*primogenito universae creaturae*).

691. Ps 88:28 LXX (κἀγὼ πρωτότοκον θήσομαι αὐτόν, ὑψηλὸν παρὰ τοῖς βασιλεῦσιν τῆς γῆς); Gen 4:22; *Constitutiones Apostolorum*, 6.11.1–2 (ἕνα μόνον θεὸν καταγγέλλομεν . . . , θεὸν καὶ πατέρα τοῦ μονογενοῦς καὶ πρωτοτόκου πάσης δημιουργίας); Ignatius of Antioch, *Epistle to the Smyrnaeans* 1.2; Justin Martyr, *Dialogus cum Tryphone* 85.2; Origen, *De principiis* 1.4 (*ante omnem creaturam natus ex patre est*).

692. John 1:4; Acts 17:28; Ps 32:6 LXX (τῷ λόγῳ τοῦ Κυρίου οἱ οὐρανοὶ ἐστερεώθησαν καὶ τῷ πνεύματι τοῦ στόματος αὐτοῦ πᾶσα ἡ δύναμις αὐτῶν); Wis 9:9.

693. Gen 1:1, 2:1; 14:19; Rev 10:6; Pseudo-Athanasius, *Expositio fidei* 4 (ὥς φησιν ὁ Παῦλος περὶ τοῦ κυρίου· Ὅτι ἐν αὐτῷ ἐκτίσθη τὰ πάντα, καί· Αὐτός ἐστι πρὸ πάντων); cf. Sir 1:4.

694. Niceno-Constantinopolitan Creed.

695. Jer 52:32; Ezek 1:26; 9:3; 10; 11:22; Ps 18:10; Victricius of Rouen, *De laude sanctorum* 2: *credimus individuam trinitatem . . . per quam omnia visibilia et invisibilia sive throni sive dominationes sive principatus sive potestates*.

696. John 1:3, 10; 2 Pet 3:5; Heb 1:2, 10; Rev 22:13; Prov 3:19–20; Niceno-Constantinopolitan Creed; Irenaeus; *Epideixis*, 6 (δι' οὗ τὰ πάντα ἐγένετο); *Letter of Six Bishops to Paul of Samosat* 4 (Ἐν αὐτῷ ἐκτίσθη τὰ πάντα, τὰ ἐν τοῖς οὐρανοῖς καὶ τὰ ἐπὶ γῆς, εἴτε ὁρατὰ εἴτε ἀόρατα εἴτε θρόνοι εἴτε ἀρχαὶ εἴτε κυριότητες εἴτε ἐξουσίαι, πάντα δι' αὐτοῦ καὶ εἰς αὐτὸν ἔκτισται).

697. John 1:1–2; Prov 8:22–31; Sir 24:9; Niceno-Constantinopolitan Creed; Chalcedonian Statement.

> cohere,[698] the Head and Source of the Body the Church[699] the A and Ω[700]—and he is Firstborn from among the dead[701] that he have preeminence in all things,[702] it having pleased God[703] that the Totality of the Pleroma of Divine Perfection[704] should take up its dwelling in him[705] and that having made peace through the blood of the Savior's cross[706] he would through him reconcile all things back to himself, be they things on Earth or things in Heaven.[707]

Although there are considerable departures from a word-for-word rendering of the literal Greek, the core of the text remains. But I now take more careful account than I had previously of the text's intrascriptural language and imagery; its intertextuality with noncanonical materials; its effective history in credal and other formulations; and the embeddedness of its translation tradition. These are now annotated with considerable detail in order to reveal the effective history of the text. The linguistic variations and additions in this version are not meant to supersede or displace existing translations, but rather to illustrate how one might continue to fill the "free space around" the text and point the reader to overlooked and/or less available elements of its effective history.[708] For example, I reverted to Wycliffe's use of "begotten" in v. 15, even though it had been dropped in later translations, in order to preserve and reflect its use in the Niceno-Constantinopolitan Creed and the Chalcedonian Statement. I likewise reverted to Tyndale's use of "rule" in v. 16. And I added words not found in the Greek text but rather in faith formulae

---

698. John 8:58; Heb 1:3; Exod 3:14; Wis 1:7; Sir 43:26; Vulgate (*omnia in ipso constant*); Basil of Caesarea, *De fide*, prologus 8.4 (ἐν ᾧ τὰ πάντα συνέστηκεν); Gregory of Nazianzus, *On God and Christ*, oratio 30.20; John of Damascus, *Expositio fide*, 1.3; cf. "Concerning Noah's Work as a Planter," 2.9, in Philo, *Works of Philo*, 191.

699. Eph 1:22.

700. Adapted from Rev 1:8.

701. 1 Cor 15:20; *Concilium Serdicense: Professio fidei ab episcopis occidentalibus promulgata* 6 (Ὁμολογοῦμεν . . . ὅτι καὶ πρωτότοκος ἐκ τῶν νεκρῶν).

702. Rev 1:5; Sir 24:5–10.

703. Ps 67:17 LXX (ὃ εὐδόκησεν ὁ Θεὸς κατοικεῖν ἐν αὐτῷ); 2 Chron 7:1–2.

704. Athanasian Creed, §6; Irenaeus, *Adversus haereses* 17.1–5; cf. John of Damascus, *Expositio fide* 1.8, 14.

705. John 1:14; 2:19–21; Exod 40:34–35; Isa 8:18; Chalcedonian Statement; cf. Milton, *Paradise Lost*, 3.225 ("The Son of God, in whom the fulness dwels of love divine").

706. Rom 5:1.

707. Eph 1:20–23; Rev 21:1–3.

708. See Luz, *Matthew 1–7*, 99: "The texts are full of possibilities of application which do not exclude each other." And other writers would doubtless find other wording.

"canonized by the ecumenical council,"⁷⁰⁹ such as "consubstantial with the Father."

Stylistically, I attempted poetico-literary language that might be of a transporting nature, in an effort to convey the ineffability of the divine message expressed through the text's distinctive vocabulary, regardless of whether the same is found in the underlying Greek or its lengthy translation tradition. Hence a phrase like "the Totality of the Pleroma of Divine Perfection." This version also includes capitalizations, extensive marginal notations, interpolated wording, and *nomina sacra*, for methodological reasons addressed in sect. III.b, *infra*. And it is italicized and inset, thus taking account of form and source-critical scholarship concerning the text's hymnic character.

I could similarly critique (and revise) other portions of my prior translation. For example, my earlier version of John 1:1 departs considerably from the literal Greek because I wanted to elicit the temporal/atemporal aspects of the passage as possibly indicative of its inner word.⁷¹⁰ Hence I wrote, "The Word existed before all Time, timelessly present with God and himself true God. He was with God at the outset." But I might now revert to the "classical" rendering of John 1:1 in order to respect the embedded role of that formulation in church tradition, i.e., simply to write, "In the beginning was the Word and the Word was with God and the Word was God."⁷¹¹ Thus, it might just as well serve my exegetical purpose were I to address issues of temporality and atemporality in a marginal comment, while retaining the reception history of the verse in its classical form. Moreover, my earlier translation failed to take into account the complex spatial/nonspatial relations among members of the Godhead that might be implicated by John's Prologue, aspects that were further explored in the Trinitarian debates of the fifth century as well as the writings of John of Damascus and others. In other words, respect for the translation tradition sometimes justifies using the same language that has been and still is used. My point in this self-critique is that just as the Word is alive, so too is the expressive word, which

---

709. J. Kelly, *Early Christian Doctrines*, 217.

710. See, e.g., Augustine, *De Trinitate* 2.9: "And when the fulness of time came, God sent his Son made of woman, that is, made in time, in order that the Word might be shown to men incarnate; and the time at which this should happen was timelessly contained within the Word."

711. I adopted such an approach, for example, in my translation of the Lord's Prayer in Matthew, where I presented the KJV *in haec verba*.

remains open to reexamination, recapitulation, and recirculation in a "hermeneutical spiral."⁷¹²

iii. Specialized Versions

1. Amplified

The Amplified Bible is purposefully distinctive, designed to provide multiple alternative readings of given words and phrases to allow the reader to weigh them for himself rather than have all the choices fixed by the translator. It does not read smoothly as a finished translation, but neither is it intended to. That said, there is necessarily a selection process in the alternatives presented, the goal being to "reveal a word's intensity or power" and "to clarify the meaning of a theological word."⁷¹³ To the extent there is a governing translation philosophy at work, it is "literal equivalence."⁷¹⁴ So amplified, the Colossian Hymn appears as follows:

> 15 He is the exact living image [the essential manifestation] of the unseen God [the visible representation of the invisible], the firstborn [the preeminent one, the sovereign, and the originator] of all creation.
>
> 16 For by Him all things were created in heaven and on earth, [things] visible and invisible, whether thrones or dominions or rulers or authorities; all things were created and exist through Him [that is, by His activity] and for Him.
>
> 17 And He Himself existed and is before all things, and in Him all things hold together. [His is the controlling, cohesive force of the universe.]
>
> 18 He is also the head [the life-source and leader] of the body, the church; and He is the beginning, the firstborn from the dead, so that He Himself will occupy the first place [He will stand supreme and be preeminent] in everything.

---

712. Osborne, *Hermeneutical Spiral*; cf. Joyce, *Finnegans Wake*, 1: "a commodious vicus of recirculation," adverting to Giambattista Vico's attempt to systematize historical cycles.

713. "Principles," in Amplified Bible (2015). The mission and purpose of its publisher the Lockman Foundation is "to promote Bible translation, Christian evangelism, education, and benevolence." "Overview," Amplified Bible (2015).

714. Amplified Bible (2015). The term "literal equivalence" is not in general usage. However, it suggests greater adherence to the text's formal characteristics than "dynamic equivalence."

19   For it pleased the Father for all the fullness [of deity—the sum total of His essence, all His perfection, powers, and attributes] to dwell [permanently] in Him (the Son),

20   and through [the intervention of] the Son to reconcile all things to Himself, making peace [with believers] through the blood of His cross; through Him, [I say,] whether things on earth or things in heaven.

As formatted, the non-bracketed material tracks the literal Greek; the bracketed material adds synonymous, clarifying, and to some extent interpreting material. This of course can be useful in personal devotion as well as for exegesis, although the additional information could alternatively be presented in marginal notation. The non-bracketed text is thus virtually indistinguishable from other literal translations. Hence it is essentially in the intratextual bracketed material that the Amplified Bible's distinctiveness lies. Whether the material is additive or just confusing, however, is an open question. It is not clear, for example, whether adding the words "the essential manifestation" in Col 1:15 to explain the theology of the Godhead is any more illuminating to the reader. It may be that passages such as this are neither clarified nor explained by simply adding more words. Whether "amplifying" the literal text with material reflective of its effective history can provide further insight remains, of course, a question posed by this book.

2. Interlinear

A strictly interlinear presentation of the text, with an English equivalent for each word in the same sequence as it appears in the Greek, is a unique form of translation and might be considered a genre of its own.[715] It is not meant for ordinary reading, given the inherent structural differences between Greek and English (in this case), but rather as an aid to translation. For example, an online interlinear translation includes hyperlinks to *Strong's Concordance* as a source for vocabulary and syntactical forms.[716] While there is generally little dispute in identifying a given form as to number, gender, case, tense, etc., there is by definition no fixed English equivalent to many of the words. Interpretive decisions are therefore

---

715. As noted above, the term "word-for-word" is more accurately applied to an interlinear translation than to a "literal" one.

716. See https://biblehub.com/interlinear/.

often required for words with doctrinal overtones. That said, it is inherent to the interlinear genre that no words are added (unless essential to the form, such as "helping" words for certain verbs); no words are deleted; no idioms are employed; and for the vocabulary to rely on English equivalents commonly found elsewhere. The following is a readily available interlinear version of the Colossian Hymn:

15 ὅς ἐστιν εἰκὼν τοῦ θεοῦ τοῦ ἀοράτου, πρωτότοκος πάσης κτίσεως,
Who is image of God of the invisible firstborn of all creation/creatures

16 ὅτι ἐν αὐτῷ ἐκτίσθη τὰ πάντα ἐν τοῖς οὐρανοῖς καὶ ἐπὶ τῆς γῆς,
Because in him were created all things in the heavens and on the earth

τὰ ὁρατὰ καὶ τὰ ἀόρατα,
the seen and the unseen

εἴτε θρόνοι εἴτε κυριότητες εἴτε ἀρχαὶ εἴτε ἐξουσίαι· τὰ πάντα δι᾽ αὐτοῦ
whether thrones or rulers or lords or powers all things through him

καὶ εἰς αὐτὸν ἔκτισται·
and in him were created

17 καὶ αὐτός ἐστιν πρὸ πάντων καὶ τὰ πάντα ἐν αὐτῷ συνέστηκεν,
and he is before all and all things in him stand together

18 καὶ αὐτός ἐστιν ἡ κεφαλὴ τοῦ σώματος τῆς ἐκκλησίας· ὅς ἐστιν ἀρχή,
and he is the head of the body of the church who is beginning

πρωτότοκος ἐκ τῶν νεκρῶν, ἵνα γένηται ἐν πᾶσιν αὐτὸς πρωτεύων,
firstborn from the dead so that might be in all he preeminent

19 ὅτι ἐν αὐτῷ εὐδόκησεν πᾶν τὸ πλήρωμα κατοικῆσαι
because in him was pleased all the fullness to dwell

20 καὶ δι᾽ αὐτοῦ ἀποκαταλλάξαι τὰ πάντα εἰς αὐτόν, εἰρηνοποιήσας
and through him to reconcile all things into him having made peace

Elements of a Canonical-Hermeneutical Translation Approach/Test Case

διὰ τοῦ αἵματος τοῦ σταυροῦ αὐτοῦ δι' αὐτοῦ, εἴτε τὰ ἐπὶ τῆς
through the blood of the cross of him through him whether the things on
γῆς εἴτε τὰ ἐν τοῖς οὐρανοῖς.
earth or things in the heavens.

It is instructive to compare that interlinear version with the translation in the appendix in order to see how the latter remains rooted in the text, yet varies from word-for-word correspondence in vocabulary as well as phrasing. It is also instructive how *intelligible* an interlinear version can be, even if it lacks necessary articles or verbs and doesn't conform to proper English word order or other grammatical rules. There are some suggestive possibilities here. For one thing, English is less distantly removed from Greek than other languages (such as Chinese, for example) and has a large number of Greek derivatives, as well as those taken from Latin.[717] And perhaps because Koine Greek exhibits a greater linearity of word order than did the Attic, one can make decent sense of the interlinear despite its staccato form. Further, the intelligibility of an interlinear version illustrates how the underlying text safeguards against extreme or unorthodox readings. And it may likewise justify the authoritative/classical status of versions that form the heart of the English translation tradition.

Some popular interlinear versions in fact rely on the vocabulary of the KJV for the verses in question, others on the RSV. But one can imagine creating an interlinear version using less common English equivalents. And further, to the extent there are only limited options in word selection for essential words such as blood, cross, image, all, dead, heaven, or earth, a translator should be humble enough not to become overly enamored of his own vocabulary and phrasing in the process, lest he find himself so unmoored from the text as to be conveying something other than its inner word.

Finally, it might be interesting to develop a grammatically/syntactically correct form of interlinear translation. Each word would be translated and given a superscript number. The given verse would then be restructured into proper English sentence form, thus allowing the reader to see clearly what words were omitted and/or added in bridging differences between the two languages. Here's an example from Col 1:19:

717. See Nichols, "Translating the Bible," 42.

ὅτι¹ ἐν² αὐτῷ³ εὐδόκησεν⁴ πᾶν⁵ τὸ⁶ πλήρωμα⁷ κατοικῆσαι.⁸
Because¹ it pleased⁴ God that all⁵ the⁶ Fullness⁷ of the Godhead should dwell⁸ in² him.³

Presenting the English in this way illustrates some of the basic syntactical differences between the two languages and at the same time provides the reader with information on the literal meaning of each Greek word. As such, it may be an aid to further translation as well as exegesis. Whether a grammatically correct interlinear version is a useful improvement over existing interlinear versions is for anyone to judge. But the point is that there is virtue in deep familiarity with the original text as well as its translation tradition, using them as the foundation and building thereon.[718]

g. Methodological Conclusions

In this section I draw conclusions as to the viability and applicability of the theory's canonical-hermeneutical approach, based on the linguistic and literary analysis of the test passage from Colossians in sect. II.e, and the examination of its translation tradition in sect. II.f. In both instances, it became clear that considering the text as the *viva vox evangelii* may allow a modern translator to give full respect to the literal Greek while at the same time incorporating the intrascriptural and intertextual elements of its presence throughout church history and tradition—and to do so with the combined benefit of classical as well as contemporary formulations.

i. Elements Relating to Linguistic and Literary Analysis

A detailed linguistic and literary analysis indicates that there is no "one size fits all" expressive mode when it comes to the range of biblical texts. To be sure, there are certain books or portions of books in the Bible that appear reasonably homogeneous. But in a broader sense, imposition of a single governing approach—whether literal, dynamic equivalence, or paraphrastic—will likely fail to account for plain differences among or even within the individual texts as to writing style, vocabulary, and grammatical forms, as well as the occasional inclusion of hymnic, prayerful, or

---

718. Cf. 1 Cor 3:10–15.

other separately identifiable material. This would be true not only for the test passage from Colossians, but also for other texts within a given literary genre, whether Gospels, Acts, Letters, or Revelation. As such, varied translation approaches may be called for, lest prose become poetry or poetry prose.

Second, in seeking to convey a text's expressive message, a translator should avail himself of historical-critical research into situational aspects of the letter. In the example used here, that would include translationally relevant information concerning competing or contrasting worship practices, contemporaneous writings, specialized vocabulary, and the sociological composition of a given worshipping community.

Third, in assessing possible linguistic options that would sustain a given text's role within a "whole Bible" framework, it is likewise important to identify the intrascriptural presence of words and imagery from the LXX as well as other books in the New Testament.

Fourth, the same would be intertextually true with respect to a given text's subsequent trajectory in church history and tradition. Again, for exemplary purposes that effective role could be seen in the development and refinement of doctrine and liturgy by way of credal affirmations, faith formulae, and conciliar understandings.

ii. Elements Relating to the Translation Tradition

In addition to the linguistic and literary elements of the methodology, examination of the English translation tradition of the Colossian Hymn confirmed the continued presence of authoritatively classical wording in contemporary versions. As noted, numerous word choices made by Wycliffe when he translated from the Vulgate at the outset of the translation tradition have been sustained for some seven hundred years, even as subsequent translators worked directly from the original Greek, and even as the English language developed from that time. Doctrines of justification, redemption, sin, forgiveness, and faith, as well as understandings of Christ's sonship, image, blood, flesh, death, or resurrection, are thus persistently articulated in English, at least, using Greco-Latinate, Anglo-Saxon, and other wordings linguistically received over multiple centuries in multiple English-speaking communities. And the continued use of many of these "classical" formulations in such academically informed and broadly church sponsored translations as the RSV, NRSV, and NRSVue further confirms their normatively authoritative nature.

But second, as a number of the modern versions excerpted above illustrated, there remains "free space around" the text "in its revealing" of the *verbum interius*, whereby a contemporary translator may take account not only of "classical" formulations but also the varied forms in which the text has found expression throughout history. These can include credal and other doctrinal language, intratextual references, intertextual allusions, and even cultural material from literature and music. To be sure, some texts will have more free space around them than others. And it may well be that the methodology of this book finds fullest value in the more elevated, theologically complex passages of the Scripture, such as the Colossian Hymn.

Third, where fresher language appeared in the translation tradition, it tended to be by way of individual translations rather than through multiply layered committee efforts. Without in the least disregarding the importance of a wide range of scholarly input, this may reflect the natural conservatism of larger translation projects and the linguistic compromises that are inherent to such structures. That conservatism does have the virtue—as seen in the NRSV and NRSVue, for example—of sustaining the core translation tradition with its embedded theologically rooted linguistic formulations. Yet in the post-KJV era, a parallel subordination of literary style may explain the unmemorability if not blandness of certain modern translations.

Fourth, detailed analysis of christologically relevant words and phrases in Colossians indicates that texts of this nature often call for interpretive decisions on the part of a translator based on scholarship of a philological, historical, or sociological nature. But they also call for interpretive decisions as to doctrinal and theological positions. Taking account of the hermeneutical principles outlined in sect. I.b, *supra*, translators should therefore consult prior translations in order to be conscious of their own horizons within the translation tradition; weigh such scholarly input through commentary or consultation as may be appropriate in order to safeguard against obvious doctrinal errors; and assess the canonical setting of the text as well as its further trajectory in church history and tradition in order to reach conclusions how best to convey aspects of the divine message in question.

The foregoing illustrates the challenge of the translator's art, whereby he seeks to maintain a "living relationship between [himself] and the text" as a "participa[nt]" in its effective history.[719] Application of a canonical-hermeneutical approach to the linguistic, intrascriptural, and intertextual elements of the New Testament should thereby assist a contemporary translator in forging language reflective of the Word's verbal incarnation across time.

---

719. Gadamer, *Truth and Method*, 290, 331.

III. Application of the Methodology to the Text

THE CANONICAL-HERMENEUTICAL TRANSLATION METHODOLOGY advanced here is one that requires particular attention both to formal aspects of a biblical text and its effective history as revealed in church history and tradition. The theoretical justification for doing so is based on certain linguistic insights concerning the relationship of thought and language and a balanced understanding of the contributions of paleographic, philological, and sociohistorical research, all as discussed in sect. I. The elements of the methodology were identified, analyzed, and tested against Colossians as an exemplary text in sect. II. Working from a Greek text based on UBS⁵/NA²⁸ (but with certain modifications based on a preference for one variant over another), I focus in this sect. III on certain technical elements involved in producing a new translation. I first note the implications of the translation methodology for any choices of words and phrases. I then discuss various issues relating to the formal presentation of the text in English. Finally, a new translation is provided in the appendix as to how one might apply the methodology to a given text, again using Colossians as an example.

a. Words and Phrases

At its most basic level, a translator's task involves selecting appropriate words and phrases in his receptor language that bear some explicable relationship to the text as presented in the source language.[1] As noted in sect. II.a, the nature of that relationship might vary depending on one's translation methodology—whether literal, dynamically equivalent, paraphrastic, or some hybrid approach. Regardless, the underlying text imposes some limits on the selection, even if what is produced is merely

---

1. Cf. Dryden, "Preface to Sylvae": "An Author has the choice of his own thoughts and words, which a Translatour has not; he is confin'd by the sence of the Inventor to those expressions which are the nearest to it."

allusive to the source material, as might be the case with a parody. As relevant here, where the goal is a contemporary version of a sacred text, such limitations arise in the first instance out of a literal grounding in the Greek as the verbally incarnational expression of a divine communication to the writer. Thus, given the continuum of the Word in the world, words chosen for translation may be multiply sourced as to prior usage by reliance on standard philological materials, including lexicons, dictionaries, and the like. Meaning is then further elicited with reference to sociohistorical analyses of a work's contextual setting.

But understanding a biblical text *also* requires examination of its effective history in credal expressions and other faith formulae, as well as doctrinal writings, sermonic expositions, commentaries, and other theological presentations. It likewise means taking account of words, imagery, and/or phrases in the text that may be intrascripturally resonant with the LXX, as well with as other books in the New Testament. And it further requires a translator's consideration of formulations found in the text's translation tradition. Beyond all that, where the *verbum interius* of the text is such that its ineffability tests the expressive limits of human language, a translator remains tasked with forging as spiritually transporting a passage as he can.

Even so, there will from time to time be credible translation options based on the grammar and syntax, options which may or may not be resolved by taking into account the text's effective history in church doctrine and liturgy. It is particularly in such cases that translation overlaps with exegesis, because in both instances the goal is to deliver the divinely communicated message in intelligible form so that it may be actively received by the reader or listener. As such, it is essential for translators to be aware of their own cultural and conceptual horizons (or "prejudices" in the Gadamerian sense), in seeking to present the words of the text in a way that fairly embodies the inner word of which the text is a processual expression. But because a translation is not itself a sermon or theological treatise, it may best serve in aid of the same where a translator alerts the reader/interpreter to possible alternative readings by marginal note or otherwise. So while there remains "free space around" the ancient text for expression of the living presence of the Word in present-day words,[2] I do not minimize the potential difficulties of the hermeneutical task.

---

2. See Gadamer, *Philosophical Hermeneutics*, 102, 210–11.

b. Formal Matters

Finding fit words and phrases may be at the core of the translator's task, but the text's formal elements can also come into play as revelatory of inner meaning. As explained in this section, attention to form can include aspects of the manuscript history, such as the presence of *nomina sacra*. Moreover, while the original text may have been written in *scriptio continua*, its subsequent history whether in later manuscripts or its translation tradition permits of sense-unit divisions by chapters and verses, punctuation, ekthetic, or other paragraphing, headings, and/or subheadings. The same is true with respect to capitalization, italics, or other forms of emphatic distinction. Neither the literal text itself nor tradition impose great constraints on such formal matters. Moreover, a *viva vox Jesu* hermeneutic permits a degree of personal style as the Word is unfolded in contemporary language.

i. Chapter and Verse/Punctuation

Ancient Greek manuscripts were written in a form referred to as *scriptio continua*. That is, they lacked chapter divisions; they lacked verse numbers; they lacked punctuation indicating where one sentence ends and another begins; and they even lacked spacing to show where one *word* ends and another begins. Over time, spacing was added as well as punctuation. But this has also left room for numerous variants. For example, one manuscript will indicate a full stop, but another will not; or one will punctuate a sentence declaratively, another interrogatively. Likewise, at a certain point biblical texts were subdivided into chapters based on a scribal or other determination that doing so would aid in readability, intelligibility, and perhaps exegesis. The same was true as sentences or portions of sentences came to be marked as individually numbered verses (although this did not occur until as late as the mid-sixteenth century). And as chapters, verses, and punctuation stabilized into lectionaries and/or copies of the Bible, they essentially became a common mode of reference.[3]

Apart from these general developments, some editors and publishers employ their own distinctive fonts or marginal indentations to mark express quotations from the Old Testament, or to provide subheadings for material they wish separately to categorize. Indeed, there are differences between the way NA[28] indicates paragraph separations and the way UBS[5]

---

3. See generally Witherington, *New Testament Rhetoric*, 104–8.

does, even though both use the same Greek text.[4] Moreover, unlike credal language that has been "canonized by the ecumenical council,"[5] these formatting developments do not reflect such a compellingly effective history of the text as to be a consistent element of the church's interpretive tradition. Nor is there consistency within the English translation tradition. It follows that a translator coming freshly to the text is often free to make his own decisions how best to divide, format, or even punctuate the text.

To be sure, ease of reference and familiarity are factors to consider. My own translation of the New Testament[6] reflects a hybrid approach. On the one hand verse numbers are jettisoned in favor of ordinary English sentences and paragraphs.[7] This admittedly makes it harder for a reader to find a given "chapter and verse." However, my translation is not meant to substitute for the many available versions that maintain such divisions. There are also departures from punctuation decisions made over the past millennia, as to which there is in all events often disagreement in the critical apparatus. And sometimes the text is punctuated in such a way as to maintain an uninterrupted flow of language and imagery, especially where the subject matter might call for departure from strict grammatical rules.[8]

At the same time, traditional chapter divisions remain. They do not impair readability in the way verse numbers can. And the persistence of chapter divisions may now embody church tradition as to broad thematic transitions reflective of the text's inner word. Even so, where a given text is short enough (as with 1 and 2 Peter), dividing it into chapters seems less justified than allowing it to be read more cohesively. And Revelation is sufficiently distinct as to allow for an entirely different approach not only with respect to internal divisions, but also syntactically and grammatically as a means of reflecting the text's atemporal nature.[9]

---

4. These decisions have evolved over time and varied from editor to editor. Thus, "in the early Nestle editions, Westcott and Hort were followed in matters of indention, paragraphing, and highlighting OT quotations. Then Nestle began accepting suggestions from scholars who were not following printed editions." Gregory S. Paulson, email to author, 2020. See Abram, "Reader's Edition."

5. J. Kelly, *Early Christian Doctrines*, 217.

6. Straus, *New Testament*.

7. The classicist, poet, and translator E. V. Rieu did something similar. See Rieu, *Four Gospels*, xiii. There are, however, no fixed rules for English paragraphing. Many would paragraph this book itself differently than I have. And some writers paragraph not at all. E.g., Kerouac, *On the Road*.

8. E.g., Col 1:15–20; Eph 1:3–14; Revelation.

9. See Straus and Reiland, *Revelation* (with illustrations, musical notation, and hyperlinks).

ii. *Ekthesis*

As explained above, typical Greek texts of the period written in *scriptio continua* would not have had sense units demarcated by paragraphs, as is the case with standard English. However, a form of paragraphing known as *ekthesis* has recently been adopted by the editors of the Tyndale House Greek New Testament based on early manuscript evidence that "from time to time differs from modern paragraph designation" assigned by the editors of other versions.[10] As a technical matter, *ekthesis* refers to a scribal practice of "projecting the first letter of the first full line of a new paragraph/section into the left margin."[11] While there are indications of *ekthesis* in a second-/third-century papyrus,[12] the principal sources justifying its usage are the fourth-century codices Sinaiticus and Vaticanus.

Larry Hurtado speculated that *ekthesis* as well as certain other scribal practices[13] may have been designed to "mark sense units, both

---

10. See Tyndale House Cambridge, "About This Edition."
11. Hurtado, *Earliest Christian Artifacts*, 179.
12. See T. Mitchell, "Reading Aids," providing this illustration from an early manuscript of Mark:

[Greek manuscript illustration]

13. Such as a diaeresis over an initial iota in some early manuscripts and "slightly wider spaces between words at certain points." Hurtado, *Earliest Christian Artifacts*, 179.

sentences/clauses and paragraph-size units."[14] Or they may have had a liturgical function, possibly relating to how the texts were read aloud in worship.[15] Or the formatting may reflect exegetical decisions by a given scribe, even if we can no longer discern the reasoning.[16] While the Greek text of the GNT is thus ekthetically presented in ways that suggest early sense transitions, its editor, Dirk Jongkind, is cautious as to the significance of the markings. For one thing, he found insufficient evidence that the divisions were intended to function as "building block[s] in the hierarchical structure of the text" in the way we might think paragraphs function now.[17] For another, he indicated that the breaks "did not work" everywhere, such as in Revelation.[18]

That said, there seems to be sufficient evidence based on early uses of *ekthesis* to justify paragraphing the *Greek* text as does GNT.[19] However, because there is no ekthetic formatting convention in English, creating one could well look odd to the reader, yet without adding to meaning. A translator should therefore mark sense transitions in an *English* translation based on his own sense of proper usage.

iii. Capitalization and Italics

There is a striking lack of uniformity when it comes to capitalization in translating biblical texts. This is likely due, at least at its origins, to there being no "large" and "small" letters in the ancient texts, but only majuscules, i.e., what we now refer to as "capital letters." The smaller, script-like Greek letters known as minuscules with which we are now familiar did not appear until the ninth and tenth centuries. Only thereafter did it become common to combine majuscule and minuscule letters in printed forms of Greek texts, such as are now common in NA^{28}/UBS^5 and elsewhere. Once the Bible began to be translated into English, however,

14. Hurtado, *Earliest Christian Artifacts*, 180.

15. Hurtado, *Earliest Christian Artifacts*, 181. This possibility is attractive, given the limited literacy of the period and the corresponding importance of reading the documents to congregants in worship or teaching. See Col 4:16; 1 Thess 5:27.

16. Hurtado, *Earliest Christian Artifacts*, 185.

17. Jongkind, *Introduction*, 36: Sometimes it was "difficult to find any 'system' behind what is happening."

18. Jongkind, *Introduction*, 36.

19. Utter faithfulness to the presumed form of the original texts would mean presenting them in *scriptio continua*, but there would be no utility in doing so.

capitalization at the start of new sentences became the rule.[20] It likewise became conventional to capitalize proper names and places, as well as God, Jesus, Holy Spirit, and titles such as Lord.[21] To be sure, English is not uniform as to the rules; and practice has varied greatly over time.[22] There is thus no clear tradition. That said, capital letters are sometimes used for emphasis. Taking that as a premise, the translation methodology example in the appendix involves capitalizing a number of words that are not normally capitalized in translation. This may be one way orthographically to reflect an elevated register. Of course, this can be overdone if one is not careful.[23]

And the same is true of italics, which are not present in the Greek text and as to which there are no standard guidelines. As a general matter, at least in English, they may also be used for emphasis, as can be seen in my own writing in the body of this work from time to time. They may also serve to mark a distinctive register. But in that regard, when italics are used in biblical translation they are something of a hybrid: neither sourced in the text nor representing the purely original thoughts of the translator, but rather the translator's sense that something in the text reflects an emphatic element of the inner word and might appropriately be

---

20. But see Hart, *New Testament*, eccentrically capitalizing the first word of each New Testament verse, regardless of whether it begins or falls within a sentence.

21. N. T. Wright, however, provides an explanation for why he *didn't* capitalize Spirit in his translation: "I use lower-case 's' for 'spirit', not because I hold a 'low' view of the third person of the Trinity but because, in the first century, the early Christian use of the common and polysemous word *pneuma* had to make its own way without such help." Wright, "Poem Doubled," 2.

22. For example, it is hard to deduce a governing rule why "day" and "night" are capitalized in Gen 1:1–5 of this 1744 Bible but "heaven" and "earth" are not; or why "day" is capitalized in one part of v. 5 but not another:

> IN * the beginning God created the heaven and the earth.
> 2 And the earth was without form and void; and darkneſs *was* upon the face of the deep: and the Spirit of God moved upon the face of the waters.
> 3 And God ſaid, ᵇ Let there be light: and there was light.
> 4 And God ſaw the light, that *it was* good: and God divided † the light from the darkneſs.
> 5 And God called the light Day, and the darkneſs he called Night: † and the evening and the morning were the firſt day.

23. Cf. Mervosh, "Trump Uses Random Uppercase Letters."

presented as such. So again, this can easily be overdone; and there is in all events wide room for disagreement.

iv. *Nomina Sacra*

As noted above, the proposed methodology suggests reviving the ancient manuscript use of *nomina sacra* as a distinctively reverential orthography. Such markers were arguably one of the ways the early church identified Jesus with the Tetragrammatonic God of Israel, as was also the case in some of its most fundamental doxologies, e.g., that "Jesus is Lord." As such, *nomina sacra* are important paleographic elements of the text's effective history, pointing to an inner canonical and spiritual meaning perceived by the early church and developed through the living tradition of its writings. Given the theological significance of *nomina sacra*, it would thus be consistent with the hermeneutic of this work to reflect them in translation.[24]

There are various ways one might indicate *nomina sacra* in English, such as with a line or bar over certain letters in replication of the early Greek forms themselves. That would mean only using two out of a number of letters in a given word for God, Father, Lord, Jesus, Christ, or Spirit (if one were to limit oneself to the "primary" group)—either by contraction or suspension, i.e., using the first and last letters of a given word or the first two. While mimicking the Greek calligraphy in that way might be the purest form of presenting *nomina sacra*, modern word processing software requires several programming steps to create overscoring of a sort found in the early manuscripts.[25] An alternative would be to underscore the letters. Or one could dispense with any additional marking of a given combination of two letters. However, some of the resulting units are either English words themselves (like GO), or would just look strange (like SP). Or one could follow the examples in Luther's Bible of 1534, where Lord is rendered by HErr, God by GOtt, and Jesus by JEsus. The result would be an Anglicized, hybrid version similar to that of Luther's German, spelling out the full word yet capitalizing just its first two letters,

---

24. That this early reverential and canonically unifying form has largely faded from view may itself be a reason to present it anew. The GNT's editors note the presence of *nomina sacra* in early manuscripts but do not mark them in the current version because of a lack of "uniformity." At the same time, they indicate that it would be a "desideratum" to include them in future editions. See GNT, 511.

25. See "Guide to Overlining Characters."

i.e., GOd, FAther, LOrd, JEsus, CHrist, or SPirit. The problem with that option is that these forms do not obviously signal the meaningfulness that seems evident in the early manuscripts. Moreover, they are homely in English and therefore lack figurative presence.[26]

But even better, one might adopt the KJV's small-caps form of Lord for the Tetragrammaton, but now using small capitals for *all* the *nomina sacra*, not just Lord.[27] Adopting the KJV's small-caps format would nicely preserve the reverential and canonical importance of the *nomina sacra*, while also maintaining formal links both to the historic manuscripts and the translation tradition.[28] For this book's present purposes, the relevant *nomina* have been limited to forms found in early manuscripts of Colossians. These include the third-century 𝔓46 (one of the so-called Chester Beatty Papyri), the fourth-century Codex Sinaiticus, and the fifth-century Codex Alexandrinus. Hence they appear in the translation in the appendix as God, Jesus, Christ, Father, Spirit, and Lord.

c. References and Allusions

Numerous books in the New Testament contain direct quotations from the Old Testament, as well as intertestamental books or certain works whose precise origin is unknown. Apart from direct quotations, such materials are occasionally the subject of paraphrase, with what are either variances from the earlier texts or possibly reflections of earlier yet lost versions. Beyond that, the books of the New Testament are laced with intrascriptural references to passages in the LXX, as well as other New Testament materials. Many or even most of these references can be relevant to exegesis.[29]

---

26. And this is not to mention how distant they are from the aesthetics of sacramental lettering achieved through illumination in later materials. See Horsley and Waterhouse, "Greek *Nomen sacrum*." And just consider the elaborate *chi-rho* abbreviation in the ninth-century Book of Kells. Kearney, "Book of Kells."

27. See also Bokedal, "Notes on *Nomina Sacra*," 274, noting John Henry Newman's use of capital letters in his own writings to mark the divine names.

28. I relied for the most part on the Greek text of Sinaiticus as prepared by the Center for New Testament Restoration for locations of the *nomina sacra*. See https://greekcntr.org/home/index.htm. The one exception concerned Πατρός, which is in *nomina sacra* form in Col 3:17 of Sinaiticus, yet not in Col 1:2 in that same codex. However, it *is* in *nomina sacra* form in Col 1:2 in Vaticanus; and I therefore include it here as well.

29. See generally Hays, *Echoes of Scripture*; Ellis, *Paul's Use*. Again, as noted, intrascripturality of this sort can be seen as a direct influence on a given text rather than the parallel consideration of related doctrines.

Some references may be less explicit. In a recent study of Old Testament references in Colossians, for example, Christopher Beetham argues that the letter in fact has multiple "allusions" to and/or "echoes" of Old Testament themes, indirect references of which the writer was likely aware based on similarity of words or phrases.[30] To the same effect is Gregory Beale and Donald Carson's analysis of the entire New Testament, as to which there is some overlap with Beetham's study of Colossians, but also some divergence.[31] Others have also identified such allusions.[32] Some of these references may only be "within a field of whispered or unstated correspondences,"[33] the allusions by one text "to an earlier text in a way that evokes resonances of the earlier text beyond those explicitly cited."[34]

The extent to which Paul's first readers and listeners perceived such references or allusions is a separate question. For example, while it is not possible to know with any certainty what familiarity members of the Colossian assembly brought to bear, it seems to have been comprised of a number of Jewish Christians, see sect. II.d.i, *supra*, for whom the LXX would have been an embedded liturgical source.[35] Catechesis of new gentile believers may well have included instruction in the Old Testament. And today there are many readers and listeners who are familiar with the Old Testament through their own faith community's teaching, preaching and liturgical worship, all with the effective history of some two thousand years of accrued interpretation and tradition.

Taking the foregoing as a set of guidelines, my annotated example translation freely identifies numerous possible sources, references, or allusions in Colossians across a range of biblical and nonbiblical materials. This is consistent with the proposed translation theory's interpretive principle recognizing canonically unified themes of promise and fulfillment, obedience and disobedience, and judgment and redemption as essential

---

30. Beetham, *Echoes of Scripture*, 15–24, 263. See also 24–27 (proposing a general category of "parallels" as a nonliterary mode of reference); but see Sandmel, "Parallelomania" (criticizing "parallelomania"); cf. Alter, Review of *Great Code* (criticizing the overbreadth of Northrop Frye's literary categories).

31. Beale and Carson, *Commentary*.

32. E.g., as marginally noted in Alford, *Greek New Testament*; NA^{28}/UBS^{5}; and M. Robinson and Pierpont, *New Testament*.

33. Hays, *Echoes of Scripture*, 20, 29.

34. Hays, *Conversion*, 2 (emphasis omitted).

35. Where the numbering of a given passage in the Septuagint varies from the Masoretic Text as rendered in most English versions, such as in the Psalms, the LXX numbering has been followed when citing the passage in Greek.

elements of the effective history of the LXX in the New Testament and the New Testament's trajectory going forward.[36] Of course, a fresh translation need not include *every* such reference. For one thing, such cross-references are readily available in many versions.[37] A more relevant goal would be to provide additive rather than duplicative methodological results, such as by inclusion of passages from the LXX, noncanonical sources, and credal and doctrinal materials that are not as readily available. There can certainly be legitimate differences of opinion between one translator and another in deciding what references to include and what to exclude. But ideally, any such references should be selected in aid of providing an expanded means of access to the *verbum interius* of a given text.

---

36. See Stuhlmacher, *Biblical Theology*, 199, 367, 800–801; C. Campbell and Pennington, *Reading the New Testament*, 3; Baker, *Two Testaments*, 373; Schoeman, *Salvation Is from Jews*, 78–134; J. Dunn, *Partings of the Ways*, 188–201; M. Wilson, *Our Father Abraham*, 54–56, 111–13; Hengstenberg, *Christology of Old Testament*, 1.21–22, 1.245–54.

37. See, e.g., Attridge, *Harper Collins Study Bible*, 2000–2004.

IV. Research Contributions and Epilogue

a. Research Contributions and Suggestions for Future Research

As NOTED AT THE outset, I seek to fill a gap in translation theory and practice parallel to certain developments in New Testament studies. Just as Markus Bockmuehl and others argue that exegetes should take fuller account of the Bible's reception history and theological readings in order to reflect to the living nature of the Scriptures, I argue that translators should do the same. The approach taken here therefore provides contributions in several areas of biblical studies, in the first instance by applying Patristic, Scholastic, Reform, and Contemporary linguistic insights to the art of translation, developing a novel methodological approach that takes into account a text's *Wirkungsgeschichte* by incorporating elements of that living history not previously considered in this context. I further respond to developments in translation theory exemplified by Eugene Nida's dynamic equivalence approach by offering a corrective balance to its history-eliding nature. And the *viva vox evangelii* ethos of the book not only builds on paleographic, philological, and sociohistorical research as well as classically formulated material, but also allows for the creative use of contemporary language in a continued filling of the "free space around" the text.

The methodology advanced here also contributes to canon theory by taking a translational approach dependent on the "wholeness" of Scripture. It offers a contribution to church history by expanding existing translation methodologies in order to elucidate textual effects on credal, doctrinal, and liturgical development and their reciprocal revelation of textual meaning. And it offers this philologically and theologically informed approach to biblical translation in service of the church's practical work of proclamation and worship.

The work also points the way towards further exploration. Because the viability of the methodology advanced here is only tested against certain formal and substantive elements of Colossians, it does not purport to cover the entirety of that letter's effective history, as might be the case were it to be analyzed within the framework of something like the Blackwell Bible Commentary series.[1] And the extent to which the methodology may be applicable to other genres within the New Testament, such as narrative elements of the Gospels or Acts, the visionary form of Revelation, or even other epistolary presentations, also remains to be explored. The book is thus suggestive of the methodology's application throughout the New Testament, but does not fully test it; and therefore draws no conclusions as to possible modifications that would be required with respect to a given subunit of the canon.

More broadly, the book does not address the methodology's possible applicability to Old Testament texts, which may present distinctive theological, historical-critical, social-scientific, textual, and linguistic issues. And even within the Old Testament, it remains to be examined whether the answer to such questions might vary depending whether one is translating the Greek LXX or the Masoretic Hebrew.

Finally, the methodology itself would benefit in particular from further research into the nature and purpose of *nomina sacra*. While I note the potential importance of *nomina sacra* as evidence of an intentional continuity of reverence from the Old to New Testament for the divine name as well as a canonically essential affirmation of Christ as the same God of creation and Israel, there remains a good deal of research to be done into the origins and usages of this textual form. And there remain similar areas of research into the nature and purpose of *ekthesis*, or markers such as those noted by Larry Hurtado in some early manuscripts in the form of a diaeresis over an initial iota or slightly wider spaces between certain words. All of these may have possible implications as formal indicators of substantive, theological meaning.

b. Epilogue: Prolegomena to Any Future Translation

As a conclusory epilogue, I offer a series of principles as prolegomena to any future translation.[2] These are not meant to be proscriptive so

---

1. See Maier, "Colossians and Philemon" (outlining such a project).
2. *Pace* Immanuel Kant.

much as suggestive elements that translators might consider in light of the canonical-hermeneutical methodology advanced herein. These principles implicitly critique and go beyond those set forth by Eugene Nida as guidelines for translation committees. As explained above, the methodology proposed here allows room for literal, dynamic, and paraphrastic approaches to a given text, the style potentially varying depending on the genre or register involved. It likewise allows room for the intrascriptural presence of the Septuagint in New Testament materials as well as the effective history of those materials in the church's ongoing kerygmatic mission. That effective history notably includes credal and other doctrinal statements, the text's own translation tradition, and even the presence of the Scriptures in literature, music, and art. Taken together, these form elements of the conceptual "horizon" of any present-day translator, a consequence of his "situatedness within the flow of history."[3]

This approach was outlined in prior sections, first by establishing a theoretical framework based on ancient and contemporary linguistic insights together with a balanced use of historical-critical paleographical, philological, and sociohistorical research; second by constructing a translation methodology utilizing such insights and research; and third by testing the methodology's viability against Paul's Letter to the Colossians. By tracing words and imagery as present in the literal Greek, rendered into Latinate form, coined in Middle English with inputs from its several component languages, developed in credal and other materials thereafter, and retained in varied translation efforts to date, it becomes clear that the "inner word" of the text is far from remote.[4] Moreover, an understanding of that inner word may be enhanced by way of an interactive engagement between translator and text in a manner exemplary of what Gadamer terms the *wirkungsgeschichtliches Bewußtsein*—a mode of thought that is conscious of its "being affected by history."[5]

Against that background, the following are offered as guidelines relevant to future New Testament translations. While the factors are not listed in a fixed order of importance, they do reflect how the methodology might progressively be applied.

1. The ground for any translation should always be the literal Greek text, which thereby serves as a normative safeguard against imagined

---

3. Thiselton, *New Horizons*, 6.
4. See Rom 10:8.
5. Gadamer, *Gadamer Reader*, 59.

readings and interpretations. The essential form of the New Testament is quite stable notwithstanding its myriad variants, although a translator should also be familiar with text-critical scholarship in determining the text from which to translate. Whether adhering to a particular manuscript tradition or proceeding on the basis of an eclectic text, a translator should thus consider possible variants and decide whether to modify the base text accordingly.

2. A New Testament translator should consult Septuagint materials to identify intrascriptural elements that might have a direct influence on the text, i.e., the extent to which given passages in the LXX may provide direct wording, allusions, and/or themes expressed in the text at hand.

3. A translator might likewise consult the Masoretic Text to identify any such intrascripturality, with particular reference to possible Hebraicisms.

4. A translator should further take account of any intrascripturality within the New Testament itself as an aid to discerning word meaning, including the extent to which one usage may influence or be parallel to another, and where one usage may diverge from, supplement, or elucidate another.

5. With respect to the meanings and usages of particular words, a translator will necessarily avail himself of the extensive scholarship reflected in a multitude of specialized dictionaries, lexicons, grammatical analyses, and concordances. In that context, classical as well as New Testament usage may be relevant. Hence the varied citations above to the LSJ, *CGL*, *BDAG*, *PGL*, *TDNT*, and other linguistic resources. And where a translator adopts a plainly novel rendering using slang, parachronisms, alternative graphics, additional wording, or the like, he should consider alerting the reader that he is doing so and why in marginal notation, perhaps also providing the more literal option.

6. A translator should likewise become familiar with a text's contextual setting, availing himself of historical-critical scholarship to the extent it may shed light on usage and meaning.

7. A translator should give serious attention to the text's *Wirkungsgeschichte*, examining how textual meaning is revealed and applied in church tradition, with consciousness of his own situatedness within

the flow of history. This aspect includes consideration of a given text's presence in writings of the apostolic fathers, apologists, and other commentators; and more broadly on any effect it may have in the development of credal or other liturgical materials.

8. A translator may further consider whether to reflect particularly notable elements of the text's effective history by incorporating credal or other post-textual language into the translated form itself and/or by providing marginal notation, quotes, and commentary.

9. If and to the extent there is a translation tradition in the receptor language, it too forms an essential element of any translator's literary and linguistic horizon. He should therefore be conscious of the inertial force exerted by prior translations by virtue of their reception, ecclesial endorsement, and/or language-formative impact. And in that context, a translator should focus on formulations that have taken on an authoritatively "classical" role in church tradition, such that they might be retained as such in any future translation regardless of the stated translation methodology. Examples in the New Testament might include the Lord's Prayer, portions of John's Prologue, or aspects of Paul's doctrine of justification; just as Ps 23 might be in the Old. In this context as well, a translator should consider the possible influence of the Latin Vulgate, whether as a source for classical formulations, early understandings, or even possible misreadings.

10. Taking such substantive factors into consideration, it will from time to time be the case that lexical as well as contextual information allows for more than one credible reading. In some instances, different readings may implicate varying doctrinal positions. It is in such cases in particular that translation overlaps with exegesis, in that in both instances the goal is to deliver the divinely communicated message in intelligible form so that it may be actively received by the reader or listener. As such, it is essential for a translator to be aware of his own cultural and conceptual horizons (or "prejudices" in the Gadamerian sense), in seeking to present the words of the text in a way that fairly embodies the inner word of which the text is a processual expression. But because a translation is not itself a sermon or theological treatise, it may best serve in aid of the same where a translator alerts the reader/interpreter to possible alternative readings by marginal note or otherwise.

11. From a stylistic point of view, a translator should consider reflecting the multiplicity of genres and registers within the New Testament by adopting varied forms of the receptor language, whether narrative, liturgical, lyrical, poetic, rhetorical, didactic, prosaic, or paracletic. And where a translator determines he should depart from standard usage, he should consider alerting the reader that he is doing so and why.

12. A translator should also consider whether or how to reflect formal aspects that are not present in all Greek texts, such as *nomina sacra*, punctuation, *ekthesis*, capitalization, italics, chapters, paragraphs, or verses.

13. As a broader consideration, a translator should be prepared to take a position in translation whether or how to account for possible gender-, race-, and/or power-based presuppositions that may be discerned in a given text.

14. There are also important procedural aspects to consider. In that regard much depends on the origination of a given translation effort, such as whether it is an individual undertaking, one sponsored denominationally/interdenominationally, a publisher's venture, or some combination thereof. Each has distinctive factors relating to relevant skills, oversight, and decision making. But regardless of the originating structure, it behooves translators to give enhanced importance to literary quality as well as clarity, so as to avoid wording that is mere "translationese." And even where the style is principally that of an individual translator, he should of course avail himself of the linguistic and theological insights of others.

15. From a "whole Bible" perspective, if a given project involves translation of both Testaments, translators should consider how to maintain canonical unity while taking account of distinctive scholarship relating to the Hebrew and the Greek texts.

16. Regardless of whether a given translation project adopts or rejects any of the foregoing guidelines, the translator(s) should provide their listeners and readers with a prefatory statement of the translation approach employed, including its relationship to other methods, in order to provide them with maximum edification from the version.

The foregoing are thus suggestive principles derived from the canonical-hermeneutical methodology of this work and its illustrative application. They are offered as such for consideration in structuring future translation projects. And because they are guidelines, there remains room for great variation in any resulting translation. Indeed, one virtue of the plethora of existing translations, the wide availability of Greek texts, the diversity of church traditions, the broad readership demand for the Bible, and the extensive pool of persons with the requisite linguistic, literary, and theological skills to undertake translation projects, is that multiple needs can be met, such as those of youthful readers, persons with only limited language capacity, or those who desire a relentlessly literal version.

In that regard Eugene Nida was right to note the value of translations prepared for readers of varied linguistic skills or interests,[6] even though he may have underestimated the general reader's ability to appreciate and derive meaning from complex doctrines or elevated language, or discounted the continued validity of classical formulations that by time and tradition have become inseparably woven into the church's "ongoing recapitulation of the event of salvation in the kerygma."[7] It therefore remains fully open to be seen where the methodology advanced here might lead a given translator—save my submission that his overarching goal should be continuing to fill the "free space around" the text, whose very meaning is found "in its revealing" of the Word's "inner mental word."[8]

---

6. Nida and Taber, *Theory and Practice*, 31.
7. Arthos, *Inner Word*, 358.
8. Gadamer, *Philosophical Hermeneutics*, 211; Gadamer, *Truth and Method*, 421.

Appendix
To the Colossians

PAUL, AN APOSTLE OF CHRIST JESUS in accordance with the Will of GOD, and Brother Timothy—to the saints in Colossae, steadfast brothers and sisters in CHRIST, we send grace and peace from our FATHER GOD and the LORD JESUS CHRIST.

We give thanks always to GOD, FATHER of our LORD JESUS CHRIST, in our prayers for you, having heard of your faith in CHRIST JESUS and the love you have toward all the saints on account of the hope stored up for you in Heaven, that hope of which you have heard before in the True Word[1] of the gospel made present among you[2] as it becomes fruitful and multiplies through the whole Earth,[3] just as it has in you from the very first day you heard and fully understood the Grace of GOD, being instructed truthfully in the Word by Epaphras, our beloved fellow laborer. He is CHRIST's faithful servant on your behalf; and has made plain to us your love in the SPIRIT.

Therefore we too from the time we first heard about you have not ceased in our prayers for you, imploring GOD that you be filled with perfect knowledge of his Will in all wisdom and SPIRIT-given discernment;[4] that you conduct yourselves in a manner worthy of the LORD in all things, seeking to please him, bearing fruit in every good work, increasing in the knowledge of GOD, strengthened with all power according to the might

---

1. John 1:1. Literally, "the word of the truth of the gospel."
2. John 1:14.
3. Cf. Gen 1:28 (αὐξάνεσθε καὶ πληθύνεσθε καὶ πληρώσατε τὴν γῆν); 9:1; Isa 27:6 (ἐξανθήσει Ἰσραὴλ καὶ ἐμπλησθήσεται ἡ οἰκουμένη τοῦ καρποῦ αὐτοῦ); Acts 6:7; 12:24.
4. Exod 31:3 (ἐνέπλησα αὐτὸν πνεῦμα θεῖον σοφίας καὶ συνέσεως καὶ ἐπιστήμης); Isa 11:2; Eph 1:17–18.

of his Glory;[5] and that you endure to the end with all patience, giving thanks with joy to the FATHER, who enabled us to share in the inheritance of the saints in the Realm of Light and translated us in exodus[6] from the tyranny of darkness to the Kingdom of his Beloved Son,[7] in whom we have redemption through his blood,[8] the forgiveness of sins.[9]

> He is the Radiant[10] Image[11] of the Invisible GOD[12] consubstantial with the FATHER[13] eternally begotten not made[14] Firstborn[15] above all Creation[16] by whom[17] all things in Heaven and on Earth

---

5. Ambrose, *De fide* 1.16.

6. Literally, "rescued us." Hence a gloss on Exod 6:6 (λυτρώσομαι ὑμᾶς); Deut 7:8; Matt 2:15.

7. Pss 88:27–28 LXX (πατήρ μου εἶ σύ, Θεός μου), 39 (χριστός), 52 (same); Exod 14:30; 2 Sam 7:10–16; Hos 11:1; Matt 3:17.

8. Eph 1:7; Deut 15:15.

9. Isa 44:22.

10. Added from Niceno-Constantinopolitan Creed: Φῶς ἐκ Φωτός.

11. 2 Cor 4:4; Heb 1:3; Gen 1:27 (κατ᾽ εἰκόνα Θεοῦ ἐποίησεν αὐτόν); Wis 7:26; Gregory of Nazianzus, *On God and Christ*, oratio 30.20; Second Decree of the Council of Antioch (τοῦ πατρὸς ἀπαράλλακτον εἰκόνα); cf. Creed of Basil of Ancyra (Τοῖς ἀποκαλοῦσι τὰς ἱερὰς εἰκόνας εἴδωλα ἀνάθεμα).

12. John 1:18; Irenaeus, *Adversus haereses* 1.10.1; Hilary of Poitiers, *Liber (II) ad Constantium Imperatorem* 11 (*qui est imago dei invisibilis*); Basil of Caesarea, *Epistula* 38.8; cf. Plato, *Timaeus* 92c.

13. Added from Niceno-Constantinopolitan Creed; Chalcedonian Statement; Hilary of Poitiers, *De synodis* 84 (*unius substantiae cum patre* (*quod Graeci dicunt omousion*)); Athanasius, *Against the Arians* 1.1.9 (μονάδα δὲ θεότητος ἀδιαίρετον καὶ ἄσχιστον).

14. Added from Niceno-Constantinopolitan Creed; Chalcedonian Statement; Pss 2:7 (υἱός μου εἶ σύ, ἐγὼ σήμερον γεγέννηκά σε); 110:4 (σὺ εἶ ἱερεὺς εἰς τὸν αἰῶνα).

15. John 3:16; Rom 8:29; Heb 1:6; Exod 4:22; Num 3:12–13; Prov 8:22; Niceno-Constantinopolitan Creed; Origen, *In Matthaeum commentariorum series* 33 (*primogenito universae creaturae*).

16. Gen 4:22; Pss 88:28 LXX (κἀγὼ πρωτότοκον θήσομαι αὐτόν, ὑψηλὸν παρὰ τοῖς βασιλεῦσιν τῆς γῆς); *Constitutiones Apostolorum*, 6.11.1–2 (ἕνα μόνον θεὸν καταγγέλλομεν . . . , θεὸν καὶ πατέρα τοῦ μονογενοῦς καὶ πρωτοτόκου πάσης δημιουργίας); Ignatius of Antioch, *Epistle to the Smyrnaeans* 1.2; Justin Martyr, *Dialogus cum Tryphone* 85.2; Origen, *De principiis* 1.4 (*ante omnem creaturam natus ex patre est*).

17. John 1:4; Acts 17:28; Ps 32:6 LXX (τῷ λόγῳ τοῦ Κυρίου οἱ οὐρανοὶ ἐστερεώθησαν καὶ τῷ πνεύματι τοῦ στόματος αὐτοῦ πᾶσα ἡ δύναμις αὐτῶν); Wis 9:9.

were created[18] *be they seen or unseen*[19] *thrones or dominions rulers or powers*[20] *all were created by him*[21] *and for him who is himself before all things*[22] *and in whom all things cohere,*[23] *the Head and Source of the Body the Church*[24] *the* A *and* Ω[25]—*and he is Firstborn from among the dead,*[26] *that he might have preeminence in all things,*[27] *it having pleased* GOD[28] *that the Totality of the Pleroma of Divine Perfection*[29] *should take up its dwelling in him,*[30] *and that having made peace through the blood of the Savior's cross*[31] *he would through him reconcile all things back to himself, be they things on Earth or things in Heaven.*[32]

And you Gentiles, who once were estranged and at enmity with GOD by your thoughts and the wicked things you did,[33] have now been

18. Gen 1:1; 2:1; 14:19; Rev 10:6; Pseudo-Athanasius, *Expositio fidei* 4 (ὥς φησιν ὁ Παῦλος περὶ τοῦ κυρίου· Ὅτι ἐν αὐτῷ ἐκτίσθη τὰ πάντα, καί· Αὐτός ἐστι πρὸ πάντων); cf. Sir 1:4.

19. Niceno-Constantinopolitan Creed.

20. Jer 52:32; Ezek 1:26; 9:3; 10; 11:22; Ps 18:10; Victricius of Rouen, *De laude sanctorum*, 2 (*credimus individuam trinitatem . . . per quam omnia visibilia et invisibilia sive throni sive dominationes sive principatus sive potestates*).

21. John 1:3, 10; 2 Pet 3:5; Heb 1:2, 10; Rev 22:13; Prov 3:19–20; Niceno-Constantinopolitan Creed; Irenaeus, *Epideixis* 6 (δι' οὗ τὰ πάντα ἐγένετο); *Letter of Six Bishops to Paul of Samosat* 4 (Ἐν αὐτῷ ἐκτίσθη τὰ πάντα, τὰ ἐν τοῖς οὐρανοῖς καὶ τὰ ἐπὶ γῆς, εἴτε ὁρατὰ εἴτε ἀόρατα εἴτε θρόνοι εἴτε ἀρχαὶ εἴτε κυριότητες εἴτε ἐξουσίαι, πάντα δι' αὐτοῦ καὶ εἰς αὐτὸν ἔκτισται).

22. John 1:1–2; Prov 8:22–31; Sir 24:9; Niceno-Constantinopolitan Creed; Chalcedonian Statement.

23. John 8:58; Heb 1:3; Exod 3:14; Wis 1:7; Sir 43:26; Vulgate (*omnia in ipso constant*); Basil of Caesarea, *De fide, prologus* 8.4 (ἐν ᾧ τὰ πάντα συνέστηκεν); Gregory of Nazianzus, *On God and Christ*, oratio 30.20; John of Damascus, *Expositio fide* 1.3; cf. "Concerning Noah's Work as a Planter," 2.9, in Philo, *Works of Philo*, 191.

24. Eph 1:22; Augustine, *Sermo* 133.8.

25. Adapted from Rev 1:8.

26. 1 Cor 15:20; *Concilium Serdicense: Professio fidei ab episcopis occidentalibus promulgata* 6 (Ὁμολογοῦμεν . . . ὅτι καὶ πρωτότοκος ἐκ τῶν νεκρῶν).

27. Rev 1:5; Sir 24:5–10.

28. Ps 67:17 LXX (ὃ εὐδόκησεν ὁ Θεὸς κατοικεῖν ἐν αὐτῷ); 2 Chron 7:1–2.

29. Expanded from Athanasian Creed, §6; Irenaeus, *Adversus haereses*, 17.1–5; cf. John of Damascus, *Expositio fide* 1.8, 14.

30. John 1:14; 2:19–21; Exod 40:34–35; Isa 8:18; Chalcedonian Statement; cf. Milton, *Paradise Lost*, 3.225 ("The Son of God, in whom the fullness dwels of love divine").

31. Rom 5:1. Literally, "of his cross."

32. Eph 1:20–23; Rev 21:1–3.

33. Eph 2:1–3.

reconciled by his material body[34] through death that he might present you holy, unblemished, and irreproachable in his sight—*if*,[35] that is, you hold steadfast in faith, well grounded and seated, not shifting away from the Hope afforded by the gospel you have heard, that which was heralded to every creature under Heaven, of which I Paul am become a servant.

I rejoice now in the things I suffer for the sake of the Body of CHRIST, his Church, supplementing in my own flesh what lacks of the Savior's afflictions.[36] In GOD's Ordered Plan I was made a servant of his Church, gifted with the privilege of fulfilling GOD's Word toward you, the Mystery[37] hidden in past ages and generations but now revealed to his holy ones[38]—GOD wishing all people and nations to know the richness of the glorious manifestation of this Mystery—that CHRIST is within and among you all.[39] He is the Hope of Glory, the one whom we proclaim as we admonish and initiate every person into all Wisdom in order to present each perfected[40] in CHRIST.[41] And this is the same goal to which I also strive, battling in the arena by virtue of his energy working powerfully in me.

2

I want you to know how much I have agonized over you, your neighbors in Laodicea and all others who have not yet seen me in person, that with your hearts made one in love you may be confirmed abundantly in rich fullness of discernment, attaining perfected[42] knowledge of the Mystery of GOD,[43] even the SAVIOR,[44] who comprehends all apocryphal treasures of wisdom and understanding.[45] I say this so that no one leads you astray

---

34. Literally, "in the body of his flesh."
35. Emphasis supplied.
36. 2 Cor 11:23–28; 2 Tim 4:6; Augustine, *Enarrationes in Psalmos* 51.21.
37. Matt 13:11; Rom 11:25–26; 16:25–26; cf. Dan 2:19–21, 22, 28–30.
38. 1 Cor 2:7.
39. Acts 10; Eph 1:9–10; 3:3–6; Isa 2:2–4; Zech 2:11; 8:22–23.
40. Cf. Plato, *Phaedrus* 249c, 250b–c.
41. 1 Cor 2:6–7.
42. Added to reflect the intensifying prefix of ἐπίγνωσιν.
43. Isa 45:3; 1 Macc 1:23.
44. Literally, "CHRIST," hence the use of a form of a form of *nomen sacrum* here.
45. Prov 2:1–6 (σοφία, σύνεσις, ἐπίγνωσις, θησαυρός); 2 Bar. 44:14; 54:13; see Augustine, *Contra Faustum* 11.2.

with sophistic persuasion, for while I may not be there in person I am present with you in the SPIRIT, rejoicing as I behold you in ordered ranks shoulder-to-shoulder firm in your Christian faith.[46]

Live your lives the way you have received CHRIST JESUS the LORD: solidly rooted and built up in him, strengthened by the faith as you were taught it, overflowing with thanksgiving. But *watch out*[47] for those who'd lead you down the primrose path with casuistic deceit,[48] captivating you with mundane rituals.[49] None of this comes from the SAVIOR,[50] in whom the Immensurable[51] Plenitude of Deity dwells corporeally.[52]

You are fulfilled in the Fountainhead of every potentate and power,[53] he in whom you were circumcised with the circumcision not made by human hands,[54] the circumcision of CHRIST, that is, stripping off the whole body of your carnal affections. You were buried with him in the act of baptism, by which you also were raised up through faith in the energizing power of GOD, who raised him from among the dead—because though you were dead in your transgressions and the uncircumcision of your corrupted self[55] yet he made you alive with him, having forgiven us all our sins, cancelling the graven decrees that stood in hostility against us,[56]

---

46. Xenophon, *Anabasis* 1.2.18. Literally, "your faith in/towards CHRIST."

47. Emphasis supplied.

48. Eph 4:14; see, e.g., "That Every Good Man Is Free," 11, 13, in Philo, *Works*, 74, 88.

49. Josephus, *Jewish Antiquities* 18.1.2–4. There is no consensus as to the meaning of τὰ στοιχεῖα τοῦ κόσμου, translated here as "mundane rituals."

50. Literally, "CHRIST." The invented *nomen sacrum* is used as a way to sustain the reverential import of the manuscript form notwithstanding the alternative term.

51. Added from Athanasian Creed, §9 (*immensus pater, immensus filius, immensus spiritus sanctus*).

52. John 1:14; Niceno-Constantinopolitan Creed; Chalcedonian Statement (ὁμοούσιον τῷ πατρὶ κατὰ τὴν θεότητα καὶ ὁμοούσιον τὸ αὐτὸν ἡμῖν κατὰ τὴν ἀνθρωπότητα); Athanasian Creed, §§29–37; Ambrose, *De fide* 1.16 (*plenus e pleno*); *Letter of Six Bishops to Paul of Samosat* 8 (χωρῆσαν πᾶν τὸ πλήρωμα τῆς θεότητος σωματικῶς); Irenaeus, *Adversus haereses* 1.26.1 and 3.11.1; Cyril of Alexandria, *Epistula tertia ad Nestorium*; Hilary of Poitiers, *Liber (II) ad Constantium Imperatorem* 11 (*in quo habitat omnis plenitudo divinitatis corporaliter*).

53. Literally, "you are made complete in him, the head/source of every rule and power."

54. Deut 30:6 (περικαθαριεῖ Κύριος τὴν καρδίαν σου); cf. Lev 26:1; Isa 21:9.

55. Gen 17:11 (περιτμηθήσεσθε τὴν σάρκα τῆς ἀκροβυστίας ὑμῶν), 14, 24, 25; cf. Eph 2:11.

56. Deut 27:14–26; Rev 20:12; Apoc. Zeph. 3:6–9.

erasing our debt once and for all, nailing it to the cross[57] and through the cross disarming all sovereigns and dominions, exhibiting them boldly in his triumph over them.[58]

Therefore do not let anyone take you to task for what you eat or what you drink[59] or how you deal with feast days or new moons or Sabbaths,[60] all of which are a shadow of things to come,[61] while that which is typified by them, the true substance, belongs to CHRIST alone.[62] In the same way do not let anyone cheat you of your prize by insisting you abase yourselves in pompous worship of angels.[63] Such a person is suffused with vanity in his carnal mind, treading the void[64] of mystical sights[65] rather than clinging to the Head, from whom the whole Body derives, with every joint and ligament providing nourishment and strength as it knits together growing in godly increase.[66]

So why, if you died with CHRIST to childish things, do you still subject yourselves to man-made dogmas[67] as though you lived worldly lives—"don't handle, don't taste, don't touch"[68]—all concerning foods that perish in the eating?[69] These are but human commandments and teachings.[70] So while some people think it's "spiritual" to deny their natural passions with self-imposed asceticism and fleshly mortification, none of this properly honors the body.

57. Eph 2:15; Rom 5:18–21.

58. Ps 109:1 LXX (ἕως ἂν θῶ τοὺς ἐχθρούς σου ὑποπόδιον τῶν ποδῶν σου); Dan 7:27 LXX/Theodotion (πᾶσαι αἱ ἀρχαὶ αὐτῷ δουλεύσουσιν καὶ ὑπακούσονται).

59. Mark 7:14–23.

60. Isa 1:13–14 (τὰς νουμηνίας ὑμῶν καὶ τὰ σάββατα καὶ ἡμέραν μεγάλην); 1 Chron 23:31; 2 Chron 2:4; 31:3; Num 28:11; Gal 4:8–10.

61. Origin, *De principiis* 4.13.

62. Matt 5:17; 1 Cor 5:7; 10:1–11; Heb 8:5; 10:1; Calvin, *Institutes*, 2.11.4.

63. Josephus, *Jewish Wars*, 2.8.7; Hippolytus of Rome, *The Refutation of All Heresies*, 5.21; Apoc. Ab. 17:1–21; 2 En. 22:1–11; 3 En. 1:12.

64. Irenaeus, *Adversus haereses* 1.4.1–2; 2.3.1.

65. Cf. Aristophanes, *Nubes* 224–25; Plato, *Apology* 19c. There is no consensus as to the form or meaning of this verse. The ESV's translation is "going on in detail about visions, puffed up without reason by his sensuous mind."

66. Eph 4:15–16.

67. As noted, there is no consensus as to the meaning of τὰ στοιχεῖα τοῦ κόσμου, translated above as "mundane rituals" and here as "man-made dogmas."

68. Let. Aris. 142–43.

69. Mark 7:1–19; Tertullian, *Contra Marcionem* 5.19.

70. Matt 15:1–20; Mark 7:1–23; Isa 29:13 (διδάσκοντες ἐντάλματα ἀνθρώπων καὶ διδασκαλίας).

3

If you were raised up together with CHRIST, seek now the things that are above, where CHRIST is seated at the right hand of GOD,[71] setting your minds on heavenly not earthly things: for you died and your life is hidden safe with CHRIST in GOD.[72] When CHRIST (who is our life) is revealed, you will be revealed in glory with him.[73]

Therefore, put to death all that is earthly in your lives: licentiousness, pollution, ardor, cupidity—but especially avarice (which is idolatry). It's because of these things that GOD's wrath falls on the children of disobedience. I know these are behaviors in which you reveled in times past. But now you must set them aside, along with any kind of ire, rage, depravity, sacrilege, obscene mockery. Do not lie to one another either, now that you have divested yourself of your old nature with its practices and clothed yourselves with the new,[74] that which is being ever renewed into perfected knowledge[75] according to the Image of its Creator,[76] where there is no Greek or Jew, circumcised or uncircumcised, privileged or untouchable, labor or capital,[77] but CHRIST is all and in all.[78]

As GOD's Chosen People, holy and beloved,[79] be clothed with robes of compassion, kindliness, humility, docility, long-suffering.[80] Be charitable and tolerant towards each other (even if you have a legitimate grudge), because just as the Savior[81] absolved you, so must you one another.[82] But above all adorn yourselves with love,[83] which is the bond of perfection. Let the LORD's peace hold sway in your hearts, because to this you have been called in one Body. And be thankful. Let the word

---

71. Ps 109:1 LXX (κάθου ἐκ δεξιῶν μου); Matt 22:44; Mark 12:36; Luke 20:42–43; Eph 1:20; see also Acts 7:55–56, 58.

72. Cf. 2 Bar., 52:6–7.

73. Rom 8:18–19.

74. Eph 4:22–24.

75. Cf. Gen 2:17.

76. 1 Cor 15:49; 2 Cor 4:16; Eph 4:24; cf. Gen 1:26–27.

77. Literally, "barbarian, Scythian, slave, or free."

78. Gal 3:28–29; Rom 3:29; John 11:52.

79. Deut 7:6–8 (λαὸς ἅγιος εἶ Κυρίῳ τῷ Θεῷ σου . . . καὶ ἐξελέξατο Κύριος ὑμᾶς . . . παρὰ τὸ ἀγαπᾶν Κύριον ὑμᾶς); 14:2; Rom 9:4–5; Acts 13:17.

80. Gal 5:22–23.

81. In the text as CHRIST.

82. Matt 6:14–15.

83. Cf. Gen 3:21.

of CHRIST dwell richly among you, teaching and encouraging one another with all wisdom, singing in the SPIRIT with grace in your hearts in psalms, songs, and hymns to GOD.[84] And whatever you do in word or in deed do all in the Name of the LORD JESUS, giving thanks to GOD the FATHER through him.

Wives, yield the right of way to your husbands, as becomes members of CHRIST. And husbands, you'd better love your wives—don't even *think* of treating them harshly! Children, always listen to your parents, because this is pleasing to the LORD. Fathers, do not provoke your children, lest they feel beaten down. Workers, obey those who supervise you as far as worldly affairs go, not just to look good in their eyes but with sincerity and in godly fear. Whatever your task, labor heart and soul as for the LORD, not men, knowing you'll receive the inheritance from the LORD as your reward—you serve the LORD CHRIST! But whoever works injustice will reap what he's sown: the LORD is no respecter of persons. So Bosses, treat your employees with fairness and equity, seeing as you both have a Boss[85] in Heaven.[86]

4

Devote yourselves to prayer. Stay vigilant in your petitions, with thanksgiving. Pray for us here as well. I'm in prison on account of the gospel; but pray GOD to find more openings for me to proclaim the Mystery of CHRIST, in the hope of making the Word manifest to all. It's what I'm bound to do.[87] Please use good sense when dealing with those outside our fellowship: use the time well;[88] season your speech with salt;[89] have a gracious answer for everyone.

Tychicus—a beloved brother, faithful servant and my fellow bondsman—will fill you in on my situation. That is in fact why I sent

---

84. Ps 6:1 (Εἰς τὸ τέλος, ἐν ὕμνοις, ὑπὲρ τῆς ὀγδόης· ψαλμὸς τῷ Δαυῒδ); Eph 5:19; Rev 19:1–8; cf. 1 Cor 14:15 (ψαλῶ τῷ πνεύματι, ψαλῶ δὲ καὶ τῷ νοΐ).

85. The same Greek word κύριος appears in this verse, either as such to refer to secular supervisors or and sometimes as a *nomen sacrum*. In order to bring out linguistic contrast but without using words like "master" or "lord," the colloquial "boss" is used for secular overseers and the *nomen*-like BOSS adopted for the LORD.

86. Eph 5:22—6:9.

87. 1 Cor 9:16.

88. Eph 5:16; cf. Dan 2:8.

89. Lev 2:13; Cicero, *On Oratory* 1.34, line 159.

him. I promise you'll be comforted in your hearts once you know how things are with us, how it's all going here. With that in mind I also sent Onesimus along with him. He's a faithful and beloved brother, as well as one of your own.[90]

My cellmate Aristarchus greets you, as does Barnabas' cousin Marcus. You have already gotten letters from me about him, so don't fail to welcome him when he arrives. He and Jesus (the brother they also call Justus) are my only fellow Jews still here, but they've been a great comfort to me, co-working for the Kingdom of GOD. CHRIST JESUS' servant Epaphras greets you—he's also your *landsman*[91]—always toiling on your behalf in his prayers to the end you stand perfected, fully settled in the whole Will of GOD. And I can testify how much he's labored both for you and those in Laodicea and Hierapolis. Lucas the beloved physician hails you, as does Demas.

Salute the brothers in Laodicea, along with Nympha and her house church. After this letter has been read by you be sure it gets to the brethren there for them to read as well. Likewise, I want you to read the letter that was left for you at Laodicea. And one more thing: I want the assembly to tell Archippus, "See that you fully discharge the ministry you received from the LORD!"

I write this last salutation with my own hand: Remember my chains. Grace be with you,

Paul

---

90. Phlm 10.
91. Yiddish gloss on the literal phrase "one of your own."

Acknowledgments

THE PREMISE OF THIS work is that the Scriptures are the divinely communicated Word of God made incarnationally present in the words of the Bible. The translation theory that flowed from that premise seeks to capture, recapitulate, and incorporate the living sweep of the timeless Word in words that cross time, with the Word continuously revealed in the world as the text is made effective in Church history and tradition. In the first instance I therefore acknowledge and give thanks to God, who inspires me through the Son.

I am also grateful to the teachers and advisers who, in the course of my studies at Columbia University, Beeson Divinity School, and the University of Cambridge, afforded me the privilege of becoming immersed in the Scriptures not only in my native English but also in the original Greek. Those studies led to my undertaking my own translation of the New Testament over the course of several years, a project which then led me to reexamine my own approach, as a result of which I developed the translation theory presented here through my doctoral studies at the University of Aberdeen. I therefore owe particular thanks to my Doktorvater Tomas Bokedal for his meticulous commentary, scholarly critique, and pointed suggestions throughout the process. His insightful contributions at each stage of the thesis from proposal to completion were simply indispensable to the conceptualization, structuring, and realization of the work. My thanks also to my thesis examiners, Arthur A. Just Jr. and J. Thomas Hewitt, for their own acute insights and suggestions. As I turned to the task of reformulating the thesis into book form, I had the benefit of Mason Hicks' detailed technical and stylistic assistance in preparing the manuscript for submission to the publisher. And I am likewise grateful to

Robin A. Parry, my editor at Wipf & Stock, whose contributions together with those of the firm's proofreading, formatting, and typesetting team were key to realizing the final product.

All that said, this book would not have been possible without the support, encouragement and above all patient tolerance of my family. I therefore dedicate this work to Philippa, Philippa, and Marc, as with all that I do.

Bibliography

Aasgaard, Reidar. "Paul as a Child: Children and Childhood in the Letters of the Apostle." *JBL* 126 (2007) 129–59. https://www.jstor.org/stable/27638423.

Abram, K-J. "Reader's Edition of the UBS^5 Greek New Testament: An Illustrated Review." Words on the Word, June 18, 2017. https://abramkj.com/2017/06/18/an-illustrated-review-of-the-readers-edition-of-the-ubs5-greek-new-testament/.

ACNS. "Archbishop of Canterbury's Sermon at Westminster Abbey—400th anniversary of the King James Bible." ACNS, Nov. 16, 2011. https://www.anglicannews.org/news/2011/11/archbishop-of-canterburys-sermon-at-westminster-abbey-400th-anniversary-of-the-king-james-bible.aspx.

Aland, Kurt, and Barbara Aland. *The Text of the New Testament*. 2nd ed. Grand Rapids: Eerdmans, 1989.

Alexander, Phillip. "Jews and Judaism in the Apostolic Fathers." In *The Cambridge Companion to the Apostolic Fathers*, edited by Michael F. Bird and Scott D. Harrower, 29–49. Cambridge Companions to Religion. Cambridge: Cambridge University Press, 2021.

Alford, Henry. *The Greek New Testament*. 4th ed. London: Gilbert and Rivington, 1859.

Alter, Robert. *The Art of Bible Translation*. Princeton, NJ: Princeton University Press, 2019.

———. *The Hebrew Bible: A Translation with Commentary*. 3 vols. New York: Norton, 2018.

———. Review of *The Great Code: The Bible and Literature*, by Northrop Frye. *Blake* 17 (1983) 20–22.

Anatolios, Khaled. *Retrieving Nicaea*. Grand Rapids: Baker Academic, 2011.

Andrie, Leonard W. "The Christ Hymn of Colossians 1:15–20: Drawing from the Wisdom Tradition in Hellenistic Judaism to Tidy Up the Church at Colossae." MATh thesis, University of St. Thomas, 2013.

Aquinas, Thomas. *Commentary on the Gospel of John (Books 1–5)*. Translated by Fabian Larcher, OP, and James A. Weisheipf, OP. Introduction and notes by Daniel Keating and Matthew Levering. Washington, DC: Catholic University of America Press, 2010.

Arnold, Clinton E. "Returning to the Domain of the Powers: 'Stoicheia' as Evil Spirits in Galatians 4:3, 9." *NovT* 38 (1996) 55–76. https://www.jstor.org/stable/1561523.

Bibliography

Arthos, John. *The Inner Word in Gadamer's Hermeneutic*. Notre Dame, IN: University of Notre Dame Press, 2009.

Attridge, Harold W., ed. *Harper Collins Study Bible: New Revised Standard Version*. New York: HarperCollins, 2006.

Baker, David L. *Two Testaments, One Bible: A Study of Some Modern Solutions to the Theological Problem of the Relationship between the Old and New Testaments*. 3rd ed. Downers Grove, IL: IVP Academic, 2010.

Balchin, John F. "Colossians 1:15–20: An Early Christian Hymn? The Arguments from Style." *VE* 15 (1985) 65–94.

Banks, E. J. "Colossae." Bible Atlas, n.d. https://bibleatlas.org/colossae.htm.

Barclay, John M. G. *Obeying the Truth: A Study of Paul's Ethics in Galatians*. Edinburgh: T&T Clark, 1988.

Barclay, William. *The Letters to the Philippians, Colossians, and Thessalonians*. Rev. ed. Philadelphia: Westminster, 1975.

Barr, James. *The Semantics of Biblical Language*. Repr., Eugene, OR: Wipf & Stock, 2004.

Barton, Stephen C. "Many Gospels, One Jesus?" In *The Cambridge Companion to Jesus*, edited by Markus Bockmuehl, 170–83. Cambridge Companions to Religion. Cambridge: Cambridge University Press, 2001.

Bauckham, Richard. "For Whom Were Gospels Written?" In *The Gospels for All Christians: Rethinking the Gospel Audiences*, edited by Richard Bauckham, 9–48. New Testament Studies. Grand Rapids: Eerdmans, 1998.

Baugh, Steven M. "The Poetic Form of Col. 1:15–20." *WTJ* 47 (1985) 227–44.

Beale, G. K., and D. A. Carson, eds. *Commentary on the New Testament Use of the Old Testament*. Grand Rapids: Baker Academic, 2007.

Beasley-Murray, Paul. "Colossians 1:15–20: An Early Christian Hymn Celebrating the Lordship of Christ." In *Pauline Studies: Essays Presented to Professor F. F. Bruce on His 70th Birthday*, edited by Donald A. Hagner and Murray J. Harris, 169–83. Grand Rapids: Eerdmans, 1980.

Beer, Jeanette, ed. *A Companion to Medieval Translation*. ARC Companion. Leeds: ARC Humanities, 2019.

Beetham, Christopher A. *Echoes of Scripture in the Letter of Paul to the Colossians*. BibInt. Atlanta: Society of Biblical Literature, 2008.

Belloc, Hilaire. "On Translation." *Bookman* (1931) 32–39.

Benedict XVI, Pope. "General Audience." Vatican, May 2, 2007. https://www.vatican.va/content/benedict-xvi/en/audiences/2007/documents/hf_ben-xvi_aud_20070502.html.

Berkhof, Louis. *The History of Christian Doctrines*. Grand Rapids: Baker Academic, 1985.

Bhatia, Vijay K. "A Generic View of Academic Discourse." In *Academic Discourse*, edited by John Flowerdew, 21–39. Applied Linguistics and Language Study. Harlow, UK: Longman, 2002.

Biber, Douglas, and Susan Conrad. *Register, Genre, and Style*. Cambridge Textbooks in Linguistics. Cambridge: Cambridge University Press, 2009.

Bible Researcher. "ESV Translators." Bible Researcher, n.d. http://www.bible-researcher.com/esv-translators.html.

Biblica. "Committee on Bible Translation." Biblica, n.d. https://www.biblica.com/niv-bible/niv-bible-translators/.

Bird, Michael F. *Colossians and Philemon*. New Covenant Commentary. Eugene, OR: Cascade, 2009.

Bird, Michael F., and Scott D. Harrower, eds. *The Cambridge Companion to the Apostolic Fathers*. Cambridge Companions to Philosophy and Religion. Cambridge: Cambridge University Press, 2021.

Bird, Michael F., and Kirsten H. Mackerras. "The Epistle to Diognetus and the Fragment of Quadratus." In *The Cambridge Companion to the Apostolic Fathers*, edited by Michael F. Bird and Scott D. Harrower, 309–31. Cambridge Companions to Philosophy and Religion. Cambridge: Cambridge University Press, 2021.

Bird, Michael F., and Preston M. Sprinkle, eds. *The Faith of Jesus Christ: Exegetical, Biblical and Theological Studies*. Peabody, MA: Hendrickson, 2010.

Bissell, Edwin C. *Historic Origin of the Bible*. New York: Randolph and Co., 1873.

Blackwell, Ben C. "You Are Filled in Him: Theosis and Colossians 2–3." *Journal of Theological Interpretation* 8 (2014) 103–23.

Bloom, Harold. *The Anxiety of Influence*. New York: Oxford University Press, 1973.

Bockmuehl, Markus, ed. *The Cambridge Companion to Jesus*. Cambridge Companions to Religion. Cambridge: Cambridge University Press, 2001.

———. "'The Form of God' (Phil. 2:6) Variations on a Theme of Jewish Mysticism." *JTS*, n.s., 48 (1997) 1–23. https://www.jstor.org/stable/23966754.

———. "Is There a New Testament Doctrine of the Church?" In *Scripture's Doctrine and Theology's Bible: How the New Testament Shapes Christian Dogmatics*, edited by Markus Bockmuehl and Alan J. Torrance, 29–44. Grand Rapids: Baker Academic, 2008.

———. "A Note on the Text of Colossians 4:3." *JTS*, n.s., 39 (1988) 489–94. https://www.jstor.org/stable/23964213.

———. Review of *Cosmic Christology in Paul and the Pauline School: Colossians and Ephesians in the Context of Graeco-Roman Cosmology, with a New Synopsis of the Greek Texts* (WUNT 2, Reihe 171), by George H. Van Kooten. *Bib* 86 (2005) 441–45. https://www.jstor.org/stable/42614616.

———. Review of *Gospel Writing: A Canonical Perspective*, by Francis Watson. *JTS*, n.s., 65 (2014) 195–211. https://www.jstor.org/stable/23970765.

———. *Seeing the Word: Refocusing New Testament Study*. STI. Grand Rapids: Baker Academic, 2006.

Bockmuehl, Markus, and Alan J. Torrance, eds. *Scripture's Doctrine and Theology's Bible: How the New Testament Shapes Christian Dogmatics*. Grand Rapids: Baker Academic, 2008.

Bodleian Library. "Manifold Greatness: Oxford and the Making of the King James Bible." Bodleian Library, Apr. 11, 2011. http://www.bodleian.ox.ac.uk/news/2011/2011-apr-11. Link discontinued.

Bokedal, Tomas. "The Bible Canon and Its Significance." In *Canon Formation: Tracing the Role of Sub-Collections in the Biblical Canon*, edited by W. Edward Glenny and Darian Lockett, 7–32. London: T&T Clark, 2021.

———. *Christ the Center: How the Rule of Faith, the* Nomina Sacra, *and Numerical Patterns Shape the Canon*. Bellingham, WA: Lexham Academic, 2023.

———. "The Early Rule-of-Faith Pattern as Emergent Biblical Theology." *Theofilos Supplement* 7 (2015) 57–75.

———. *The Formation and Significance of the Christian Biblical Canon: A Study in Text, Ritual and Interpretation*. London: Bloomsbury Academic, 2014.

———. "Notes on the *Nomina Sacra* and Biblical Interpretation." In *Beyond Biblical Theologies*, edited by Heinrich Assel et al., 263–95. WUNT 295. Tübingen: Mohr Siebeck, 2012.

———. "The Rule of Faith: Tracing Its Origins." *Journal of Theological Interpretation* 7 (2013) 233–55.

Bratcher, Robert G., and Eugene A. Nida. *A Handbook on Paul's Letters to the Colossians and to Philemon*. New Testament Handbooks. Stuttgart: United Bible Societies, 1977.

Bremer, J. M. "Greek Hymns." In *Faith, Hope and Worship: Aspects of Religious Mentality in the Ancient World*, edited by Henk Versnel, 193–215. Studies in Greek and Roman Religion 2. Leiden: Brill, 1981.

Brewer, Todd H. W. "Welcome." Gospel Writing—A Canonical Perspective, Feb. 16, 2012. https://gospelwriting.wordpress.com/.

Brown, Colin, ed. *The New International Dictionary of New Testament Theology*. 4 vols. Grand Rapids: Zondervan, 1975–85.

Bruce, Frederick F. *The Epistles to the Colossians, to Philemon, and to the Ephesians*. Grand Rapids: Eerdmans, 1984.

———. *The Letters of Paul: An Expanded Paraphrase*. Grand Rapids: Eerdmans, 1965.

———. *The New Testament Documents: Are They Reliable?* Grand Rapids: Eerdmans, 2003.

Brueggemann, Walter. *Worship in Ancient Israel: An Essential Guide*. Nashville: Abingdon, 2005.

Bujard, Walter. *Stilanalystische Untersuchungen zum Kolosserbrief als Beitrag zur Methodik von Sprachvergleichen*. Göttingen: Vandenhoeck und Ruprecht, 1973.

Burke, David G., et al., eds. *The King James Version at 400: Assessing Its Genius as Bible Translation and Its Literary Influence*. BSNA. Atlanta: Society of Biblical Literature, 2013.

Burnet, Gilbert. *An Exposition of the Thirty-Nine Articles of the Church of England*. 3rd ed. London: Chiswell, 1705.

Burney, C. P. "Christ as the ΑΡΧΗ of Creation." *JTS* 106 (1926) 160–77. https://biblicalstudies.org.uk/pdf/jts/027_160.pdf.

Burridge, Richard A. "Priorities, Principles, and Prefaces: from the KJV to Today (1611–2011)." In *The King James Version at 400: Assessing Its Genius as Bible Translation and Its Literary Influence*, edited by David G. Burke et al., 195–226. BSNA. Atlanta: Society of Biblical Literature, 2013.

Cadwallader, Alan H., and Michael Trainor, eds. *Colossae in Space and Time: Linking to an Ancient City*. NTOA/SUNT. Göttingen: Vandenhoeck und Ruprecht, 2011.

Calvin, John. "The Bible and the Word of God." In *Readings in Christian Thought*, edited by H. T. Kerr, 157–69. 2nd ed. Nashville: Abingdon, 1990.

———. *On the Christian Faith: Selections from the "Institutes," "Commentaries" and "Tracts."* Edited by John T. McNeil. Library of Liberal Arts. New York: Liberal Arts, 1957.

Campbell, Constantine R. "Response to Macaskill." *ExAud* 33 (1977) 108–12.

Campbell, Constantine R., and Jonathan T. Pennington. *Reading the New Testament as Christian Scripture: A Literary, Canonical and Theological Survey*. Reading Christian Scripture. Grand Rapids: Baker Academic, 2020.

Campbell, Douglas A. *Paul: An Apostle's Journey*. Grand Rapids: Eerdmans, 2018.

Carr, Wesley. "Two Notes on Colossians." *JTS*, n.s., 24 (1973) 492–500. https://www.jstor.org/stable/23962131.

Carson, D. A., ed. *The Enduring Authority of the Christian Scriptures*. Grand Rapids: Eerdmans, 2016.

Casey, Michael. *Sacred Reading: The Ancient Art of Lectio Divina*. Liguori, MO: Liguori/Triumph, 1995.
Castelli, Elizabeth A. "Les Belles Infidèles/Fidelity or Feminism? The Meanings of Feminist Biblical Translation." *JFSR* 6 (1990) 25–39. https://www.jstor.org/stable/25002133.
Castelli, Elizabeth A., et al., eds. *The Postmodern Bible*. New Haven, CT: Yale University Press, 1995.
Catholic Church. *Catechism of the Catholic Church*. Vatican, 1993. https://www.vatican.va/archive/ENG0015/_INDEX.HTM.
Charlesworth, James H., ed. *The Old Testament Pseudepigrapha*. 3 vols. Garden City: Doubleday & Co., 1983.
Chauran, Alexandra. "Understanding Elementals." Llewellyn, Nov. 11, 2013. https://www.llewellyn.com/journal/article/2399.
Childs, Brevard S. *Biblical Theology of the Old and New Testaments: Theological Reflection on the Christian Bible*. Minneapolis: Fortress, 1992.
———. *The Church's Guide for Reading Paul*. Grand Rapids: Eerdmans, 2008.
———. "The Old Testament as Scripture of the Church." *CTM* (1972) 709–22.
———. *Old Testament Theology in a Canonical Context*. Philadelphia: Fortress, 1985.
Church of England, The. "Articles of Religion." Church of England, 1562. https://www.churchofengland.org/prayer-and-worship/worship-texts-and-resources/book-common-prayer/articles-religion.
———. *Book of Common Prayer, and Administration of the Sacraments, and Other Rites and Ceremonies of the Church, According to the Use of the Church of England: Together with the Psalter or Psalms of David, Pointed as They Are to Be Sung or Said in Churches*. Cambridge: Baskerville, 1762. https://www.churchofengland.org/sites/default/files/2019-10/the-book-of-common-prayer-1662.pdf.
Collins, Adela Y. "Psalms, Philippians 2:6–11, and the Origins of Christology." *BibInt* (July 2003) 361–72. https://brill.com/abstract/journals/bi/11/3/article-p361_10.xml.
Combs, William W. "The Preface to the King James Version and the King James-Only Position." *Detroit Baptist Seminary Journal* 1 (1996) 253–67.
Cone, James H. *A Black Theology of Liberation*. Maryknoll, NY: Orbis, 2010.
Council Fathers. "Council of Constance 1414–18." Papal Encyclicals, 1414–18. https://www.papalencyclicals.net/councils/ecum16.htm.
Cyril of Jerusalem. *The Catechetical Lectures of S. Cyril, Archbishop of Jerusalem*. Edited by E. B. Pusey et al. Vol. 2 of *A Library of Fathers of the Holy Catholic Church, Anterior to the Division of the East and West*. Oxford: Parker, 1838. https://holytrinity-oca.org/wp-content/uploads/2020/05/The-Catechetical-Lectures-of-St-Cyril.pdf.
Daley, Brian E., SJ. *God Visible: Patristic Christology Reconsidered*. Changing Paradigms in Historical and Systematic Theology. Oxford: Oxford University Press, 2018.
Dana, H. E., and Julius R. Mantey. *A Manual Grammar of the Greek New Testament*. Toronto: Macmillan, 1957.
Davis, Ellen F., and Richard B. Hays. *The Art of Reading Scripture*. Grand Rapids: Eerdmans, 2003.
Decock, Paul B. "On the Value of Pre-Modern Interpretation of Scripture for Contemporary Biblical Studies." *Neot* 39 (2005) 57–74. https://www.jstor.org/stable/43048528.

DeMaris, Richard E. *The Colossian Controversy: Wisdom in Dispute at Colossae.* JSOTSup. Sheffield: Sheffield Academic, 1994.

Denniston, John D. *The Greek Particles.* 2nd ed. Oxford: Clarendon, 1966.

Derrida, Jacques. *Limited Inc.* Edited by Gerald Graff. Translated by Jeffrey Mehlman and Samuel Weber. Evanston, IL: Northwestern University Press, 1977.

Devlin, Nicola G. "The Hymn in Greek Literature." PhD diss., University of Oxford, 1994.

Dibelius, Martin. "The Isis Initiation in Apuleius and Related Initiatory Rites." In *Conflict at Colossae: A Problem in the Interpretation of Early Christianity Illustrated by Select Modern Studies*, edited and translated by Fred O. Francis and Wayne A. Meeks, 61–121. Missoula, MT: Scholars, 1975.

Dibelius, Martin, and Hans Conzelmann. *The Pastoral Epistles.* Philadelphia: Fortress, 1972.

Diggle, James, ed. *The Cambridge Greek Lexicon.* Cambridge: Cambridge University Press, 2021.

Dines, Jennifer M. *The Septuagint.* Understanding the Bible and Its World. London: T&T Clark, 2004.

Dix, Gregory. *The Shape of the Liturgy.* Rev. ed. New York: Continuum, 2005.

Donovan, Richard Niell. "Hymns for Colossians 1:15–28." Sermon Writer, 2013. https://www.sermonwriter.com/hymn-list/colossians-115-28-hymns/.

Dormeyer, Detlev. "The Hellenistic Letter-Formula and the Pauline Letter-Scheme." In *The Pauline Canon*, edited by Stanley E. Porter, 59–63. Pauline Studies 1. Heidelberg: Springer Berlin, 2004.

Doty, Stephen H. "The Paradigm Shift in Bible Translation in the Modern Era, with Special Focus on Thai." PhD diss., University of Auckland, 2007. https://researchspace.auckland.ac.nz/bitstream/handle/2292/2458/02whole.pdf.

Dunn, James D. G. "The Colossian Philosophy: A Confident Jewish Apologia." *Bib* 76 (1995) 153–81. https://www.jstor.org/stable/42611452.

———. *The Partings of the Ways: Between Christianity and Judaism and Their Significance for the Character of Christianity.* London: SCM, 1991.

Dunn, Patrick. "'What If I Sang': The Intonation of Allen Ginsberg's Performances." *Style* 41 (2007) 75–93. https://www.jstor.org/stable/10.5325/style.41.1.75.

Dryden, John. "Preface to Sylvae, or the Second Part of Poetical Miscellanies, 1685." Bartleby, 1685. https://www.bartleby.com/204/180.html.

Easton, Burton S. "The Pauline Theology and Hellenism." *AmJT* 21 (1917) 358–82. https://www.jstor.org/stable/3155524.

Ebeling, Gerhard. *The Problem of Historicity.* Philadelphia: Fortress, 1967.

Eberhard, Philippe. "The Mediality of Our Condition: A Christian Interpretation." *JAAR* 67 (1999) 411–34. https://www.jstor.org/stable/1465743.

Eco, Umberto. *Interpretation and Overinterpretation.* Edited by Stefan Collini. Tanner Lectures in Human Values. Cambridge: Cambridge University Press, 1992.

Edsall, Benjamin, and Jennifer R. Strawbridge. "The Songs We Used to Sing? Hymn 'Traditions' and Reception in Pauline Letters." *JSNT* 37 (2015) 290–311. https://doi.org/10.1177/0142064X14567054.

"Elemental." Wikipedia, last edited Oct. 1, 2023. https://en.wikipedia.org/wiki/Elemental.

Ellis, Earle E. *Paul's Use of the Old Testament.* Grand Rapids: Eerdmans, 1957.

Epp, Eldon J. "It's All about Variants: A Variant-Conscious Approach to New Testament Textual Criticism." *HTR* 100 (2007) 275–308. https://www.jstor.org/stable/4495120.
———. "The Multivalence of the Term 'Original Text' in New Testament Textual Criticism." *HTR* 92 (1999) 245–81. https://www.jstor.org/stable/1510127.
Evans, Craig A. "The Colossian Mystics." *Bib* 63 (1982) 188–205. https://www.jstor.org/stable/42707113.
———. "The Meaning of πλήρωμα in Nag Hammadi." *Bib* 65 (1984) 259–65. https://www.jstor.org/stable/42707233.
Faulkner, William. *Requiem for a Nun*. New York: Vintage, 1951.
Fee, Gordon D. "Modern Text Criticism and the Synoptic Problem." In *J. J. Griesbach: Synoptic and Text-Critical Studies 1776–1976*, edited by Bernard Orchard and Thomas R. W. Longstaff, 154–69. Cambridge: Cambridge University Press, 1979.
Fee, Gordon D., and Douglas Stuart. *How to Read the Bible for All Its Worth*. 4th ed. Grand Rapids: Zondervan, 2014.
Felber, Stefan. "Die Bibelübersetzung 'Hoffnung für alle' im kritischen Textvergleich." *TBei* 35 (2004) 181–201.
———. "Chomsky's Influence on Eugene Nida's Theory of Dynamic Equivalence in Translating." In *Bibelübersetzung als Wissenschaft. Aktuelle Fragestellungen und Perspektiven. Beiträge zum Forum Bibelübersetzung aus den Jahren 2005–2011*, edited by Eberhard Werner, 253–62. Stuttgart: Deutsche Bibelgesellschaft, 2012.
———. *Kommunikative Bibelübersetzung*. Stuttgart: Deutsche Bibelgesellschaft, 2013.
———. "A Moratorium on Dynamic-Equivalent Bible Translating." *Unio cum Christo* 4 (2018) 215–26.
Forshall, Josiah, and Frederic Madden, eds. *The Holy Bible Containing the Old and New Testaments with the Apocryphal Books in the Earliest English Versions Made from the Latin Vulgate by John Wycliffe and His Followers*. Oxford: Oxford University Press, 1850.
Foster, Paul. *Colossians*. BNTC. London: Bloomsbury T&T Clark, 2016.
Fowl, Stephen. "The Canonical Approach of Brevard Childs." *ExpTim* (1985) 173–76. https://doi.org/10.1177/001452468509600604.
Francis, Fred O. "Humility and Angel Worship in Colossae." In *Conflict at Colossae: A Problem in the Interpretation of Early Christianity Illustrated by Select Modern Studies*, edited and translated by Fred O. Francis and Wayne A. Meeks, 163–95. Rev. ed. Missoula, MT: Scholars, 1975.
Francis, Fred O., and Wayne A. Weeks, eds. *Conflict at Colossae: A Problem in the Interpretation of Early Christianity Illustrated by Select Modern Studies*. Rev. ed. Missoula, MT: Scholars, 1975.
Frei, Hans W. *The Eclipse of Biblical Narrative: A Study in Eighteenth and Nineteenth Century Hermeneutics*. New Haven, CT: Yale University Press, 1974.
Frye, Northrop. *The Great Code: The Bible and Literature*. New York: Houghton Mifflin Harcourt, 1983.
Fuchs, Ernst. *Zum hermeneutischen Problem in der Theologie. Die existentiale Interpretation*. Tübingen: Mohr Siebeck, 1959.
Furley, William D., and Jan Maarten Bremer, eds. and trans. *Greek Hymns: A Selection of Greek Religious Poetry from the Archaic to the Hellenistic Period*. 2 vols. Studien und Texte zu Antike und Christentum/Studies and Texts in Antiquity and Christianity 9. Tübingen: Mohr Siebeck, 2001.
Gadamer, Hans-Georg. *The Beginning of Philosophy*. New York: Continuum, 1998.

———. "Boundaries of Language." In *Language and Linguisticality in Gadamer's Hermeneutics*, edited and translated by L. K. Schmidt, 9–18. New York: Lexington, 2000.

———. *Gadamer in Conversation: Reflections and Commentary*. Edited and translated by Richard E. Palmer. Yale Studies in Hermeneutics. New Haven, CT: Yale University Press, 2001.

———. *The Gadamer Reader: A Bouquet of the Later Writings*. Edited and translated by Richard E. Palmer. Topics In Historical Philosophy. Evanston, IL: Northwestern University Press, 2007.

———. "Grenzen der Sprache." In *Ästhetik und Poetik I*, 350–61. Vol. 8 of *Gesammelte Werke*. Tübingen: Mohr Siebeck, 1993.

———. *Philosophical Hermeneutics*. Edited and translated by David E. Ling. Berkeley: University of California Press, 1976.

———. *The Relevance of the Beautiful and Other Essays*. Edited by Robert Bernasconi. Translated by Nicholas Walker. Cambridge: Cambridge University Press, 1986.

———. *Truth and Method*. Translation revised by Joel Weinsheimer and Donald G. Marshall. 2nd ed. New York: Continuum, 1994.

———. *Wahrheit und Methode. Grundzüge einer philosophischen Hermeneutik*. Vol. 1 of *Gesammelte Werke*. 6th ed. Tübingen: Mohr Siebeck, 1990.

Gathercole, Simon J. *Where Is Boasting? Early Jewish Soteriology and Paul's Response in Romans 1–5*. Grand Rapids: Eerdmans, 2002.

Gibbs, John G. "The Cosmic Scope of Redemption According to Paul." *Bib* 56 (1975) 13–29. https://www.jstor.org/stable/42611469.

Giles, John A., ed. *The Venerable Bede's Ecclesiastical History of England*. London: Bohn, 1897.

Gignilliat, Mark. "Paul, Allegory, and the Plain Sense of Scripture: Galatians 4:21–31." *Journal of Theological Interpretation* 2 (2008) 135–46.

Gitlin, Todd, and Liel Leibovitz. *The Chosen Peoples: America, Israel, and the Ordeals of Divine Election*. New York: Simon & Schuster, 2010.

Glasson, T. Francis. "Colossians I 18, 15 and Sirach XXIV." *NovT* 11 (1969) 154–56. https://www.jstor.org/stable/1560218.

Glenny, W. Edward. "The Septuagint and Biblical Theology." *Them* 41 (2016) 263–78.

Gopnik, Adam. "How to Read the Good Books." *New Yorker*, Jan. 29, 2019. https://www.newyorker.com/magazine/2019/01/28/how-to-read-the-good-books.

Gorday, Peter J., and Thomas C. Oden, eds. *Colossians, 1–2 Thessalonians, 1–2 Timothy, Titus, Philemon*. ACCS 9. Downers Grove, IL: IVP Academic, 2000.

Gordley, Matthew. "The Johannine Prologue and Jewish Didactic Hymn Traditions: A New Case for Reading the Prologue as a Hymn." *JBL* 128 (2009) 781–802. https://www.jstor.org/stable/25610219.

Gordley, Matthew E. *New Testament Christological Hymns: Exploring Texts, Contexts and Significance*. Downers Grove, IL: IVP Academic, 2018.

Granados Rojas, Juan M. "Is the Word of God Incomplete? An Exegetical and Rhetorical Study of Col. 1,25." *Bib* 94 (2013) 63–79. https://www.jstor.org/stable/42614729.

Gregory of Nazianzus. *On God and Christ*. Translated by Frederick Williams and Lionel Wickham. Crestwood, NY: St. Vladimir's Seminary Press, 2002.

"A Guide to Overlining Characters in Microsoft Word." WikiHow, last updated Mar. 19, 2024. https://www.wikihow.com/Overline-Characters-in-Microsoft-Word.

Hagner, Donald A., and Stephen E. Young. "The Historical-Critical Method and the Gospel of Matthew." In *Methods for Matthew*, edited by Mark Allan Powell, 11–43. Methods in Biblical Interpretation. Cambridge: Cambridge University Press, 2009.

Harding, Mark. "Disputed and Undisputed Letters of Paul." In *The Pauline Canon*, edited by Stanley E. Porter, 129–68. Pauline Studies 1. Heidelberg: Springer Berlin, 2004.

Hardy, Edward R., ed. *Christology of the Later Fathers*. Louisville: Westminster John Knox, 2006.

Harnack, Adolf. *Marcion: The Gospel of the Alien God*. Translated by John E. Steely and Lyle D. Bierma. Eugene, OR: Wipf & Stock, 1990.

Harrison, J. R., and L. L. Welborn, eds. *Colossae, Hierapolis, and Laodicea*. The First Urban Churches 5. WGRWSup. Atlanta: Society of Biblical Literature, 2019.

Hart, David Bentley. *The New Testament: A Translation*. New Haven, CT: Yale University Press, 2017.

———. "A Reply to N. T. Wright." A. F. Kimel, Jan. 16, 2018. https://afkimel.wordpress.com/2018/01/16/a-reply-to-n-t-wright/.

———. *That All Shall Be Saved: Heaven, Hell, and Universal Salvation*. New Haven, CT: Yale University Press, 2019.

Hartman, Lars. "On Reading Others' Letters." *HTR* 79 (1986) 137–46. https://www.jstor.org/stable/1509406.

Harvard Law Review Association. *The Bluebook: A Uniform System of Citation*. 15th ed. Cambridge, MA: Harvard Law Review Association, 1991.

Hatina, Thomas R. "The Perfect Tense-Form in Colossians: Verbal Aspect, Temporality and the Challenge of Translation." In *Translating the Bible: Problems and Prospects*, edited by Stanley E. Porter and Richard S. Hess, 225–52. JSNTSup 173. Sheffield: Sheffield Academic, 1999.

Hawking, Stephen. *Brief Answers to the Big Questions*. New York: Bantam, 2018.

Hays, Richard B. *The Conversion of the Imagination: Paul as Interpreter of Israel's Scripture*. Grand Rapids: Eerdmans, 2005.

———. *Echoes of Scripture in the Letters of Paul*. New Haven, CT: Yale University Press, 1989.

———. *The Faith of Jesus Christ: The Narrative Substructure of Galatians 3:1—4:11*. Biblical Resource. Grand Rapids: Eerdmans, 2002.

Heath, S. B., and Juliet Langman. "Shared Thinking and the Register of Coaching." In *Variation in English: Multi-Dimensional Studies*, edited by Susan Conrad and Douglas Biber, 171–84. Studies in Language and Linguistics. London: Longman, 2001.

Helyer, Larry L. "Cosmic Christology and Col. 1:15–20." *JETS* 37 (1994) 235–46. https://www.etsjets.org/files/JETS-PDFs/37/37-32/JETS_37-2_235-246_Helyer.pdf.

Hemphill, Ken. *The Names of God*. Tigerville, SC: Auxano, 2015.

Hengel, Martin. *The Son of God*. Philadelphia: Fortress, 1976.

Hengel, Martin, with Roland Deines. *The Septuagint as Christian Scripture: Its Prehistory and the Problem of Canon*. Grand Rapids: Baker Academic, 2002.

Hengstenberg, Ernst W. *Christology of the Old Testament*. 2 vols. Alexandria, DC: Morrison, 1839.

Hincks, Edward Y. "The Meaning of the Phrase τὰ στοιχεῖα τοῦ κόσμου in Gal. 4.3 and Col. 2.8." *JBL* 15 (1896) 183–92. https://www.jstor.org/stable/3268841.

Holloway, Paul A. "The Enthymeme as an Element of Style in Paul." *JBL* 120 (2001) 329–39. https://jstor.org/stable/3268298.

Horace. *The Works of Horace*. Edited by Theodore Alois Buckley. Translated by C. Smart. New York: Harper & Brothers, 1863. http://www.perseus.tufts.edu/hopper/text?doc=Perseus%3Atext%3A1999.02.0065%3Acard%3D1.

Horsley, G. H. R., and E. R. Waterhouse. "The Greek *Nomen sacrum XP* in some Latin and Old English Manuscripts." *Scriptorium* 38 (1984) 211–30. https://doi.org/10.3406/scrip.1984.1358.

Housman, A. E. "The Application of Thought to Textual Criticism." *Proceedings of the Classical Association* 18 (1922) 67–84. http://cnx.org/contents/cbe1bb93-f304-43ca-abfe-a243c55b6597@2/%22The-Application-of-Thought-to.

Humphrey, Edith M. *And I Turned to See the Voice: The Rhetoric of Vision in the New Testament*. STI. Grand Rapids: Baker Academic, 2007.

Hurtado, Larry W. "Another New Article on Philippians 2:6–11." Larry Hurtado's Blog, May 7, 2015. https://larryhurtado.wordpress.com/2015/05/07/another-new-article-on-philippians-26-11/.

———. "Are Philippians 2:6–11 and Colossians 1:15–20 Christ-Hymns?" Larry Hurtado's Blog, May 5, 2015. https://larryhurtado.wordpress.com/2015/05/05/are-philippians-26-11-and-colossians-115-20-christ-hymns/.

———. *The Earliest Christian Artifacts: Manuscripts and Christian Origins*. Grand Rapids: Eerdmans, 2006.

———. "'Nomina Sacra': Further Observations." Larry Hurtado's Blog, Mar. 6, 2017. https://larryhurtado.wordpress.com/2017/03/06/nomina-sacra-further-observations/.

———. "On 'Hymns' in the New Testament: A Suggestion." Larry Hurtado's Blog, May 11, 2015. https://larryhurtado.wordpress.com/2015/05/11/on-hymns-in-the-new-testament-a-suggestion/.

———. "The Origin of the *Nomina Sacra*: A Proposal." *JBL* 117 (1998) 655–73. https://www.jstor.org/stable/3266633.

Hymnary. "Hymns for Colossians." Hymnary, n.d. https://hymnary.org/browse/scripture/Colossians.

Idioms, The. "A Place for Everything and Everything in Its Place." The Idioms, n.d. https://www.theidioms.com/a-place-for-everything-and-everything-in-its-place/.

Johnson, Luke Timothy. *The First and Second Letters to Timothy: A New Translation with Introduction and Commentary*. AB. New York: Doubleday, 2001.

Johnson, Sherman E. "Laodicea and Its Neighbors." *BA* 13 (1950) 1–18. https://www.jstor.org/stable/3209323.

Jongkind, Dirk. *An Introduction to the Greek New Testament*. Cambridge: Tyndale, 2019.

Jongkind, Dirk, and Peter J. Williams, eds. *The Greek New Testament*. Cambridge: Tyndale, 2017.

Jordan, Mark D. "Words and Word: Incarnation and Signification in Augustine's *De Doctrina Christiana*." *AugStud* 11 (1980) 177–96.

Jowett, Benjamin. *The Interpretation of Scripture and Other Essays*. London: Routledge & Sons, 1897.

Joyce, James. *Finnegans Wake*. New York: Macmillan, 1939.

Just, Arthur A., Jr. *Heaven on Earth: The Gifts of Christ in the Divine Service*. St. Louis: Concordia, 2008.

———. "Today in Our Hearing: The Living Voice of Jesus in the Gospel of Luke." *Touchstone,* Apr. 2004. https://www.touchstonemag.com/archives/article.php?id=17-03-036-f&readcode=&readtherest=true.

Kagan, Elena. "The 2015 Scalia Lecture: A Dialogue with Justice Elena Kagan on the Reading of Statutes." YouTube, Nov. 18, 2015. https://www.youtube.com/watch?v=dpEtszFToTg&ab_channel=HarvardLawSchool.

Kaiser, Walter C., Jr. "The Canon of the Old Testament." *Unio cum Christo* 5 (2019) 13–26.

Käsemann, Ernst. "A Primitive Christian Baptismal Liturgy." In *Essays on New Testament Themes,* 149–68. London: SCM, 1971.

Kearney, Martha. "The Book of Kells: Medieval Europe's Greatest Treasure?" BBC, Apr. 26, 2016. https://www.bbc.com/culture/article/20160425-the-book-of-kells-medieval-europes-greatest-treasure.

Kehl, Nikolaus. *Der Christushymnus im Kolosserbrief.* Stuttgart: Katholisches Bibelwerk, 1967.

Keister, Lane. "Too Many to Choose From? The English Translation Controversy." *Unio cum Christo* 5 (2019) 61–76.

Kelly, Henry A. "Bible Translation and Controversy in Late Medieval England." In *A Companion to Medieval Translation,* edited by Jeanette Beer, 51–62. ARC Companion. Leeds: ARC Humanities, 2019.

Kelly, J. N. D. *Early Christian Creeds.* 3rd ed. New York: Continuum, 2006.

———. *Early Christian Doctrines.* Rev. ed. Peabody, MA: Prince, 2007.

Kennedy, George A. *New Testament Interpretation through Rhetorical Criticism.* Chapel Hill: University of North Carolina Press, 1984.

Kenyon, F. G. "*Nomina Sacra* in the Chester Beatty Papyri." *Aeg* 13 (1933) 5–10. https://www.jstor.org/stable/41214231.

Kerouac, Jack. *On the Road: The Original Scroll.* New York: Viking, 2007.

Kerridge, Benjamin. "A Reading of Ephesians in the Light of the Hermeneutics of Paul Ricoeur." MPhil thesis, University of Sheffield, 2015.

Kilgallen, John J. "A Complicated Apostle: Who Was St. Paul?" *America Magazine,* Nov. 10, 2008. https://www.americamagazine.org/issue/675/article/complicated-apostle.

Kim, Seyoon. *Paul and the New Perspective: Second Thoughts on the Origin of Paul's Gospel.* Grand Rapids: Eerdmans, 2002.

Kinzig, Wolfram. *Faith in Formulae: A Collection of Early Christian Creeds and Creed-Related Texts.* 4 vols. Oxford Early Christian Texts. Oxford: Oxford University Press, 2017.

———. "Καινὴ διαθήκη: The Title of the New Testament in the Second and Third Century." *JTS* 45 (1994) 529–44.

Kinzig, Wolfram, and Markus Vinzent. "Recent Research on the Origin of the Creed." *JTS* 50 (1999) 535–59.

Kirkland, Alastair. "The Beginnings of Christianity in the Lycus Valley: An Exercise in Historical Reconstruction." *Neot* 29 (1995) 109–24. https://www.jstor.org/stable/43049047.

Klein, William W., et al. *Introduction to Biblical Interpretation.* Nashville: Thomas Nelson, 1993.

Kruger, M. A. "Law and Promise in Galatians." *Neot* 26 (1992) 311–27. https://www.jstor.org/stable/43048040.

Kümmel, W. G. *Promise and Fulfillment: The Eschatological Message of Jesus*. London: SCM, 1956.
Lawn, Chris, and Niall Keane. *The Gadamer Dictionary*. New York: Continuum, 2011.
Lightfoot, Joseph B. *St. Paul's Epistles to the Colossians and Philemon*. Repr., Peabody, MA: Hendrickson, 1995.
"The Living Bible." Wikipedia, last edited Oct. 31, 2023. https://en.wikipedia.org/wiki/The_Living_Bible.
Lohse, Eduard. *A Commentary on the Epistles to the Colossians and Philemon*. Philadelphia: Fortress, 1971.
Lonergan, Bernard J. *Verbum: Word and Idea in Aquinas*. Notre Dame, IN: University of Notre Dame Press, 1967.
Longenecker, Richard N. *The Epistle to the Romans*. NIGTC. Grand Rapids: Eerdmans, 2016.
Loubser, J. A. "Orality and Literacy in the Pauline Epistles: Some Hermeneutical Implications." *Neot* 29 (1995) 61–74. https://www.jstor.org/stable/43049045.
Lowe, Philip J. "The Premise and Paraenesis: Rhetorical Studies and the Connection of the Christ Hymn with the Corresponding Paraensis of Colossians." Humanities Commons, 2019. http://dx.doi.org/10.17613/1nr8-vb11.
Luther, Martin. "An Open Letter on Translating." Project Wittenburg, June 25, 1995. From "Sendbrief von Dolmetschen," in *Dr. Martin Luthers Werke* (Weimar: Hermann Boehlaus Nachfolger, 1909), 30:632–46. Translated by Gary Mann. https://archive.org/stream/anopenletterontr00272gut/ltran11.txt.
———. *Word and Sacrament I*. Edited by Ernest T. Bachmann. Vol. 35 of *Luther's Works*. Philadelphia: Muhlenberg, 1960.
Luz, Ulrich. *Matthew 1–7: A Commentary*. Edited by Helmut Koester. Translated by James E. Crouch. Hermeneia. Minneapolis: Fortress, 1989.
Lyonnet, S. "Paul's Adversaries in Colossae." In *Conflict at Colossae: A Problem in the Interpretation of Early Christianity Illustrated by Select Modern Studies*, edited and translated by Fred O. Francis and Wayne A. Meeks, 147–61. Rev. ed. Missoula, MT: Scholars, 1975.
Macaskill, Grant. "Union(s) with Christ: Colossians 1:15–20." *ExAud* 33 (2017) 92–107.
Mace, Emily R. "Feminist Forerunners and a Usable Past: A Historiography of Elizabeth Cady Stanton's The Woman's Bible." *JFSR* 25 (2009) 5–23. https://www.jstor.org/stable/10.2979/fsr.2009.25.2.5.
Mack, Burton L. *Rhetoric and the New Testament*. GBS. Minneapolis: Fortress, 1990.
Maier, Harry O. "Colossians and Philemon through the Centuries: A Proposal for the Blackwell Bible Commentary Volume on Colossians and Philemon." Unpublished paper, n.d. Email in possession of author.
———. "A Sly Civility: Colossians and Empire." *JSNT* 37 (2005) 323–49.
———. "Vision, Visualization, and Politics in the Apostle Paul." *MTSR* 27 (2015) 312–32. https://www.jstor.org/stable/43907205.
Marcos, Natalio Fernández. *The Septuagint in Context: Introduction to the Greek Versions of the Bible*. Translated by Wilfred G. E. Watson. Boston: Brill, 2000.
Markham, Robert P., and Eugene A. Nida. *An Introduction to the Bible Societies' Greek New Testament*. New York: American Bible Society, 1966.
Marlowe, Michael. "The Literal Character of the Vulgate." Bible Researcher, Sept. 2010. https://www.bible-researcher.com/vulgate4.html.
Martin, Ralph P. *Carmen Christi: Philippians 2:5–11 in Recent Interpretations and in the Setting of Early Christian Worship*. Rev. ed. Grand Rapids: Eerdmans, 1983.

———. "An Early Christian Hymn—Col. 1:15–20." *EvQ* 36 (1964) 195–205.
Marvel Database. "Elementals." Marvel Database, n.d. https://marvel.fandom.com/wiki/Elementals.
Marx, Karl, with Friedrich Engels. *The German Ideology*. Great Books in Philosophy. Amherst, NY: Prometheus, 1998.
Mathison, Keith A. *The Shape of Sola Scriptura*. Moscow: Canon, 2001.
McKnight, Scot. *The Letter to the Colossians*. NICNT. Grand Rapids: Eerdmans, 2018.
McLay, R. Timothy. *The Use of the Septuagint in New Testament Research*. Grand Rapids: Eerdmans, 2003.
McLuhan, Marshall. *Understanding Media: The Extensions of Man*. Cambridge: MIT Press, 1964. https://web.mit.edu/allanmc/www/mcluhan.mediummessage.pdf.
McNally, Robert E. *The Bible in the Early Middle Ages*. Atlanta: Scholars, 1986.
Melanchthon, Philip. *Commonplaces: Loci Communes 1521*. Edited and translated by Christian Preus. St. Louis: Concordia, 2014.
Melville, Herman. *White-Jacket, or The World in a Man-of-War*. New York: United States, 1892. https://www.gutenberg.org/files/10712/10712-h/10712-h.htm.
Mervosh, Sarah. "Trump Uses Random Uppercase Letters, but Should You? An Issue of Capital Importance." *New York Times*, July 4, 2018. https://www.nytimes.com/2018/07/04/us/trump-capitalization-tweets-nyt.html.
Metzger, Bruce M. *Chapters in the History of New Testament Textual Criticism*. Grand Rapids: Eerdmans, 1963.
———. *The Text of the New Testament: Its Transmission, Corruption and Restoration*. 3rd ed. New York: Oxford University Press, 1992.
———. *A Textual Commentary on the Greek New Testament*. Stuttgart: United Bible Societies, 1971.
———. *A Textual Commentary on the Greek New Testament*. 2nd ed. Stuttgart: German Bible Society, 1994.
Metzger, Bruce M., and Bart D. Ehrman. *The Text of the New Testament: Its Transmission, Corruption, and Restoration*. 4th ed. Oxford: Oxford University Press, 2005.
Miller, Merle. *Plain Speaking: An Oral Biography of Harry S. Truman*. New York: Berkley, 1974.
Milton, John. *Paradise Lost*. Repr., London: Routledge and Sons, 1905. https://books.google.com/books/about/Paradise_Lost.html?id=FgdbAAAAMAAJ&printsec=frontcover&source=kp_read_button&hl=en#v=onepage&q&f=false.
Mitchell, Margaret M. "The Continuing Problem of Particularity and Universality within the *Corpus Paulinum*." *ST* 64 (2010) 121–37. https://doi.org/10.1080/0039338X.2010.523217.
Mitchell, Timothy N. "Reading Aids in Early Christian Manuscripts." The Textual Mechanic, Apr. 30, 2013. http://thetextualmechanic.blogspot.com/2013/04/reading-aids-in-early-christian.html.
Modern Language Association of America. *MLA Handbook*. 8th ed. New York: Modern Language Association of America, 2016.
Montgomery, Helen Barrett. *Montgomery New Testament: The New Testament in Modern English*. Nashville: Holman, 1988.
Moore, Edward. "Gnosticism." *Internet Encyclopedia of Philosophy*, n.d. https://iep.utm.edu/gnostic/.
Morgan, Robert. "Can the Critical Study of Scripture Provide a Doctrinal Norm?" *JR* 76 (1996) 206–32. https://www.jstor.org/stable/1204406.

Moule, Charles F. D. *The Epistles of Paul the Apostle to the Colossians and to Philemon*. Cambridge: Cambridge University Press, 1957.

Mouton, Elna. "Reimagining Ancient Household Ethos? On the Implied Rhetorical Effect of Ephesians 5:21–33." *Neot* 48 (2014) 163–85. https://www.jstor.org/stable/43926977.

Moyo, Ambrose M. "The Colossian Heresy in the Light of Some Gnostic Documents from Nag Hammadi." *JTSA* 48 (1984) 30–44.

Mueller-Vollmer, Kurt, ed. *The Hermeneutics Reader: Texts of the German Tradition from the Enlightenment to the Present*. Repr., New York: Continuum, 1989.

Nakagawa, Hideyasu. "On the Christology of Colossians 1:15–20." *Bulletin of the Society for Near Eastern Studies in Japan* 9 (1966) 121–45, 230. https://www.jstage.jst.go.jp/article/orient1960/6/0/6_0_1/_pdf.

NASA. "Dark Matter & Dark Energy." NASA, n.d. https://science.nasa.gov/astrophysics/focus-areas/what-is-dark-energy.

Nash, H. S. "Θειότης—Θεότης, Rom. 1.20; Col. 2.9." *JBL* 18 (1899) 1–34. https://www.jstor/stable/3268966.

National Council of the Churches of Christ in the USA. "Version Information." Bible Gateway, n.d. https://www.biblegateway.com/versions/New-Revised-Standard-Version-Updated-Edition-NRSVue-Bible/#vinfo.

Naudé, Jacobus A. "The Role of the Metatexts in the KJV." In *The King James Version at 400: Assessing Its Genius as Bible Translation and Its Literary Influence*, edited by David G. Burke et al., 157–95. BSNA. Atlanta: Society of Biblical Literature, 2013.

Neufeld, Dietmar, ed. *The Social Sciences and Biblical Translation*. SymS. Atlanta: Society of Biblical Literature, 2008.

Newbold, R. F. "Nonverbal Communication and Parataxis in Late Antiquity." *L'antiquité classique* 55 (1986) 223–44. https://www.jstor.org/stable/41656351.

The New-England Primer Improved: For the More Easy Attaining the True Reading of English, to Which Is Added, the Assembly of Divines, and Mr. Cotton's Catechism. Boston: Ellison, 1773. https://www.loc.gov/resource/rbc0001.2015juv23945.

New Living Translation. "Meet the Scholars." New Living Translation, n.d. https://www.tyndale.com/nlt/meet-the-scholars.

New Revised Standard Version Bible. "New Revised Standard NRS." Bible Study Tools, 1989. https://www.biblestudytools.com/nrs/.

Newman, Sara. "Aristotle's Notion of 'Bringing-before-the-Eyes': Its Contribution to Aristotelian and Contemporary Conceptualizations of Metaphor, Style and Audience." *Rhetorica* 20 (2002) 1–23. https://www.jstor.org/stable/10.1525/rh.2002.20.1.1.

Nichols, Anthony H. "Translating the Bible." PhD diss., University of Sheffield, 1996. https://etheses.whiterose.ac.uk/5994/1/262848.pdf.

Nida, Eugene A. "The Sociolinguistics of Translating Canonical Religious Texts." *Traduction, Terminologie, Rédaction* 7 (1994) 191–217.

Nida, Eugene A., and Charles Taber. *The Theory and Practice of Translation*. Helps for Translators 8. Leiden: Brill, 1969.

Nielsen, Jon, and Royal Skousen. "How Much of the King James Bible Is William Tyndale's?" *Reformation* 3 (1998) 49–74. https://www.tandfonline.com/doi/abs/10.1179/ref_1998_3_1_004.

Noble, Terence P., ed. *Wycliffe's New Testament*. Vancouver, Can.: Noble, 2001.

Norton, D. "The KJV at 400: Assessing Its Genius as Bible Translation and Its Literary Influence." In *The King James Version at 400: Assessing Its Genius as Bible Translation and Its Literary Influence*, edited by David G. Burke et al., 3–27. BSNA. Atlanta: Society of Biblical Literature, 2013.

O'Gorman, Ned. "Longinus's Sublime Rhetoric, or How Rhetoric Came into Its Own." *Rhetoric Society Quarterly* 34 (2004) 71–89. http://www.jstor.org/stable/40232412.

O'Keefe, John J., and R. R. Reno. *Sanctified Vision: An Introduction to Early Christian Interpretation of the Bible*. Baltimore: Johns Hopkins University Press, 2005.

Old, Hughes Oliphant. *The Biblical Period*. Vol. 1 of *The Reading and Preaching of the Scriptures in the Worship of the Christian Church*. Grand Rapids: Eerdmans, 1998.

Osborne, Grant R. *The Hermeneutical Spiral: A Comprehensive Introduction to Biblical Interpretation*. Downers Grove, IL: InterVarsity, 1991.

Oxenham, John. "In Christ There Is No East or West." Hymnary, 1908. https://hymnary.org/text/in_christ_there_is_no_east_or_west_oxenh.

Page, Hugh R., Jr., ed. *The Africana Bible: Reading Israel's Scriptures from African and the African Diaspora*. Philadelphia: Fortress, 2009.

Pagels, Elaine. *The Gnostic Gospels*. New York: Random, 1979.

———. *The Gnostic Paul*. Harrisburg, PA: Trinity, 1975.

Pamuk, Orhan. *My Name Is Red*. New York: Vintage, 2001.

Pannenberg, Wolfhart. *Systematic Theology*. Translated by Geoffrey W. Bromiley. 3 vols. Grand Rapids: Eerdmans, 1991–98.

Parsenios, George L. "Anamnesis and the Silent Narrator in Plato and John." *Religions* 8 (2017) 47. https://doi.org/10.3390/rel8040047.

Pascal, Blaise. *The Provincial Letters*. Translated by T. M'Crie. Edinburgh: Johnstone, 1847. https://archive.org/details/provincialletter00pascuoft/page/n7/mode/2up.

Paul VI, Pope. "*Dei Verbum*: Dogmatic Constitution on Divine Revelation." Vatican, Nov. 18, 1965. https://www.vatican.va/archive/hist_councils/ii_vatican_council/documents/vat-ii_const_19651118_dei-verbum_en.html.

Payne, Philip B. *Man and Woman, One in Christ: An Exegetical and Theological Study of Paul's Letters*. Grand Rapids: Zondervan, 2009.

Peppard, Michael. "'Poetry,' 'Hymns' and 'Traditional Material' in New Testament Epistles or How to Do Things with Indentations." *JSNT* 30 (2008) 319–42.

Pernot, Laurent. "The Rhetoric of Religion." *Rhetorica* 24 (2006) 235–54. https://www.jstor.org/stable/10.1525/rh.2006.24.3.235.

Phillips, John B. *Letters to Young Churches*. New York: Macmillan, 1952.

———. "The New Testament in Modern English." Bible Researcher, 1958. From *The New Testament in Modern English*, by John Bertram Phillips (London: Bles, 1958). http://www.bible-researcher.com/phillips.html#preface.

———. "Translating the Gospels: A Discussion between Dr. E. V. Rieu and the Rev. J. B. Phillips." *BT* 6 (1955) 150–59.

Philo. *The Works of Philo*. Translated by Charles D. Yonge. Peabody, MA: Hendrickson, 1993.

Pickering, Wilbur N. "In Defense of Family 35." Revised Standard, n.d. https://www.revisedstandard.net/text/WNP/InDefenseOfFamily35.pdf.

Piñero, Antonio, and Jesús Peláez. *The Study of the New Testament: A Comprehensive Introduction*. Tools for Biblical Study. Leiden: Deo, 2003.

Pizzuto, Vincent A., ed. *A Cosmic Leap of Faith: An Authorial, Structural and Theological Investigation of the Cosmic Christology in Col. 1:15–20*. CBET 41. Leuven: Peeters, 2006.

Plater, William F., and H. J. White. *A Grammar of the Vulgate*. Oxford: Clarendon, 1926. https://archive.org/details/AGrammarOfTheVulgateByPlaterAndWhite/mode/2up.

Plutarchus, Lucius M. *Plutarch's Lives*. Translated by John Dryden. Revised by Arthur M. Clough. 5 vols. Boston: Little, Brown, and Company, 1888.

Pontifical Biblical Commission. *The Interpretation of the Bible in the Church*. Vatican City: Libreria Editrice Vaticana, 1993.

Porta, Fred R. "Greek Ritual Utterances and the Liturgical Style." PhD diss., Harvard University, 1999.

Porter, Stanley E., ed. *The Pauline Canon*. Pauline Studies 1. Atlanta: Society of Biblical Literature, 2004.

Price, Reynolds. *Three Gospels*. New York: Simon & Schuster, 1996.

Pulleyn, Simon. *Prayer in Greek Religion*. Oxford Classical Monographs. Oxford: Clarendon, 1997.

Rahlfs, Alfred. *Septuaginta*. Stuttgart: Deutsche Bibelgesellschaft, 1979.

Rastell, John. "A New Interlude and a Merry, of the Nature of the Four Elements." In *English Miracle Plays: Moralities and Interludes*, edited by Alfred W. Pollard, 98–105. Oxford: Clarendon, 1923.

Reasoner, Mark. *Romans in Full Circle: A History of Interpretation*. Louisville: Westminster John Knox, 2005.

Rhodes, Ron. *The Complete Guide to Bible Translations: How They Were Developed; Understanding Their Differences; Finding the Right One for You*. Eugene, OR: Harvest, 2009.

Ricoeur, Paul. *On Translation*. Thinking in Action. New York: Routledge, 2006.

Ridderbos, Herman. *Paul: An Outline of His Theology*. Grand Rapids: Eerdmans, 1975.

Rieu, Emile V. *The Four Gospels*. Baltimore: Penguin, 1953.

Risser, James. "Hermeneutics and the Linguisticality of the Christian Word." Paper presented at Christian Reasoning Colloquium, Trinity Western University, Langley, Can., Oct. 2008. https://www.academia.edu/19821488/Hermeneutics_and_the_Linguisticality_of_the_Christian_Word.

Roberts, C. H. *Manuscript, Society and Belief in Early Christian Egypt*. Schweich Lectures on Biblical Archaeology. Oxford: Oxford University Press, 1979.

Robinson, James M. "A Formal Analysis of Colossians 1:15–20." *JBL* 76 (1957) 270–87. https://www.jstor.org/stable/3261897.

Robinson, Maurice A., and William G. Pierpont. *The New Testament in the Original Greek*. Southborough, MA: Chilton, 2005.

Rohrbaugh, R. L. "Foreignizing Translation." In *The Social Sciences and Biblical Translation*, edited by Dietmar Neufeld, 11–24. SymS. Atlanta: Society of Biblical Literature, 2008.

Rösel, Martin. "Towards a 'Theology of the Septuagint.'" In *Septuagint Research: Issues and Challenges in the Study of the Greek Jewish Scriptures*, edited by Wolfgang Kraus and R. Glenn Wooden, 239–52. SCS. Atlanta: Society of Biblical Literature, 2006. https://www.academia.edu/26404961/Towards_a_Theology_of_the_Septuagint_.

Rosner, Brian S., et al., eds. *Paul as Pastor*. London: T&T Clark, 2017.

Rosten, Leo. *The New Joys of Yiddish*. New York: Three Rivers, 2001.

Rowland, Christopher. "Apocalyptic Visions and the Exaltation of Christ in the Letter to the Colossians." *JSNT* 6 (1983) 73–83.

———. "A Pragmatic Approach to *Wirkungsgeschichte*: Reflections on the Blackwell Bible Commentary Series and on the Writing of Its Commentary on the Apocalypse." Unpublished paper, 2004. PDF in the author's possession.

Royal Shakespeare Company. "Written on the Heart." Royal Shakespeare Company, n.d. https://www.rsc.org.uk/written-on-the-heart.

Royalty, Robert M., Jr. "Dwelling on Visions: On the Nature of the So-Called 'Colossians Heresy.'" *Bib* 83 (2002) 329–57. https://www.jstor.org/stable/42614382.

Royse, James R. *Scribal Habits in Early Greek New Testament Papyri*. NTTSD. Leiden: Brill, 2008.

Sampley, J. Paul, and Peter Lampe, eds. *Paul and Rhetoric*. T&T Clark Biblical Studies. New York: Continuum, 2010.

Sanders, E. P. *Paul and Palestinian Judaism: A Comparison of Patterns of Religion*. Philadelphia: Fortress, 1977.

Sanders, Jack T. *The New Testament Christological Hymns: Their Historical Religious Background*. SNTSMS 15. Cambridge: Cambridge University Press, 1971.

Sandmel, Samuel. "Parallelomania." *JBL* 81 (1962) 1–13. http://www.jstor.org/stable/3264821.

Sappington, Thomas J. *Revelation and Redemption*. LNTS. Sheffield: Sheffield Academic, 1991.

Scalia, Antonin. *A Matter of Interpretation: Federal Courts and the Law*. Edited by Amy Gutmann. University Center for Human Values. Princeton, NJ: Princeton University Press, 1997.

Scanlin, Harold P. "Revising the KJV: Seventeenth through Nineteenth Century." In *The King James Version at 400: Assessing Its Genius as Bible Translation and Its Literary Influence*, edited by David G. Burke et al., 141–55. BSNA. Atlanta: Society of Biblical Literature, 2013.

Schaff, Philip. *The History of Creeds*. Vol. 2 of *Creeds of Christendom*. Christian Classics Ethereal Library, 1876. https://ccel.org/ccel/schaff/creeds2.

———. *Nicene and Post-Nicene Christianity, AD 311–600*. Vol. 3 of *History of the Christian Church*. Christian Classics Ethereal Library, 1889. https://www.ccel.org/ccel/s/schaff/hcc3/cache/hcc3.pdf.

Schleiermacher, Friedrich. *On Religion*. Translated by John Oman. London: Kegan Paul, Trench, Trübner & Co., 1893. https://www.google.com/books/edition/On_Religion/lH1AAAAAIAAJ?hl=en&gbpv=1.

Schmemann, Alexander. *The Eucharist: Sacrament of the Kingdom*. Translated by Paul Kachur. Crestwood, NY: St. Vladimir's Seminary Press, 1987.

Schoeman, Roy H. *Salvation Is from the Jews: The Role of Judaism in Salvation History from Abraham to the Second Coming*. San Francisco: Ignatius, 2003.

Schüssler Fiorenza, Elizabeth. "Apocalyptic and Gnosis in the Book of Revelation and Paul." *JBL* 92 (1973) 565–81. https://www.jstor.org/stable/3263124.

Schweizer, Eduard. "Colossians 1:15–20." *RevExp* 87 (1990) 97–104. https://journals.sagepub.com/doi/10.1177/003463739008700108.

———. "Slaves of the Elements and Worshippers of Angels: Gal 4:3, 9 and Col 2:8, 18, 20." *JBL* 107 (1988) 455–68. https://www.jstor.org/stable/3267580.

Seitz, Christopher. *The Character of Christian Scripture: The Significance of a Two-Testament Bible*. STI. Grand Rapids: Baker Academic, 2011.

Selby, Gary S. *Not with Wisdom of Words: Nonrational Persuasion in the New Testament*. Grand Rapids: Eerdmans, 2016.

Sendrey, Alfred. *Music in Ancient Israel*. New York: Philosophical, 2007.
Siegal, Allan M., and William G. Connolly. *The New York Times Manual of Style and Usage: The Official Style Guide Used by the Writers and Editors of the World's Most Authoritative Newspaper*. New York: Random, 1999.
Silva, Moisés. *Biblical Words and Their Meaning: An Introduction to Lexical Semantics*. Rev. ed. Grand Rapids: Zondervan, 1994.
———. "Faith versus Works of the Law in Galatians." In *The Paradoxes of Paul*, edited by D. A. Carson et al., 217–48. Vol. 2 of *Justification and Variegated Nomism*. WUNT, 2nd ser., 181. Grand Rapids: Baker Academic, 2004.
Smith, David. *The Epistles for All Christians: Epistolary Literature, Circulation, and "The Gospels for All Christians."* BibInt 186. Leiden: Brill, 2020.
Smith, James K. A. *The Fall of Interpretation: Philosophical Foundations for a Creational Hermeneutic*. Downers Grove, IL: InterVarsity, 2000.
Smyth, Herbert W. *Greek Grammar*. Cambridge, MA: Harvard University Press, 1963.
Sokupa, Michael. "The Calendric Elements in Colossians 2:16 in Light of the Ongoing Debate on the Opponents." *Neot* 46 (2012) 172–89. https://www.jstor.org/stable/43048850.
Standhartinger, Angela. "The Origin and Intention of the Household Code in the Letter to the Colossians." *JSNT* 79 (2000) 117–30. https://doi/pdf/10.1177/0142064X14567054.
Stanton, Elizabeth C. *The Woman's Bible*. Seattle: Pacific, 2010.
Stark, Ryan J. "Some Aspects of Christian Mystical Rhetoric, Philosophy, and Poetry." *Philosophy & Rhetoric* 41 (2008) 260–77. https://www.jstor.org/stable/25655316.
Starr, James. "Paraenesis." Oxford Bibliographies, last modified July 24, 2013. DOI: h10.1093/OBO/9780195393361-0143.
Steiner, George. *After Babel*. 3rd ed. Oxford: Oxford University Press, 1998.
Steinmetz, David C. "The Superiority of Pre-Critical Exegesis." In *Taking the Long View: Christian Theology in Historical Perspective*, 3–14. New York: Oxford Academic, 2015. https://doi.org/10.1093/acprof:osobl/9780199768936.003.0001.
Stendahl, Krister. "The Apostle Paul and the Introspective Conscience of the West." *HTR* 56 (1963) 199–215. https://doi.org/10.1017/S0017816000024779.
Straus, Michael, trans. and Jennifer Reiland illus. *The Book of Revelation: A New Translation*. New York: Spuyten Duyvil, 2018.
———, trans. *The New Testament: A 21st Century Translation*. Eugene, OR: Wipf & Stock, 2019.
———. "Psalm 2:7 and the Concept of περιχώρησις." *SJT* 67 (2014) 213–29. https://doi.org/10.1017/S0036930614000076.
Strawbridge, Jennifer R. *The Pauline Effect: The Use of the Pauline Epistles by Early Christian Writers*. SBR 5. Berlin: de Gruyter, 2015.
Strunk, William, Jr., and E. B. White. *The Elements of Style*. 4th ed. Harlow: Pearson Education, 1999.
Stuhlmacher, Peter. *Biblical Theology of the New Testament*. Edited and translated by Daniel P. Bailey. Grand Rapids: Eerdmans, 2018.
———. *Historical Criticism and Theological Interpretation: Toward a Hermeneutics of Consent*. Translated by Roy A. Harrisville. Eugene, OR: Wipf & Stock, 2003.
———. *How to Do Biblical Theology*. Edited by Dikran Y. Hadidian. Princeton Theological Monograph 38. Eugene, OR: Pickwick, 1995.
———. *Revisiting Paul's Doctrine of Justification: A Challenge to the New Perspective*. Special ed. Downers Grove, IL: IVP Academic, 2001.

Bibliography

Sumney, Jerry L. *Colossians: A Commentary*. NTL. Louisville: Westminster John Knox, 2008.

———. "Those Who 'Pass Judgment': The Identity of the Opponents in Colossians." *Bib* 74 (1993) 366–88. https://www.jstor.org/stable/42611339.

Swales, John M. *Research Genres: Explorations and Applications*. Cambridge Applied Linguistics. New York: Cambridge University Press, 2004.

Taylor, Daniel. "Chief Stylist's Edits on Draft Translation of Colossians." Unpublished paper, Feb. 2001. In the author's possession.

Thielman, Frank. *From Plight to Solution: A Jewish Framework for Understanding Paul's View of the Law in Galatians and Romans*. Eugene, OR: Wipf & Stock, 1989.

———. *Romans*. ZEC. Grand Rapids: Zondervan, 2018.

Thiselton, Anthony C. *Colossians: A Short Exegetical and Pastoral Commentary*. Eugene, OR: Cascade, 2020.

———. *Hermeneutics: An Introduction*. Grand Rapids: Eerdmans, 2009.

———. *New Horizons in Hermeneutics*. Grand Rapids: Zondervan, 1992.

———. *The Two Horizons: New Testament Hermeneutics and Philosophical Description*. Grand Rapids: Eerdmans, 1980.

Thompson, Michael B. *The New Perspective on Paul*. Grove Biblical 26. Cambridge: Grove, 2002.

Thornton, T. C. G. "Jewish New Moon Festivals, Galatians 4:3–11 and Colossians 2:16." *JTS*, n.s., 40 (1989) 97–100. https://www.jstor.org/stable/23963765.

Tomlin, Graham. "Luther's Approach to Bible Translation and the KJV." In *The King James Version at 400: Assessing Its Genius as Bible Translation and Its Literary Influence*, edited by David G. Burke et al., 125–40. BSNA. Atlanta: Society of Biblical Literature, 2013.

Trobisch, David. *The First Edition of the New Testament*. Oxford: Oxford University Press, 2000.

———. "The KJV and the Development of Text Criticism." In *The King James Version at 400: Assessing Its Genius as Bible Translation and Its Literary Influence*, edited by David G. Burke et al., 227–34. BSNA. Atlanta: Society of Biblical Literature, 2013.

———. *Paul's Letter Collection: Tracing the Origins*. Minneapolis: Fortress, 1994. https://archive.org/details/paulslettercolleooootrob.

Tulsa 2011. "King James Version Was Edited by Rosicrucians and/or Masons?" Talk Jesus, June 6, 2015. https://www.talkjesus.com/threads/king-james-version-was-edited-by-rosicrucians-and-or-masons.52781/.

Tyndale House Cambridge. "About This Edition." Greek New Testament, n.d. https://www.thegreeknewtestament.com.

Ullmann, Stephen. *Semantics: An Introduction to the Science of Meaning*. Oxford: Basil Blackwell, 1962.

University of Chicago Press Editorial Staff. *The Chicago Manual of Style*. 17th ed. Chicago: University of Chicago Press, 2017.

University of Oxford. "The King James Bible Lecture Series." University of Oxford, Mar. 8, 2011–July 25, 2011. https://podcasts.ox.ac.uk/series/king-james-bible-lecture-series.

Ure, Jean. "Introduction: Approaches to the Study of Register Range." *International Journal of the Sociology of Language* 35 (1982) 5–23. https://doi.org/10.1515/IJSL.1982.35.5.

Vanhoozer, Kevin J. *Is There a Meaning in This Text? The Bible, the Reader, and the Morality of Literary Knowledge*. Grand Rapids: Zondervan, 1998.

Van Kooten, George H. *Cosmic Christology in Paul and the Pauline School*. Tübingen: Mohr Siebeck, 2003.

Van Leeuwen, Raymond C. "On Bible Translation and Hermeneutics." In *After Pentecost: Language and Biblical Interpretation*, edited by Craig Bartholomew et al., 284–311. Grand Rapids: Zondervan, 2001.

Van W. Cronjé, J. "The Stratagem of the Rhetorical Question in Galatians 4:9–10 as a Means towards Persuasion." *Neot* 26 (1992) 417–24. https://www.jstor.org/stable/43048047.

Vasileiadis, Pavlos D. "Aspects of Rendering the Sacred Tetragrammaton into Greek." *Open Theology* 1 (2014) 56–88. https://www.degruyter.com/document/doi/10.2478/opth-2014-006/pdf.

Vawter, F. Bruce. "The Colossians Hymn and the Principle of Redaction." *CBQ* 33 (1971) 62–81. https://jstor.org/stable/43714980.

Venuti, Lawrence, ed. *The Translation Studies Reader*. 3rd ed. London: Routledge, 2000.

Vergeer, Wim C. "Σκιά and Σῶμα: The Strategy of Contextualisation in Colossians 2:17." *Neot* 28 (1994) 379–93. https://www.jstor.org/stable/43048153.

Vincent of Lérin. *Commonitorium*. Translated by C. A. Heurtley. From *Nicene and Post-Nicene Fathers*, edited by Philip Schaff and Henry Wace, 2nd ser., 11. Buffalo, NY: Christian Literature, 1894. Revised and edited for New Advent by Kevin Knight. http://www.newadvent.org/fathers/3506.htm.

Voelz, James W. *What Does This Mean?* 2nd ed. St. Louis: Concordia, 2003.

Wagner, J. Ross. "The Septuagint and the 'Search for the Christian Bible.'" In *Scripture's Doctrine and Theology's Bible: How the New Testament Shapes Christian Dogmatics*, edited by Markus Bockmuehl and Alan J. Torrance, 17–28. Grand Rapids: Baker Academic, 2008.

Wainwright, Arthur W. *The Trinity in the New Testament*. London: SPCK, 1962.

Wallace, Daniel B. "The Majority Text and the Original Text: Are They Identical?" Bible, June 3, 2004. https://bible.org/article/majority-text-and-original-text-are-they-identical#_ftn23.

Warren, Michelle. "Modern Theoretical Approaches to Medieval Translation." In *A Companion to Medieval Translation*, edited by Jeanette Beer, 165–73. ARC Companion. Leeds: ARC Humanities, 2019. https://digitalcommons.dartmouth.edu/cgi/viewcontent.cgi?article=4970&context=facoa.

Wasserman, Emma. "Gentile Gods at the Eschaton: A Reconsideration of Paul's 'Principalities and Powers' in 1 Corinthians 15." *JBL* 136 (2017) 727–46. https://jstor.org/stable/10.15699/jbl.1363.2017.290006.

Watson, Francis. *Text and Truth: Redefining Biblical Theology*. Grand Rapids: Eerdmans, 1997.

Webster, John. *Holy Scripture: A Dogmatic Sketch*. Current Issues in Theology 1. Cambridge: Cambridge University Press, 2003.

Wedderburn, Alexander J. M. *The Reasons for Romans*. London: T&T Clark, 1988.

Wessels, G. Francois. "The Eschatology of Colossians and Ephesians." *Neot* 21 (1987) 183–202. https://www.jstor.org/stable/43070391.

Westerholm, Stephen. *Israel's Law and the Church's Faith: Paul and His Recent Interpreters*. Eugene, OR: Wipf & Stock, 1988.

Willett, Elizabeth A. R. "Feminist Choices of Early Women Bible Translators." *Open Theology* (2016) 400–404. https://www.degruyter.com/view/journals/opth/open-issue/article-10.1515-opth-2016-033/article-10.1515-opth-2016-033.xml.

Willi, Andreas. *The Languages of Aristophanes: Aspects of Linguistic Variation in Classical Attic Greek*. Oxford Classical Monographs. Oxford: Oxford University Press, 2003.

Williams, A. L. "The Cult of the Angels at Colossae." *JTS* 10 (1909) 413–38. https://www.jstor.org/stable/23948824.

Williams, Rowan. "Augustine and the Psalms." *Int* 58 (2004) 17–27. https://doi.org/10.1177/002096430405800103.

———. "Celebrating the 1611 King James Bible." *Guardian*, Nov. 16, 2011. https://www.theguardian.com/commentisfree/belief/2011/nov/16/1611-king-james-bible-400th-anniversary.

Wilson, Marvin R. *Our Father Abraham: Jewish Roots of the Christian Faith*. Grand Rapids: Eerdmans, 1989.

Wilson, Robert McL. *Colossians and Philemon*. ICC. London: T&T Clark, 2005.

Witherington, Ben, III. *New Testament Rhetoric: An Introductory Guide to the Art of Persuasion in and of the New Testament*. Eugene, OR: Wipf & Stock, 2009.

Wittgenstein, Ludwig. *Philosophical Investigations*. Translated by Gertrude E. M. Anscombe. Oxford: Blackwell, 1967.

———. *Zettel*. Translated by Gertrude E. M. Anscombe. Oxford: Blackwell, 1967.

Wonderly, William L. "Crib, Transposition, and Dynamic Equivalence." *BT* 19 (1968) 6–13. https://journals.sagepub.com/doi/10.1177/000608446801900102.

Worman, Nancy. *Abusive Mouths in Classical Athens*. Cambridge: Cambridge University Press, 2008.

Wright, N. T. *Colossians and Philemon*. TNTC 12. Downers Grove, IL: InterVarsity, 1986.

———. *The Kingdom New Testament: A Contemporary Translation*. New York: HarperCollins, 2012.

———. "The New Testament in the Strange Words of David Bentley Hart." *ChrCent*, Jan. 15, 2018. https://www.christiancentury.org/review/books/new-testament-strange-words-david-bentley-hart.

———. "A Poem Doubled: Pauline Reflections on Theology and Poetry." Photocopy, University of St. Andrews [since published].

———. "Poetry and Theology in Colossians 1:15–20." *NTS* 36 (1990) 444–68. https://doi.org/10.1017/S002868850001585X.

———. "Reading Paul, Thinking Scripture." In *Scripture's Doctrine and Theology's Bible: How the New Testament Shapes Christian Dogmatics*, edited by Markus Bockmuehl and Alan J. Torrance, 59–71. Grand Rapids: Baker Academic, 2008.

Zahl, Paul F. M. *The First Christian: Universal Truth in the Teachings of Jesus*. Grand Rapids: Eerdmans, 2003.

Zahl, Simeon. *The Holy Spirit and Christian Experience*. Oxford: Oxford University Press, 2020.

Zondervan. "Translation Committee." Zondervan, n.d. https://www.zondervan.com/p/nrsv-2/#committee.

Zwicky, Fritz. "Die Rotverschiebung von extragalaktischen Nebeln." *Helvetica Physica Acta* 6 (1933) 110–27.

Subject Index

Adam, 118, 118n370
admonitory register, 106
affirmations, 78
afflictions, from union with Christ, 135
Alexander the Great, 156n569
"all the Fullness was pleased to dwell,"
    139
all things, held firmly together by or in
    Christ, 126–27
allegorical readings, 23, 23n29
allusions, to the Old Testament in the
    New, 215
"Alpha and Omega," Christ as, 124–25
Alter, Robert, 56
American Standard Version (ASV), 168
Amplified Bible, 198–99
anamnestic function, of the Eucharist,
    112n346
ancient texts. *See* biblical text(s)
ancillary liturgies, kinds of, 131
angels, 148, 149, 150, 156, 156n569
apocrypha, 17
apocryphal treasures of wisdom and
    knowledge, found in Christ, 144
Apostles' Creed, 29
apostolic teaching, on Christ, 7
Aquinas, Thomas, 2, 19–20
Archippus, 104
Arians, 119, 125
Aristotle, 96, 98
asceticism, 68, 142
Asia Minor, worship of angels in, 156

ASV (American Standard Version), 168
Athanasian Creed, 34, 133
Augustine of Hippo
    on access to divine self-disclosure, 19
    on Jesus, 73n153
    on the Old and New Testaments,
        72–73
    reading of the Vulgate, 192
    on the translation of the LXX,
        72n149
    Trinitarian analogy to relationship
        of thought and language, 2–3,
        19–25
    understanding of biblical wholeness,
        7
    used *verbum interius* describing
        inner thought, 2
    on the Word shown to men
        incarnate, 197n710
authorial intent, discerning, 4

Balchin, John, 84–85
"barbarians," as south of Greece, 108
Baugh, Stephen, 84
"being affected by history,"
    consciousness of, 157
Benedictus, 81
biblical text(s)
    capitalization and italics in, 211–13
    dialogic engagement with, 4
    interpreting through dialogue with
        tradition, 158n577
    chapters, 208

biblical text(s) (*cont.*)
   in translation, 161
   understanding, 31, 207
biblical translation, informed approach to, 217
biblical words, as "events," 112
binary distinctions, translation theory and, 37
Bockmuehl, Markus, 33
Body of Christ, church as, 135
Bruce, Frederick F., 176

canon, 17, 32, 217
canonical integrity, translation methodology premised on, 35
canonical relationships, retaining in translation, 94
canonical unity, maintaining, 222
canonical-hermeneutical approach
   application of, 107, 113, 205, 206
   elements of, 35–205
   suggestive elements for translators, 219
   testing the viability of, 158
   viability and applicability of, 202–5
canonized, by ecumenical council, 78
capital letters, uses of, 90, 212
Chalcedonian Statement, 34, 140, 196
charismatic gifts, range of displayed in the church, 156
children
   place in the family, 105
   understanding of Bible versions, 187
Chomsky, Noam, 43n37
Chosen People, capitalized, 139
Christ. *See also* Jesus; Son
   actively holding all things together, 126, 127
   authority of, 123
   believer's relationship to, 136–38
   "completeness" of, 131
   conquest of "principalities and powers," 150
   "consubstantial/of one substance" with the Father, 119
   defeat of death by, 130
   "divest[ed] all sovereigns and dominions," 146
   as firstborn, 128, 129, 130
   greatness of God shown forth in him, 118n372
   as the Head of the Body, the Church, 122–23
   humiliation of, 147
   identification with God, 118n371
   as the "interpretative key for understanding the Old Testament," 7
   in John 1:1, 141
   kingdom of, 146
   making his "dwelling among us," 134
   nature of vis-à-vis the Father, 77
   as the one by whom all things were made, 113
   as ontologically equal to God the Father, 139
   presence in his people, the church, 137–38
   presented in elevated language, 112–36
   as the source for true knowledge and wisdom, 143
   superior with respect to all creation, 129
   as true Wisdom, 114
   two natures of, 121
   as the "unparalleled/matchless image of the Godhead," 120
   as the very Impress of God's Being, 118
Christian doctrine, terms with special meaning in, 46
Christian faith, summaries of belief, 76
Christian theology, as a form of poetry, 186
christological crises, of the fourth century, 77
Christological language, 113, 136–43
Christology
   of the Colossian Hymn, 188
   of Paul, 68–69, 104
church councils or synods, series of, 77
church history and tradition, text's trajectory in, 203
Church/ the Body, Christ as "head" of, 122–23

Subject Index

"classical" formulations
    continued use of many, 203
    excursus on, 50–53
    inertial force of, 177
    retained in, 5
classical references, detecting in Paul's letters, 144n507
Clement of Alexandria, 49n67
Colossae, 63–71
Colossian church, 65
"Colossian heresy," 65, 83
Colossian Hymn
    disagreements about, 82
    English translation tradition of, 203
    as an exemplary application of the model, 9
    faith formulae canonized by conciliar decrees, 9
    focusing on, 75, 80–81, 190
    illustrating options available to a translator, 82
    as the letter's most distinctive portion, 13
    literature concerning, 82n202
    on the lordship of Jesus, 128
    "Mystery of Christ" reflected in, 120
    as theologically complex, 204
    vocabulary and style as markedly distinct, 85–86
    on who God "is," 140–41
Colossian Hymn (translations of)
    in the Amplified Bible, 198–99
    Bratcher and Nida's (GNB) translation of, 178
    Bruce's version of, 176–77
    ESV's version, 171–72
    Hart's translation of, 192–93
    interlinear version of, 200–201
    Jerome's rendering of, 160
    Jordan's translation of, 183–84
    in the KJV, 167
    N. T. Wright's translation of, 185–86
    NIV translation of, 180
    NLT rendering of, 189–90
    NRSV's translation of, 170
    Peterson's translation, 181
    RSV's translation of, 169
    Straus' 2019 published version, 194
    Straus' new translation of, 194–96
    TLB translation of, 187–88
    translated by Phillips, 174
    translated into English as a test case, 158
    translation of in the appendix, 87
    Tyndale's translation of, 164–65
    Wycliffe's translation of, 162
"Colossian philosophy," 66, 154
Colossians, urged into ascetic abasement, 155
Colossians (book of)
    addressed to a specific concern, 63–67
    authored by Paul, 60n102
    authorization for others to "read," 71
    elements common to other Pauline letters, 61
    examination of key language in, 111–57
    as an example of history methodology, 59
    as an exemplary text, 32
    as exhortation and encouragement, 67–69
    literary and linguistic elements, 80
    as more varied than many New Testament texts, 58
    Nida failing to perceive canonically essential elements of, 45–46
    nomina sacra appearing in manuscripts, 91
    Old Testament references in, 215
    personal aspect of the closing, 111
    relationship to other writings, 69–79
    Straus' translation of with extensive notes, 225–33
    as a "test case" for the proposed translation methodology, 9, 12, 13, 60
committee process, 54, 56, 192
"complete intelligibility," of biblical translation, 48n59
completeness
    Christ and, 131, 146–47
    general sense of, 132
    resulting of having been filled, 137

congregation, disqualifying members of, 156
consensus, 48–49, 58
contemporary translation approaches, examples of, 172–98
contextual settings, translators becoming familiar with, 220
core translation tradition, sustaining, 204
"corporeal aspect of God," Paul seeing manifest, 141
corpus Paulinum, expanded readership of, 44
"cosmic Christology," 70, 128
"cosmic lordship," of Christ, 130
The Cotton Patch Gospel, 183–85
Council of Chalcedon (AD 451), 77, 120
Council of Constantinople (AD 381), 77, 120
Council of Nicaea (AD 325), 77, 119, 125
"covenanted presence," of Christ, 134
created beings, worshiping those inferior to the Creator, 157
creation, Christ's role in, 125
creation story, 127
credal and liturgical formulations, in New Testament translation, 75–79
credal expression, incorporating relevant, 126
credal language, translators incorporating, 122, 221
creeds
  brief in words but great in mysteries, 78n184
  "canonized" words of, 122
  defined, 77, 78
Cretans, comparison to "slow bellies," 144n507
cultural and conceptual horizons, translators being aware of, 207

"dark matter," holding the universe together, 127n420
Dedication Creed, of the Council of Antioch, 119–20
defeated powers, Christ's humiliation of, 147
"deficiency," as a gnostic term, 138

deitas Latin word, into use after Jerome published the Vulgate, 140n489
"Deity," not clearly embedded in the English translation tradition, 139–40
deliberative argument, 96
dialogic interaction, between linguistic past and present, 109
dialogic participation, in kerygmatic presence, 31
Dibelius, Martin, 66
Dilthey, Wilhelm, 27
"distancing of form from meaning," avoiding, 93, 185
doctrinal and theological positions, interpretive decisions, 204
doctrinal development, highlighting the dialogic nature of, 94
doctrinal horizon, of Nida affecting his choices, 46
doctrinal positions, taking into account, 193
doctrine
  Christological language as, 136–43
  persistently articulated, 30
Douay-Rheims version, place in the Catholic translation tradition, 166n607
dynamic equivalence approach
  defined, 17
  of Eugene Nida, 10, 26
  Phillips anticipating, 174
  of theological concepts and, 133
  to translation, 42–48
  translation projects geared to, 57
  in translation theory, 217
"dynamic equivalent," of the Colossian Hymn, 181

each age translating anew, 39
Eastern Orthodox perspective, of Hart, 192
"ecstatic" transport, vehicle for, 100
ecumenical council, canonized by, 78
effective history hermeneutic, applying to the text, 47
effective history (*Wirkungsgeschichte*), 4, 17, 138

Subject Index

ekthesis, 210–11, 218
elements
    of earth, water, air and fire, 149
    melting with fervent heat at the day of the Lord, 148n525
    of the world, 148
elevated language, Christ presented in, 112–36
English
    of the KJV, 166
    as less distantly removed from Greek, 201
English Revised Version (ERV), 168
English Standard Version (ESV), 39n22, 171
English translation tradition, of Colossians, 158
English translations, impact of Wycliffe, 162
Enlightenment, rational analysis and, 23–24
"enthusiasm," Luther's concerns about, 80n192
enthymemes (inferred propositions), use of, 96
Epaphras, 67, 71, 110
Ephesians, 69–70
epideictic speech, reflecting similar forms, 96
"epistolary" genre, characteristics of, 60
epithets, in Colossians, 89
equivalent effect principle, 47, 173
"errorist/heresy" view, of Christ, 124
ERV (English Revised Version), 168
ESV (English Standard Version), 39n22, 171
Eucharist, anamnestic function of, 112n346
events, occurring in the eternal present, 102
"excess of meaning," 3, 52
exegesis, translation overlapping with, 8, 207, 221
explanatory language, use of, 49
expressions, freshly coined providing fuller understanding, 52
expressive affirmations, 77
expressive word, should embody the inner one, 185
extended "blessing" of Eph 1:3–14, compared to the Colossian Hymn, 99

faith-in-translation, Christianity as, 35
false teaching, concerns raised by Paul about, 68
Father. *See* God
fellowship, of the Colossians, 68–69
"filling" words, contrasting with "emptiness," 138
"firstborn"
    Christ's priority as, 128
    placed "over" all, 129
"firstborn from among the dead," Christ as, 130
"foreignizing translation," 45n46
"forerunner," Jesus' perfect offering as, 130
form elements, of the "horizon" of any present-day translator, 219
"formal correspondence." *See* literal approach
formal elements, of the text as revelatory, 208
forms, of the receptor language, 222
formulations, with a "classical" role in church tradition, 221
"Fountainhead," conveying that all power and rule comes from Christ, 137
"free space around" the text
    allowing for novel expressions, 53
    ancient text for expression of the living presence of the Word, 207
    filling of, 11, 217, 223
    "in its revealing" of the *verbum interius*, 204
    recognizing, 1, 83
    translator exploring, 112
fullness, 132, 133, 153, 154
"functional equivalence" approach, 42–48
future research, suggestions for, 218

Gadamer, Hans-Georg, 2–3, 21, 27

Geneva Bible, extensive interpretive notes of, 168n611
genitive construction, 41–42
genre, 17, 59, 60–69
genre analysis, 59, 62
genres and registers, translators reflecting, 222
gentile Christians, worship practices reverting, 153n556
gentile members, of the Colossian community, 87
Gloria in Excelsis, 81
GNB. *See* Good News Tradition (GNB)
gnostic sources, 153
goals, of Paul in his letters, 103–4
God
    dwelling between the cherubim on high, 133–34
    enfleshed in the man Jesus, 141
    fullness of, 89
    maintaining the cosmos, 126
    of the Old Testament, Christ's identity with, 125
    sense of reciprocal obligation, 88
    will of knowing "in all wisdom," 115
Godhead, 116, 139–40
Godhead/Deity/Divine Essence, dwelling bodily in Christ, 141–42
gods, 87, 89
Good News Tradition (GNB), 177, 178, 179
Gospel readings, providing access to the life and ministry of Jesus, 112n346
governing approach, imposition of a single, 202
Graham, Billy, 177
Greek philosophy, theological concepts considered in, 143n502
Greek text
    biblical translations must be grounded in, 79–80
    elements of reflected in translation, 81
    as the ground for any translation, 219–20
    literal as inconsistent with contemporary sensibilities, 106
    paragraphing as does GNT, 211
    translators reflecting formal aspects not present in, 222
Gregory of Nazianzus, on the Son as "Word," 19
guidelines
    of Nida, 57
    for the "Organization of Translation Programs," 53
    reflecting a mission-driven desire to translate, 54n80
    relevant to future New Testament translations, 219–23
    for stylistic input, 55

Hart, David Bentley, 191, 192, 193
Head of the Body, the Church, Christ as, 122–23
"hearing," importance of the letters being read aloud, 95
heavenly things, setting minds on, 105
Hebrew Scriptures, as the framework for Jesus' own hermeneutic, 6
Hebrews (book of), reading less like a letter than a treatise, 60
"hermeneutical spiral," 11, 198
hermeneutical principles, 34
hermeneutics, defined, 18
Herodotus, on Colossae as "a great city in Phrygia," 64
Hierapolis, medicinal benefits of its spas, 64
historical phenomenon, translation as, 6
historical-critical approaches, 4, 22–31, 44
historical-critical approaches, limitations of, 25–27
historical-critical research, 203
historical-critical scholarship, distancing the text, 4n21
history, textual revealing in the continuum of, 3, 26–28
Holy Spirit, demonstration of the power of, 95
homosexuality, Bible's position on, 107
"horizon," of modern listeners and readers, 29
horizons (or "prejudices"), translators being aware of, 221

Subject Index

"household code" guidelines, Colossians including, 104
household code instructions, to parents, 105
"household" instructions of Paul, 68
human language, expressive limits of, 132
human relationships, corresponding to the Trinity, 21
humiliation, of defeated powers and principalities, 147
hybrid approach, for Straus' translation of the New Testament, 209
hymnic aspects, in Colossians, 80–87, 111

icons, long and traditionally venerated, 121
idolatry, condemnation of throughout the Bible, 178
image and likeness of God, mankind's creation in, 118
"image of the invisible God," Christ as, 117, 120
images, devotion to as "pointless and misleading," 121
imaginative projections, 27, 46
imprisonment, of Paul, 67
incarnation, mystery of, 120, 133, 134
individual translators, committee of, 58
inertial force, exerted by prior translations, 221
"the infinity of dialogue," scriptural understanding achieved in, 79
inflection, relative absence of in English, 38
initiation, into the Christian faith, 67
initiation practices, in Ovid's *Metamorphoses*, 66
inner meaning, 63, 179
"inner word"
    concerning Christ's preeminence, 129
    defined, 18
    as far from remote, 219
    means of access to, 18
    noncanonical material revelatory of, 79
    perceiving "in its revealing," 32
    providing further access to, 50
    referring to the meaning communicated, 112
    revealing of, 21
"inspired literalism," of the KJV, 10
intelligibility, 47, 201
intended audience, of Paul's letters, 44
"intentional ambiguity," 47
interlinear genre, 200
interlinear presentation, of the text, 199
interlinear translation, 201
intrascriptural account, of a given text, 69
intrascriptural elements, identifying, 220
intrascriptural presence of words and imagery, 203
intrascriptural reference, bringing out parallel, 118n371
intrascriptural usages and resonances, translator examining, 124, 152
intrascripturality, 31n82, 129n432
intratextual bracketed material, in the Amplified Bible, 199
invisible God, as visibly present in the world, 120
invocation, opening of Colossians not beginning with, 88
Irenaeus, on credos, 76
Isis cult, initiation into, 154–55
Islam, on the Koran as "untranslatable," 160n584
italics, in biblical translation, 212

Jerome of Stridon
    apostolic renderings of Old Testament passages, 7
    on Greek transferred literally into Latin, 38n15
    Latin Vulgate as the source for Wycliffe's Latinate renderings, 9, 158
    mistranslation leading to doctrinal error, 192
    not including verse numbers in his translation, 160n585
    rendering texts on a "sense for sense" basis, 159
    tracing Augustine's doctrine of original sin, 191
Jerome/Wycliffe/Tyndale, alignment of words and phrases, 165

Jesus. *See also* Christ
    identity as the same God of creation and Israel, 32–33
    on the nature of the incarnate person of, 120
    reference to "the temple that was his body," 134
"Jesus is Lord," as "the basic confession," 75
Jewish members of the congregation, familiar with Hebrew prayers, 87
Jewish Scriptures, in the New Testament, 31
Jewish sources, on the "presence of the fullness of divinity in bodily form," 141
Jews, living in the Phrygian Cities, 65
Jews and gentiles, within the Colossian congregation, 152
Jordan, Clarence, 183–85
Josephus, on schools of Jewish thought, 145
"Judaizers," in Galatians, 66
judicial argument, seeking to persuade the audience, 96
Justin Martyr, on the word remaining in us, 19

"kernels," all languages sharing, 43n37
King James translators, 40, 56, 159, 166
King James Version (KJV)
    compilers read their drafts aloud to one another, 166
    methodology of as "inspired literalism," 166n604
    not using the same English word to translate the same Greek word every time, 39–40
    phrases originating with Wycliffe incorporated in, 163, 167–68
    as the product of a "committee" of fifty-four scholars, 165–68
    70 percent of Tyndale's Old Testament phrasing and 80 percent of the New, 9
    small-caps form of LORD for the Tetragrammaton, 92, 214

The Kingdom New Testament, stated goal of accessibility, 185–86
"knowledge," Christ as the source of, 115–17
Koine Greek, exhibiting linearity of word order, 201

language
    of God, Origen on, 113n347
    imposing limits with respect to the "unsaid and inexpressible," 45n47
    opting for reflecting a mutuality of respect among family members, 107
    of Wycliffe remaining as substrate, 163
"language-shaping power"
    of Jerome's wordings, 160
    of the translation tradition of the KJV, 167
Laodicea, 64
Latin Vulgate, translators considering the influence of, 221
Letter to the Laodiceans, 71n145
letters/epistles, 93
    of Paul, 60, 61, 71n147, 103
licentiousness, Paul's rejection of, 68
Lightfoot, Joseph, 66
linguistic and literary analysis, elements relating to, 202–3
linguistic forms, categorizing, 59
linguistic insights, applying to the art of translation, 217
linguistic theory, as a point of departure, 19–22
listenability, of the KJV, 166
literal approach, 1, 38
"literal equivalence," as a translation philosophy, 198
literal text, 159, 199
literal translation methodology, 18, 40
literary analysis, revealing intrascriptural aspects, 80
literary characteristics, in translation, 58–111
literary documents, in early Christianity intended to be read aloud, 95

Subject Index

literary quality, translators giving enhanced importance to, 222
literary talents, of Tyndale, 164
liturgical language and structure, Colossians as a useful example of other forms of, 87
liturgical texts, celebrating God, 81
Living Bible, 187–91
living history, 5, 8
living Word approach, 62, 112n346
"living Word" of God (the *viva vox Jesu*), 26, 28, 29
"Logos," as another possible translation for Word, 51
Lord's Prayer, Wycliffe's version of, 162
lordship, of Jesus, 127, 128
Luther, Martin, on Holy Scripture urging Christ, 7
Luther's Bible of 1534, 213–14
LXX. *See* Septuagint (LXX)
Lycus River Valley, 64

Magnificat (Luke 1:4–55), 81
majuscules, as "capital letters," 211
male authority, tension with Paul's understanding of equality in Christ, 106n320
Martin, Ralph, 85
Masoretic Text, translators consulting, 220
McKnight, Scot, 85
media salutis (the means of salvation), risk of diminishing, 45
medium, as the message, 45n45
mens auctoris, imaginatively reconstructing, 47
mental words, perfected in verbal or written formation, 20
The Message (MSG), as a personal paraphrase, 181–83
metaphors, Paul's use of, 105n315
methodological approach, taking into account a text's *Wirkungsgeschichte*, 217
methodological reactions, against the WYC/TYN/KJV translation tradition, 10
methodology, 206–16, 218, 219

Middle English, of Wycliffe, 163
military vocabulary and imagery, in Colossians, 97
mimesis, sense-producing potential of, 99
mimetic form, 112n346
minuscules, not appearing until the ninth and tenth centuries, 211
modern reader and an ancient text, relating to each other, 27
Montgomery, Helen Barrett, 174n627
Mosaic purity laws, 151–52
Mount Zion, God's indwelling presence on, 137
MSG (The Message), 182
musicality, in biblical texts, 82
"mystery"
  embodied in the words themselves for Jerome, 160
  of the gospel, 135–36
  subordinating to "intelligibility," 45
  of the Word, 57
  of word order in the Scriptures, 159
mystery and other sects, restrictions practiced by, 154
"Mystery of Christ," in the Colossian Hymn, 120
"mystery religions," initiation rites involved in, 135
"mystical enthymemes," 99
mystical views, Paul fully negativizing, 147

negative consequences, of giving credence to subordinate powers, 146
negativizing rhetoric, 143–56
New International Version (NIV), applying dynamic equivalence theory, 180–81
New Living Translation (NLT), 55, 187–91
New Revised Standard Version (NRSV), 169–70
New Testament
  background information in various noncanonical texts, 79
  difficulties of common to the Greek and the English, 49

New Testament (cont.)
- diversities in tone or register found in, 80
- form of as quite stable, 220
- intrascriptural references to passages in the LXX, 74, 214, 220
- letters/epistles, 60n100, 61, 62
- lived responses to historical and eternal realities, 8
- passages expressive of the essential truths of the faith, 75
- presenting within a church framework, 11
- relationship to Colossians, 69–72
- studies reframing, 4

The New Testament: A 21st Century Translation, 193–98

The New Testament for Everyone, 185

Niceno-Constantinopolitan Creed, 34, 120, 140, 196

Nida, Eugene
- assuming the translator can discern the original writer's intent, 44, 176
- guidelines for translation committees, 54, 219
- on his "dynamic equivalence" methodology, 26
- seeking to render the text as fully "intelligible" to the modern reader, 10
- on translations prepared for readers of varied linguistic skills or interests, 223

NIV (New International Version), 180–81

NLT. *See* New Living Translation (NLT)

nomina sacra
- in Colossians, 89–93
- in early Christian codices of the LXX, 74
- in Patristic writings, 36
- research into the nature and purpose of, 218
- reviving the ancient manuscript use of, 213–14
- in some of the earliest manuscripts, 35, 76

noncanonical writings, information found in, 79

NRSV. *See* New Revised Standard Version (NRSV)

NRSVue, 170, 170n616

Nunc Dimittis, 81

"occasional" nature, of correspondence, 94

"occasional" type, 61

Old Testament
- Christological readings of, 33
- language and imagery of in the New Testament, 8
- marking express quotations from, 208
- methodology's possible applicability to, 218
- in the New, 175
- references and allusions to, 133, 214–16
- varied names for the God of creation and Israel, 89

"On Translating," by Martin Luther, 49

Onesimus, 67, 72

online interlinear translation, 199

organizational principles, for translation committees, 53

Origen, on the language of God, 113n347

"original receptors," identifying, 43

originating priority, Christ having, 124

overscoring, for *nomina sacra*, 213

pagan practices, 156

paracletic tone, adoption of, 104

paragraphing, no fixed rules for English, 209n7

paraphrase translation methodology, 18

paraphrasing
- of the Old Testament in the New Testament, 214
- as a translation method, 48–49

particles, complexity in Greek, 38

passages, translating using rhetorical imagery, 147

pastoral side, of Paul, 68, 103

Patristic thinking, 33

Subject Index

Patristic writings, 134
Paul
    on all the fullness of God dwelling in Christ, 132
    allegorical interpretation of Sarah and Hagar, 23n33
    condemning those seeking to worship angels, 157
    connecting Colossians and Laodiceans, 71
    criticizing overly florid speech, 95
    imprisonment of, 67
    insistence on the absolute fullness of the Godhead abiding in Christ, 154
    interpreting the exodus and the manna and water provided in the desert, 23n34
    on the "large letters" penned in closing Colossians, 111
    "lawful" vision of, 156
    praying, 32, 88
    rebuke of the Galatians, 152–53
    referring to Christ as the Word, 114
    series of predicates concerning Christ, 32
    stereotype as a harsh authoritarian, 105
    sufferings in his physical body, 135
    using clothing vocabulary to contrast the "putting off" of old behaviors, 97
"Pauline theology," 93
Pax Romana, Paul using imagery of, 108
"penitential *stelai*," 151
peoples of the earth, core biblical division among, 107
"personal supernatural forces," detecting a reference to, 148
persuasive liturgy, of Paul, 99
Peterson, Eugene, 181–83
phantasia, placing the vision "before the eyes," 99
Pharisee, Paul's training as, 98
Philemon, 71
Phillips, J. B., translation of the New Testament, 173–75
Philo of Alexandria, 145, 148

philosophy, 142, 145–46
phrasings
    in the receptor language, 206–7
    of Tyndale, 164
Phrygian Cities, in the Roman District known as "Asia," 64
Phrygians, in Jerusalem at Pentecost, 65n125
"physicality," questions of God's, 120n381
Plato, 118n371, 144
plerophoric style
    of Colossians, 88, 132
    striving to capture, 116
Plutarch, 148
poetic register, passages with, 186
"poetic texts," of the New Testament, 98–99
poetico-literary language, conveying ineffability, 197
Post-Enlightenment scholarship, on Judaism's and Christianity's historical origins, 24
practical theologian, Paul as, 103
prayer, in Colossians, 87–89, 103
"pre-critical" exegesis, relied on historicity of the Scriptures, 22
predicate adjective, the Lord described by use of a, 89
"preeminent" "in all things," Christ as, 130–31
pre-existence, idea of, 128
presuppositions, 27, 42, 46, 222
primary words, of the Scriptures, 50
"principalities and powers," Christ's conquest of, 150
principles
    as prolegomena to any future translation, 218–23
    theoretical and interpretative, 17–34
priority, of Christ, 124
probability, arguments from, 99
procedural aspects, of translation efforts, 222
"processual" nature of language, insights into, 26
"processual" point of view, translation made from, 21

prolegomena, to any future translation, 218–23
prosaic/"everyday" language, in Scripture, 109–11
protean translators, 44–45
proto-gnostic views, Paul fully negativizing, 147
Psalms, not following Greek poetic/hymnic forms, 81
punctuation, none in ancient Greek manuscripts, 208
purity and food ordinances, described by Paul, 152
Purvey, John, Wycliffe's secretary, 161
Pythagorean soul-purifying rituals, 153

question "behind the text," as "Who is Christ?" 32

readers, engaging in dialogue with a text, 3
receptor language, presenting the source text in, 43
reductionist assumption, of Nida, 47
Reformers, 20, 21, 23
register
    defined, 18
    identification of a given, 59–60
    referring to linguistic and syntactical features, 18
    varieties of, 59, 79–111
regula fidei
    traceable to Apostolic teaching, 6–7
    building blocks of, 91
    content in "material agreement" with, 6
    emerging by the second century, 33
    rearticulated by various church fathers, 78
    relationship of early Christian with *nomina sacra*, 90n231
religious register, 82n201
resurrection to life, only through Jesus, 130n439
revealing, of the Word's inner mental word, 11
Revelation (book of), 100, 101, 102, 209
Revised Standard Version (RSV), 50, 169

rhetoric, negativizing, 143–56
rhetorical elements, 97, 98
rhetorical modes, employed by Paul, 98n275
rhetorical nature, of the epistolary form, 94–103
rhetorico-poetical devices, 102
Robinson, James, 83–84
Roman "triumph," Paul referencing, 146
Romans (book of), "as some sort of treatise," 93
Rome, Paul under house arrest, 67
RSV. *See* Revised Standard Version (RSV)
"Rule of Faith," affirmations as, 76

sacred writings style, replacement of, 45n44
"salvation-meaning of a scriptural text," not limited to "'actual' horizon[s]," 28
Schleiermacher, Friedrich, 26
scribal practice, *ekthesis* as, 210–11
scriptio continua, in ancient Greek manuscripts, 208
scriptural texts, "non-rational" responses to, 98
Scripture
    as the divinely communicated Word of God, 1–2
    essential not to "twist," 106
    faithful readers of undergoing inspiration, 100
    as having ongoing presence and effect in the world, 3, 26
    imposing limits on interpretation and translation, 29
    as inspired expression, 159
    literal reading of, 23
    meaning not limited to the original author, 62
    proclaiming Christ and enjoining love, 7
    as the property of the people for Wycliffe, 161
    reflecting the living nature of, 217
    textual mediation depending on, 48
    unifying approach to, 6
Second Adam, Jesus as, 118

Subject Index

Second Council of Nicaea (AD 757), 77, 121
"Second Iconoclastic Period," Synod of the Hagia Sophia in AD 815 and, 121
"self-imposed asceticism," persons engaged in, 155–56
sense-for-sense approach, of Jerome, 159
sentences, as individually numbered verses, 208
separation, walls of broken down in Christ, 108
Septuagint (LXX)
  Augustine of Hippo on the translation of, 72n149
  defined, 18
  effective history (*Wirkungsgeschichte*) of passages from, 138
  intrascriptural language and imagery from, 11, 129n432
  New Testament intrascriptural references to, 214
  relationship to Colossians, 72–75
Septuagint materials, New Testament translators consulting, 220
serial greetings, susceptible of individualized style, 110
sin, each newborn person having a capacity to, 191
situatedness, within the flow of history, 219
slaves, treating as equal members, 109
sociohistorical setting, of a given text, 63
Son, 77, 119n375, 126. *See also* Christ
"song" or "hymn" or "psalm," passages self-identifying as, 81
Sophists, Paul not expressly referring to, 144
spacing, lacking in ancient Greek manuscripts, 208
specialized versions, 198–202
Spirit, pleading before God on our behalf, 133n453
Spirit of God, bridging the ontological gap, 99
"spirit-guided apostolic freedom," in construing the LXX, 73

Steinmetz, David, 28
Straus, Michael, translation methodology of, 193–98
Strong's Concordance, 199
structural parallels, highlighting in the Colossian Hymn, 86
style, 18, 56, 59, 59n98
stylist, 55
Synod of Hierea, ban on all religious images, 121n388

Taylor, Kenneth, 187
terminology, glossary of, 17–19
terms, in the New Testament reflecting the Old Testament, 31
Testament of Solomon, referring to spirits summoned, 150–51
Testaments, God as inspirer and author of both, 74n160
text
  adding words to, 122
  application of the methodology to, 206–16
  defined, 18
  departing from risking personal opinion or bias, 48
  dialogue with, 3
  imposing limits on the selection of words and phrases, 206–7
  itself remaining the fixed point of relation, 102n297
  meaning of deeply intertwined with its own tradition, 157
  meaning of revealed in the continuum of church history and tradition, 44, 50
  original operating as a guardrail, 80
  retaining authoritative/normative significance, 50
  revealing early understandings of, 73
  seeking to convey meaning, 174
  seeking to express the inexpressible, 112
text varieties, describing different perspectives on, 59
text's inner word. *See* "inner word"
textual language, developing church doctrine and liturgy, 34

textual meaning, not fully captured if limited to its original context, 147
textual mediation, 2, 20, 28
theological clarity, adhering to "classical" terms, 107
theological questions, 138
theological terms, 40–41, 49–50
theological words, owing to Christian Latin, 160n586
theology
  biblical, 62
  Christian, 186
  Pauline, 93
  whole Bible, 72
"things invisible," evoking, 143
"This is my body," as the real presence of Christ in the elements, 142
Thiselton, Anthony, 114
thought, as imperfectly realized in human language, 112
thought and word, relationship between, 19
"time-bound" premises, Enlightenment-derived, 25
timeless being, of Jesus, 118
TLB (The Living Bible), 187
Today's English Version. *See* Good News Tradition (GNB)
tradition
  consistent with Gadamer's "concept of the classical," 50
  defined, 18
  as essential to the unfolding of the Word of God, 3
  on images functioning in sacramental terms, 122
  as an incremental process, 28
  as a process of transmission mediating between past and present, 27
  safeguarding textual meaning, 29
translation
  examining prior, 157
  as a historical phenomenon, 31
  implications of scholarly developments for, 25
  new incorporating passages from prior versions, 36
  options based on grammar and syntax, 207
  overlapping with exegesis, 221
  prolegomena to any future, 218–23
  relevance of a cross-temporal approach to, 3
  reproducing from among a multiplicity of possible meanings, 39
  taking into account the origin of a given text, 62
  theories focusing on particular concerns, 37n12
translation approaches, 37–49, 203, 222
translation committees, excursus on, 53–58
translation methodology
  applicable to the New Testament, 1
  calling for a "voice" sensitive to communicating, 69
  defined, 18
  embracing effective history of the Old Testament in the New, 35
  New Testament text's trajectory and, 4
  presenting for modern translators of the New Testament, 17
translation projects, 25, 204
translation theory and practice, 217
translation tradition, 157–202
  defined, 18
  elements relating to, 203–5
  essential for any translator, 221
  respect for justifying using the same language, 197
translational approach, dependent on the "wholeness" of Scripture, 217
translator(s)
  alerting the reader/interpreter to possible alternative readings, 207, 221
  coming freshly to the text, 209
  considering a range of historical evidence, 67
  conveying that which is beyond words, 87
  examining creedal materials, 79
  identifying forms of persuasive rhetoric, 98

Subject Index

maintaining a "living relationship between [himself] and the text," 204–5
as participant in the text's effective history, 112
providing sufficient information to a reader or interpreter, 39
reproducing stylistic specialties, 43
seeking the best solution, 39n18
"situatedness within the flow of history," 75
task of bringing the "then to now," 183
Tridentine Mass, churches still using, 142
Trinitarian analogy, as perceived by Augustine, Justin Martyr, Gregory of Nazianzus, Aquinas, and Gadamer, 22–25
Trinity, 20, 34
True, capitalizing alluding to Christ as the True Word, 114
Truman, Harry, on the King James Version, 169n615
"truth," using adjectivally, 113–14
"twofoldness," of the Bible, 32
Tychicus, dispatched by Paul, 70
Tyndale, William, 9, 56, 164
Tyndale House Greek New Testament, editors adopted *ekthesis*, 210
typological readings, allowing the literal and the figural to be interpreted, 22

United Bible Societies, published a *Translator's Hand-book on Paul's Letters to the Colossians and Philemon*, 177–78
"unknown god," Paul's gloss on, 118n371
"unseen" God, Christ revealing, 118

variations, of Straus' translation, 194
Venerable Bede, 161n588
verbum cordis, 31, 112
verbum interius
existing in the mind before its expression, 19
as more than a mere metaphor, 20, 112

not constrained by time, place, and circumstances, 62
not limited to speech, 100
of a text, 53, 109, 207, 216
vision, experienced by John, 100
viva vox evangelii, 2, 12, 42, 202
viva vox Jesu, 122, 208
"vivid actuality," 100, 103

warnings, Paul balancing with encouraging words, 105–6
"who Christ is," 66, 111
"who God is," 140
the whole, understanding, 25
"whole Bible," 72, 222
Wirkungsgeschichte
canonical integrity as a consistent element of, 7
defined, 20
essential elements of the text's, 36
essential to translation as well as exegesis, 5
taking into account a text's, 217, 220–21
text's translation tradition and, 13, 50
"Wisdom," Christ as, 114
wisdom and knowledge, Christ as the locus of, 142–43
Witherington, Ben, III, 95
Word
capitalized, 18, 114
expressed in the words of the Bible, 2
revealing of the "inner mental word," 223
who or what is, 51
words expressive of that which is beyond words, 89
word
choice of depending on doctrinal position, 42
in continual formation when being actively understood, 2, 21, 100
most frequently used as the most appropriate, 115
uncapitalized, 18
Word of God, 2, 3, 18–19
the word of the Word, gospel message as, 114
the word of truth, of the gospel, 113

"word-for-word." *See* literal approach
words
    adding to the text, 122
    making sense of as the parts of a whole, 20
    persuading by means of, 144
    revealing intensity or power, 198
    revealing the *verbum cordis* of a text, 132
    selecting appropriate, 206–7
    translators availing themselves of scholarship, 220
words and phrases, detailed analysis of key, 111–57

Wright, N. T., 185–86, 212n21
Wycliffe, John, 51, 56, 115, 161–63, 203
Wycliffe/Tyndale/ King James translation tradition, continuity and, 159–72
WYC/TYN translation tradition, KJV's refinements of, 168
WYC/TYN/KJV translation tradition, 10, 172, 179, 194–96

YHWH, marking the reverential nature of, 92

Ancient Document Index

OLD TESTAMENT

Genesis

1	125n409, 127, 127n420
1:1	124n400, 195n693, 227n18
1:1 LXX	125n408
1:1–5	212n22
1:3	2n6
1:5	212n22
1:6	2n6
1:9	2n6
1:11	2n6
1:14	2n6
1:20	2n6
1:24	2n6
1:26–27	231n76
1:27	94, 195n686, 226n11
1:27 LXX	118n368, 119n374
1:28	225n3
2:1	195n693, 227n18
2:17	231n75
3:21	231n83
4:22	195n691, 226n16
9:1	225n3
14:19	195n693, 227n18
17:11	229n55
17:14	229n55
17:24	229n55
17:25	229n55
22:14	89n228
22:18	175
49:24	89n228

Exodus

3:14	196n698, 227n23
4:22	94, 129n432, 195n690, 226n15
6:6	226n6
11:5	129n432
12:29	129n432
14:30	226n7
15:1–21	82n200
15:26	89n228
16:13	89n228
17:15	89n228
25:8	134n456
25:22	134n456
29:45	134n457
31:3	225n4
40:34–35	196n705, 227n30

Leviticus

2:13	232n89
11:1–47	154n562
26:1	229n54

Numbers

3:12–13	195n690, 226n15
8:16	129n432
28:11	230n60

Deuteronomy

4:19	148n530, 156n571
6:4–9	74n162, 103n305
7:6–8	231n79
7:6–8 LXX	138n482
7:8	226n6
14:2	231n79
14:2 LXX	138n482
15:15	226n8
17:3	156n571
27:14–26	229n56
30:6	229n54

2 Samuel

7:10–16	226n7
23:2	110n334

1 Chronicles

23:31	154n562, 230n60

2 Chronicles

2:3	154n562
2:4	230n60
7:1–2	196n703, 227n28
31:3	154n562, 230n60

Ezra

3:11	82n200

Nehemiah

8	190

Psalms

	81, 82n200, 88, 215n35
2:7	195n689, 226n14
4	87n221, 88n223
5	88n223
6	88n223
6:1	232n84
7	88n223
10	87n221
13	87n221
17	87n221
18:10	195n695, 227n20
22	87n221
23	221
25	87n221
28	87n221
32:6	113
32:6 LXX	113n349, 195n692, 226n17
33:6	2n6
39	87n221
42	87n221
43	87n221
44	87n221
51	87n221
67:17 LXX	131, 193n681, 196n703, 227n28
68:16	134n458, 137
70	87n221
71	87n221
82	87n221
85	87n221
88:27–28 LXX	226n7
88:28 LXX	195n691, 226n16
88:39	226n7
88:52	226n7
99:1	134n456
109:1 LXX	230n58, 231n71
110:1	128
110:4	195n689, 226n14
143	87n221

Proverbs

	83
2:1–6	228n45
2:1–6 LXX	116n358
2:5	117n365
3:19–20	195n696, 227n21
8	114
8:22	195n690, 226n15
8:22–31	195n697, 227n22
10:1	83n207

Song of Solomon

	82n200

Isaiah

1:13–14	230n60
2:2–4	228n39
7:14	73, 171n622
8:18	134n458, 137, 196n705, 227n30
9:6	89n228
11:2	225n4
21:9	229n54
27:6	225n3
29:13	230n70
33:6	116n358
33:6 LXX	143n503
37:16	134n456
42:1 LXX	138n482
44:22	226n9
45:3	116n358, 228n43
55:10–11	21n18
55:11	2n6, 20

Jeremiah

8:2	156n571
19:13	156n571
33:16	89n228
52:32	195n695, 227n20

Ezekiel

1:26	195n695, 227n20
9:3	195n695, 227n20
10	195n695, 227n20
11:22	195n695, 227n20

Daniel

2:8	232n88
2:18–19	136n473
2:19–21	228n37
2:22	228n37
2:27	136n473
2:28–30	228n37
2:30	136n473
2:47	136n473
7	146
7:10 LXX/Theodotian	152n549
7:27 LXX	146n517
7:27 LXX/Theodotian	230n58
10:13	147n520

Hosea

2:12	154n562
4:1	117n365
4:6	117n367
6:6	117n365
11:1	226n7

Joel

2:28–36	6n36, 33n88

Amos

9:11–12	73

Zephaniah

1:5	156n571

Zechariah

2:11	228n39
3:1–2	147n520
8:22–23	228n39

DEUTEROCANONICAL BOOKS

1 Enoch

	79n189, 128n431
75:3	148n528

Book of the Watchers

	128n431

1 Maccabees

1:23	116n358, 228n43
9:14	97n270

2 Maccabees

4:47	108n325

3 Maccabees

7:5	108n325

4 Maccabees

	145
12:13	148n525

Jubilee

	128n431

Martyrdom and Ascension of Isaiah

	79n189
7:21	157n573

Sirach

	130n441
1:4	195n693, 227n18
24:5–10	196n702, 227n27
24:5–10 DRA	131n441
24:9	195n697, 227n22
43:26	196n698, 227n23

Wisdom of Solomon

1:7	196n698, 227n23
7:17	148n525
7:26	195n686, 226n11
9:9	195n692, 226n17
19:18	148n525

APOCRYPHA (OLD TESTAMENT)

Apocalypse of Moses (Life of Adam and Eve)

13-15	157n573

2 Baruch

	79n189
44:14	116n358, 143n503, 228n45
52:6–7	237n72
54:13	116n358, 143n503, 228n45

3 Enoch

1:12	230n63

Apocalypse of Abraham

	79n189
§10f	141n493
17:1–21	230n63
17:2	157n573

Apocalypse of Zephaniah

3:6–9	152n549, 229n56
6:15	157n573

Letter of Aristeas

	72n149
142–43	230n68

Prayer of Joseph

	79n189, 129n432

Testament of Solomon

	79n189, 150

ANCIENT JEWISH WRITERS

Josephus

	145

Jewish Antiquities

	79n189
18.1.2–4	229n49
18.1.2–5	145n513

Jewish Wars

	79n189
2.8.7	230n63

Philo of Alexandria

	117, 145, 148

Ancient Document Index

Concerning Noah's Work as a Planter

	79n189
2.9	196n698, 227n23

Eternity of World

	79n189

Life of Moses

	79n189

Life of Moses II

7	72n149

Quis rerum divinarum heres

23:188	127n420

That Every Good Man Is Free

	79n189
11	229n48
13	229n48

Theodotion

	152n549, 230n58

RABBINIC WORKS

Talmudic Literature
Mishna

Ketubot 8a	119n374

NEW TESTAMENT

Matthew

	197n711
1:1–17	175
1:22–23	6n35
1:23	73
2:14–15	6n35
2:15	226n6
3:1–3	6n35
3:17	226n7
5:3–11	83n207
5:17	230n62
5:21–26	6n34
6:9–13	162
6:14–15	231n82
13:11	228n37
15:1–20	230n70
22:44	231n71
27:29	147
27:51	136n470
28:18–20	35n2
28:19	76n178, 92n246

Mark

	210
7:1–19	230n69
7:1–23	230n70
7:14–23	230n59
8:30	75n169
12:36	110n334, 231n71
16:9–20	180n647
16:15–17	35n2

Luke

	117
1:1–4	2n6, 7n41
1:4–55	81
1:47–55	81n197
1:68–79	81
1:70	110n334
2:14	81
2:29–32	81
4:16–20	190
4:16–21	6n33
9:32	126
10:16	7n41
10:17	92n246
11:31–30	86n216
12:11	123
17:26–30	86n216
20:42–43	231n71
22:19	112n346
24:13–27	6n33
24:13–32	32n87
24:44	32n87

John

	114
1:1	3n13, 21n20, 51, 52n73, 57, 58, 113, 124, 141, 143n504, 225n1
1:1–2	195n697, 227n22
1:1–17	81
1:3	125n408, 195n696, 227n21
1:4	195n692, 226n17
1:10	195n696, 227n21
1:14	134n460, 141, 196n705, 225n2, 227n30, 229n52
1:16	133n451
1:18	118, 125, 195n687, 226n12
2:19–21	196n705, 227n30
2:21	134n459
3:16	180n647, 195n690, 226n15
5:29	130
5:39	6n33, 32n87
6:9	161n588
8:58	196n698, 227n23
11:25–27	75n169
11:43	2n6
11:52	231n78
13:21	182
14:6	2n6
14:13–14	92n246
14:26	110n334
18:6	2n6
19:30	138n479

Acts

	203, 218
1:1–3	7n41
1:16	110n334
2:4	35n3
2:10	65n125
2:14–26	6n37
2:14–36	6n36, 33n88
2:36	76n174
2:44–45	109n331
3:16	41n31
4:30	92n246
4:32	109n331
6:7	225n3
7	6n38
7:55–56	231n71
7:58	231n71
8:36–38	75n169
9:3–6	2n6
10	156, 228n39
10:43	75n169
12:24	225n3
13:17	138n482, 231n79
15:16–18	73
16:9	156
16:30–34	75n169
17:22–31	118n371
17:28	195n692, 226n17
18:4	144n506
19:8	144n506
22:3	98n277
26:1	95n259
26:28	144n506
28:23	144n506

Romans

	93, 96n262, 192n678, 193
1:3–4	75n171, 76n174
1:8–17	61n105
1:9–10	103n305
1:16–17	61n103
1:17	41n31, 42n32
1:20	139, 140, 140n489
1:21	117
1:21–25	156n571
1:28–31	106n317, 106n319
1:38	117
2:14–15	150n539
2:20	117n367
2:26–27	150n539
3:2	33n88
3:22	41n31
3:28	49
3:29	231n78
5:1	196n706, 227n31
5:11	46
5:12	191

5:18–21	230n57	8:10	117n367
7:12	154n563	8:11	117n367
8:5–12	41n27	9:7–14	98n276
8:18–19	237n73	9:10	73
8:26	133n453	9:16	232n87
8:29	195n690, 226n15	10:1–4	23n34
8:34	128n430	10:1–11	175n630, 230n62
9:4–5	231n79	10:10	95n257
9:6	138	11:3	106n320, 124n399
9–11	111n338, 175n631	11:24–25	112n346
10:8	219n4	12	156
10:9	75n169	12:8	117n367
10:13	92n246	12:27	123
10:14–17	20	13	61, 96n265
10:17	189n668	13:2	117n367
11:14	41n29	13:8	117n367
11:15	46	13:12	117
11:25–26	228n37	14:15	232n84
11:33	116, 117n367	14:26	81n198
12:9–21	105n316	15	129nm431
15:14	117n367	15:3–4	33n88, 75n169
16	110n335	15:20	124n403, 196n701, 227n26
16:1–23	61		
16:25–26	228n37	15:20–28	128n426
		15:25	128n430
1 Corinthians		15:27	139
		15:39	41n25
1:2–5	95n258	15:49	231n76
1:4–9	61n105	15:51	136
1:9	61n103		
2:4	95n259	**2 Corinthians**	
2:6–7	228n41		
2:7	115n355, 143, 228n38		60n101
		1:1	71n146
2:7–13	136n469	3:6	39n21
2:8	147n520	3:13–16	136n470
2:9	73	4:4	195n686, 226n11
3:10–15	202n718	4:16	231n76
4:11–13	135n466	4:17	182
4:14–15	105n310	5:14	41n31
5:7	230n62	5:18	46
5:9–11	106n317	5:19	46
6:9–10	106n317	6:4–10	135n466
8:1	117n367	6:16	138n477
8:2	143n502	8:13–15	109n331
8:6	33n88, 75n171, 76n178	11:23–28	228n36
		11:24–30	135n466
8:7	117n367		

Galatians

	60n101, 66, 98n278, 147, 151, 152n550
1:6–9	69
2:5	113
2:14	113
2:16	41
2:20	41n31
2:22	41n31
3:1–4	69
3:13	150n538
3:24	153
3:27	97n273
3:28	105n316, 106n320
3:28–29	231n78
4:3	147
4:8–10	230n60
4:9	147
4:9–10	152
4:14–15	111n339
4:19–20	105n310
4:20	153
4:21–31	23n33, 98n276
5:19–21	106n317
5:22–23	105n316, 231n80
5:26—6:6	110n335
6:11	111n339

Ephesians

	60n101, 69, 70, 132
1:1	70n143
1:3–14	99, 209n8
1:7	226n8
1:9–10	228n39
1:15–16	103n305
1:17	117n365
1:17–18	225n4
1:19–23	128n426
1:20	128n430, 231n71
1:20–23	196n707, 227n32
1:22	196n699, 227n24
1:22–23	123n395, 137n474
1:23	88n225, 132
2:1–3	227n33
2:11	229n55
2:14–15	105n316
2:14–16	81
2:15	230n57
2:16	123n395
3:3–6	228n39
3:10	123
3:19	70n141, 117n367, 132
4:4	76n178, 123n395
4:4–6	75n169
4:12	123n395
4:13	117n365
4:14	229n48
4:15–16	123, 230n65
4:22–24	231n74
4:24	231n76
4:25–32	70n136
5:1–18	70n139
5:14	73
5:16	232n88
5:19	70n140, 232n84
5:19–20	81n198
5:21–24	107
5:21–32	70n136
5:22—6:9	232n86
5:23	124n399
5:32	136
6:1–4	107
6:1–9	70n136
6:4	105n312
6:11	129nm431
6:12	123, 129nm431, 149

Philippians

1:3–11	61n105
2:6	119n373
2:6–8	139n484
2:6–11	81, 85n213, 186
2:9–11	92n246, 128n426
2:22	105n311
3:8	117n367
3:9	41n31
4:8	105n316

Colossians

	9, 9n56, 10, 12, 13, 34, 37, 45, 58, 59, 60, 60n102, 61, 61n102, 62, 63, 66, 67, 68, 69, 70, 71, 75n168, 77, 79, 80, 87, 88, 89, 91, 93, 94, 96, 97, 98, 98n279, 103, 105n316, 106n317, 109, 110, 111, 119, 124, 124n404, 125n409, 128, 130, 132, 134, 143, 148, 150, 151, 158, 162, 185, 190n671, 192n678, 194, 203, 204, 206, 215, 218, 219, 225–33
1:1	89, 111
1:2	214n28
1:2–4	61n105
1:3	88
1:4–8	67
1:5	113, 114
1:6	88n224, 97n268, 132n449
1:9	32, 88, 88n224, 97n267, 103, 115, 116, 132n449
1:9–10	117n367
1:9–11	88n224, 97n268, 132n449
1:9–12	103
1:10	103, 104, 116
1:11	104
1:12	104
1:13–20	104
1:14	180n647
1:15	3n13, 21n20, 32, 34n96, 40, 84, 85, 86, 94, 117, 118, 119, 120, 121, 125, 128, 129, 130, 160, 162, 164, 167, 168, 169, 170, 171, 178, 180, 185, 187, 189, 192, 196, 198, 199, 200
1:15–16	84, 137
1:15–18	181
1:15–20 ("Colossian Hymn")	9, 57, 61, 75n169, 80, 81, 81n199, 82, 82n202, 83, 86n215, 86n216, 87, 88n224, 97n268, 99, 102, 119n377, 120, 128, 132n449, 134, 139, 140, 158, 162, 164–65, 167, 169, 170, 171–72, 175, 176–77, 178, 180, 181, 183–84, 185, 187, 189–90, 192–93, 194, 195–96, 198–99, 200–201, 204, 209n8
1:16	34n96, 83, 84, 85, 119, 124n400, 125, 129nm431, 150, 160, 162, 164–65, 164n598, 167, 169, 170, 171, 178, 180, 184, 185, 187, 189, 192, 196, 198, 200
1:16–18	146
1:16a	86
1:16c	86
1:17	84, 85, 126, 126n414, 133, 160, 162, 165, 167, 168, 169, 170, 172, 178, 179, 180, 184, 186, 187, 189, 192, 198, 200
1:17a	84
1:17a–18	84

Colossians (*cont.*)

1:17b	84
1:18	32, 83, 84, 85, 88, 123, 124n399, 130, 143, 160, 162, 165, 167, 168, 169, 170, 170n618, 172, 178, 180, 186, 187, 189, 192, 198, 200
1:18–20	181
1:18a	84, 122, 123, 186
1:18b	85, 86, 123, 124, 124n403
1:18b–20	84
1:19	19n4, 32, 34, 34n94, 70n141, 84, 85, 86, 88n224, 97n267, 131, 132, 132n449, 133, 136, 139, 153, 160, 162, 165, 167, 169, 170, 172, 178, 180, 182, 186, 188, 189, 192, 193n681, 199, 200, 201–2
1:19–20	83
1:20	32, 45, 47, 84, 85, 86, 160, 162, 165, 167, 169, 170, 172, 178, 180, 184, 186, 188, 190, 192, 199, 200
1:21	65
1:23	88n224, 97n268, 132n449
1:24	41n26, 134, 135, 135n465
1:24–25	88n224, 97n267, 132n449
1:24–29	98n276
1:26	32, 135, 184
1:26–27	115n355, 135–36, 188n664
1:28	88n224, 97n268, 106n318, 132n449
1:29	97
2	143
2:2	88, 88n224, 97n267, 104n308, 116n360, 132n449
2:2–3	88n224, 97n268, 116, 116n358, 132n449
2:3	115, 117n367, 142, 144
2:4	67, 144
2:5	41n28, 97, 97n270
2:6–23	61n103
2:8	67, 113, 142, 145, 147, 154
2:9	32, 34, 70n141, 132, 133, 136, 137, 139, 140, 140n489, 142, 153
2:9–10	34n94, 88n224, 97n267, 97n268, 132n449, 137n474, 139
2:10	32, 123, 123n396, 129nm431, 137, 151
2:10–11	146
2:13–15	97
2:14	88n224, 97n268, 98n274, 132n449, 145n509, 151
2:15	97, 98n274, 123, 129nm431, 145n509, 146, 149, 150
2:16	98n274, 145n509
2:16–17	151
2:16–23	154
2:17	144, 154
2:18	66, 67, 98n274, 145n509, 154, 155, 156
2:19–20	88n224, 97n268, 132n449
2:20	98n274, 113, 145n509, 149n531, 153n555
2:20–22	152
2:21	154

2:22	88n224, 97n268, 98n274, 132n449, 145n509	4:9	67, 88n224, 97n268, 132n449
2:23	68, 98n274, 145n509, 154	4:12	67n131, 71, 88n224, 97n267, 110, 132n449
3:1	105, 128n430	4:13	71
3:1–4	105	4:15	71
3:1–15	70n139	4:16	61n102, 70, 71n147
3:1–25	97		
3:2	105	4:17	88n224, 97n267, 104, 132n449
3:5	88n224, 106n319		
3:5–7	68	4:18	71n148
3:5–9	105	15:45–47	179n640
3:5–25	104		
3:8	88n224, 97n268, 132n449	**1 Thessalonians**	
3:8–10	97	1:2–3	61n105, 103n305
3:10–11	106, 109	1:4–5	61n103
3:11	88, 88n224, 97n268, 107, 108n324, 132n449	2:7	104
		2:11–12	104
		4:3–7	106n317
3:12	138, 138n482, 154	5:12–28	110n335
3:14	88n224, 97n268, 132n449	5:27	95n256
3:16	70n140, 81, 88n224, 97n267, 114, 132n449	**2 Thessalonians**	
		1:3–4	61n105
		1:5–10	61n103
3:17	88n224, 97n268, 132n449, 214n28	2:2	71n146
		3:17	71n146
3:18–25	70n136		
3:19–20	106	**1 Timothy**	
3:20	88n224, 97n268, 132n449		60n101
		3:16	75n169, 81
3:21	105	4:13	190
3:22	88n224, 97n268, 132n449	6:13–16	128n426
		6:16	53n76
3:22—4:1	107	6:20	116n357, 117n367, 142
4:1	70n136, 97, 104, 108, 109		
4:2–18	104	**2 Timothy**	
4:3	67	3:16	62n110, 109
4:6–7	88n224, 97n268, 132n449	4:6	228n36
		4:9–21	110n335
4:7	70	4:13	70n135
4:7–9	67n132		
4:7–17	72		
4:8	104n308		

Titus

	60n101
1:12	144n507
2:3–10	70n138
3:1	123

Philemon

	61n102, 67, 71
1:2	72
1:10	105n311, 233n90
1:23	67n131, 72

Hebrews

	60, 126
1:1	190
1:1–4	81
1:1–13	128n426
1:2	195n696, 227n21
1:3	40, 118, 118n371, 126, 195n686, 196n698, 226n11, 227n23
1:5–13	6n35
1:6	73, 195n690, 226n15
1:10	195n696, 227n21
1:12	126n417, 126n418
2:14–15	146
3:1–7	6n36, 33n88
3:5	88n226
4:12	20, 103n302
4:15	135n464
5:8–9	20n7
6:11	88n226
6:20	130
7–9	6n39
8:5	230n62
10:1	230n62
10:22	88n226
12:2	147

James

2:1	41n31
4:5–6	73

1 Peter

	60n101, 209
1:1	138n481
1:21	75n169
2:1	106n317
2:18—3:7	70n138
3:18–22	81
3:21–22	128n426
4:1	41n26
4:2–3	106n317

2 Peter

	209
1:2	117n365
1:8	117n365
1:20–21	110n334
1:21	62n110
2:20	117n365
3:5	126, 195n696, 227n21
3:10	126n417, 126n418, 148n525
3:12	148n525
3:15–16	6n40
3:16	62n110, 106n321

1 John

1:1	113, 124
2:22	75n169
4:14–15	75n169

2 John

1:1	138n481
1:13	138n481

3 John

2	60n101

Jude

1:6	129nm431

Ancient Document Index

Revelation

	100, 102, 194n684, 203, 209, 209n8, 211, 218
1:3	190
1:5	196n702, 227n27
1:8	124, 196n700, 227n25
3:14	124n401, 129
5:5–14	128n426
5:9	81n196
5:9–10	81
6:1–7	101
6:1–17	102
10:4	100n293
10:6	102n298, 195n693, 227n18
14:12	41n31
15:3–4	81, 81n197
19:1–8	232n84
19:10	6n36, 33n88
19:11–16	128n426
20:12	152n549, 229n56
21:1–3	196n707, 227n32
21:6	124
21:22	138n478
22:13	124, 195n696, 227n21

APOCRYPHA (NEW TESTAMENT)

2 Enoch

22:1–11	230n63

EARLY CHRISTIAN

Alexander of Alexandria

Epistula ad Alexandrum Thessalonicenseum

46	125n412

Ambrose

De fide

1.16	141n496, 226n5, 229n52

Ambrosiaster

	152n550

Amphilochius of Iconium

On the Orthodox Faith

2	122n392

Apostles' Creed

	29

Aquinas, Thomas

	2, 19–20, 21, 72, 93, 100, 185

Commentary on Aristotle

§1229	20n12

Commentary on John

| 15 | 3n13 |
| 15 (§29) | 21n20 |

De natura verbi intellectus

	2n11
§277	3n15, 19n6, 20n8, 21n21, 100n291, 112n340, 112n345

Arius

Epistula ad Alexandrum Alexandrinum

| 4 | 119n375 |
| 5 | 119n375 |

Epistula ad Eusebium Nicomediensem

5	179n640

Ancient Document Index

Athanasian Creed

	34, 133n455
§6	196n704, 227n29
§9	133n450, 229n51
§9.29–37	141n496
§29–37	34n95, 229n52

Athanasius
Against the Arians

1.1.9	195n688, 226n13

Augustine of Hippo

2, 7, 19, 20, 22n26, 72, 72n149, 100, 185, 191

Confessions

9.2	95n258

Contra Faustum

11.2	228n45

De catechizandis rudibus

2.3	20n10, 100n292, 112n343
4.8	7n46, 73n153

De civitate Dei

ch. 17	32n84
ch. 43	72n149

De doctrina christiana

1.13	2n8, 19n2
1.16.40	7n46
1.40.44	7n46

De Trinitate

	34n95
2.9	1n4, 197n710
9:5	20n13
15	2n8
15.24–25	19n2, 112n340

Enarrationes in Psalmos

51.21	228n36
51.4	135n465
144.8	7n46

Sermones

119.7	2n9, 19n3
133.8	227n24
213	78n184

Basil of Caesarea
De fide

prologus 8.4	126n415, 196n698, 227n23

De Spiritu Sancto

§18.45	121n387

Epistula

38.8	195n687, 226n12

Bernard of Clairvaux

	23n30

Chalcedonian Statement

34, 141n496, 195n689, 195n697, 196, 226n13, 226n14, 227n22, 227n30, 229n52

Chrysostom, John

	152n550

Clement of Alexandria
Stromata

6.15	33n89, 74n160
7.16	49n67
7.6	75n170

Ancient Document Index

Clement of Rome
1 Clement
1:3	104n307
21:6–9	104n307
46:6	76n178

Concilium Sedicense
6	196n701, 227n26

Constitutiones Apostolorum
6.11.1–2	128n427, 195n691, 226n16

Council of Chalcedon
120

Council of Trent
29n69

Creed of Basil of Ancyra
226n11

Cyril of Alexandria
Epistula tertia ad Nestorium
141n496, 229n52

Cyril of Jerusalem
Catechetical Lectures
58 (lecture 5.12)	78n187

Damasus I, Pope
159

Dedication Creed
119

Didache
4:9–11	104n307

Gregory of Nazianzus
19, 72, 185

On God and Christ
oratio 30.20	126n415, 195n686, 196n698, 226n11, 227n23

Gregory Thaumaturgus
Confessio fidei
118n371

Hilary of Poitiers
De synodis
84	119n376, 195n688, 226n13

Liber (II) ad Constantium Imperatorem
11	120n378, 142n40, 195n687, 226n12, 229n52

Hippolytus of Rome
The Refutation of All Heresies
5.21	230n63

Ignatius of Antioch
Epistle to the Smyrnaeans
1.2	128n427, 195n691, 226n16

Irenaeus
Adversus haereses
1.10.1	76n176, 118n371, 195n687, 226n12
1.22.1	125n409
1.26.1	141n496, 229n52
1.4.1–2	230n64
1.8.1	7n43
2.28.3	7n43

Adversus haereses (cont.)

2.3.1	230n64
3.1.1	7n41
3.11.1	141n496, 229n52
3.4.1	76n176
5.praefatio	76n173
17.1–5	196n704, 227n29

Epideixis

6	125n409, 195n696, 227n21

Jerome of Stridon

7, 9, 13, 40, 52, 119, 140n489, 158, 159–60, 160n585

Letter to Pammachius

5	159n580
7	159n579
7–10	7n45
11	38n15

John of Damascus

197

Expositio fide

1.3	126n415, 196n698, 227n23
1.8.14	34n95, 196n704, 227n29

Justin Martyr

19, 33, 72, 185

Dialogus cum Tryphone

85.1–2	33n89
85.2	128n427, 195n691, 226n16

Letter of Six Bishops to Paul of Samosat

4	195n696, 227n21
8	141n496, 229n52

Melito of Sardis
Peri Pascha

104	74n160

Niceno-Constantinopolitan Creed

34, 74n162, 120, 128n427, 140, 141n496, 195n685, 195n688, 195n689, 195n690, 195n694, 195n696, 195n697, 196, 226n10, 226n13, 226n14, 226n15, 227n19, 227n21, 227n22, 229n52

Origen
De principiis

1.4	128n427, 195n691, 226n16
4.13	22n26, 33n89, 230n61
4.16–18	22n25
4.6	113n347

In Matthaeum commentariorum series

33	128n427, 195n690, 226n15

Pseudo-Athanasius
Expositio fidei

4	195n693, 227n18

Pseudo-Augustine
Sermones
242   78n184

Pseudo-Hippolytus of Rome
Traditio apostolica
21:1–20   97n273
21.11–18   76n177

Second Council of Nicaea
                              121

Acta
1.135–36   121n387

Second Decree of the Council of Antioch
                   195n686, 226n11

Tertullian
De praescriptione haereticorum
13, 20–22   7n41, 29n69
20–21   32n87
37   32n87

Theodore of Mopuestia
                              118n372

Theodoret of Cyrus
Interpretation of the letter to the Colossians
                              156n569

Victricius of Rouen
De laude sanctorum
§2   34n96, 195n695, 227n20

GREEK AND ROMAN LITERATURE

Appian
                              97n272

Apuleius
Metamorphosis
9.23   155n564
9.28   155n564
9.30   155n564

Aristophanes
Nubes
224–25   157n572, 230n65

Aristotle
                    96, 98, 99n281

Nicomachean Ethics
1.1   143n502

Politics
1.1252a   104n307

Rhetoric
1355a–57a   99n284

Callimachus
Hymn to Zeus
                              144n507

Cassius
                              97n272

Cicero
"For Flaccus"
                              65

On Oratory
1.34 line 159   232n89

Ancient Document Index

Dio
97n272

Empedocles
148

Epimenides
144n507

Euripides
Iphigenia in Aulis
1400 — 108n324

Gorgias
144

Herodotus
64
Histories
7.30–32 — 64n121

Hesiod
Theogony
26 — 144n507

Homer
175n629

Horace
Works of Horace
line 133 — 185n657

Isocrates
144

Livy
97n272

Ovid
Metamorphoses
148n525
book 11 — 66

Plato
144
Apology
19c — 230n65
Phaedrus
249c — 228n40
250b–c — 228n40
Sophist
144
243c — 144n508
Theaetetus
162e — 144n505
Timaeus
92C — 118n371
92c — 195n687, 226n12

Pliny the Elder
Natural History
21.27.9 — 64n120

Pliny the Younger
Letter to Trajan
10.96.7 — 81n198

Plutarch (Plutarchus)
148, 156n569
Plutarch's Lives
4:160–61 — 156n569

Protagoras

144

Strabo
Geography

12.8.16   64n118, 64n120

Suetonius

97n272

Tacitus
Annals

14.27   65n123, 65n124

Tertullian
Contra Marionem

5.19   230n69

Xenophon

64

Anabasis

1.2.6   64n122
1.2.18   97n270, 229n46

www.ingramcontent.com/pod-product-compliance
Lightning Source LLC
Chambersburg PA
CBHW071234230426
43668CB00011B/1428